THE BRANCH DAVIDIANS OF WACO

The Branch Davidians of Waco

The History and Beliefs of an Apocalyptic Sect

KENNETH G. C. NEWPORT

OXFORD
UNIVERSITY PRESS

OXFORD
UNIVERSITY PRESS

Great Clarendon Street, Oxford OX2 6DP

Oxford University Press is a department of the University of Oxford.
It furthers the University's objective of excellence in research, scholarship,
and education by publishing worldwide in

Oxford New York

Auckland Cape Town Dar es Salaam Hong Kong Karachi
Kuala Lumpur Madrid Melbourne Mexico City Nairobi
New Delhi Shanghai Taipei Toronto

With offices in

Argentina Austria Brazil Chile Czech Republic France Greece
Guatemala Hungary Italy Japan Poland Portugal Singapore
South Korea Switzerland Thailand Turkey Ukraine Vietnam

Oxford is a registered trade mark of Oxford University Press
in the UK and in certain other countries

Published in the United States
by Oxford University Press Inc., New York

British Library Cataloguing in Publication Data

Data available

Library of Congress Cataloging–in–Publication Data

Newport, Kenneth G. C.
The Branch Darvidians of Waco: the history and beliefs of an apocalyptic sect/Kenneth G. C. Newport.
p. cm.
ISBN–13: 978–0–19–924574–1 (alk. paper)
ISBN–10: 0–19–924574–6 (alk. paper)
1. Branch Davidians. I. Title.
BP605. B72N49 2006 299'. 93–dc22
2005 0 33133

Typeset by SPI Publisher Services, Pondicherry, India
Printed in Great Britain
on acid-free paper by
Biddles Ltd., King's Lynn
ISBN 0–19–924574–6   978–0–19–924574–1

1 3 5 7 9 10 8 6 4 2

In memory of Baby Gyarfas and Baby Gent, whose lives were ended almost before they began.

Preface

This is a book about religious belief. It is about the kind of religious belief that may lead a person to come to the conviction that God has called him or her to lead a community of the faithful and to teach them the ways of God. It is about belief that may lead a person to take action—to move thousands of miles, to establish a place on earth where people may be prepared for heaven, to devote oneself to the writing and spreading of religious tracts. It is about belief that looks for the self-revelation of God in scripture and in the spoken word of living prophets. It is about the kind of belief for which one may choose to die.

The story told here is the story of 'Waco'—the name of a pleasant enough Texan town now synonymous in many people's minds with religious extremism and/or government heavy-handedness. What took place there in the spring of 1993 is now etched upon the American psyche, and despite the passing of a dozen years 'what really happened' continues to be a matter of grave concern. It was, for example, of grave concern to Timothy McVeigh, who on the second anniversary of the Waco fire bombed the Alfred P. Murrah building in Oklahoma City in an act of revenge. It continues to be of grave concern to those who lost loved ones at Waco, the mothers, fathers, sons, daughters, other family members, and friends of the eighty-four who died during the fifty-one days.

It is hoped that this book will contribute to the understanding of 'Waco' in a number of ways. First, every attempt has been made to set the events in context. The Branch Davidians were not a new movement in 1993 and to understand them it is necessary also to understand something of their history. Even more important, however, is the need to understand something of their theology, for it was theology that drove them; it was theology for which they lived and theology for which so many of them died. My task has been to understand some of that theology and some of that history in an effort to see beneath the surface of events that for a while so dramatically hit the world's TV screens. It has not always been an easy task nor always a pleasant one. I remain convinced, however, that it was necessary. There will be other Wacos, and if this book assists in some small way in understanding the one we have already had, there is some hope, even if only a small one, that it might assist too in seeking to avert the kind of outcome we witnessed on 19 April 1993. In this case my time will have been well spent.

This book has grown considerably in the writing and the end product is nearly fifty per cent longer than had originally been contracted. In the end

I had to decide on what it was that I might most profitably bring to this discussion. My own background being in history and biblical studies I chose to focus on two primary tasks: the attempt to piece together as fully as possible the history of this trajectory and the more complicated matter of outlining its theology, especially its use of the Bible. I hope that I have done these two things tolerably well. I have, however, had to leave it to others to reflect more theoretically on the nature of this movement, the reason for the course of its development, and the role it has played in recent American cultural and political life. If this study assists in that wider task, again I believe that my time will have been well spent.

A website that supports this book and provides a good deal of the documentary and other evidence that undergirds it can be found at: *www.hope. ac.uk/humanities/theology/branchdavidians.*

Acknowledgements

I could not have written this book without the help of numerous individuals. Great practical assistance and fruitful conversation was provided by Mark Swett who for many years has been involved in his own investigations into Waco, despite which he still found time to provide me with a mass of information and hard data. My debt to him is very large indeed.

Other conversation partners include my long-time friends Malcolm Bull and Keith Lockhart, both of whom have found time to read draft material and offer detailed feedback. This book would be very much weaker without their input.

I have been very fortunate in being able to call upon the assistance of a number of really quite superb archivists and librarians. Lynda Baildam of Newbold College provided me with archive material and also very helpfully tracked down the publication details of some of the more obscure Seventh-day Adventist works mentioned in this volume. At Baylor University in Waco, Texas, I was very well looked after by Ellen Brown. The Texas Collection (which now includes the private archive built up by Mark Swett) has been the most important source of material for much of what I have been working on these past few years. Working on a book which draws so heavily upon an archive some 4,500 miles away has its own challenges. Ellen Brown made those challenges manageable, even giving up her own time so that I might work late on the collection during my visits. Kent Keeth and Bill and Ruth Pitts all extended traditional Texan hospitality to me whenever I was in town, and for interesting conversation (and some very good food) I am indebted.

I have tried in this research to be as open as possible and to consult directly with at least a few of those who were centrally involved in the 1993 stand-off. FBI negotiator Byron Sage was generous in giving up an entire Saturday to explain to me his side of the story, and has provided detailed responses to some of the chapters in this book. My thanks are due also to Marie Hagen who similarly has been generous in sharing comments with me and drawing my attention to documents that I might easily otherwise have missed. On at least two major points she has saved me from serious factual error. The contents of this book will reveal also that I have been able to speak with a number of surviving Branch Davidians. These include Derek Lovelock, a resident of my own home city of Manchester, UK. Derek and I have spent many hours together in conversation and he has kindly permitted me to publish as an appendix to this book a summary of a much longer manuscript he has been working on which gives a glimpse into his own association with the Branch Davidian community. Livingstone Fagan has also been very generous in finding the time to write to me and explain his system of belief. Clive Doyle was kind enough to ask me to speak at the tenth anniversary meeting held at Mt. Carmel in April 2003. Not all the contents of this book will meet with Branch Davidian approval, and I am deeply aware that what I have ended up saying will be a disappointment to some of the persons I have named here. I hope, however, that at least the energy and time I have put into this volume will meet with their approval.

This is the third major book I have completed while at Liverpool Hope University, which is a testimony to the institutional support I have received. I have again been provided with more than I could reasonably wish for. At an institution such as mine, one obvious and soft target for cutbacks is research and I have been fortunate indeed that neither the previous Rector and Chief Executive, Professor Simon Lee (now Vice-Chancellor at Leeds Metropolitan University), nor the present one, Professor Gerald Pillay, has opted for the relatively easy financial option of going down this route. An institution that is proud, as Hope is, of its Christian foundation ought to be doing study in theology and religion and doing it well. It will be for others to judge whether the study in this book has been 'done well', but independent of that judgement the fact that the senior management team at Liverpool Hope has consistently given me the space and the encouragement to take on a task of this size illustrates an institutional commitment to such study.

My colleagues in the department of Theology and Religious Studies at Liverpool Hope have offered valuable advice as this work has progressed, and have been subjected to a number of trial runs of chapters in the form of papers. Dr J'annine Jobling in particular has spent rather longer than might be good for her listening to me thinking out loud. I also owe a truly enormous debt to my research and teaching assistant, Ursula Leahy, who has worked with me on this book as she has on others. Her eye for detail has spared me many errors and has made the job of the reader rather less arduous than it might otherwise have been by improving my style. She has worked late at night and early in the morning in an effort to meet deadlines and for this I am deeply appreciative.

The real heart of this book was written during the period of a Leverhulme Research Fellowship, the granting of which enabled me to concentrate on this project. Without the generous support of the Trust the writing of the book would still have several years to go and I am very grateful that I (and my family) have been spared that! In the course of writing this book I was also awarded a grant by the British Academy. This enabled me to make one of the visits to Waco and to purchase some highly specialized research materials.

My wife, Rose-Marie, and my children, Matthew, Stephen, and Sarah have put up with me over the past several years as I have sought to bring this project to a close. 'Dad's book on Waco' has been very much a part of the Newport household for the past few years, for too long in fact, and I am fortunate in having a family that has been as patient as has mine. Mitzy, our cat, has kept me company during some very late nights.

Eastertide, 2004   K.G.C.N.

Contents

Plates

Abbreviations

ATF	[Bureau of] Alcohol, Tobacco, and Firearms
CEV	Combat Engineer Vehicle
FLIR	Forward Looking Infrared [technology]
HRT	Hostage Rescue Team
KJV	King James Version
KRLD	The news radio station at Dallas-Fort Worth, Texas
MRE	Meal-ready-to-eat
NRSV	New Revised Standard Version
NT	Negotiation tapes
SDA	Seventh-day Adventist
SWAT	Special Weapons and Tactics
TXC	Texas Collection at Baylor University, Waco, Texas

1

'A Mad Man in Waco': David Koresh in Popular Perspective

On 19 April 1993, what was to become one of the lasting images of the late twentieth century appeared on television screens across the globe. 'Mt. Carmel', a rather ramshackle set of buildings about twelve miles from Waco, Texas, the headquarters of the Branch Davidian movement, was ablaze. Inside were eighty-nine members of the community including its leader, David Koresh,[1] sixty-eight adults and twenty-one children,[2] all but nine of whom were to die.[3]

The events of that day were the climax of a siege that had been in progress for fifty-one days. The stand-off had started on 28 February with the arrival of two cattle trucks carrying some seventy-five agents from the Bureau of Alcohol, Tobacco, and Firearms (ATF),[4] who had come to serve a search-and-arrest warrant and to inspect the Branch Davidian premises for alleged illegal weapons. That initial raid was itself the climax of a very long period of investigation during which evidence was gathered relating to the Branch Davidians' purchase of guns, hardware that might be used to convert those guns into fully automatic weapons, and other materials that the ATF suspected had been purchased for the production of destructive devices (grenades).[5] Two warrants were in place, one authorizing the search of the Mt. Carmel property and another address,[6] the other for the arrest of David Koresh aka Vernon Wayne Howell.[7]

Despite careful planning on the part of the ATF, which included training at a military base and a month-long surveillance operation conducted at close range, the initial raid on Mt. Carmel was a disaster. A gun battle ensued in which four ATF agents and a number of Branch Davidians died. After this initial shootout, a ceasefire was brokered. The ATF retrieved their injured and dead colleagues, and the pictures of their retreat, like those of the later fire, became an image played and replayed on TV screens around the world. Within hours the whole situation was effectively in the hands of the FBI. One of the most significant stand-offs between American government agencies and US citizens had begun. It would end in tragedy.

For all sorts of reasons what was happening at Waco caught the media's attention and the response was intense. The events themselves were dramatic enough and made powerful news stories: dead and wounded ATF agents being carried away from the battle scene, footage of the initial raid, including extensive gunfire involving both parties, images of the 'compound' silhouetted against the Texan skyline, all made spectacular television. But the interest probably went a good deal deeper than just this, and the appeal of the Waco TV pictures was of more than simply immediate, individual, and visual interest. What was happening at Waco on that cold February morning played, rather, directly on collective fear. Here, surely, if ever it were needed, was evidence of just how dangerous religious 'cults'[8] can be. (And to some subsections of society, here, surely, was evidence of a government gone amok.) Here we see the enemy within.[9]

In the days that followed, the world's media indulged in a feeding frenzy. In much reporting, David Koresh was portrayed as the archetypal leader of such movements: a man whose hold over his followers was complete, to the point of his being able, if he so wished, to order them to commit suicide in the knowledge that they would do so. Charges of 'brainwashing' abounded, giving extra emphasis to the worrying point that society was not safe while such madmen lived in its midst, especially if both the brainwasher and the brainwashed happened also to have an interest in, and a stockpile of, guns. Fear and loathing were heightened further once tales of Koresh's sexual appetite got out (including his interest in under-age girls).[10] There were some more balanced reports, of course, and these became more frequent and substantial as the siege wore on, but the immediate media coverage fixed (perhaps one might better say 'confirmed') in the minds of the world's public the view that what was happening at Waco was fundamentally a case of a religious maniac who, together with his followers, had finally gone right off the rails.[11] It was not long before the same public was reminded of Jim Jones and the People's Temple, and hence the prospect of another mass suicide similar to that in Jonestown, Guyana, was raised.

As the siege continued, media interest waned somewhat, though the familiar images of the Mt. Carmel centre, perhaps now with banners such as 'Rodney King we understand' or 'God help us, we want the press' hanging from an upstairs window, were never entirely absent from news bulletins. When, on 19 April, the fire broke out and Mt. Carmel was razed to the ground, its occupants either perishing amid the flames or arrested as they fled from the burning buildings, public interest understandably revived.[12] Mt. Carmel once again commanded the front pages of the world's newspapers. A similar tale was told to that of fifty-one days before: Koresh, it seemed, had engineered his own death and that of his followers. News bulletins and talk shows covered aspects of the siege and discussed the evident danger such 'cults' posed to society at large. Public interest is, however, notoriously fickle and before too long Waco had again ceased to be of major interest.

For a small group, however, what happened at Waco was of more lasting concern. First and foremost there were those who had survived the siege and the fire, and the friends and families of those who had not. And there were others for whom Waco had struck a particular chord. Among these were people quick to produce the first wave of books seeking to treat what had happened in fuller detail. Perhaps the most widely known of these was by Marc Breault and Martin King, a book with the eye-catching title *Preacher of Death*.[13] The book built upon King's documentary on Koresh, filmed before the siege and screened in 1994.[14] That documentary has provided some excellent footage of life inside Mt. Carmel, and the book, too, contains some useful first-hand material from Breault. Neither the book nor the documentary, however, has any claim to being even an attempt at an unbiased account of Koresh and his followers. That is made very clear indeed in what King has to say about his motives in travelling from Australia to talk to Koresh in person. He had quite clearly made up his mind on Koresh well before he visited Waco. (One suspects of course that his views were largely those transmitted to him by Breault.) Near the beginning of the book King states just what his purpose was:

Vernon believed we'd travelled half-way across the world on a public relations exercise so he could strike back at his disenchanted former followers ... The truth was that we had come to Mount Carmel to expose him as a cruel, maniacal, child-molesting, pistol-packing religious zealot who brainwashed his devotees into believing that he was the messiah.[15]

Throughout the book such a view is developed with, one has to say, some obvious concern for those of Koresh's followers who were, in the authors' view, hoodwinked by Koresh and led to their deaths as a consequence. There is a good deal of unsubstantiated assertion in this book, however, and it has the feel of the haste with which it was composed.

A somewhat better researched book is that of David Leppard.[16] As a journalist (he was deputy editor of the British newspaper the *Sunday Times* when he wrote the book), he was able to ferret out a good deal of information on Koresh. Regrettably, however, almost nothing is referenced, so the academic reader will be frustrated in being largely unable to check the assertions—at times potentially very significant—that are made. Some of the material seems to have been recycled from such sources as Mark England at the *Waco Tribune-Herald* (the person largely responsible for 'The Sinful Messiah' series of articles in that newspaper), Michelle Coffey of the

Melbourne Sun Times, and Geordie Greig, a fellow worker on the *Sunday Times*.[17] Leppard pays particular tribute to the work of the *Washington Post's* Curt Suplee, who, says Leppard, 'has written exclusively on berserkers and other mass murderers'.[18] To be sure, there are more substantial sources in evidence in the book, and Leppard is at pains to point out that where possible he has used court and other official documentation.[19] But the influence of Breault and other ex Branch Davidians is apparent. Indeed Leppard himself states that his account of life at Mt. Carmel has drawn heavily on such material.[20] The use of these sources is understandable, though academic researchers may be more wary of them than Leppard. What is also clear is that whatever strengths Leppard might have as a journalist, he appears to have seriously misunderstood the way religious groups such as the Branch Davidians work and the kind of people attracted to them. He wrote:

> Cults such as the Branch Davidians attracted the lonely, the lost, the unloved and the naive. Their members came from all over but had at least one thing in common: they were alienated from modern society and were searching for a replacement. Many were society's losers with nowhere else to go. Others sought spiritual salvation and believed they would discover it by joining a cult. A few, like George Roden, were simply mad.[21]

There may have been some at Mt. Carmel who fitted this description, but the majority did not: Wayne Martin was a Harvard-trained lawyer, Steve Schneider had a master's degree from the University of Hawaii, Livingstone Fagan had degrees from Manchester Metropolitan University and had been trained as a Seventh-day Adventist (SDA) pastor at Newbold College in England, and Paul Fatta had a highly successful business with an annual turnover running into millions of dollars. Most came from loving homes with strong family ties and were active members of their local SDA Church. These were not social misfits, lacking intelligence or material success.

A similar book by another journalist, Tim Madigan,[22] was written in four weeks, and as with the efforts of King and Breault the haste shows. Again the researcher will be infuriated by the lack of references. In the preface Madigan indicates that most of the material has come from private interviews and the work of fellow reporters. Again, however, a good deal appears to have come from sources that can hardly be thought of as independent; these include grieving family members such as Samuel Henry and Lloyd Hardial.[23] Most problematic of all is the fact that Rick Ross, who wrote the foreword to the book, was quite obviously a source of great importance to Madigan. Ross's role as a 'deprogrammer' of ex-'cult' members is well known and his views on the members of such groups is as one-sided as it is vociferous. One might think that at the very least Madigan should have sought a counterbalance to the views he was here repeating. He did not.

Within just a few months of the ending of the Waco siege, then, there were at least three reasonably substantial books already available to the public. These were soon to be joined by a film, the shooting of which had begun within days of the fire, namely *Ambush in Waco*.[24] This repeated much of what had by now become the popular line: Koresh was a sex-crazed maniac who duped his followers into accepting his twisted views on life, death, and the world that is to come.[25]

Better by far is the book by Brad Bailey and Bob Darden which, though it carries a similarly provocative title, *Mad Man in Waco*, is much more balanced than the others, and contains evidence of some considerable research, despite having been written in a matter of months.[26] Indeed, on matters relating to Koresh's tradition it remains an exceptionally valuable source, its one real weakness being the very hit-and-miss nature of its referencing of sources. Much of the book's considerable value derives from the use the authors have made of the superlative collection of primary materials now located in the Texas Collection (hereinafter 'TXC') at Baylor University in Waco itself.

Bailey and Darden made a particularly valuable contribution to Branch Davidian studies in that they saw the need not to begin their account simply with the arrival at Mt. Carmel of David Koresh. This is a movement that goes back a long way. The 'Branch' Davidians were an offshoot of the older 'Davidian' tradition which had started (under a different name) in 1929; it had been in Waco since 1935. Other books mention this fact, and essays such as that by Pitts give an excellent (mainly historical) overview.[27] But it was to Bailey and Darden, and still, prior to the publication of this present book, largely to them alone, that the task of exploring the wider history and theology of the trajectory as a whole was left.[28]

The sources accessed by Bailey and Darden and now located in TXC are varied. They range from secondary literature through press cuttings spanning the entire period with which we are here concerned to primary sources, documentary and otherwise.[29] Some are particularly illuminating of the early period in the story of the Davidian movement. Chief among these is a really quite remarkable volume, the oral memoirs of long-time Davidian George Saether.[30] Saether went to Mt. Carmel in September 1937 and remained there until at least early 1961.[31] The memoirs provide a rare insight into the workings of the community, its prophet, its troubles, and its near collapse leading up to the formation of the Branch Davidians in *c.* 1962, when Saether left. TXC also holds a mass of material relating to the times of the first leaders of the Branch Davidians, Ben and Lois Roden and their son George. Before February 2003 TXC was much weaker on materials relating to Koresh (a fact perhaps reflected in Bailey and Darden's book, where the specifically

Koresh-related section is noticeably weaker). However, this gap has now been filled.[32]

Bailey and Darden used material generated by the Davidians and Branch Davidians themselves, rather than being almost wholly dependent upon the testimony of ex-members and others likely to be hostile to Koresh and his followers, and this is welcome. The sections on Houteff and the Rodens are fundamentally sound, and a good deal more balanced than one might expect given the speed at which the volume was produced. The Rodens get a worse press than the Houteffs, but this seems to reflect the evidence itself, a point that will become apparent later in this volume. The overall tone of the section on Koresh remains essentially negative and it does not appear that the authors really understood the internal workings of this group. Koresh is still portrayed as fundamentally bad: a manipulative, sex-crazed, power hungry, and downright wicked person who duped his followers. In fact the community of Koresh's Mt. Carmel is portrayed not as a community at all, but rather as a boot-camp in which Koresh himself barks out the orders to his near-terrified, and near zombie-like, followers.

The immediate published response to what happened at Waco, then, was fundamentally negative: Koresh was a maniac and his followers were brainwashed, just plain stupid, and/or social misfits who were prepared to give up anything in order to gain a sense of belonging. These possibilities are not mutually exclusive. But there was another aspect of this reaction which was, if anything, even more lopsided and extreme. This was the view that what happened at Waco was at the very best a massive blunder on the part of government agencies (both ATF and FBI), followed by a cover-up; at worst it was a conspiracy from start to finish. While there were rumblings of this during the siege itself, the view that the government agencies were either grossly and criminally negligent or else murderers plain and simple took a bit longer to get off the ground. However, the view is now a force to be reckoned with. The internet, for example, is saturated with it, as even the shallowest of trawls using the most neutral of search words will quickly reveal. Numerous sites claim to give 'the truth' about what really happened at Mt. Carmel; this turns out to be that the Branch Davidians—innocent, God-fearing people who were simply exercising their right to bear arms—were ruthlessly and viciously attacked by the ATF. The FBI, so some claimed, went even further; they purposely set fire to the Mt. Carmel property and shot at any Branch Davidians seeking to exit the building by any route not open to public view. The evidence of these crimes was quickly destroyed. All this was done with the full approval of the highest authorities in the White House. In addition to web sites that propose this sort of view, which are numerous,[33] there are also a number of films and books. The films include *Waco: The Rules of Engagement*

(1997),[34] *Waco: A New Revelation* (1999),[35] *The FILR Project* (2001),[36] and two films put out by Linda Thompson: *Waco the Big Lie* (*c.*1993)[37] and *Waco: The Big Lie Continues* (*c.*1994).[38] Particularly worthy of note among the books that argue the case are Carol Moore's *The Davidian Massacre* (1995),[39] David Hardy and Rex Kimball's *This is not an Assault*,[40] and Reavis's *The Ashes of Waco*.[41]

While one may wish to disagree with some of the 'findings' of such films and books and the views put forward so aggressively on some of the web sites, all these expressions are at least physically peaceful. One individual who felt strongly about what had happened at Waco, and had a very clear view on who was to blame for the perceived infringements of individual rights, however, took no time to write a book or produce a video, but went for more direct action. Timothy McVeigh bombed the Alfred P. Murrah building in Oklahoma City on the second anniversary of the Waco fire, claiming that he was acting partly as a result of his anger over Waco.[42]

With the exceptions of Bailey and Darden's work and that of Moore, Hardy and Kimball, the bulk of the work mentioned is of a fundamentally popular kind. Indeed, in a more leisurely academic book such as this such contributions would not normally be reviewed in any detail. However, they are important here; not so much for what they might tell us about Koresh and the Branch Davidians (though the King–Breault volume is useful in this respect), but rather for what they tell us about the way Waco was interpreted by those whose job it is to keep the rest of us reliably informed on news events. It is worth underscoring again that King, Leppard, and Madigan are all professional journalists.

Academic monographs on Waco are not numerous, but of generally good quality. The first was a collection of materials and very short essays edited by James R. Lewis.[43] Here the initial work on Waco by some of the foremost experts in the field was collected together and augmented by a helpful collection of primary documents and responses from those centrally involved in the conflict. There is much in this volume of value and it is cited throughout this present study. The overall tone of the work is striking. The editor's own essay 'Showdown at the Waco Corral: ATF cowboys shoot themselves in the foot', for example, is a withering attack on the ATF's lack of professionalism in dealing with the Branch Davidians, a lack that was, in Lewis's view, at least partly driven by a concern to get good media coverage of the raid ahead of Department of Treasury decisions. Other essays point out what the authors view as the failure of the FBI negotiators to understand the mindset of the Branch Davidians inside Mt. Carmel, despite (as the essay by Tabor in particular points out) the efforts of religious studies scholars to assist the FBI in their understanding of the group.[44]

The generally negative portrayal of the ATF and the FBI found in many of the essays in Lewis's book was a sign of what was to come in the professional academic response to Waco. James Tabor and Eugene Gallagher argued a similar case.[45] According to them, the FBI simply failed to understand what was going on inside Mt. Carmel during the siege and made next to no attempt to understand even the basics of Branch Davidian theology. Misunderstandings of the group, its dynamics, and its theology led, so the authors argue, to the use of inappropriate methods in seeking to get the Branch Davidians out. This was not a hostage situation and should not have been treated as such.

On some of these points Tabor and Gallagher are surely right. For example, the tape recordings of the FBI–Branch Davidian negotiations during the fifty-one days demonstrate that the FBI understood almost nothing of Branch Davidian theology, and there is no indication that negotiators did anything to try to change this situation. One has to ask why; but one has to ask also what difference it might have made if the negotiators had understood Koresh's thought world. Would it actually have made a difference if, for example, the FBI negotiators had been able to debate with Koresh the (biblical) strengths and weaknesses of his view that he was the Lamb of Revelation 5, or had been able to talk on his wavelength regarding the fulfilment of the seals? It might have been an interesting exchange of views, but would any practical advantage have been gained? This is taken up further in Chapter Thirteen of this book.

It is argued here that the FBI may have been less to blame than is often imagined. The Branch Davidians were a volatile group under Koresh, whose leadership had changed the nature of the community significantly. It is true that the Davidians under Victor Houteff (Chapters Three and Four) and the Branch Davidians under the Rodens (Chapters Six and Seven) were fundamentally a millennial group with expectations that the millennium would come about violently. However, in these cases the expected violence would be the work of God and God alone and in any case would be first targeted only on the hypocritical members of the SDA Church. Houteff and the Davidians expected to be players in this drama only in so far as it was their job to mark out those who were *not* to be slain. Roden had the same view, though he appears to have differed from Houteff in arguing that the slaying agents would be human beings not angels.[46] Koresh, on the other hand, seems to have taken the view that it was he who (with the army of righteous martyrs) would one day slay the wicked.[47]

Neither should one underestimate the significance of 28 February to the Branch Davidian scheme of things. The ATF decided to 'raid' Mt. Carmel using dynamic entry techniques. The element of surprise was lost and the plan went terribly wrong. What had been planned as a well-executed operation which would secure the Branch Davidians' arsenal while the group were still in a state of shock from the force of entry was transformed, by blunder and poor judgement rather than by design, into an attempt to enter the property of a well-armed group of eschatologically confident and religiously determined individuals forewarned of an impending assault by those they considered to be on the side of Satan. When the FBI arrived they were not simply facing a religious group with some views that most of the rest of the world would find very odd. They were facing also a group effectively already under siege whose underlying world view was eschatological and who expected one day to be a part of an army that would wreak God's vengeance upon the wicked. Worse still, their home had been attacked by the very forces they identified as one of the book of Revelation's apocalyptic beasts. This was now a highly volatile situation and the FBI were right to think that the worst might come about, even if they thought it for the wrong reasons. One suspects that however well-informed and however well-meaning they might have been, had Tabor, Gallagher, and others been granted access to the telephone lines, they would have been hard-pressed to persuade Koresh and the other Branch Davidians to come out. One suspects too that they would have had their work cut out in seeking to make Koresh adjust the eschatological timetable that he had evidently drawn up in his mind from an early point in the siege. Given the stakes, however, it might have been worth a try.

In general, then, the literature on the Waco siege falls into three main genres.[48] First there is the popular material, in which Koresh is portrayed as either mad or bad or both and his followers characterized as being largely unable to resist the force of his will. Second there is what is again largely popular material, found mostly on the internet. Here the government agencies are seen as being almost entirely to blame. Some of that material goes so far as to argue that the whole chain of events, from the planning of the initial raid to the alleged cover-up after the fire, was planned. Here we have oppressive government agencies planning and executing an infringement of civil liberties. Finally there is the academic literature, which is closer to the second category than to the first, but less extreme in its understanding of the dynamics of the situation. The events at Waco were, according to many scholars, more the result of (perhaps wilful) ignorance and blunders than any presumed conspiracy.

These three positions are reflected in the way the fire is explained. According to those of the 'anti-cult' persuasion, the Branch Davidians set fire to the place themselves. Why they should have done this is not clear. Perhaps it was the last insane act of the madman in charge. The conspiracy theorists quite often argue that the fire was set deliberately by the FBI, either by using tanks that had flame-throwers attached, or by people who sneaked up to the compound and torched it; perhaps both. The scholarly community has been more likely to argue that the FBI were responsible for the fire, but that it was accidental. Kerosene lamps used by the Branch Davidians may have been knocked over during the move to insert the CS gas, or else 'pyrotechnic' tear gas rounds caused the fire inadvertently. It will be argued (especially in Chapters Fourteen and Fifteen) that none of these explanations is satisfactory.

The other major criticism to be made of almost all the literature referred to is that it is focused almost exclusively on the period of David Koresh, more specifically on the period of the siege, and more specifically again on two days of the siege: 28 February and 19 April. By comparison little attention has been paid to the group as a religious trajectory, in terms of what went before it or what followed (neither the Davidian nor the Branch Davidian tradition has as yet reached its end). This is a serious gap since no account of what happened at Waco can really hope to make sense outside the broader Davidian and Branch Davidian context. It is true that Koresh took the movement in some new directions and introduced into the tradition some elements previously lacking. These include the two things for which the Branch Davidians under Koresh became most infamously known: guns and odd sexual arrangements; though in fact even these could be explained in terms of a development of the tradition to which Koresh belonged.

The Davidian/Branch Davidian tradition as a whole has followed an interesting path. Its story is one of survival in the face of near overwhelming odds: internal dispute, prophetic disappointment, and significant fragmentation being among the things it had somehow to survive. But survive it did and survive it still does, for despite the destruction of one major part of the Davidian and Branch Davidian tradition, other parts continue to live on— the Branch Davidians only just, but the older Davidian Seventh-day Adventists with more confidence. At the same time the trajectory has at all points refused even for a moment to move towards any accommodation with the wider world. There never has been even the slightest hint of denominalization; indeed, if anything the groups become even more distant from society as they mature. That is certainly the case with the Branch Davidians, a tradition that seems now more or less, and quite literally, to have burnt itself out.

Before this story begins in detail, however, another aspect of the reaction to what happened at Waco in 1993 needs to be considered. As will quickly become apparent, just as the Branch Davidians emerged from the older 'Davidians', so the 'Davidians' emerged from the SDA Church, and throughout their history neither Davidians nor Branch Davidians have felt the need to cut the umbilical cord to the original movement. Indeed theologically they could not, for despite some fairly major differences both the Davidians and Branch Davidians have only ever wished to define themselves with reference to mainstream Seventh-day Adventism, with which they have developed an antagonistic and entirely parasitic relationship.[49]

For their part, the Seventh-day Adventists have not looked with favour upon their Davidian and Branch Davidian offspring. This may be because the mainstream Seventh-day Adventists, unlike the Davidians and Branch Davidians, have sought accommodation with the world and have moved towards denominalization. This is particularly true of those employed in a professional capacity by the SDA Church. Far from being a 'cult' or a 'sect', so it has been collectively argued, and far too from being less than fully Christian, SDA academic professionals have sought, with some success, to present their Church as being a full and entirely legitimate member of the wider Christian family. Consequently attempts have been made to reduce SDA tensions with both the world and the wider Christian Church. An event like Waco and the dragging of the good name of the SDA Church through the subsequent blood-soaked mud could set this process back years. Professional Seventh-day Adventists hence reacted quickly. One can understand this. The Waco story was a big one and the level of public interest high. The last thing that the professionals in this Church wanted was for the movement to which they belonged to be judged guilty by (the in fact indisputable) association.

But the SDA response was not entirely uniform and the varied reactions of the Church to the events of Waco themselves make an interesting study into the competing pressures, objectives and self-understandings operative within the SDA fold. This has been adequately summarized and discussed in a useful essay by Ronald Lawson, who has noted the most important literature.[50]

As Lawson indicates, there was an 'official' response: that the Branch Davidians had nothing whatsoever to do with Seventh-day Adventism, to which they were at best very distantly related. No effort or expense was spared on the Church's part in an effort to distance itself from the Waco 'cultists'. A public relations firm was hired and something in the order of $100,000 was spent in an effort to drive a wedge in the public perception of the good Seventh-day Adventist folk and those gun-toting maniacs holed up at Mt. Carmel. The strategy worked well, and the message was reinforced time and time again: Seventh-day Adventists and Branch Davidians had no connection. Such a view can be seen in, for example, a press release sent out by the British Union of Seventh-day Adventists in the immediate aftermath of the initial raid, which stated categorically that the Church was not connected to the Branch Davidians.[51] Just as clear was the press release put out by the General Conference, whose first line read ' "Branch Davidians" in the news today have no connection with the Seventh-day Adventist Church'.[52] The report went on to state that 'no one of them [i.e. the Branch Davidians] is known to hold membership in a Seventh-day Adventist Church at Waco or any other place'.

(It may have been true that none of the Branch Davidians were 'known' to hold membership in the SDA Church, but it is extremely unlikely that none of them did.) As the days and weeks and months went by the 'official' line did not soften. In a special report on Waco published in the *Adventist Review* in June 1993 a series of near rhetorical questions was addressed by William G. Johnsson, the editor. The first of these is, 'Can we truly say that the Seventh-day Adventist Church had no connection with David Koresh's group?' The answer given is, 'Absolutely'.[53]

In a formal sense the position taken by the SDA leadership was right. Mt. Carmel was not an SDA-owned property, Koresh and others, including Steve Schneider, had been disfellowshipped from the Church, and on a number of significant points there was a chasm between the teachings of Koresh and those of the mild-mannered (if theologically aggressive) SDA Church. The response was also understandable: the professional leadership of no Church would wish to be associated with the events of Waco, least of all perhaps one that has sought, as the SDA leadership has, to swim with the current of denominalization, only to find itself periodically pushed back by the opposing tides of traditionalism. However, the overall cumulative impression given in the official SDA response was wrong. Mt. Carmel was not an SDA campus and some of those who lived there were not members of the SDA Church. However, the brute fact is that almost all of those at Mt. Carmel had once been Seventh-day Adventists, and, furthermore, the movement, formally an 'offshoot of an offshoot' (as SDA sources at the time were at pains to point out)[54] nevertheless continued to draw its vitality from the original stock and root. This is a point that will become apparent in later chapters; we note here only in brief that the Davidian/Branch Davidian trajectory of Seventh-day Adventism has remained substantially shackled to its SDA mother faith. For example, there has never been any significant development of a non-Seventh-day Adventist Branch Davidian leadership—Victor Houteff was a Seventh-day Adventist and the Rodens and Koresh were recruited directly from the ranks of the SDA Church. Other key figures such as Schneider, Livingstone Fagan, Cliff Sellors, and Wayne Martin were direct ex-Seventh-day Adventists. Similarly, while there were major points of theological difference between mainstream Seventh-day Adventism and the Branch Davidians under Koresh, there were also points of highly distinctive similarity. These will emerge in later chapters of this book. To say that what happened at Waco, then, was nothing to do with the SDA Church is just simply wrong.

In fact such a view comes across fairly clearly in one of the Church's own publications, namely *The Messenger*, a journal for the SDA Church in the British Isles. To its credit, *The Messenger* printed a letter which voiced dissent from the official position. The author wrote:

Dear Editor,

I am concerned at the Church's attitude towards the Davidian Cult. Over the past few weeks the Church has been at pains to disassociate itself from this group, and rightly so as we do not accept their radical teachings, but I do [not][55] feel that our responsibility towards them can be dismissed so easily. In actual fact the nine from the Manchester area were, until just two years ago, members in good and regular standing, not just fringe members but active within the Church.[56]

Also to be noted is the very candid work of Dennis Hokama. A short summary of some of what he had to say was published in *Adventism Today*,[57] and in two unpublished papers he went into more detail in outlining his concerns and making it clear that, in his view, the church could not shirk its responsibility so easily.[58] It is regrettable that those papers were never published.

The 'official' response of the Church is not the only one that can be detected in SDA sources, however. In particular there were two other sections within Adventism which for various reasons had rather less hostile reactions to the Waco group. These were, rather ironically, those on the very conservative, and those of the more liberal, wings of the Church.

The conservatives tended to view the whole episode as an opportunity, squandered some said by the Church's leaders, to get across to the general public the true content of SDA apocalypticism as opposed to the aberrant form put forward by Koresh. Such a view comes across in a number of sources. One example is found in *Our Firm Foundation*—an interesting publication which gives voice to a particularly conservative form of Seventh-day Adventism. The June 1993 issue was entirely given over to the events at Waco, and while, as would be expected, there is little sympathy for the theological position taken by the Branch Davidians, the issue as a whole certainly sought to make the most of a bad episode in the Church's history. One writer, for example, argued that the events of Waco, while tragic, had nevertheless provided the Church with a golden opportunity to get across its message to the general public, a public which, especially in Britain, had to that point been virtually unaware even of the existence of the SDA Church, let alone in possession of an understanding of its divinely inspired doctrines.[59]

Such sentiments were not limited to those of the Firm Foundation section of the Church. George W. Reid, then director of the very conservatively inclined Biblical Research Institute of the General Conference of Seventh-day Adventists, speaking before the fire of 19 April, is reported in a Church source as expressing the view that Waco would be to the long-term benefit of the Seventh-day Adventists. This was so, the report stated, since in Reid's view the media coverage of Waco had provided the opportunity for the Church to point out publicly the differences between its official theology and that taught at Mt. Carmel, and hence get 'the truth' across (the absolute truth that is, not just the truth about what Seventh-day Adventists really teach).[60] In the same report Cyril Miller, president of the South-western Union Conference, noted that 'the focus of attention may cause more individuals to seek more information about the Church. This will enable us to share the truth'.[61]

Some other conservatives went even further. To them Koresh was himself an eschatological sign, for, they argued, the Bible clearly states that before the end false prophets and false Christs will appear (cf. Matt. 24.24);[62] distressing as the events of Waco were, then, they must also be seen positively, for they show just how close the end really is.

The liberal wing of the SDA Church, on the other hand, had views so distant from those of Koresh that he was not a threat to them in any way. For this group Waco posed the question of how helpful the traditional SDA interpretation of the book of Revelation was. The publication *Spectrum* gave voice to this liberal concern, and in a remarkably candid issue several SDA commentators spoke their minds.[63] The response is best summed up by the editorial headline: 'We didn't start the fire, but the tinder was ours'.[64] Thus for this part of the Church, Waco was at least a good stick with which to beat the conservatives.

Somewhat surprisingly there has been no full-scale attempt on the part of the SDA Church to investigate Waco from a rigorously academic standpoint. The substantial publications that have appeared from Church sources have largely been for home consumption, written with pastoral rather than academic intent.[65] A good deal of the material is, understandably, highly defensive in tone, with much space given to an explanation of how Koresh erred on points of biblical interpretation and to the extent to which what he had to say was out of tune with SDA doctrine. The only sure guard against the likes of Koresh, so one Seventh-day Adventist commentator put it, is for people 'to know the scriptures better'.[66]

Perhaps the closest one comes to a full SDA account of what happened at Waco is the popular-level book by Cari Hoyt Haus and Madlyn Lewis Hamblin: *In the Wake of Waco: Why Were Adventists among the Victims?*[67] Chapter 18 of this work is quite illuminating and indeed is a helpful statement of some of the points of obvious theological contact between mainstream Seventh-day Adventists and the Branch Davidian tradition. Much of the book, however, is concerned to build up a case, usually without any evidence that can be checked, that Koresh was the kind of person that traditional anti-cult propagandists and the media at the time have generally made such leaders in general and Koresh in particular out to be: somewhat insane, certainly very manipulative, sexually deviant, arrogant, and entirely lacking any moral code that would make him take into consideration the good of others. For example, claims that Koresh exercised mind control are frequent in the book,[68] despite the fact that such claims run counter to the evidence of internal dissent the authors themselves discuss.[69] At one point they go so far as to suggest that Koresh may even have brainwashed himself,[70] while at another they describe him as 'mentally unbalanced'.[71]

Some of the points Haus and Hamblin make may be worth further consideration. For example, the charge that Koresh was arrogant and somewhat manipulative appears to be not too far from the truth. Unfortunately, however, Haus and Hamblin provide no real evidence to back up their assertions, and the presence in the book of a number of factual errors rather weakens one's confidence in the judgements to which they come. This is not a particularly scholarly volume and the level of research it contains is below what one would expect of an academic monograph. In fact it would not have come under scrutiny here had other more substantial material existed. Such material might have been written by those in the Church whom one might reasonably expect to take on the task of addressing the question that Haus and Hamblin have properly identified: just why *were* so many Seventh-day Adventists among the dead at Waco? It is indeed surprising, given the number of professional Seventh-day Adventists who hold posts in SDA seminaries and universities, that the task of seeking to answer this question in a full monograph was left to two individuals not so employed.[72] But that is the situation. It is a shame both academically and pastorally; academically because only a Seventh-day Adventist could really answer the question, and pastorally because the leadership has, one suspects, let the membership down.

Such then was the SDA response, a response by no means uniform. If there is a unity at all it is in the high level of agreement in these sources that Koresh was manipulative, deviant, and possibly insane, and that his followers were, by and large, duped. In making such claims the Seventh-day Adventists are in the company of the majority of commentators who similarly see the whole Waco tragedy as a (literal) flare-up of religious insanity.

There has of course also been a US government response to Waco. The first substantial documentary incarnation of this was the *Report to the Deputy Attorney General on the Events at Waco, Texas, February 28 to April 19, 1993* (hereinafter '*Report*'). This is largely an account of what in the view of its authors actually happened during the siege, and is defensive in tone. On pages 14–17 there is a woefully inadequate account of the origins of the Branch Davidians, together with some brief remarks on the theology of Koresh. There are factual errors even in those brief remarks, for example that Houteff founded the Davidians in 1934. This, it is true, was the date of the 'first convention', but the movement had been in existence since 1930. The statement that the group 'believed strongly in both the second coming of Christ, and the battle of Armageddon' (15) is so simplistic as to be (unintentionally perhaps) misleading. Nevertheless, the report is helpful and unless one is prepared to go down the route of the conspiracy theorists the information it gives must be taken seriously. The authors lack the theological and biblical tools with which to fashion a rounded response to what Koresh had to say and the way this was taken on board by those to whom he spoke, and so the picture of Koresh is at best lopsided. Here again, as in the sensationalist literature already noted, we find a Koresh who is both mad and bad; a sexually deviant man who exercises mind control through material deprivation. It will be argued in this book that Koresh may have been astonishingly arrogant and not a little insensitive, but whether he could actually control people's minds and get them to do and believe things they would not have done had their minds and wills been free is open to serious question. People could and did leave Mt. Carmel even after Koresh took over the leadership in 1987. The evidence is that the Branch Davidians were not a group of weak-minded (still less stupid) dropouts. Many were well-educated, several had higher degrees and a number were really quite exceptionally articulate. Even the video footage shot inside Mt. Carmel during the siege gives the clear impression of a self-confident group who knew what they believed, knew why they believed it, were able to explain it to others, and were not under any undue pressure from Koresh or anyone else to stay in Mt. Carmel against their better judgement.[73] Treating the incident as a hostage situation was a significant error of judgement on the part of the authorities; it did not allow adequately for the kind of group dynamics operative inside Mt. Carmel or the extent to which this group was fully cohesive (especially after the weaker members were sent out in the days following the initial raid). Later Government sources, while providing far more detailed evidence relating to the outbreak of the fire, the actions of ATF and the FBI and similar matters, do not move much past this point and seem to make the same basic errors.[74]

This book gives a full account of the Davidians and Branch Davidians, including a substantial and documented history of the movement from its beginnings in 1844 to the present day. Throughout, however, there is an even greater emphasis upon theology, for while one might want to disagree with the Davidians and Branch Davidians on almost every theologically distinctive point, one thing is clear: for them theology was life itself. Theology, talk about God, an understanding of God, and an understanding of God's purposes for the world were what made them tick. It was for theology that these believers lived. It was for theology too that some of them died.

For the most part the book is arranged chronologically. Hence in the next chapter an account is given of the origins of the movement within the Millerite and SDA traditions, beginning in 1844. Chapter Three pieces together the development of the Davidians (not yet the 'Branch' Davidians) under Victor T. Houteff, their founder. Chapter Four treats Houteff's theology and in particular his emphasis on the establishment of the antitypical (but literal) kingdom of David in Israel. Chapter Five looks at the movement's near collapse following Houteff's death in 1955 and the crisis that came as a result of a prediction that the world would see the outbreak of the battle of Armageddon some time close to 22 April 1959. That date was also expected to see the resurrection of Houteff himself and the establishment of the kingdom. In the next three chapters attention is given to the leadership and theology of Ben and Lois Roden and the birth of the 'Branch' Davidians. Chapters Nine and Ten introduce the figure of Vernon Wayne Howell (David Koresh), and his ultimately successful quest for the leadership of the Branch Davidian movement. Chapter Eleven explores in some detail the often misunderstood world of Koresh's theology. With Chapter Twelve something of a turning point is reached. In that chapter an account is given of the reasons for and events leading to the initial ATF raid on the Branch Davidian headquarters. This chapter draws more extensively than previous chapters on the available secondary literature. Its conclusion is not particularly radical, but it is important: the ATF did have probable cause to believe that crimes within their jurisdiction (weapons offences) were being committed at Mt. Carmel. With hindsight it is reasonably plain that they made some errors of judgement about how best to serve the search and arrest warrants. Most obviously, on the morning of 28 February, they made what was almost certainly the biggest tactical error of the whole episode, the decision to go ahead with the dynamic entry plan even though the element of surprise had been lost. By the time the FBI took over the Branch Davidians had dug in their eschatological heels and, one suspects, a catastrophe was already on the cards. The FBI's handling of the negotiations is the subject of Chapter Thirteen. In Chapters Fourteen and Fifteen the question of the fire is dealt with in some detail. The conclusion to Chapter Fourteen is not pleasant. The balance of evidence seems to indicate very clearly that the Branch Davidians themselves set Mt. Carmel ablaze. In Chapter Fifteen it is argued that this was not simply an act of suicide, but one of almost unparalleled faith, since for them the death that was to ensue was the gateway to life— not in some celestial realm, but here and now on earth. Their belief was that like the phoenix, though without the extended temporal delay, they would be reborn out of the fire to live as God's righteous ones in the new kingdom. Chapter Sixteen summarizes what has happened in the Branch Davidian movement since 1993 and hence brings their story up-to-date. The final chapter seeks to draw together the whole of the book and offer some specific conclusions.

There are four appendices, two of them substantial. Appendix A contains the testimony of Derek Lovelock, a survivor of the Waco fire. Here he gives a fascinating and important insight into the course of and reasons for his initial attraction to the Branch Davidian message, his visits to Waco, his experience of David Koresh, and his survival of the fire. In many ways it is that appendix that explains the reason for the writing of this book, and the reader may wish to tackle it at this point rather than leaving it until near last. Appendix B takes something of a step backwards and summarizes developments in the Davidian (as opposed to the Branch Davidian) tradition since *c.*1962. The final two appendices present a summary of Waco deaths (Appendix C) and Waco survivors (Appendix D). Regrettably Appendix C is much the longer.

NOTES

1. Somewhat ironically the song 'Mad Man in Waco' was written and produced by David Koresh himself. The 'Mad Man' in question was George Roden, with whom Koresh was in dispute when the song was composed. The proceeds from the sale of the recording were earmarked by Koresh for the payment of defence expenses for himself and his followers who were at that time being prosecuted for various weapons offences arising from a shoot-out with Roden.
2. The count does not include two unborn children; Nicole Gent Little and Aisha Gyarfas Summers were pregnant when they died.
3. For details of Branch Davidian deaths at Mt. Carmel see Appendix C. Details of those who survived are given in Appendix D.
4. In this book the abbreviation 'ATF' rather than 'BATF' is used throughout. The point is rather more than stylistic; in general those who write from an anti-government stance tend to use 'BATF' while those more favourably disposed towards the US Government use 'ATF'. What one calls the [B]ATF has hence become something of a political point in writing about Waco, though no such politics should be read into the usage here.
5. There were also allegations of child abuse. Though these lay outside of the jurisdiction of the ATF, they nevertheless surfaced in the affidavit which was the basis on which the warrants were issued. The details of the investigation are examined more fully in Chapter Ten.
6. This was a garage rented by the Davidians and used for their automobile repair business. It was also used as a delivery address for some of the weapons for which the ATF wished to search.
7. In this book 'David Koresh' will normally be used (Ch. Nine is the exception) regardless of whether the period in focus was before or after Vernon Howell changed his name to David Koresh in August 1990 (on which see further, Ch. Eleven).

8. A brief note on terminology: in popular terms the word 'cult' is generally used to refer to any religious group that holds views that are seen as very strange and/or very extreme. It is often used loosely and more or less interchangeably with the word 'sect'. In so far as these words are used in this book (unless in quotations or, as here, in the context of summarizing the views of others), the word 'cult' is used in the way defined in Rodney Stark and William Sims Bainbridge, *The Future of Religion: Secularization, Revival, Cult Formation* (Berkeley Calif.: University of California Press, 1985), 24–5. According to this definition a 'cult' is a religious group that is fundamentally alien to the culture in which it exists, either because it is brand new or because it has been imported from outside. The word 'sect' is used to refer to groups which, while they exist in a state of tension with the society in which they are found, are not entirely alien to it and in general have split off from another more established and widely accepted religious body. Hence the Mormons are neither a sect nor a cult in Utah, while they are a cult in Italy. Accordingly the Branch Davidians may be referred to as a 'sect', being a splinter group that separated from the Seventh-day Adventists, a group which has achieved a measure of acceptance by its host, at least in North America.

9. On this point see further in particular Stuart A. Wright, 'Construction and Escalation of a Cult Threat: Dissecting Moral Panic and Official Reaction to the Branch Davidians', in Stuart A. Wright, ed., *Armageddon in Waco: Critical Perspectives on the Branch Davidian Conflict* (Chicago and London: The University of Chicago Press, 1995), 75–94; the role of the anti-cult movement in whipping up public hysteria still further is explored in James R. Lewis, 'Self-fulfilling Stereotypes, the Anticult Movement, and the Waco Confrontation', in Wright, ed., *Armageddon in Waco*, 95–110.

10. This charge is examined in detail in Chapter Ten (and see further in particular Christopher G. Ellison and John P. Bartowski, 'Babies were Being Beaten: Exploring Child Abuse Allegations at Ranch Apocalypse', in Wright, ed., *Armageddon in Waco*, 111–49). In essence, while the media much exaggerated the extent to which Koresh engaged in sex with underage girls, that he did so on a number of occasions with at least two minors seems certain. The more general charges of physical and psychological abuse seem groundless.

11. On the media response to Waco in general see especially James T. Richardson 'Manufacturing Consent about Koresh: A Structural Analysis of the Role of Media in the Waco Tragedy', in Wright, ed., *Armageddon in Waco*, 153–76; Anson Shupe and Jeffrey K. Hadden, 'Cops, News Copy and Public Opinion: Legitimacy and the Social Construction of Evil in Waco', in Wright, ed., *Armageddon in Waco*, 177–202.

12. A significant number of those who died at Mt. Carmel died not, it seems, from the effects of the fire itself, but from gunshot wounds. Nine escaped the fire; see Appendices C and D for brief details.

13. Martin King and Marc Breault, *Preacher of Death: The Shocking Inside Story of David Koresh and the Waco Siege* (Victoria, Australia: Signet Books, 1993).

14. *Madman of Waco*, A Current Affair Special (Nine Network Australia, 1994).

15. King and Breault, *Preacher of Death*, 12.

16. David Leppard, *Fire and Blood: The True Story of David Koresh and the Waco Siege* (London: Fourth Estate, 1993).

17. Ibid. vii.

18. Ibid. 182.

19. Ibid. 182.

20. Ibid. 182.

21. Ibid. 7.

22. Tim Madigan, *See No Evil: Blind Devotion and Bloodshed in David Koresh's Holy War* (Fort Worth, Texas: The Summit Group, 1993). At the time of writing the book, Madigan was on the staff of the *Fort Worth Star-Telegram*.

23. Samuel Henry was the only member of the Henry family from Old Trafford, England, who was not a Branch Davidian. His wife and five children died in the fire. Lloyd Hardial was a relative of Sandra Hardial, another British Branch Davidian who perished in the Waco fire.

24. *Ambush in Waco: In the Line of Duty* (Culver City, Calif.: Patchett Kaufman Entertainment, 1993).

25. Clifford L. Linedecker's book *Massacre at Waco, Texas: The Shocking True Story of Cult Leader David Koresh and the Branch Davidians* (New York: St Martin's Paperbacks, 1993) might also be added to this list of basically anti-Koresh literary productions appearing within months of the siege. In places the book opens up the other side of the debate, but in general it reflects the anti-cult agenda seen more clearly in King, Leppard, and Madigan.

26. Brad Bailey and Bob Darden, *Madman in Waco: The Complete Story of the Davidian Cult, David Koresh and the Waco Massacre* (Waco: WRS, 1993).

27. William Pitts, 'Davidians and Branch Davidians: 1929–1987', in Wright, ed., *Armageddon in Waco*, 20–42.

28. Dick J. Reavis's book *The Ashes of Waco: An Investigation* (Syracuse: Syracuse University Press, 1995), for example, has only one short (eight-page) chapter dealing with Victor Houteff, Florence Houteff, Ben Roden, and Lois Roden. James D. Tabor and Eugene V. Gallagher, *Why Waco? Cults and the Battle for Religious Freedom in America* (Berkeley, Los Angeles, and London: University of California Press, 1995), is better; although still only a sketch, it gives some account at least of the principal Davidian and Branch Davidian doctrine prior to Koresh's coming on the scene (33–40).

29. Such sources include audio tapes of Koresh's teachings (his principal method of communication with his scattered followers) and collected video and audio tapes relating to the siege and its aftermath. There is also a good number of photographs.

30. George Saether, *Oral Memoirs* (hereafter 'OM'), TXC. This volume contains transcripts of ten interviews conducted between 12 July 1973 and 30 June 1975 by Dr Dan McGee as part of the Program for Oral History at Baylor University. Similar, but not as extensive, are a series of four interviews also conducted at Baylor University on 1 Feb. 1989 as part of the project, with Glen Green, Sidney

Smith, and Bonnie Smith. The first interview, with all three together, was conducted by David Stricklin and Bill Pitts (hereafter 'GSS1'). There were then three further separate interviews, one each with Sidney Smith only, conducted by Jaclyn Jeffrey (GSS2), Bonnie Smith only, conducted by David Stricklin (GSS3), and with Glen Green only, conducted by Bill Pitts (GSS4). The first interview is recorded also on video tape and all materials are available in draft copies from the Institute of Oral History at Baylor University. Page numbers of the transcripts are given here, but it is important to note that that numbering is likely to change as further work is done by the Institute of Oral History.

31. *OM* 125. The last clear reference to his being at Mt. Carmel is in January 1961 (*OM* 441). He appears to have fallen out with the community shortly after that.
32. In February 2003 TXC was augmented significantly by the addition of the private collection of Mark Swett. Swett, to whom all Waco researchers are indebted, had spent the best part of ten years building up a huge archive of primary and other materials, much of it focused upon Koresh himself. His collection is now at Baylor, which is hence the most important source of primary sources for the study of this aspect of American history. Future researchers will benefit from having the materials in one place.
33. Web sites are inherently unstable and hence no addresses are given here. A quick trawl of the internet using almost any search engine will quickly find examples of such sites.
34. *Waco—The Rules of Engagement* (Los Angeles, Calif.: COPS/Somford Productions, 1997).
35. *Waco: A New Revelation* (Fort Collins, Col.: MGA films Inc., 1999).
36. *The FLIR Project* (Los Angeles, Calif.: COPS, 2001).
37. *Waco: The Big Lie* (Indianapolis, Ind.: American Justice Federation, *c.*1993).
38. *Waco II: The Big Lie Continues* (Indianapolis, Ind.: American Justice Federation, *c.*1994).
39. Carol Moore, *The Davidian Massacre: Disturbing Questions about Waco which Must be Answered* (Franklin, Tenn.: Legacy Communications, and Springfield, Va.: Gun Owners Foundation, 1995).
40. David T. Hardy with Rex Kimball, *This is Not an Assault: Penetrating the Web of Official Lies Regarding the Waco Incident* (Philadelphia: Xlibris, 2001).
41. Reavis, *Ashes of Waco*. This book is exceptionally well written and makes an interesting read. Some of the material Reavis unearthed is potentially important, and a number of references to his work will be found later in this volume. Again, however, the lack of precise detail on sources is frustrating. The book has no footnotes, though the bibliographical note (301–4) is useful.
42. On the link see Mark S. Hamm, *Apocalypse in Oklahoma: Waco and Ruby Ridge Revenged* (Boston: Northeastern University Press, 1997).
43. James R. Lewis, ed., *From the Ashes: Making Sense of Waco* (Lanham, Md.: Rowman and Littlefield, 1994).
44. James D. Tabor, 'The Waco Tragedy: An Autobiographical Account of One Attempt to Avert Disaster', in Lewis, ed., *From the Ashes*, 13–21; also J. Phillip

Arnold, 'The Davidian Dilemma—To Obey God or Man?', in Lewis, ed., *From the Ashes*, 23–31.

45. Tabor and Gallagher, *Why Waco?*

46. This is taken from an interview with Don Adair as part of a series of three he gave to the Baylor University Institute of Oral History (hereinafter 'Adair, "Interviews" '). The first and second were conducted by Dan McGee on 20 Aug. 1993; the third, conducted by Glenn Jonas, took place on 6 Apr. 1994. All were held at the headquarters of the General Association of Davidian Seventh-day Adventists, 282 Davidian Way, Tamassee, South Carolina 29686. The three interviews are numbered consecutively. The reference to the role of men and not angels in the slaying work of God is found on 120–1. (The transcripts of these interviews are still in draft form, so the page numbering is likely to change as further work is undertaken by the Institute of Oral History.)

47. See further Chapter Fifteen.

48. There are three other academic volumes on Waco that ought to be mentioned here. Two relating to the siege in particular are David B. Kopel and Paul H. Blackman, *No More Wacos: What's Wrong with Federal Law Enforcement and How to Fix it* (New York: Prometheus Books, 1997) and Jayne Seminare Docherty, *Learning Lessons from Waco: When the Parties Bring their Gods to the Negotiation Table* (Syracuse: Syracuse University Press, 2001). A useful insight into the logic of the kind of millennialism operative at Waco is found in James D. Faubion, *The Shadows and Lights of Waco: Millennialism Today* (Princeton and Oxford: Princeton University Press, 2001).

49. One exception came in 1959 in the wake of a failed prophecy under which the Davidians were expecting the onset of Armageddon in that year. When it did not happen, one explanation was that God had given the Davidians time to take the message to all Protestants and not just the Seventh-day Adventists alone. This 'new' doctrine caused a major split in the community. See further Chapter Five and Appendix B.

50. Ronald Lawson, 'Seventh-day Adventist Responses to Branch Davidian Notoriety: Patterns of Diversity within a Sect Reducing Tension with Society', *Journal for the Scientific Study of Religion*, 34 (1995), 323–41.

51. See letter of Paul D. Tompkins to SDA ministers in the British Union Conference, 4 Mar. 1993 (Newbold College ref. DF367-b 10; Newbold College is an SDA institution in Bracknell, Berkshire, England), and the press release itself (ref. DF 367-b 15); see also DF 367-b 15 (which comprises several items stapled together); letter of D. W. McFarlane, then president of the South England Conference of Seventh-day Adventists, which urges 'departmental directors, pastors, elders, Bible instructors and institutional heads' to 'emphasize, as the General Conference has already done, that the Church is in no way connected with the "Branch" '.

52. Newbold College ref. DF 367-b 15.

53. William G. Johnsson, 'Pain and Perspective', *Adventist Review*, (3 June 1993), 4.

54. The phrase 'an offshoot of an offshoot' is historically accurate since the Branch Davidians were one of the groups that emerged after the near collapse of the Davidian Seventh-day Adventists. As the weeks went by, however, in some SDA sources the phrase became 'an offshoot of an offshoot of an offshoot' (see, e.g. *Our Firm Foundation*, June 1993, 5; *The Messenger*, 2 Apr. 1993, 1), which is in error.

55. Interestingly the word 'not' is not actually found in the letter, but is unquestionably called for in context.

56. *The Messenger*, 7 May 1993, 6 (Newbold ref. DF 367-b 30).

57. Dennis Hokama, 'Koresh and Ellen White', *Adventism Today*, May–June 1993.

58. Dennis Hokama, 'Converting the Very Elect: Why SDAs Believed David Koresh', unpublished MS, n.d.; id., 'The Ghost from Adventism's Past: Vernon Howell and the LA/SDA Connection', unpublished MS, March, 1993). Copies of both are located in TXC, Mark Swett Collection, folder Hokama.

59. Colin Standish, 'Lessons from Waco', *Our Firm Foundation*, June 1993, 5–6.

60. *Adventist Review*, 18 Mar. 1993, 7.

61. Ibid.

62. See further Lawson, 'Responses', 331–2.

63. *Spectrum: The Journal of the Association of Adventist Forums*, 23/1 (May 1993).

64. Roy Branson, editorial in *Spectrum*, 23/1 (May 1993), 2.

65. Some attempt is made to outline the process by which British Seventh-day Adventists were recruited, in Albert C. Waite, 'From Seventh-day Adventism to David Koresh: The British Connection', *Andrews University Seminary Studies*, 38 (2000), 107–26.

66. The comment is attributed to Pastor Barry Whelan, then pastor of one of the SDA Churches in Melbourne. It is published in 'A Cult that Infiltrated the Church', [*Australian*] *Record*, 8 May 1993, 12.

67. Hagerstown, Md.: Review and Herald Publishing Association, 1993.

68. Haus and Hamblin, *In the Wake of Waco*, see, e.g. 21, 29, 30, 33.

69. Ibid. 35.

70. Ibid. 163.

71. Ibid. 10.

72. At the time of writing, Haus was editor of *Creative Parenting* while Hamblin operated a printing company.

73. A copy of this video footage is in my personal possession.

74. There are a number of other government documents that could be surveyed here. This seems hardly necessary, however, since there is little change in the basic position already clear in the *Report*. Arguably the most important is the *Final Report to the Deputy Attorney General Concerning the 1993 Confrontation at the Mt. Carmel Complex, Waco, Texas* (Washington, DC: Office of Special Counsel, 8 Nov. 2000; hereinafter *Final Report*). The main difference between this and the earlier reports is the addition of some truly enormous appendices. The central findings of the report, however, remain largely the same, though it should be

noted that this final report does criticize a number of government agencies and individuals for lack of attention to detail and/or actual concealment of evidence. This document and others are discussed in significant detail in Chapters Twelve to Fifteen of this book. (Danforth's earlier *Interim Report* (21 July 2000) is not used here since it was superseded by *Final Report* a few months later.)

2

'A Sure Word of Prophecy' (cf. 2 Peter 1.19):
the Bible, Prophecy Belief, and the
Seventh-day Adventist Church

The picture of David Koresh and the Branch Davidians reflected in the more popular sources surveyed in the previous chapter was and is almost entirely wrong. To be sure, they did hold some beliefs and engage in some actions which few (including the FBI) could understand, but this is not necessarily to say that either Koresh as an individual or the group as a whole were mentally unbalanced. That said, getting to grips with the theology of this group is not easy and is not a task that has been undertaken by most of those who have written on Waco. As a consequence the general impression one gets as a result of reading much of what has been written on the Branch Davidians is that their views cannot be fathomed since they are at heart deranged. If this was not true of all of them, so some forms of the argument run, it was certainly true of Koresh himself, who subsequently drew others into his crazed world. The only other explanation that gets significant space in popular level literature is that Koresh was not mad but bad, and those upon whom he inflicted his world view were in fact simply being used by him for his own megalomaniacal and sexually perverse ends.

On the other hand, the kind of understanding of Branch Davidian theology that is evident in some of the more academic work on Waco is also less than fully adequate. These were not simply a group of peace-loving Bible students who had chosen to live a semi-monastic life in order to devote themselves to spiritual concerns. This was an apocalyptic group, with violent expectations, and heavily armed. Koresh was extreme; he did have sex with minors and, it seems, did seek to prepare his community for a violent, if temporary, death.

The theological reality of the Mt. Carmel community was, then, a good deal more complicated than has generally been appreciated. Koresh and the Branch Davidians in general developed a highly complex scheme of biblical interpretation which, if one accepts the underlying principles upon which it is based, both makes sense and exhibits a quite rigorous internal consistency. Above all the Branch Davidians sought to base their beliefs upon the Bible, which, they argued, was the inspired and therefore infallible word of God. (They are not the only ones who have taken this view.) If we are to understand the Branch Davidians and thereby be able to conceive better how it was that a large number of perfectly sane persons chose to defy what others might well judge to be the rational dictates of the situation in which they found themselves during the 1993 stand-off, we are going to need to sojourn in their thought world. This will require first and foremost an appreciation of their understanding of the biblical text. This is true whether, as some might say, their understanding of that text was dictated by their preconceived notions of the world and their place within it, or, as others might argue, they genuinely drew from the Bible (rather than reading into it) their understanding of the role of their community in what they believed to be the last days. Probably the truth lies somewhere between these two poles, but in any case what is surely true is that, by meeting the Branch Davidians on the common ground of the biblical text and then seeking to understand what they made of it, one is able to get at least a partial view of their understanding of the world in which they lived and the significance of the events that were happening. This is no less difficult than indispensable, and a good deal of what follows in this book is concerned with this often-times frustrating task.

One particularly important part of Branch Davidian biblical interpretation was their view of the end times and, to use a popular expression, 'the end of the world'. This is a topic about which the Bible, especially the New Testament, speaks often. Indeed a number of scholars have argued that Jesus himself was an eschatological prophet, perhaps one who looked confidently for the destruction of the Jerusalem temple of his day and its rebuilding, and with it the restoration of Israel as a whole.[1] Certainly many of the New Testament writers were interested in matters pertaining to 'the end of the world'. The author of the gospel of Matthew emphasizes again and again both the nearness of the end, and its cataclysmic nature (see for example Matt. 10.23; Matt. 24), while Mark's gospel contains both the 'little apocalypse' (Mark 13) and two other references to the apocalyptic coming of the Son of Man at the end of time (Mark 8.38; 14.62). Even Luke, who generally softens end-time expectation,[2] does not excise it altogether (see for example Luke 17.22–37), while John, who is sometimes said to have reinterpreted end-time expectation so as to make it relate to the incarnation of the Logos in the past and present, still has some references to the end time (for example John 14.3).[3] Paul can say in what are clearly eschatological contexts 'the appointed time has grown short' (1 Cor. 7.29) and 'the night is far gone, the day is near' (Rom. 13.12), while to the church in Thessalonica he wrote:

the Lord himself, with a cry of command, with the archangel's call and with the sound of God's trumpet, will descend from heaven, and the dead in Christ will rise first. Then we who are alive, who are left, will be caught up in the clouds together with them to meet the Lord in the air; and so we will be with the Lord forever (1 Thess. 4.16–17).

And the story does not stop there. The author of 2 Peter thinks that the end is coming (e.g. 2 Pet. 1.19) as does that of 1 John (e.g. 1 John 2.28), and the author of Ephesians speaks of 'the age that is to come' (Eph. 1.21). The Old Testament[4] is no less plain on the issue. The phrase 'the Day of the Lord', for example, is often used with apparent reference to an eschatological point to which this world is moving (see e.g. Isa. 13.6; Joel 1.15; 2.1, 11), while in the book of Daniel numerous references are made to times when, for example, the dead will rise (Dan. 12.2) and the kingdom of God will come (Dan. 2.44).

Thus the Bible, Old and New Testament alike, does refer to the end of this age and the approach of some kind of eschatological rite of passage into the next. One finds this in the gospels (which may reflect the actual teaching of Jesus on this point), in Paul, in the deutero-Pauline tradition,[5] and elsewhere. The Branch Davidians, who believed that the Bible was the inspired word of God, took such passages with the utmost seriousness. To them the argument was simple: the Bible says that this age will not last for ever, the Bible is the inspired word of God, therefore some sort of transition into 'the age/world to come' is to be anticipated. To be sure the Branch Davidians differed from other Christian millennialists both on the nature of the new kingdom and on the detail of the way in which it would come about, but on the basic issue there is a fundamental consistency: this age will be transformed into some other.

While talk of a new kingdom/age pervades a good deal of scripture, it is arguably in the final book of the Bible, the book of Revelation, that one finds the most dramatic and extensive treatment of matters relating to the end time, and it was this book that really caught the Branch Davidians' attention.[6] Here is found a description of the powers that do currently exist and that will in the future continue to rule humankind. For example, the career of terrible beasts, symbols it seems for world powers, is dramatically outlined in places such as Revelation 13.1–10:

And I stood upon the sand of the sea, and saw a beast rise up out of the sea, having seven heads and ten horns, and upon his horns ten crowns, and upon his heads the name of blasphemy. And the beast which I saw was like unto a leopard, and his feet were as the feet of a bear, and his mouth as the mouth of a lion: and the dragon gave him his power, and his seat, and great authority. And I saw one of his heads as it were wounded to death; and his deadly wound was healed: and all the world wondered after the beast. And they worshipped the dragon which gave power unto the beast: and they worshipped the beast, saying, Who is like unto the beast? who is able to make war with him? And there was given unto him a mouth speaking great things and blasphemies; and power was given unto him to continue forty and two months. And he opened his mouth in blasphemy against God, to blaspheme his name, and his tabernacle, and them that dwell in heaven. And it was given unto him to make war with the saints, and to overcome them: and power was given him over all kindreds, and tongues, and nations. And all that dwell upon the earth shall worship him, whose names are not written in the book of life of the Lamb slain from the foundation of the world. If any man have an ear, let him hear. He that leadeth into captivity shall go into captivity: he that killeth with the sword must be killed with the sword. Here is the patience and the faith of the saints.

This is followed later in the book by a description of the destruction of the beasts at the battle of Armageddon and the entry of the saved people into the 'New Jerusalem' prepared for them by God.

It is very easy for the secular and/or academic mind to underestimate the power such material has in certain faith communities, and not just the Branch Davidians. Certainly a general belief in the eventual return of Jesus to this earth is found extensively in many parts of the Christian world, especially, it seems, North America. So, for example, Paul Boyer refers to a Gallup survey conducted in America in 1983 which indicated that some 62 per cent of Americans had 'no doubts' that Jesus would come to earth again. A later poll (1988) showed that 80 per cent of all respondents expected to appear before God 'on judgement day'. Such results are hardly surprising when two others are taken into account: in 1980 a survey revealed that 40 per cent of Americans regarded the Bible as 'the actual Word of God ... to be taken literally word for word', while a further 45 per cent thought that the Bible was divinely inspired, even if not literally inerrant. As with the Branch Davidians, it seems, so more widely, there is a simple reasoning evident: the Bible is the inerrant word of God, the Bible speaks of the coming of an 'end time', therefore that 'end time' will come. Boyer goes on to describe in detail the boom in prophecy book sales and the growth of evangelical Christianity, which is itself often highly supportive of what he calls 'prophecy belief'.[7]

To Boyer's detailed statistics we might add many more, and some that are particularly relevant here. These include the fact that in 2002 the SDA Church, the parent of Davidianism and the grandparent of Branch Davidianism, had a total membership of almost 13 million, with something like 981,000 new members added to the Church in 2002 alone; even allowing for losses through death and apostasy this figure still represents net growth at the staggering rate of 4.65 per cent (though significantly less than the 2001 growth statistics).[8] The beliefs of the Seventh-day Adventists are considered in some detail in this book, for many of them are presupposed by the Branch Davidians. Suffice it to say here, however, that that Church adopts a very clear-cut line on the interpretation of biblical prophecy, and remains ever expectant of the Lord's return.

To anyone who reads Boyer's book or takes time to look at some of the areas of the Christian church that are currently growing, it will be plain that a fervent belief in the end of the world is today held by millions across the globe. Such beliefs are not the preserve of an extremist few; they are, even today, accepted by tens, perhaps hundreds, of millions.

But such expectation is not a new phenomenon. Indeed, as we have seen, such belief is clearly present in the biblical texts themselves and it is plain also that the post-biblical Christian tradition has always taken seriously a belief in the impending end of the world from an early point in its history. While this is not the place to engage in an extended discussion on this issue, which has in any case received such treatment before,[9] a few comments regarding the history of Christian apocalypticism are called for. It is a basic component of the argument presented in this book that if the Branch Davidians are to be understood, they need to be seen in the context of the tradition to which they firmly belong. Their immediate context is Seventh-day Adventism, but the more general one is the long tradition both in America and Europe of belief in the fulfilment of what are perceived to be the biblical prophecies. Since Koresh and his followers were particularly concerned with the book of Revelation (though the centrality of the book of Psalms and many other Old Testament books is also important),[10] the comments here are focused on the ways in which this book has been understood by Christians down through the centuries.[11] One must be aware, however, that the ways in which the book of Revelation has been read are symptomatic of a much more general belief in the approach of the end and the dawn of the new age.

In the early church the book of Revelation was much discussed and much disputed; it entered into the canon only after some significant debate. What is clear, however, is that by the second half of the second century it had been accepted by the western church as part of scripture; the eastern section of Christianity was less certain.[12] It was generally assumed that the work had been written by John the Beloved Disciple, the author of the fourth gospel and the three epistles, in the context of Roman persecution.

Quite when the book of Revelation began to be the object of detailed exposition is not entirely clear. Chiliasm, belief in the coming of a thousand-year period which would be qualitatively different from the age in which humankind now lives, was a view to which a significant number of the early church writers were drawn. They include Justin Martyr (*c.*100–165), who in his *Apology* made clear his acceptance of the coming of a literal millennium, preceded by a bodily resurrection.[13] Irenaeus of Lyons (*c.*130–*c.*202) also argued such a case and, like Justin, looked for the coming of a millennial period preceded by a literal, bodily resurrection.[14] Tertullian (*c.*160–*c.*240) had a similar scheme, as did Hippolytus (*c.*170–*c.*236).[15] All such expositors were as much concerned with the book of Daniel as with Revelation, but the outcome was much the same: this world was to be transformed into some other. Chiliasm, and with it a literalist reading of the prophetic books of the Bible, can thus be demonstrated to have a firm foothold in the Christian tradition from its outset.

It was Augustine (354–430) who was to bring about fundamental change to the Church's understanding of the book of Revelation, a change that was to last for nearly a thousand years.[16] While Augustine held to the view that this present world would one day end and that Christ would return, he argued that only a relatively small part of the book of Revelation actually deals with these aspects of God's plans for the salvation of humankind. The bulk, he argued, refers to the present state of the world and the place and role of the Church in it. Hence he famously argued that the millennium was not a time yet future, but the period of the Church even now present. This 'millennium' refers, he said, to a long but indefinite time span between the first appearance of Christ and his second coming.[17]

The Augustinian model of interpreting Revelation soon became dominant and remained largely without significant challenge until the work of Joachim of Fiore (*c.*1135–1202).[18] Joachim's importance to the history of the interpretation of Revelation is enormous, although much of the detail of what he had to say seems to have enjoyed only very limited popularity. In many ways Joachim's overall paradigm simply harks back to the pre-Augustinian tradition, though the detail of his scheme was rather novel. In outline he argued that the history of the human race is to be divided into three ages, the age of the Father (the age of Law), the age of the Son (the age of gospel), and the age of the Spirit (the age of freedom). The book of Revelation, Joachim argued, gives a detailed account of the course of these three ages (or 'states' as he referred to them). As such the book refers not only to what was (from John's perspective) future, but also to what was past. Joachim held that the third age had dawned with the coming of St Benedict (*c.*480–550). Thus the Church and people are currently living in the third and final stage in the course of history.

It is plain, then, that for Joachim the book of Revelation deals with matters contained within the course of human history. It is not just about the past, not just about the present, and not just about the future. Rather, he proposed, this book outlines the entire course of human history. This view was to become central during and after the Reformation, when Protestants in general argued that the book of Revelation is a panorama of human history from the time of

John himself to the dawn of the millennium, and perhaps even a little beyond. (Joachim's view that it spoke also of the pre-Christian period was not one that gained much support.) As one reads Revelation, then, and considers what one finds there, so the Protestants argued, one may see how prophecy has been fulfilled in the past, is being fulfilled in the present, and will reach its final fulfilment in the future. Careful analysis might even reveal just where one is on the map of world time.[19] Central to this whole scheme was the view that the Pope and/or the Roman Catholic Church in general was the Antichrist predicted in scripture, most particularly Daniel 7, 2 Thessalonians 2, and Revelation 13.[20]

Such views are ubiquitous in the literature and virtually any work concerned with the interpretation of Revelation and written by a Protestant between about 1550 and 1850 falls within this basic 'historicist' interpretative paradigm. Needless to say, Roman Catholic writers were not impressed with the view that the Pope was the Antichrist, and sought to defend the Church from such attack. In part this defence could take the form of simple restatement of the older Augustinian view, but in addition to this a number of very substantial volumes were written in an effort to shift the paradigm once more. The most important of these were aimed at establishing two other methods of interpretation: preterism and futurism.

In outline preterists argued that the book of Revelation falls into two parts. One deals with the first three or four centuries of the Christian church and ends with the victory of Christianity over Judaism and Paganism and the establishment of the Church. The second part, a relatively small section, deals with the events that are to occur in the three and a half literal years of Antichrist immediately before the end of the world. Futurists basically reversed this pattern and argued that almost all of Revelation pertains to the last few years of the earth's history, while the first three chapters or so deal with John's own day. In either case the present is devoid of prophetic fulfilment.[21]

Preterism has not survived in any significant form among prophecy believers today, though one might argue that an extreme form of it has transmuted to become the scholarly consensus (Revelation speaks only of John's own time and not about the future at all). Futurism, however, is a real force to be reckoned with. This method, which has now broken free from its Roman Catholic historical moorings, exercises considerable influence, not least in North America. For example, Hal Lindsey's work *The Late Great Planet Earth*[22] presents a basically futurist reading of the book of Daniel. This became the best seller of the 1970s with something like 27 million copies in print. More recently the *Left Behind* series has achieved quite phenomenal success, with tens of millions of copies being sold. The books in this series present a basically futurist reading of the biblical prophecies and chart the rise of Antichrist and his rule prior to the end of the world.[23] As we shall see, under the leadership of Koresh the Branch Davidian interpretation of the book of Revelation (and with it many other parts of scripture including the Psalms) veered significantly towards a futurist reading. The futurist reading was an inaugurated one (in the person of Koresh the fulfilment of the prophecies had begun), but there was much left to be fulfilled in the prophetic scheme.

It is plain, then, that down the Christian centuries the book of Revelation and with it several other parts of scripture have been interpreted in many ways. As part of this brief overview we have noted how in the Protestant tradition one of the main interpretative paradigms has been historicism. Indeed, as we have seen, the historicist approach was *the* way of interpreting this text in Protestant circles from *c.*1550 to 1850, and is almost ubiquitously employed in the relevant literature. While it is true that such thinking has been largely abandoned even in Protestant circles in post-war prophecy belief, to be replaced by a modified (often inaugurated) futurism, in some few but important Church communities the historicist method lives on. One of these is the Jehovah's Witnesses, a group with which we are not directly concerned here.[24] There is another major group, however, that similarly holds to a very clear historicist hermeneutic. These are the Seventh-day Adventists.

Despite its low public profile, Seventh-day Adventism is a hugely successful and numerically very significant movement. The statistics are impressive: as was seen above Church membership in 2002 was 13 million and growth is strong. The Church operates a very significant educational system, including almost 100 tertiary institutions and 4,407 primary schools. The medical wing is similarly substantial: the 2002 Church report stated that it had 166 hospitals, 395 clinics and dispensaries, and 160 retirement centres and orphanages. Even allowing for the fact that the above data have been collected from the Church's own web site and could possibly be somewhat inflated (though there is no evidence that they are), this is still a very impressive set of figures. It was from this highly successful movement that Koresh himself and almost all of those who died at Waco directly came.[25]

From its beginnings the SDA Church has had a particular interest in the interpretation of biblical prophecy. This is more than just an optional part of the SDA message: it lies at the heart of the movement and is central to its sense of identity. As such it cannot be dispensed with easily. The very name of the movement indicates this. They are 'Seventh-day', that is they observe the seventh day of the week as a Sabbath (as instructed to do by the fourth commandment), but they are also 'Adventists', that is, they look expectantly for the second advent of the Lord. Eschatological expectation is underscored further by the continued focus on biblical prophecy in SDA publications,[26] web sites, and evangelistic methodology. In this latter context, for example, one may note the continued use of the 'Revelation seminar' as a means of public evangelism. This is, as its name suggests, concerned with outlining to potential converts the Church's views on the interpretation of the book of Revelation, and is replete with the standard images of beasts and dragons, trumpet-blowing angels, and earthquakes, scarlet-clad women, and the various horsemen—including the one on the white horse from Revelation 19, which, as we shall see in Chapter Eleven, Koresh identified as himself. This emphasis upon the nearness and catastrophic nature of the end is important in the context of Waco. Indeed, the evidence is that Koresh was himself heavily influenced by such imagery when he attended the evangelistic meetings held by SDA pastor Jim Gilley.[27]

This continued emphasis upon matters apocalyptic is somewhat surprising in a sect that is now more than 150 years old, for, one would think, such hard-line apocalypticism, especially when coupled with Seventh-day Adventism's 'remnant' theology, would be one of the first offerings made upon the altar of denominalization. This has not been the case, however. Indeed if the kind of evidence presented here is anything to go by, the SDA church shows little sign of being able, willing, or interested in cutting loose from the biblical-prophetic tradition to which it has always been tied.

The reason for this continued stress on biblical prophecy, indicative of the role such matters play in SDA self-identity, is first and foremost historical. The Church grew out of what has become known as 'the great disappointment', that is the anticlimactic failure of the Millerite predictions that Jesus was to return visibly to the earth on 22 October 1844. The Millerites, of whom there may have been some 50,000,[28] were the followers of William Miller (1782–1849), a New England farmer turned prophetic expositor whose attention had been caught by the book of Daniel. Koresh, and indeed all of his predecessors in the line of Davidian/Branch Davidian leadership, placed great emphasis upon the importance of Miller as one who had begun the work of God which they were to complete.

Miller's attention was caught especially by the words of Daniel 8.14 and the context of those words found in the preceding verse. Here (in Dan. 8.13) a question is asked by a certain 'saint': 'Then I heard one saint speaking, and another saint said unto that certain saint which spake, How long shall be the vision concerning the daily sacrifice, and the transgression of desolation, to give both the sanctuary and the host to be trodden under foot?' To which the answer comes, in verse 14, 'unto two thousand and three hundred days; then shall the sanctuary be cleansed'. Miller came to the conclusion that these 2,300 prophetic 'days' (which he understood as literal years)[29] began in 457 BCE and would hence end in 1843. This was adjusted to 1844 when Miller spotted his mistake of not allowing for the absence of a year '0'. The end of these days, Miller argued, would see Christ come to cleanse the sanctuary, that is, the earth. The reasoning behind this calculation has been extensively discussed elsewhere and there is no need to go into detail here.[30]

Miller had hence set the year, but was wary of setting a precise day; after all Jesus himself had said that the 'day and hour' of the coming of the Son of man (it does not mention 'year') was known to no one but the Father (Mark 13.32; Matt. 24.36). However, others in the Millerite movement took up the challenge and fine-tuned Miller's predictions to 22 October of the year in question, a date that Miller himself finally accepted.

The reason for determining 22 October for Jesus's return is detailed and somewhat complex. However, it is important that some account be given, since it illustrates how from the very beginning of this religious-traditional trajectory the typological method of interpretation of biblical prophecies was central. It has remained so, and much of the Davidian and Branch Davidian theological system is entirely dependent upon it.

The typological method of biblical interpretation centres upon the belief that certain parts of the Old Testament are 'types' or 'foreshadowings' of what was or is yet to come.[31] The method has a long and distinguished pedigree. Indeed, it forms the backbone of the argument of the letter to the Hebrews, where the author argues in great detail that the Old Testament sacrificial system was but a foreshadowing of the ministry and sacrifice of Christ himself (see especially Heb. 8–10). The author of the Fourth Gospel is probably arguing the same with regard to the Passover lamb, which, he seems clearly to imply, was a type of Christ himself (John 19.36, cf. Exod. 12.46; and note especially Paul's statement in 1 Cor. 5.7). Further, the story of Jonah's three days in the belly of the fish are seen as a 'sign' of Jesus's three days in the tomb in the Q tradition (Matt. 12.40; Luke 11.29–32).[32] Typology was also an important method of interpretation in the early church, used by, among others, Justin, Melito, and Irenaeus, and it has continued to be important as a way of Christianizing the Old Testament ever since. In using it, then, the Millerites were on some very well trodden ground.

This typological method gave rise to the date for Christ's return. A key aspect was the debate in Millerism regarding the extent to which the Old Testament sanctuary service was a type of Christ's ministry. All, including Miller himself, agreed that it was in general, but not all agreed on some of the finer details. Samuel Sheffield Snow (1806–70), who was largely responsible for fixing the date, took a particular view on this issue.[33] He accepted the general view that Jewish feasts pointed forward to the ministry of Christ, but went one step further. According to him the Day of Atonement, which had not found its fulfilment or 'antitype' in the earthly ministry of Christ, was a type of the second coming, when Christ, like the Old Testament priest coming out of the holy of holies to proclaim forgiveness to Israel, would come from heaven bringing with him the salvation of God. Hence, Snow argued, Christ would return on the antitypical Day of Atonement, which chronologically would be the same day as the actual Day of Atonement in 1844, the tenth day of the seventh month. A calculation was made and, following the Karaite rather than the Rabbinic calendar, the date of 22 October was arrived at.[34]

This 'Seventh Month' movement quickly gained a following in Millerism and in the end was endorsed by Miller himself. The result was intense excitement that was very precisely focused. One of the numerous first-hand accounts is worth citing.

We confidently expected to see Jesus Christ and all the holy angels with him; and that his voice would call up Abraham, Isaac and Jacob, and all the ancient worthies, and near and dear friends which had been torn from us by death, and that our trials and sufferings with our earthly pilgrimage would close, and we should be caught up to meet our coming Lord to be forever with him to inhabit the bright golden mansions in the golden home city prepared for the redeemed.[35]

Jesus did not appear. However, as students of prophetic movements know well, such disappointments, while effecting a crisis in the movement, will not necessarily lead to its total collapse,[36] and out of Millerism there came a number of groups that dealt in one way or another with the problem of the apparent failure of the prophecy.[37] One such, indirectly at least, was the Jehovah's Witnesses.[38] Another, of direct concern here, was later to become the SDA Church.

The transition from disappointed Millerite to SDA is not particularly complicated, but it did require some imaginative theology. The first major step was taken the very next day by Hiram Edson (1806–82), the leader of a group of Millerites in Port Gibson, New York. On the morning of 23 October he and some few others of the disappointed Millerites had spent time praying in a barn, asking for strength and understanding in what must have been an hour of particular need and psychological stress. After prayer Edson set off to visit another group of believers. As he was walking something happened, though quite what is unclear; his own account seems to suggest a visionary experience. The claimed means, however, are relatively unimportant. What matters here is the content of this 'revelation'. As we have seen, Miller expected that at the end of the 2,300 days of Daniel 8.14 Jesus would 'cleanse the sanctuary'—that is, so Miller argued, come to earth. On the morning of 23 October, however, Edson came to a different conclusion. The 'cleansing of the sanctuary' was not, he now understood, the return of Christ to earth, but his entry into the heavenly 'holy of holies', there to begin the final phase of his heavenly ministry prior to coming to his eschatological return. This was a masterstroke and effectively threw a theological lifeline to those who now found themselves in some very uncertain waters as a result of the sinking of the Millerite ship. Perhaps the date had been right after all; maybe it was the event that had been misunderstood. What is more, unlike the uncompromising claim 'Jesus will return visibly to this earth on 22 October 1844', this new one, 'yesterday Jesus moved into the heavenly holy of holies', could in no way be proved wrong, since there is no conceivable way in which it could be tested. The potential long term viability of the movement was hence assured.

It was from these unpromising beginnings that the now exceptionally impressive SDA Church eventually grew. Edson's initial 'revelation' was built upon so that in the end (and the process was quite a long one) it was argued that God had raised up a movement, the SDA Church, to proclaim to the world a number of important messages in this last phase of the world's history. Even the birth of the movement itself, so it was argued, was reflected in scripture. In Revelation 10.9–11 we read:

And I went unto the angel, and said unto him, Give me the little book. And he said unto me, Take it, and eat it up; and it shall make thy belly bitter, but it shall be in thy mouth sweet as honey. And I took the little book out of the angel's hand, and ate it up; and it was in my mouth sweet as honey: and as soon as I had eaten it, my belly was bitter. And he said unto me, Thou must prophesy again before many peoples, and nations, and tongues, and kings.

This, so members of the SDA Church believe, is an account of their experience as a part of the 'Great Disappointment'. The 'little book' mentioned in verse 9 is the book of Daniel, the Millerite interpretation of which was 'sweet' as the message of the return of Christ in 1844 was joyously proclaimed; the 'bitterness' in the belly is that of the disappointment itself.[39]

For present purposes, however, it is the final verse that is most significant. It is here that we find the heart of SDA self-identity. It must be remembered that in keeping with the underlying historicist methodology, Seventh-day Adventists will read these three verses in simple chronological sequence. First comes the description of Millerite excitement (the taste of honey in the mouth); then follows the bitter disappointment (the bitterness in the stomach); and finally comes the charge to 'prophesy again before many peoples, and nations, and tongues, and kings'. This, they argue, is a charge to themselves: they are a Church raised up by God to announce a final warning to the world. Eschatology provides the basis for self-identity, and to sacrifice the former is hence to risk seriously undermining the latter. This is why, in all probability, Seventh-day Adventists have resisted any temptation to mute their prophetic voice.

The content of the warning which the Seventh-day Adventists believe they must give to the world is very specific. They have, so members of the Church believe, been raised up by God to 'prophesy again' and the content of that prophecy is also found in the text. At this point, they refer specifically to Revelation 14.6–12:

And I saw another angel fly in the midst of heaven, having the everlasting gospel to preach unto them that dwell on the earth, and to every nation, and kindred, and tongue, and people, Saying with a loud voice, Fear God, and give glory to him; for the hour of his judgment is come: and worship him that made heaven, and earth, and the sea, and the fountains of waters. And there followed another angel, saying, Babylon is fallen, is fallen, that great city, because she made all nations drink of the wine of the wrath of her fornication. And the third angel followed them, saying with a loud voice, If any man worship the beast and his image, and receive his mark in his forehead, or in his hand, The same shall drink of the wine of the wrath of God, which is poured out without mixture into the cup of his indignation; and he shall be tormented with fire and brimstone in the presence of the holy angels, and in the presence of the Lamb: And the smoke of their torment ascendeth up for ever and ever: and they have no rest day nor night, who worship the beast and his image, and whosoever receiveth the mark of his name. Here is the patience of the saints: here are they that keep the commandments of God, and the faith of Jesus.

If Revelation 10.11 provides the imperative for the eschatological message that this raised-up community will announce, Revelation 14.6–12 outlines its content. These three angels' messages are of fundamental importance to the Church, for they outline its end-time mission. In addition to standard Christian doctrine, such as righteousness by faith, the three angels' messages are understood by the SDA Church to include some highly distinctive elements. These include 'worship the creator', a part of which is the observance of the Seventh-day Sabbath, which, according to Exodus 20.8–11, is a memorial of God's creative act.[40] The second angel announces that 'Babylon is fallen', that is that apostate religion, Catholic and Protestant, has fallen away and that God's people must 'come out of her'. (Seventh-day Adventists emphasize that it is only when the first angel's message has gone out that the second may follow. But the crisis is coming; individuals and churches will hear the voice of the first angel as the church preaches the message, and those who reject it will by virtue of their rejection become part of fallen Babylon). Similarly, the final message will relate to the number '666', that is, according to the Church's understanding, the 'mark of the beast' (cf. Rev. 13.18). This again ties in with eschatological expectation, for the time will come, so the Church argues, when a choice will have to be made either to worship the creator or to worship human institutions. When this happens the choice, in essence, will be to join the Sabbath-keeping remnant or the leagues of Antichrist. Antichrist, one is not surprised to learn, is identified as the Roman Catholic Church, on the basis of whose power the Sabbath was replaced by Sunday worship and whose head, the Pope, goes by the title *Vicarius Filii Dei* ('vicar of the Son of God'), the numerical value of which is 666.[41]

Central to this kind of thinking is of course a fervent belief in the nearness of the end and the ability of the scriptures, properly interpreted, to give at least a rough guide to the days that lie ahead. Such details crossed over from Seventh-day Adventism into Davidianism and from there into Branch Davidianism. Less obvious perhaps, but of central importance in the context of what was going on at Waco, is the extent to which this kind of interpretation requires of the one who adopts it the notion of a 'remnant' community. God has raised up an end-time Church that will remain true to his word when others are 'fallen'. This concept of the 'remnant' is very strong in Seventh-day Adventism; it was if anything even stronger in Davidianism and it was and still is central to Branch Davidianism.

Intertwined with this concept of the remnant, and very much part of it, is the continuation of the prophetic gift. It would be easy to underestimate the centrality of this concept to the SDA Church, but such a danger must be avoided if we are to gain a rounded picture of this movement and thereby an appreciation for the immediate context out of which the Davidians and Branch Davidians came. The Church's views on the 'gift of prophecy' are outlined clearly and, presumably, authoritatively in *Seventh-day Adventists Believe*. Here the seventeenth fundamental belief of the Church is discussed in some detail:

One of the gifts of the Holy Spirit is prophecy. This gift is an identifying mark of the remnant church and was manifested in the ministry of Ellen G. White. As the Lord's messenger, her writings are a continuing and authoritative source of truth which provide for the church comfort, guidance, instruction and correction. They also make clear that the Bible is the standard by which all teaching and experience must be tested.[42]

As is clear from the form this statement takes, Seventh-day Adventists see this 'gift of prophecy' as tied to the identity of the true remnant who are destined to keep the flame of truth flickering in the otherwise dark days of the pre-Advent period of tribulation. Like the observance of the Sabbath, then, it is both a mark of divine approval and an eschatological sign. In fact, Seventh-day Adventists argue, the two are brought together in Revelation 12.17 and 19.10. The first of these reads: 'And the dragon was wroth with the woman, and went to make war with the remnant of her seed, which keep the commandments of God, and have the testimony of Jesus Christ.' Here, Seventh-day Adventists note, the 'remnant', which is persecuted by Satan (the dragon), is described as being made up of those who 'keep the commandments of God' and 'have the testimony of Jesus'. Jumping straight to

Revelation 19.10 we read that 'the testimony of Jesus is the spirit of prophecy'. The reasoning is plain: the remnant keep the Sabbath (one of the commandments of God) and have a prophet(ess).

It is important in the context of this book to note that while Seventh-day Adventists do make the claim that Ellen G. White was a prophetess, the underlying conceptual framework is not at heart specific to White herself. In SDA literature two entirely separable arguments are put forward to support the view that White manifested the prophetic gift. First, there is the general argument that prophecy did not cease with the close of the New Testament period, but that it is a gift that God will continue to give to his Church up to and perhaps especially during the end times. Second, there is the argument that this continued gift of prophecy, always a theoretical possibility, was actually at work in the ministry of Ellen G. White.

This method of argumentation can be seen in the relevant literature. It is implied even in the wording of the twelfth fundamental belief itself, while the comments in *Seventh-day Adventists Believe* indicate that:

There is no biblical evidence that God would withdraw the spiritual gifts He gave the church before they had completed their purpose, which, according to Paul, was to bring the church 'to the unity of the faith and the knowledge of the Son of God, to a perfect man, to the measure of the stature of the fullness of Christ' (Eph. 4:13). Because the church has not yet reached this experience, it still needs all the gifts of the Spirit. These gifts, including the gift of prophecy, will continue to operate for the benefit of God's people until Christ returns. Consequently, Paul cautioned believers not to 'quench the Spirit' or 'despise prophecies'.[43]

The next three pages then go into greater detail on this point, arguing that in the first three Christian centuries the gift of prophecy was still active, but that later apostasy led to a decline in the presence of the Holy Spirit and hence a decline in the Spirit's gifts. However, the editors note, 'just before the second coming' the gift would be seen again. There is nothing in this section to indicate that it would be seen only in the ministry of Ellen G. White; she was an example of it but, in theory at least, not the only possible one. Indeed, one part of the argument given to support the view that during the last days the gift of prophecy would be active is that Christ warned against 'false prophets' (Matt. 24.11, 24). If there were to be no prophets at all, the editors argue, 'Christ would have warned against anyone claiming that gift. His warning against false prophets implies that there would be true prophets as well'.[44] The plural 'prophets' is to be noted.

This point has been stressed for good reason. Ellen G. White is understood by Seventh-day Adventists as a prophetess, but behind that belief there lies an even more fundamental one, namely that the gift of prophecy is active in the remnant Church. Numerous publications outline the various 'tests' that an individual must pass in order to be accepted as a true prophet, again giving expression to the view that there could be another one.[45] Those in mainstream Seventh-day Adventism would probably wish to argue quite rigorously that Koresh (and for that matter Victor Houteff and Ben and Lois Roden) would not have passed those tests. Koresh's followers presumably thought otherwise. But the fundamental point is not to be missed: if the kind of publications referred to above are to be taken at face value, Seventh-day Adventists are open to the idea of the rise of a new prophet. Koresh claimed he was just that. His claim may have sounded radical to the SDA ear; it would not have sounded deranged. In fact there is hard evidence to support this conclusion: when Marc Breault, who was at the time training for the SDA ministry at Loma Linda University, was told by Perry Jones (a long-time Branch Davidian and Koresh's father-in-law) that a new prophet had arisen, his response was, 'Well, the Seventh-day Adventist Church was founded by a prophet ... who says God can't raise up another one. Sure, I'll talk to him'.[46]

The nature of Ellen White's presumed prophetic status is also worth further consideration at this point. Seventh-day Adventists are uncompromising in their insistence that Ellen White is not above the Bible and that the latter is the true standard by which truth may be judged. This is seen in the twelfth fundamental belief, which ends with the statement '[Seventh-day Adventists] also make clear that the Bible is the standard by which all teaching and experience must be tested'.[47] Many SDA publications quote with enthusiasm Ellen White's own statement that she was 'a lesser light to lead men to a greater light' in the context of describing the relationship between her writings and those of scripture.[48] Hence, while Ellen White claimed many visionary experiences and did provide 'new light' on many issues, for example her voluminous writings on health, for Seventh-day Adventists a key feature of her ministry was the attempt to promote the biblical text and to make its meaning clear.

This latter point is important. In *Seventh-day Adventists Believe* the editors state that the writings of Ellen White are 'a guide in understanding the Bible'.[49] They go on quickly to say that this does not mean that she brings additional truth out of the writings, but rather that she makes plain what is already revealed. It would be improper to bring into question the integrity or consistency of the editors on this point, and that is not intended; however one might conceivably argue, as Hoekema did in the past,[50] that although Seventh-day Adventists claim to base their beliefs on the Bible, in fact they base them on the Bible-as-interpreted-by-Ellen-White. There is a court of appeal higher than the text itself, namely Ellen White's interpretation of the text.

Seventh-day Adventists would of course deny this charge, though it must be said that the format of some works such as the *Seventh-day Adventist Bible Commentary* does suggest that, even if Hoekema misunderstood their exegetical theory, he adequately described what many do in practice.[51] It is not necessary to get into this debate here. The issue has been brought to the surface only to illustrate the centrality in Seventh-day Adventism of the role of an inspired interpreter of an inspired text. Koresh certainly claimed to be that, as did Houteff and the Rodens, each following in the line of the tradition to which they had previously belonged. The gift of prophecy has not been removed from the church, in fact it is one of the defining marks of the remnant. What is more, in substantial part that 'prophecy' will focus not so much upon new revelations through visions (though Koresh, like White, claimed that this was part of his ministry), but rather upon the correct interpretation of the Bible.

In this chapter an attempt has been made to place the Branch Davidians in a wider context. The context identified is not insanity or downright wickedness, but rather a religious tradition focused upon the fulfilment of biblical prophecy. On a myriad of details, and even on some very fundamental underlying principles, Koresh and his followers differed from what had gone before, and in the remainder of this book many of those differences will become apparent. Indeed, Koresh even differed from the more specific SDA context from which he and the vast majority of his followers had directly come. This is to be expected, for the Branch Davidian trajectory of mainstream Seventh-day Adventism can claim its own history and, as will be shown, the Houteffs and the Rodens took it into theological waters uncharted by the Seventh-day Adventists themselves. However, the end-time scenario at the heart of SDA thinking almost since the movement began, including concepts such as the remnant, the continuation of the prophetic gift, and the nearness of the end, provides the basic canvas upon which the distinctively Branch Davidian apocalyptic images can be painted. More broadly, Koresh differed in degree and detail more than in kind from countless millions of his fellow Americans who, the statistics indicate, have 'no doubt' that Jesus will one day come to earth again. To begin to see Koresh in this context is to begin to understand him, and to understand him is to begin to understand what his followers found so attractive about his message, a message which would in the end require that they be faithful unto death (cf. Rev. 2.10).

NOTES

1. This is the position put forward by E.P. Sanders, for example, in his highly influential book *Jesus and Judaism* (London: SCM, 1985).
2. Such a view is standard in New Testament scholarship, and is based upon such evidence as Luke's apparent editing of his Marcan and Q sources, as for example in

Chapter 21, where he is careful to distinguish between the destruction of Jerusalem and the eschatological coming of Jesus.

3. Not all would agree with this statement. Bultmann, for example, argued that John 14.3 refers to the evangelist's expectation of the personal coming of Christ to the believer at death (Rudolf Bultmann, *The Gospel of John*, tr. G. R. Beasley-Murray (Oxford: Blackwell, 1971), 601–3), whereas the references to the 'last day' found four times in John 6, he argued, are the work of a later editor (Bultmann, *Gospel of John*, 219).

4. This term is used, rather than the increasingly common 'Hebrew Scriptures', simply because the older term was so entirely part of the mindset of the people being discussed throughout this book.

5. The deutero-Pauline tradition is found in letters attributed to Paul but which are probably not his own work. These are Ephesians, Colossians, 2 Thessalonians, 1–2 Timothy and Titus; dispute of course surrounds each case.

6. It is not necessary here to enter into discussion of what, precisely, the author of Revelation was actually trying to achieve, or the literary genre of the work that he composed in an effort to meet his objectives. For a concise analysis and further references see John M. Court, *Revelation* (Sheffield: Sheffield Academic Press, 1994).

7. Paul Boyer, *When Time Shall be no More*, 2.

8. These statistics are taken from the Church's annual statistical report for 2002, a copy of which can be accessed via the Church's official website, www.adventist.org.

9. The literature is extensive. Among the works most relevant to the present inquiry are David Brady, *The Contribution of British Writers between 1560 and 1830 to the Interpretation of Revelation 13.16–18 (The Number of the Beast): A Study in the History of Exegesis* (Tübingen: J. C. B. Mohr (Paul Siebeck), 1983); Le Roy Edwin Froom, *The Prophetic Faith of Our Fathers*, 4 vols. (Washington, DC: Review and Herald Publishing Association, 1946–1954); J. A. Oddy, 'Eschatological Prophecy in the English Theological Tradition, c.1700–c.1840' (University of London, Ph.D. thesis, 1982); Kenneth G. C. Newport, *Apocalypse and Millennium: Studies in Biblical Eisegesis* (Cambridge: Cambridge University Press, 2000).

10. It was with the leadership of Koresh that the Psalms came clearly into focus as central to the Branch Davidian tradition. Extensive comment on this is found in Chapter Eleven.

11. A good general survey is found in Arthur W. Wainwright, *Mysterious Apocalypse* (Nashville: Abingdon Press, 1993).

12. The book of Revelation is among those books listed on the Muratorian Fragment. This document, dated to the second century but discovered in the eighteenth century by L. A. Muratori, is the oldest list of New Testament books known. It is not complete (hence 'fragment') but even so lists all the books now found in the NT except Hebrews, James, 1 and 2 Peter and one of John's epistles, usually thought to be 3 John.

13. Justin Martyr, *First Apology*, chapter 52; cited in Froom, *Prophetic Faith*, i: 232.

14. Irenaeus, *Against Heresies*, book 5, chapter 30, section 4, cited ibid. 250.

15. Tertullian, *On the Resurrection of the Flesh*, cited ibid. 255–6; Hippolytus, *Treatise on Christ and Antichrist*, chapter 65, cited ibid. 276.

16. Augustine's understanding of the book of Revelation owed a great deal to the earlier work of the fourth century writer, Tychonius. Tychonius's commentary itself is no longer extant, but its influence upon a number of writers is plain. These include Augustine himself, the English theologian Bede (*c*.673–735) and the Spanish writer Beatus (eighth century).

17. Hence according to Augustine, who seems to be following Tychonius here, the binding of Satan and his being cast into the Abyss (Rev. 20.1–3) is the driving out of Satan from the hearts of Christian believers and the church and his subsequent retreat into the hearts and minds of the 'countless multitude of the wicked' (Augustine, *The City of God Against the Pagans*, book xx, chapter 8, cited in Froom, *Prophetic Faith*, i: 482). Similarly, the many negative images in the book of Revelation, those of the beasts in Rev. 13, for example, for Augustine are symbols of the unregenerate world as a whole in which the Church exists and to which it bears witness (ibid., bk. xx, ch. 14, cited in Froom, *Prophetic Faith*, i: 485).

18. On Joachim see further Wainwright, *Mysterious Apocalypse*, 49–53, Bernard McGinn, *The Calabrian Abbot: Joachim of Fiore in the History of Western Thought* (New York: MacMillan Publishing Company, 1985), 145–60. A full and detailed study of Joachim and his legacy is to be found in Marjorie Reeves, *The Influence of Prophecy in the Later Middle Ages: a Study in Joachimism* (Oxford: Clarendon Press, 1969).

19. A good example, as the title of the work demonstrates, is Samuel Petto's *The Revelation Unvailed: Or, an Essay Towards the Discovering I. When Many Scripture Prophecies had Their Accomplishment and Turneth into History II. What Are Now Fulfilling III. What Rest Still to be Fulfilled, with a Guess at the Time of Them with and Appendix Proving that Pagan Rome Was not Babylon, Rev 17, and that the Jews Shall be Converted* (1693).

20. See further Newport, *Apocalypse and Millennium*, 48–65.

21. On Roman Catholic interpretations of the book of Revelation see Newport, *Apocalypse and Millennium*, 66–90.

22. Zondervan, 1970.

23. The 'Left Behind' series is written by Tim LaHaye and Jerry B. Jenkins. As of early 2004 some twelve volumes in the series have either been published or are soon to be released. See further www.leftbehind.com.

24. The historical as well as the theological links between the Jehovah's Witnesses and the Seventh-day Adventists will be noted later in this chapter.

25. It is not clear precisely how many of the Waco group were not formerly Seventh-day Adventists. There were at least two: Jaime (Jamie) Castillo, a Pentecostal, joined the Branch Davidians after Koresh answered an advertisement Castillo had placed saying that he was interested in joining a Christian musical band (Reavis, *Ashes of Waco*, 292–3 has the details). Castillo's mother was a Jehovah's Witness. David Thibodeau, a Waco survivor who was in Mt. Carmel for the whole of the siege, had no religious affiliation at all when he met Koresh and Steve Schneider in

a music shop (David Thibodeau and Leon Whiteson, *A Place Called Waco* (New York: Public Affairs, 1999), 17–18, 29–30).

26. Sources here are in abundance. See for example Jon Paulien, *What the Bible Says about the End-Time* (Hagerstown, Md.: Review and Herald Publishing Association, 1998). The author is an SDA professor of New Testament who teaches at the Church's theological seminary. What he says, therefore, has some claim to being authorized.

27. Thomas Robbins and Dick Anthony, 'Sects and Violence: Factors Enhancing the Volatility of Marginal Religious Movements', in Wright, ed., *Armageddon in Waco*, 236–59, 239.

28. David L. Rowe, 'Millerites: A Shadow Portrait' in Ronald L. Numbers and Jonathan M. Butler, eds., *The Disappointed: Millerism and Millenarianism in the Nineteenth Century* (Bloomington and Indianapolis: Indiana University Press, 1987), 7. Rowe is commenting upon the work of Francis D. Nichol, *The Midnight Cry: A Defense of William Miller and the Millerites* (Washington, DC: Review and Herald Publishing Association, 1944), 204, who is himself quoting Miller on the issue.

29. The 'year-day' principle, i.e. the view that in prophecy a 'day' means a literal year was standard in historicist interpretation. Among those who accepted it were Sir Isaac Newton, who once stated that 'in *Daniel's* Prophecies days are put for years' (Sir Isaac Newton, *Observations on the Prophecies* (1733), 123). See further Newport, *Apocalypse and Millennium*, 9–10.

30. For a fuller discussion see Newport, *Apocalypse and Millennium*, 159–65; Kai Arasola, *The End of Historicism: Millerite Hermeneutic of Time Prophecies in the Old Testament* (Uppsala: University of Uppsala, 1990), and Steen Raabjerg Rasmussen, 'Roots of the Prophetic Hermeneutic of William Miller' (MA thesis, Newbold College, Bracknell, Berkshire, 1983).

31. For a summary see e.g. R. J. Coggins and J. L. Houlden, eds., *A Dictionary of Biblical Interpretation* (London: SCM Press, 1990), 713–14.

32. See further Yvonne Sherwood, *A Biblical Text and its Afterlives: The Survival of Jonah in Western Culture* (Cambridge: Cambridge University Press, 2000), 11–21.

33. On Snow and the Seventh-Month Movement, see further Froom, *Prophetic Faith*, iv: 801–26; Nichol, *Midnight Cry*, 213–16.

34. This calendar was adopted by the Karaite Jews, an eighth-century Jewish sect which rejected the Oral Law. According to this the festival of New Year may fall on any day of the week, and as a consequence the Karaite and Rabbinate calendars may differ on the celebration of the Day of Atonement. See further *Encyclopedia Judaica*, 17 vols. (Jerusalem: Keter Publishing House, 1972–82), x: 778–9.

35. Hiram Edson, undated MS fragment, printed in *The Disappointed*, 215.

36. The standard study is that of Leon Festinger, H.W. Riecken, and S. Schachter, *When Prophecy Fails* (Minneapolis: University of Minnesota Press, 1956). More recent is Jon R. Stone, ed., *Expecting Armageddon: Essential Readings in Failed Prophecy* (London: Routledge, 2000).

37. The precise number of Miller's denominational offspring is unclear. However, Stark and Bainbridge claim to have identified at least 33 different groups that followed in the wake of Millerism's collapse (Stark and Bainbridge, *The Future of Religion*, 457).

38. The Jehovah's Witnesses can be traced back to the work of Charles Taze Russell (1852–1916), who was significantly influenced by Nelson H. Barbour, a follower of William Miller. Barbour accepted the broad outline of Miller's scheme, including the 1844 terminus for the 2,300 days of Dan. 8.14. Building further on the work of Miller, Barbour eventually came to the conclusion that to this period must be added the 70 years of the Gentiles (cf. Luke 21.24) and that the close of the period would hence come in 1914. The outbreak of the first world war in that year was then understood as the fulfillment of the prophecy in Matt. 24.7 that 'nation shall rise against nation', which marked the dawn of the final stage in world history. In accordance with their understanding of Matt. 24.34 ('this generation will by no means pass away until all these things occur' (*New World Translation of the Holy Scriptures*)), the Jehovah's Witnesses remain convinced that not everybody who was alive in 1914 will die before the second advent. See further M. James Penton, *Apocalypse Delayed: The Story of the Jehovah's Witnesses* (Toronto: University of Toronto Press, 1985), 18–22, 44–6. A recent example of their continued historicist reading of the scriptures can be found in *Pay Attention to Daniel's Prophecies* (New York: Watch Tower and Bible Tract Society of New York Inc., 1999).

39. See further Froom, *Prophetic Faith*, iv: 877–905.

40. See, e.g. *Seventh-day Adventists Believe: A Biblical Exposition of 27 Fundamental Doctrines* (Washington, DC: The Ministerial Association of the Seventh-day Adventist Church, 1988), 164–5, 255.

41. Ibid., chs. 12, 19. Such views are absolutely standard in Seventh-day Adventist literature.

42. Ibid. 216.

43. Ibid. 219–20.

44. Ibid. 220.

45. See for example Richard Rice, *The Reign of God* (Berrien Springs, Mich.: Andrews University Press, 1985), 196–8; *Seventh-day Adventists Believe*, 223–4.

46. King and Breault, *Preacher of Death*, 49.

47. *Seventh-day Adventists Believe*, 216.

48. White made this statement in an open letter published in *Review and Herald*, 12 Jan. 1903, 15. It is quoted with approval in many places, including *Seventh-day Adventists Believe*, 228.

49. *Seventh-day Adventists Believe*, 228.

50. Anthony Hoekema, *The Four Major Cults* (Grand Rapids: Zondervan, 1963).

51. Thus when commenting on Rev. 13.14 and the deception that Satan works according to that verse, the editors state that 'The whole world will be led captive'; to support this claim the editors write, 'See 9T 16, GC 589, 624; EW 88', where

these references are to White's books *Testimonies to the Church, The Great Controversy,* and the compilation of her works published as *Early Writings* respectively. (See *A Verse-by-Verse Commentary on the Book of Revelation: A Section of Volume VII of the Seventh-day Adventist Bible Commentary* (Washington, DC: Review and Herald Publishing Association, 1957), 821.)

3

'Hear Ye the Rod' (cf. Micah 6.9): Victor T. Houteff, the Shepherd's Rod, and the Davidian Seventh-day Adventists

In the previous chapter the general context of the Branch Davidian movement was briefly sketched, with particular attention to the origin and early development of the SDA Church—the group that provides the immediate context of Branch Davidianism. It was from the Seventh-day Adventists that the 'Shepherd's Rod' movement (later to be known as 'the Davidian Seventh-day Adventists') emerged and from that movement in turn that 'the Branch Davidians' came. It would therefore be true to say, as many Seventh-day Adventists did, that the Branch Davidians are an 'offshoot of an offshoot' of Seventh-day Adventism. What ought not to be missed, however, is that despite institutional distance Davidians and Branch Davidians alike have always seen themselves as Seventh-day Adventist reformers; their missionary activity is focused almost exclusively on members of the SDA Church. (The theological reasoning for this self-definition will be made plain in this and the following chapter.) Almost all those who lived at Mt. Carmel during the period of Koresh's leadership had been previously connected with Seventh-day Adventism, or were the first generation offspring of parents who had an SDA background but had become Davidians/Branch Davidians. Further, the main leaders of both the Davidians and the Branch Davidians (Victor and Florence Houteff, Ben and Lois Roden, and David Koresh) were former Seventh-day Adventists. The following chapters, then, present an account of the life and teachings of these five principal leaders of the Davidian/Branch Davidian trajectory, and the continuity and the discontinuity between what they had to say and what had gone before is explored.

The first of these is the founder of the Davidians, Victor Tasho Houteff (1885–1955).[1] This chapter gives an account of his career, tracing his development from successful immigrant, businessman, and disaffected reformer of the Seventh-day Adventists to his taking on of the role of prophet and leader of the group that was to become known as the 'Davidian Seventh-day Adventists'. The institutional structures he founded to support his religious

PLATE 1 Victor and Florence Houteff (date unknown)

vision, especially the Mt. Carmel centre in Waco, Texas (established 1935), are an important part of this story and are hence also outlined here. Chapter Four will focus on his theology.

Houteff was born in Raikovo, Bulgaria, on 2 March 1885.[2] Relatively little is known of his early life, except that he was raised as a member of the Greek Orthodox Church, hardly surprising given his cultural context.[3] A little more information can be gained from George Saether, who reported that Houteff had told him something further of his early background, including the fact that his uncle was in business trading attar (an oil produced from flowers, especially the damask rose, used as a base for perfumes).[4] For reasons that are not clear, though probably as a result of his uncle's death, the business came to Victor and his cousin.[5] From Saether we learn also that the attar trading business was the root of Houteff's initial problems in Bulgaria, problems which resulted in his leaving his homeland and emigrating to America. Precisely what the problems were is unclear, but it seems that he was accused of unfair trading practices in Turkey, a charge he denied and eventually took to the Bishop in an effort to find mediation.[6] Houteff's own report of these events leaves much to the imagination:

Some years ago while in Europe, I heard that one of my cousins had left for America. I then said to myself, 'Poor cousin, I will never leave home and go to live anywhere as far away as America for any reason.' But about that time, I, along with others, was falsely accused of conspiracy. It was in the season when the nights were long, and as we put on the lights in our store one morning before daylight, a mob gathered with guns and stones, and stormed the windows. So it was that just a few months after I took pity on my poor cousin's estrangement from his homeland I found myself in America in the same house with him. It was a great disappointment at first, no not lesser than Joseph's of old, but what a favor at last! God bless the mob![7]

Whatever the truth of the matter it is perhaps unsurprising that Houteff later put it all down to providence.

I came to America, not because I wanted to, but because God wanted me to. And since I knew not my future work, and as God could then no more make me understand than He could at first make Joseph understand his trip to Egypt, I was therefore driven out of the country at the point of a gun as was Moses driven out of Egypt.[8]

The fact that Houteff was in effect forced to leave Bulgaria was something of a gift to his later critics, who could with some justification use it to suggest that there was something suspicious about his background.[9]

For whatever reason, then, Houteff left Bulgaria and arrived in America in 1907.[10] His early years there brought prosperity. He worked first in a restaurant in New York, but later joined his brother in Milwaukee. He apparently married at this time; his later marriage to Florence was hence his second.[11] There were no children from either marriage.[12]

By 1919 Houteff owned a hotel in the 'middle west back' and it was at this time that he first became acquainted with the SDA Church.[13] Saether remembers that Houteff told him he had been out walking one evening when he heard music coming from a tent; he went in to find that a religious meeting was taking place and sat down to listen to the preacher. Finding what the preacher had to say appealing, Houteff returned several times. The meeting turned out to be one organized by the Seventh-day Adventists, and Houteff subsequently joined the movement, being baptized at the church in Rockford, Illinois, on 10 May 1919.[14] The by now relatively wealthy Houteff assisted the Church financially and in effect paid for the construction of a new place of worship.[15] Some time after this he sold the hotel and went into the grocery business instead, but that business too he soon gave up, selling it at a loss. In about 1923[16] he was in California and fell sick. Following a suggestion from a retired SDA minister he presented himself at Glendale Seventh-day Adventist Sanitarium in Los Angeles.[17]

It was Houteff's experience at this health institution that seems to have marked the turning point in his relationship with the Seventh-day Adventists and set in motion the process that was to result in his gradual defection from the Church (this is not how he would have seen it) and ultimately the formation of the Davidians. According to Houteff, who was of course writing this some time after the event and from the perspective of his later stance, the first thing that happened when he arrived at the Sanitarium was that he was asked for a deposit, which he duly gave. He then spent four days waiting for the doctor to come to see him, a delay he suspected was because he had given a cheque drawn on an Illinois bank account and the Sanitarium was waiting to see if payment would be forthcoming before giving treatment. A doctor eventually did see him; he was prescribed a treatment of hydrotherapy and a special nurse was assigned to care for him. Houteff does not say how long the treatment lasted, but he was eventually well enough to leave and did so with a bank account much depleted as a result of the charges that the Sanitarium had made. It was not a happy situation; but, says Houteff,

This Sanitarium incident … produced another disappointing picture in my mind. Is that Sanitarium God's place for His sick people? I asked myself. Is this people really God's people? The answer that came to these questions was this: the Sanitarium is God's, and the church is God's, but the people that are running them are reactionaries, they are the modern priests, scribes and Pharisees, that there is a need for more Samaritans among them. This is where God's Truth is, though, and God helping me, I said, I shall stay with it. Yes, God did help me, I kept the faith, complained about nothing and stayed in the church with as good [a] record as any.[18]

Shortly after his discharge, Houteff wrote a $75 cheque for past tithes and offerings and sent it to the Church authorities on the assumption that if he did not pay it now, he would never again have sufficient funds to do so. He was left, so he thought, with the $3.50 he had in his pocket and no job. A few days later a cheque for $350 arrived from his bank in Illinois, being the remaining balance of his now closed account. (Quite how the business mind of Houteff had so badly miscalculated his remaining funds is not clear, and he himself says that he never got to the bottom of it.) Houteff by now clearly had doubts about the purity of the people in the Church that he took to be the true Church, though it would be several years before his views reached the point where he had to separate from them.

By 1923 Houteff was working as a salesman in Los Angeles for the newly formed Maytag agency, which sold washing machines and vacuum cleaners. It appears from his account that he was highly successful in this new line of work and both he and the company prospered. It was not to last, however, and after some dispute about commissions, he quit. The ever-resourceful Houteff had already been working independently of the company making and selling health sweets, a business that from this point on seems to have been his main source of income.

The outline given above is plain and there is nothing remarkable about it. Houteff's own account is more lively, being punctuated with references to presumed miracles, such as the time when he was run over by a car but escaped completely unscathed, much to the surprise of onlookers who shouted 'he must be made of rubber'.[19] He also recounts how, from his perspective, those who ignored the message that he gave to them often came to an untimely end. Two of his fellow workers at Maytag, for example, questioned him about his religion and responded that they could never become Seventh-day Adventists since if they could not work on the Sabbath they would lose their jobs. Both were dead within a short time of the discussions taking place. A convert whom Houteff had won over lost everything, including his wife, for going against Houteff's advice not to attend a business meeting on the Sabbath. Such recollections illustrate Houteff's developing sense of his own importance as one who was responsible for teaching the truth, and the dire consequences in store of those who rejected it.

This sense of destiny and prophetic responsibility began to manifest itself in Houteff's dealings with the Church from which he was soon to break. By 1928 he had become assistant Sabbath School superintendent in the Church and hence had an outlet for his developing views.[20] It was apparently during his study of Isaiah 54 that he first began to get a sense of having something very special revealed to him.[21] He later identified 6 January 1929 as the date of the first 'Present Truth' study[22] and from this point on things moved quickly. 'On

1 February 1930', he notes, 'the truth of the 144,000 was revealed' (to whom he does not say but it seems to be himself);[23] and in June of the same year a draft copy of the first volume of what was to become the major Houteff publication was handed to thirty-three leading Seventh-day Adventists.[24] This was *The Shepherd's Rod*, a book that was to take on canonical status in later Davidian and Branch Davidian thinking and from which Houteff's movement was for a number of years to take its name.[25]

Those to whom the draft copy was given included Elder F. C. Gilbert, who wrote to Houteff on 26 June outlining some of the points at which he felt Houteff to be in error.[26] There was one other respondent, though Houteff does not give the name.[27] The other thirty-one recipients seem to have ignored him.[28]

The Shepherd's Rod broke with Seventh-day Adventist doctrine in some substantial and important ways, and the viability of Houteff's long-term association with the Church was now in serious doubt. Measures had already been taken in an effort to limit his influence; these included asking him to hold his Sabbath School classes in the afternoon and eventually refusing to allow them to take place on Church property.[29]

By this point, then, the final break with Seventh-day Adventism was only a matter of time. Houteff's own account of this period is worth quoting in full:

[T]hen came the message which we are now endeavoring to take to the Laodiceans.[30] The enemies of the message then left nothing unturned in their search for something against me, rather than to make sure that they were not turning down Truth. They tried every hook and crook to pin something on me and to stop my activities, but found nothing and as a rule about 30 members of the church stayed in my special meetings each Sabbath afternoon. Then came the time that the elders of the church refused to let us use the church for our meetings, and they made us all get out. But one of the sisters who was living in a big house right across from the church offered her place for the meetings, and there was a great uproar among the people around the church premises. Some were for us and some were against us. So it was that the house across from the church was filled that afternoon and many listened from the outside through the windows. The enemies failed to break up our meetings, and the victory was ours.

Next they forbade us to attend their church services, and they began to disfellowship those who still wanted to attend our meetings. They tried to deport me, too, but failed. Then they endeavored to get a court order against any of us going to the church on Sabbath, but lost out. Once they called the police to have me arrested on false charges that I was disturbing the meetings, but after the officer in the police station heard my story and the deacon's charges against me, he commanded the two policemen who brought us to the station to put us in their car again, and to take us right back to the church where they picked me up!

After this the elders endeavored to put me in an insane asylum. The 'city manager' of Glendale[31] himself (a Seventh-day Adventist) had come to this church that Sabbath morning to lay down the charges and to see me carried away and locked in the asylum. After talking with me for a few minutes, though, the officer did nothing but to tell me that he would not bother me again! Then the 200 lb. city manager felt smaller than my 135 lb. weight.

They did all these unbecoming things and many others; besides, they talked and preached against me. And though I had no one but the Lord to defend me at any time, yet in all these the victory was mine![32]

On 23 July a motion was passed at the board of the Olympic Exposition Park SDA church in Los Angeles to recommend to the Church's business meeting that Houteff should be disciplined.[33] There was a further meeting with Houteff on 16 October at which a number of church administrators were present, together with the pastor of the Olympic Park Church, W. H. Schacht.[34] Things came to a head on 20 November when a motion was passed by the church disfellowshipping him.[35] From this point on Houteff's relationships with Seventh-day Adventism became increasingly acrimonious, though as far as one can tell he never gave up on the view that the SDA Church was the true Church and what it needed was reform. He pressed on: 5,000 copies of volume one of *The Shepherd's Rod* were published in December 1930 and the task of distribution began.

It is difficult to gauge just how successful Houteff was in gaining supporters. That he made some progress, however, is clear. One early convert was W. G. Butterbaugh MD, from Chandler, Colorado, who wrote a letter addressed 'to whom it may concern' in which he outlined how he and some others had studied Houteff's writings and come to the conclusion that they had been prepared under divine guidance.[36] Butterbaugh was to prove an important and long-term convert. By 1933 he and an associate, W. A. Eckerman, were witnessing to their faith through the tried and tested SDA means of 'health evangelism', that is, using health and health institutions as a means of contact with potential converts.[37] Butterbaugh himself soon came into conflict with the Church and the letter he wrote to his fellow believers regarding his forthcoming 'trial' gives a clear indication of the increasing tension that by now existed between the Seventh-day Adventists and their Shepherd's Rod offspring. Butterbaugh wrote:

Dear Brethren: You may not be surprised to learn that I am on record to be tried for 'heresy' on Thursday evening, July 26, at 7 P.M. in Canon City. These 'orders' come from the 'Sanhedrin' of the Colorado Conference, S.D.A. executive department! Thus far, only seven hours of time has been taken to misinterpret the message of the Shepherd's Rod in the pulpit of the Canon City Church and I presume I will be given 15 minutes' time in which to reply. I hope and pray that God may give me grace to defend the truth as it is, and at the same time to uncover error. I leave it to you to pass the word to all concerned. I do not know, but they evidently intend to make me 'an example' of what is to happen to others, and thus the poor blind sheep are to continue to be frightened to not so much as to even think for themselves! You brethren everywhere pray to the end that something will develop so as to make manifest the utter foolishness of and the weakness of the leaders in keeping the truth from the sheep.—W. S. Butterbaugh.[38]

The outcome of that meeting is unknown. However, Butterbaugh himself evidently kept the faith; he is listed as both a minister and a worker in 1943[39] and was still with the movement when Houteff died. Indeed, he was one of two who spoke at their deceased leader's funeral.[40]

   Butterbaugh was himself modestly successful in gaining converts and hence establishing in Colorado a small group of Shepherd's Rod believers. 'Sr. Bliven' reports that Butterbaugh was elected the leader of this group.[41] Those with whom Butterbaugh studied included 'brother and sister H. G. Warden'. The Wardens had evidently become Davidians[42] in their native Oregon, but went to Denver at the request of Eckerman in 1933, where they worked together.

After some weeks of vain effort trying to get an opening for the Message, we temporarily abandoned Denver and visited other Colorado cities. The Lord led us back again in February of this year and the way opened for 'the angel with the writer's inkhorn' to begin his marking. Bro. Eckerman was now free from other duties and proved himself a willing worker. Day after day we went from door to door hunting 'for the lost sheep of the house of Israel'.[43]

Warden himself speaks of his own and Eckerman's efforts in the Denver region as resulting in the establishment of a 'goodly company'.[44] The figure given in the Davidian publication *The Symbolic Code* (hereinafter *SC*), 1 *SC* 17, is 'about thirty'.[45] One of that company was R. E. Davis (perhaps the Mrs Evelyn Davis listed in the directory as a worker, or else her husband), who wrote, 'When Bro. Warden came to my house I was a backslidden SDA, having no interest in religion, and do not know what made me decide to come to a study. I fully believe now that I will, with the grace of our Lord, be one of the 144,000'.[46] From Denver, Warden moved south to continue the work. In November 1935 his address is given as 1225 10th Street, Pueblo, Colorado.[47] One of Warden's other converts was Sidney Smith, who, together with his second wife, Bonnie, was to be interviewed at Baylor University in 1989. Smith, an engineer with an SDA background, was working on what was to become Los Angeles Airport some time in the later part of the 1930s (Smith is uncertain of the date). While working on this project he met Warden and undertook Bible studies with him.[48] The result was that Smith became convinced of the truth of the Davidian message, a conviction that is still very apparent in the 1989 videotaped interview. Smith later moved to Mt. Carmel and was one of those involved in the 'hunting' campaign to be discussed later.

By 1943 the Wardens had moved to Waco, and are listed in the directory as being at the Mt. Carmel address. H. G. Warden is further listed as being on the movement's governing body, the executive council. He was later, in 1961, to become vice-president. (It should be noted that no one other than Houteff himself ever occupied the post of president of the Davidians. After Houteff's death, therefore, the office of vice-president became in reality the highest in the movement.)

Another early convert was SDA minister and Texaco conference president E. T. Wilson from Charleston, South Carolina.[49] As an ordained Seventh-day Adventist minister, and a person with considerable administrative experience, Wilson must have been a real asset to Houteff. He appears frequently in the early material: for example he wrote to Houteff on 15 December 1933 thanking him for drawing his (Wilson's) attention to 'the precious truths of the Bible, and the gems of the Spirit of Prophecy, which are so abundant throughout the two little volumes of the "Shepherd's Rod" '.[50] E. T. Wilson was later appointed by Houteff as vice-president of the Davidians, a post he held until replaced by Houteff's wife, Florence, in 1955.

The picture one gets, then, at least from the Davidian witness, is that the movement grew fairly quickly. To the evidence presented above may be added that of Fannie-Lou Woods of Georgia, who wrote to Wilson on 21 October 1934 telling him that a company of 42 (thirteen men, twelve women, and seventeen children) had formed and from this group a 'little army of workers' had been organized 'to proclaim the message of Present Truth to the churches in Georgia'.[51] It must be remembered of course that these are far from unbiased accounts, but the cumulative picture is probably not too distorted, given that much of it is pieced together from signed letters from those working in various parts of the USA. During the early few years (to 1935), Houteff himself continued to operate out of Los Angeles; his letters are sent to and from 10466 South Hoover Street.[52]

It is not necessary to trace further here the early development of the movement, except to note that, in keeping with the theology of the group, the sole emphasis was on contacting Seventh-day Adventists and alerting them to this new light that had been given. Nearly sixty years later exactly the same tactics were to be used by the Branch Davidians, including Koresh himself, whose missionary efforts were almost exclusively focused upon the members of the Seventh-day Adventist Church.

Even after his formal disfellowshipping, Houteff did not give up on the Church he considered to be the true remnant of God's people. He applied for a 'hearing' before 'a body of leading brethren' and the leaders of the Church granted it. Houteff was, however, deeply unhappy about the make-up of the committee since those who sat upon it, so he said, were already known for their opposition to the Shepherd's Rod teaching.[53] (This was certainly true in the case of committee member O. A. Graf, for already early in 1933 Graf had prepared a response to Houteff's work in the form of an unpublished manuscipt which sought to refute some of Houteff's principal teachings.)[54] In the end, however, Houteff agreed to meet with those who had been selected as the representatives of the Church. The meeting was held on Monday 19 February 1934 at 4800 South Hoover Street, Los Angeles.[55]

The meeting did not progress well. Despite the fact that there were several topics on the agenda and a week set aside for their discussion,[56] only one topic, 'The Harvest', was presented by Houteff, and the committee then adjourned the meeting to prepare a written reply. This was published several weeks later as *A Reply to the Shepherd's Rod*, a wide-ranging theological response that deals with more than just the one topic. The report was read to Houteff and about a dozen followers on Sunday 18 March. Houteff sought further clarification and further responses, but none (he says) were forthcoming. To this point the matter had been treated very much on a local level; on 19 February 1934, however (the same day as the meeting in Los Angeles) the General Conference Committee discussed Houteff's work and directed that a response be written 'counteracting the false teaching of the "Shepherd's Rod" '.[57] By this point Houteff was now occupying a familiar role in the history of Christianity: a prophet who had found himself without honour in his own country.[58] The formal organization of 'the Shepherd's Rod' under Houteff's leadership appears to have taken place between 25 February and 12 March 1934—the date he gives for 'the first convention'.[59]

By 1935 Houteff had taken the decision to relocate. To this point the movement had centred upon a leadership in California. However, in January of that year three of the leaders of the fledgling movement, Houteff, Wilson, and M. L. Deeter,[60] travelled to Texas to survey a number of properties. Texas had been chosen, it seems, because of its centrality (according to Houteff's world view) and its consequent accordance with the words of Isaiah 19.24 'In that day shall Israel be the third with Egypt and with Assyria, even a blessing in the midst of the land'.[61] Four properties seem to have been on the shortlist: in Dallas, San Antonio, Houston, and Waco. After careful consideration and of course prayer, the Waco site was chosen. Houteff borrowed (apparently from the Hermanson family)[62] the $1,000 needed for a down payment; the site was purchased on 15 March and the Davidians made preparations for the move.[63]

The original purchase was of 189 acres, but to this were added a further 188 purchased from the Southwestern Life Insurance Co.[64] It was presumed that the Davidian occupation of the Waco site would be only temporary, it being a short-term staging post where the 144,000 could gather and prepare for their eschatological role of spreading the gospel to the world.[65] However, the group, together with its most significant offshoot, the Branch Davidians, has remained in Waco to this day, although not continuously on the same site.[66]

On 19 May 1935 those who had responded to the call to move to Texas met in San Diego.[67] The fact that there were twelve volunteers from seven families filled Houteff with the assurance that the move was in accordance with God's wishes, both numbers being symbolically important in the Bible. He wrote:

Our company being composed of twelve members signifies that it is to represent the foundation of this central headquarters location of the last and everlasting spiritual government. And as number 'seven' denotes completeness, the seven families are to represent all the families that are to make up the everlasting kingdom of Christ. Hence, we see the hand of God moving in the same mysterious way even now.[68]

The names of the twelve are given as Elder E. T. Wilson,[69] Sr. Florence Charboneau,[70] Mr. C. E. Charboneau,[71] Sr. S. Hermanson,[72] Miss Florence Hermanson, Oliver Hermanson,[73] Bro. and Sr. J. Berolinger,[74] Bro. M. L. Deeter, Naoma Deeter,[75] Bro. John Knippel, Snr.,[76] and Bro. V. T. Houteff.[77] The fact that two of the group had the use of only one hand was seen as a further sign, in that it was perceived to be a fulfilment of Luke 14.21, which speaks of the 'maimed' being invited to a wedding feast, an invitation that the rich and well-to-do have rejected. This parable, says Houteff,

must find its fulfillment in the end of the world, for the fact that the call came at '*supper time*' and just before the marriage of the king's son (Matt. 22:2) when it can be truly said, 'all things are now ready,' that is, at the time when Christ is to be crowned as King of Kings and Lord of Lords, which is to take place at the close of probation.[78]

The group arrived in Waco on 24 May, which was good going considering the transport:

Three automobiles and two home made trailers composed the caravan—1924 Durant, 1926 Chevrolet, and 1932 Ford. The first two were in bad repair and, as we were able to make only about 100 miles for the first 8 hours, it appeared impossible to make the journey, but the One Who is 'taking charge of the flock' ('Testimonies to Ministers,' p. 300) and Who neither slumbers nor sleeps (Ps. 121:4) led us safely with no trouble at all save two or three minor repairs and three flats on one of the sixteen wheels that carried the caravan.[79]

For theological reasons (as always) the name chosen for the new centre was 'Mt. Carmel'. This will be explored in a little more detail in Chapter Four, but in essence Houteff argued that the Waco centre was that predicted in the prophecy of Amos 1.2: 'And he said, the Lord will roar from Zion, and utter his voice from Jerusalem; and the habitations of the shepherds shall mourn, and the top of Carmel shall wither'; this refers to a time, says Houteff, when probation has closed and the Davidians have been transported to Israel. 'Carmel' will then wither, and if it is to wither, it must first flourish.[80] And flourish it did: by August 1935 the group had grown from twelve to thirty-seven.[81] Houteff was now in charge of a movement that seemed to have a future.

On 1 January 1937 Houteff married Florence Hermanson, thirty years his junior, a marriage that was to last until his death in 1955.[82]

Exactly at the close of the seventh year of the sealing message, and, as with our father Adam, on Friday, the sixth day of the week, January 1, the outworking of Providential purpose and design, restoring type in antitype, united in holy wedlock Brother V.T. Houteff and Miss Florence Hermanson, who has been connected with the message of Present Truth from its inception, and who, for the past three years, has been in active service to this cause. The ceremony, performed by Elder E.T. Wilson, was simple, solemn, and unforgettable, beautifully befitting the occasion. Moreover, it was the first marriage on Mt. Carmel, the home of the Elijah message, which is now in the process of restoring 'every divine institution'.[83]

Florence's influence on the Davidian movement was to be profound, if negative, in that it was she who took the leadership following the death of Victor and she also who eventually sought to disband the group.

Also in 1937 Houteff instituted the system of the 'second tithe'. The 'second tithe' was in effect an insurance plan for the members of the community. Those who paid it paid an additional 10 per cent of their income into a common fund (10 per cent of the 90 per cent of their income left after they had paid the first tithe).[84] This was used to support the education of the children and in particular for the payment of medical bills incurred by members of the community. In effect it was not an 'offering to the Lord'.[85] The 'second tithers' were to become a very important group among all those who eventually became associated with the Davidian movement and the Mt. Carmel property. It was to them, in 1962, that the assets of the group, including the property in Waco, were turned over when the Davidians formally disbanded.

Some further details of life at Mt. Carmel at this time are supplied by Glen Green and Bonnie Smith.[86] The picture one gets is of an exceptionally hard-working community devoted to the service of God and the task of spreading the Davidian message and determined to make Mt. Carmel a going concern. Houteff had chosen the location in part on account of its distance from the city, a place where the gathered people of God could go about their business undisturbed and uninterrupted by the distractions of the world. Daily routine began very early, with prayer and then work. Work included construction of the buildings and looking after the dairy herd that had been brought onto the property. Meals were simple, vegetarian, and taken together. Clothing too was modest, with long sleeves, long dresses, and hats for the female members of the community.[87] Even the children were expected to do some work, but schooling was of course also provided (Saether's wife being an important person in this context) with subjects such as history, mathematics, and 'nature'. For the latter subject the children often went on long walks around the extensive Mt. Carmel property. In addition to schooling in the day, there were study sessions in the evening.

It was not all plain sailing, however. In 1938 Houteff visited his mother in Bulgaria, a trip that lasted four months.[88] By this time a rivalry had sprung up between M. J. Bingham[89] and Wilson, and in Houteff's absence this rivalry became more acute, to the point that upon his return he found two definite factions at Mt. Carmel: those who supported Wilson and those who supported Bingham. Saether recounts these events in some detail and notes how Houteff was able to bring reconciliation. The day that peace was restored, says Saether, was 25 October, a day which from that point on was celebrated each year by the community as 'the day of days', a day when all Davidians would look back over the past year, consider any differences they had with fellow believers, and remember the reconciliation of the community in 1938.[90]

The Mt. Carmel centre developed significantly over the next several years and the work progressed elsewhere as well. Saether was quite clear that in the year that he arrived, 1937, there were already some seventy-five residents and that the number jumped in 1938 to 125. This is rapid growth, and Saether's interviewer properly questioned him on the figures. Saether insisted, however, that in 1938 there were indeed about 125 residents at Mt. Carmel, though he added that this was the highest it reached and it fell back in subsequent years.[91] Saether might be overestimating somewhat. The Smiths suggested that in 1938 there were between seventy and ninety persons at Mt. Carmel, but on reflection thought it might be closer to the lower number.[92] In a later interview, Glenn Green said that in the late 1930s there were about seventy persons at Mt. Carmel.[93] According to Adair the number of residents when he arrived in 1951 was somewhere between seventy-five and one hundred.[94] By 1940 the community had fallen back from even the lower estimates; in this year Baylor researcher Mary Power visited the centre and reported that there were some sixty-four residents.[95]

Power's thesis is useful for this period more generally. In it she provides an extended first-hand external glimpse of the community as it was in 1939–40.

She visited Mt. Carmel several times during this period and reported that by the time she visited it the centre was already well advanced in terms of its physical structures. Originally two large-framed buildings provided the bulk of the accommodation, one used for living quarters, the other as a warehouse, kitchen, dining room, and sleeping quarters. There followed the addition of more adequate housing, school rooms, a laundry, a general store, 'and a home for the aged and afflicted from the "streets and the lanes" '.[96] By January 1940, the last time Power visited the community, there were ten buildings, some two stories high: a chapel had been added, as had an administration building. (It was in this building that the famous 'eleventh-hour clock' was, and indeed still is, situated.)[97] Two dirt roads had been constructed, one of which was known as 'The King's Highway'.[98] A dam alleviated the water supply problem and sewage, electricity, and telephone services were now on site.[99] This is quite an accomplishment in a relatively short space of time given the small numbers involved and the phenomenal publishing output that was going on alongside the physical construction.

This publishing work was of course vital in the life of the community. Like their SDA predecessors, the Davidians saw the written word as central to the task of distributing the truth. Even before the move to Mt. Carmel publishing had constituted a major part of Davidian evangelistic outreach. Both volumes of *The Shepherd's Rod* enjoyed wide distribution in the early 1930s, with some 5,000 copies of each coming into print. In August 1933 some 3,000 copies of the first Davidian tract, *The Pre-Eleventh Hour Extra*, were published.[100] This was followed in December by the second tract, *The Great Paradox of the Ages*, with again a first print run of 3,000.[101] Others soon followed: 5,000 copies of *The Judgment and the Harvest* were published in May 1934; 6,000 copies of *The Latest News for Mother* appeared in August of the same year; and 6,000 copies of *Final Warning* appeared in May 1935. Once the group had settled at Mt. Carmel the publications resumed. Both *Why Perish* and *The Great Controversy over the Shepherd's Rod* appeared in June 1936 (6,000 copies of each), *Mount Sion at the Eleventh Hour* appeared in November 1937 (6,000 copies), and in January 1940 some 15,000 copies of *Behold I Make All Things New* came off the press.[102] These tracts were not small: the shortest (*Pre-Eleventh Hour Mystery*) is fifty-six pages and the longest (*Final Warning*) is 120. In addition to these publications were the issues of *The Symbolic Code* from this period.

Power observed that the community at Mt. Carmel was much taken with the business of observing the Sabbath and she noted in particular that special arrangements were in place to ensure that each Davidian was able to finish work early on the Friday so that there was time to prepare properly for the Sabbath hours. On the Sabbath itself, the members of the community rose

PLATE 2 'B8'—the administration building at 'Old' Mt. Carmel

early and went to Sabbath School. Food intake was restricted on the Sabbath so that the brain might be alert. Sabbath School was followed by morning worship (a traditional Seventh-day Adventist package) and the remainder of the day was then taken up by activities such as walking, reading, instruction, or discussion (on spiritual matters no doubt) between members of the community. Evening worship brought the sacred day to a close and marked the start of the working week. Power appears to have attended the Sabbath worship sessions at least once; she notes how although in broad outline it was very similar to what one might find elsewhere, the sermon took the form of a detailed exposition of the scriptures that made use of large charts filled with symbolic drawings.[103] There was a mid-week service also on a Wednesday, preceded by a vesper service for the younger members of the community.

Power emphasized that one of the doctrines that the Davidians seemed particularly keen on was the view that the United States was prophetically portrayed as the two-horned beast in Revelation 13.11–18. The reason for her emphasis is not obvious, but given the context it seems that it figured as part of Houteff's exposition of scripture.[104] It is an interesting detail. Seventh-day Adventists in general have long taken the view that the USA is an eschatologically significant power that will one day join hands with apostate Christendom in an effort to stamp out the last of God's people on earth,[105] even if present Seventh-day Adventists, though confessing this in their literature, seem largely unconcerned by it on any practical level. In Houteff's Mt. Carmel, however, the doctrine must have had a particular resonance. As Power says, the community was geographically and socially quite isolated and this sense of living in the land of the enemy must have been real to them.[106] After all, not only did these early Davidians share the temporal disjunction with the rest of Christianity that came as a result of keeping the Sabbath ('So, as their day of sacred worship ceases[,] other Christians are making preparation for the Sunday Sabbath, and the Seventh-day Adventists of Mount Carmel Center begin their week of labour'),[107] they were distanced too from their own mother faith, Seventh-day Adventism, to which they had by now become something of an annoyance. What is more, the prophetic-interpretative tradition that they inherited told them that their own government would one day turn against them in an effort to enforce a universal Sunday law. But God was on their side. Here they were, a small community of the faithful ready to announce God's warning to his remnant people, prepared to call out the 144,000 to inhabit the kingdom and always on guard against the 'lamb-like beast' who would one day seek to destroy them. It is entirely clear that the Branch Davidians at the 'new' Mt. Carmel in February–April 1993 took the same view and this may well have been a factor in the outcome of the siege.

Other information Power includes is that the Davidians were strict tithe payers,[108] and that they shunned dancing, theatre, tobacco, 'common litera-ture', 'costly raiment', and jewellery. None of these things are surprising given the broader SDA context. She notes also that the members of the community were all strict vegetarians, a detail supplied also by Saether.[109]

Power has a good deal to say about the school established at Mt. Carmel in 1935, namely 'The Mt. Carmel Academy'. When she visited there were ap-proximately thirty-five students ranging from eight to twenty years of age.[110] The purpose of the Academy was to train workers 'to carry the group's religious beliefs to other Seventh-Day Adventists who have not accepted the message of the Shepherd's Rod . . .'[111] A variety of subjects was taught, but all were based almost exclusively on the Bible and the writings of Ellen White. Schooling was for body, mind, and spirit, and so the day was divided into four two-hour sessions. Two hours of mental work were followed by two hours of physical work in one of Mt. Carmel's departments.

Houteff's relatively brief pamphlet (twenty-nine pages), the *Mt. Carmel Training Center: Catalog Syllabus and Rules Manual*,[112] gives further details both of the programmes on offer at the centre and the educational philosophy behind its establishment. Its regulations are severe, but understandable given the context. The emphasis is upon preparing workers for the proclamation of the Davidian message and all else is subjected to that supreme goal.[113]

During the period 1935–40 there were four marriages and two births at Mt. Carmel.[114] The first marriage was that of Houteff himself. Marriage to outsiders was not permitted. By now the community was operating its own currency.[115] As Pitts notes, this was highly symbolic, for it represented an increasing sense of self-sufficiency.[116] The currency used carried two logos: the eleventh hour clock and the lion of Judah.[117]

By 1940, then, Houteff's Mt. Carmel was very much a going concern and during the next decade it would grow further. To his death Houteff remained the undisputed leader of the movement, and what he said was final. However, Houteff quickly put in place a system of government which theoretically at least meant that the community was directed by more that just one individual. Indeed, the 'Executive Council' was already in place when Power visited the community, and she described how it operated. It had been set up in a conscious attempt to mirror the council of Acts 6.2–5, which talks of a group of seven men to take care of the day-to-day business of the Church. Accordingly, seven individuals (not all men) were appointed as Council members to direct the business affairs of the community. The Council had full power to grant credentials and licenses and fill by appointment any vacancies that arose in its membership, other than that of president. It could also adjust pay and expenses for those employed by the association. There is no hint that the Council exercised any authority in doctrinal matters, which presumably rested solely with Houteff himself.[118] The first full published list of council members seems to have been the one in the 1943 *Directory*.[119] The names given are V. T. Houteff, Mrs. G. R. Bingham, M. J. Bingham,[120] E. T. Wilson, Mrs. S. Hermanson, H. G. Warden, and Mrs. F. M. Houteff.

Through the 1940s the community continued to grow both in Mt. Carmel residents and in Davidians who lived in other parts of the country. Up to this point they continued to be known generally as 'The Shepherd's Rod', the name of Houteff's principal publication, or, more properly, 'The General Association of Shepherd's Rod Seventh-day Adventists'.[121] In 1943, however, the organization was named officially as 'The General Association of Davidian Seventh-day Adventists', an organization that still exists today, and certificates of membership were introduced. These moves towards official organization may have been in response to the draft, since as a properly constituted 'Seventh-day Adventist' ecclesial community, the Davidians could claim established conscientious-objector status,[122] though in fact they were willing to register for non-combatant duties so long as their sensitivities regarding Sabbath observance and vegetarianism could be safeguarded.[123] Hence the 'Shepherd's Rod' movement became the 'Davidian Seventh-day Adventists' and on 12 February *The Leviticus of Davidian Seventh-day Adventists*, which contained the Constitution and Bye-Laws of the Association, was published.

Rather ambitiously one has to say some 5,075 copies were printed. This is an interesting little publication that provides a further glimpse of the community as it had now developed. The name 'Davidian Seventh-day Adventist', so the publication explains, is taken from the parent body, the Seventh-day Adventists, but gives unequivocal testimony to its principal concern.

The name, Davidian, deriving from the name of the king of Ancient Israel, accrues to this Association by reason of its following aspects: First, it is dedicated to the work of announcing and bringing forth the restoration (as predicted in Hosea 1:11; 3:5) of David's kingdom in antitype, upon the throne of which Christ, 'the son of David,' is to sit. Second, it purports itself to be the first of the first fruits of the living, the vanguard from among the present-day descendants of those Jews who composed the Early Christian Church. With the emergence of this vanguard and its army, the first fruits, from which are elected the 12,000 out of each of the twelve tribes of Jacob, "the 144,000" (Rev. 14:1; 7:2–8) who stand on Mount Zion with the Lamb (Rev. 14:1; 7:2–8), the reign of antitypical David begins.[124]

The implied theology of this passage will be examined in greater detail in the next chapter. Here we note only the way in which it was this concern to spread the news of the coming kingdom of David that gave the group its focus. And the focus was very clear: only those who were already Seventh-day Adventists needed to be told at this stage, for it was from them alone that the 144,000 were to come. *The Leviticus* goes on to explain in much greater detail the way in which the group sees itself and its mission and how, on a practical level, it is to be organized to achieve its task. Much of the tract is taken up with quotations from Ellen White and the Bible, which are without comment or explanation.

Around this time too a decision was taken to separate the sexes, apart from married couples. Saether recalled how this was in part the influence of Bingham and how his own children, until then living with their parents, had to live in single-sex dormitories.[125] The experiment did not last and the order was revoked two years later. This was not the last time the Davidians/Branch Davidians were separated according to sex. Koresh instituted the same regime in 1989.

For the adults, life at Mt. Carmel seems to have involved hard physical labour during the day followed by intensive Bible study at night (a pattern we shall see again in the Koreshs' time). Bingham was obviously a major influence here and did a good deal of the teaching in the evenings. Eventually he was to become involved with some of the female members of the academy, which resulted in his leaving his wife and Mt. Carmel.[126] He returned, however, and continued to work at the Academy until it was closed in 1948.

Houteff's health was failing. In 1945 he nearly died from a duodenal ulcer and though he was to survive another ten years his health was clearly giving cause for concern. The publishing work was now in full swing with some 48,000 tracts coming off the press every two weeks. In addition to *The Shepherd's Rod* volumes 1 and 2 (volume 1 had been produced also in a 'pocket edition'), *The Symbolic Code*, and the various tracts already referred to, the Mt. Carmel presses were busy with several others such as *The Sign of Jonah* (1940), *God's Titles Not Restricted to One Language* (1940), *The World Yesterday, Today and Tomorrow* (1941), *War News Forecast* (1943), *The Entering Wedge* (1946), and *To the Seven Churches* (1947). In addition Houteff's sermons at Mt. Carmel appeared in print as *Timely Greetings* from 1946 on (terminated 1953) and *The Answerer* volumes 1–5 appeared in 1944.[127]

Published materials were by now being sent to a mailing list estimated to contain the names of nearly 100,000 Seventh-day Adventists. This policy of sending out materials to every Seventh-day Adventist for whom an address could be found was not a particularly efficient means of contact and Houteff took the view that a more targeted approach was needed. Consequently in late 1952 a new plan was instituted. Houteff drew attention to Jeremiah 16.16: 'Behold, I will send for many fishers, saith the Lord, and they shall fish them; and after will I send for many hunters, and they shall hunt them from every mountain, and from every hill, and out of the holes of the rocks.' From this text it was deduced that there were two distinct phases of the work to call the 144,000. The first, 'the fishing period', had been in place since the message had come to Houteff; the presses had been set up and the literature had been sent out. Now, however, was the time of the 'hunting'; and this would be much more targeted. Davidians were to go out and seek God's people wherever they were.[128] Investment was needed for the purchase of vehicles for the 'hunters' to use in their travels and for their support. Consequently the sale of 'old' Mt. Carmel began as land was gradually sold off to fund between twenty and thirty fieldworkers who went out as 'hunters'. These were to seek out Seventh-day Adventist families in person, ascertain their level of interest, and give them the message. Six new cars were purchased and Davidian 'hunters' sent to many parts of the USA and even further afield: to Australia, England,[129] India, the West Indies, and Canada. Saether himself was sent to Ohio and Pennsylvania but was called back in 1953 since, Houteff said, funds were now getting low.[130] All the hunters were eventually recalled by Mrs Houteff in 1957.[131] Smith states: 'I went to every town in the state of Montana, and then came back down into Kansas, went through every town in the state of Kansas, but [there were] two counties to the west, the only ones I didn't get. And then they called me back to Waco again.'[132] To support the message, Houteff composed the *Jezreel Letters*, which explained in outline and somewhat simplified form the key Davidian beliefs.

By 1954 Houteff was seriously ill; from Saether's account he endured a period of illness for several months prior to his death. The report was that he had kidney failure.[133] Right up to the end his focus was on the interpretation of prophecy; if later reports are to be believed, even in the last hour or two of his life he was much concerned with the interpretation of Revelation 11 in general and the forty-two months of Revelation 11.2 in particular.[134] His wife was later to claim that he made it clear to her during this time that she should take over the leadership of the movement. According to a short obituary in the *Waco Tribune-Herald* and information given by Saether, Victor Houteff eventually died in Hillcrest Hospital at 12.05 on Saturday 5 February 1955; he was sixty-nine. Before this he had been in an oxygen tent at Mt. Carmel, where he was cared for by Saether and M. W. Wolfe.[135] He died from kidney failure.

Houteff's funeral service took place at Mt. Carmel at 3.00 p.m. on Wednesday 9 February with Wolfe and E. T. Wilson presiding.[136] Long-time member of the community Dr W. G. Butterbaugh was one of the two persons who preached at the funeral. It was by all accounts exceptionally well attended.[137] Houteff was survived by three brothers and three sisters.[138]

Houteff's death was a shock to the community. Many had thought that he would not die before the coming of the kingdom. There were perhaps around a hundred Mt. Carmel residents at the time, and there is some evidence that the crisis was so great that it led to an immediate exit from the community of some of these.[139] How the rest of the community dealt with the crisis, and the emergence of Florence as the next leader of the Davidians, is picked up in Chapter Five. Before moving on to those developments, however, a sketch of Houteff's theology is clearly called for, for it was theology that formed the heart of his life's work, and though the man was now dead his theology lived on. His dream of the coming of the kingdom, the precursory call of the 144,000, and perhaps too the slaughter of the wicked, would continue to inspire Davidians and Branch Davidians alike for at least another forty years, indeed, right down to the present day.

NOTES

1. Reliable secondary literature covering Houteff's life is not vast, but includes Bailey and Darden, *Mad Man in Waco*, 15–37. See also William Pitts, 'The Lord's Return to Mt. Carmel: Davidian Seventh-day Adventists 1935–1961', a paper presented to the South-west Meeting of the American Academy of Religion, Dallas, TX, 1987; and id., 'The Mount Carmel Davidians; Adventist Reformers 1935–1959', a paper presented at the American Academy of Religion, Kansas, 1991. These papers are

unpublished, but copies of both are available in TXC 2D212/4. Some of that material is found in id., 'Davidians and Branch Davidians: 1929–1987' in Wright, ed., *Armageddon in Waco*, 20–42. Primary material on Houteff's life (as opposed to his theology) and the development of Mt. Carmel under his leadership is more difficult to access. It includes Houteff's tract *The Great Controversy over the Shepherd's Rod* (1936) and some of the issues of his magazine *Timely Greetings* (hereinafter *TG*), to which reference is made in this chapter. *OM* is indispensable, as are the interviews with Glen Green and Sidney and Bonnie Smith (GSS1, 2, 3, 4). Also useful is Mary Elizabeth Power's work, 'A Study of the Seventh-day Adventist Community, Mount Carmel Center, Waco, Texas', an MA thesis at Baylor University completed in 1940, which has much primary material describing Mt. Carmel as Power found in during her visits. This is available in TXC. A small unpublished term paper by Herman L. Green entitled 'Community Study of the Davidian Seventh-day Adventists Mount Carmel Center, Waco, Texas' [1950], also in TXC, is based extensively on Power and has no new first-hand material. Don Adair's book *A Davidian Testimony* (privately published, 1997) is also very valuable in that it contains many first-hand recollections of Houteff. Less useful and without any references at all is J. J. Robertson, *Beyond the Flames* (San Diego, California: ProMotion Publishing, 1996), 47–52. Robertson's account of Houteff's life is based principally upon details given directly to him by Branch Davidian survivor Catherine Matteson.

2. Pitts, 'Davidians and Branch Davidians', 21.
3. *OM* 131.
4. *OM* 194.
5. *OM* 194–6.
6. *OM* 195–6.
7. 1 *TG* 50/26; in another passage Houteff speaks of the root of this problem lying with a provincial Greek Orthodox bishop, though again there is no detail (see 2 *TG* 35/30).
8. 2 *TG* 35/29.
9. Adair, *Davidian Testimony*, 36–7, presents some of the relevant material.
10. Ibid. 35.
11. *OM* 196–7. According to Saether, Houteff said almost nothing about his first marriage other than that he had the right to remarry because his first wife had committed adultery. From the way Saether reports this point, it rather looks as though in fact it was his view that Houteff might not actually have been divorced from his first wife when he married his second.
12. Houteff himself gives an account of this early period in 2 *TG* 35/12–31. It is from this, together with the Saether material, that the following account has been reconstructed.
13. Houteff wrote: 'While running a small hotel in the middle west back in 1919, I became intensely interested in religion, and providentially joined the Seventh-day Adventists. They were at the time meeting in a rented hall, not too attractive for a church. The people appeared to be very poor. Aside from the preacher I was the

only one that was driving a car, and he had a worn out Ford that I would not have given a dollar for it if I had to drive it.' 2 *TG* 35/12.

14. See 'The Committee on Defense Literature of the General Conference of Seventh-day Adventists', *The History and Teachings of 'The Shepherd's Rod'* (1955), 3 n. 3, which makes reference to the original church record book in which Houteff's reception into the Church is documented.

15. *OM* 130.

16. The precise chronological structure of Houteff's narrative is difficult to follow at this point, but the spell in the hospital seems to have happened shortly before his starting work for the Maytag agency, which he dates to 1923 (2 *TG* 35/15).

17. Glendale Sanitarium was founded in 1905, at which time it occupied a seventy-five-room former hotel. In 1924, which was after Houteff's visit, it moved to a new site. As with many Seventh-day Adventist health institutions it has grown considerably and is now a 450 bed, full-service facility operating under the name of 'Glendale Adventist Medical Center'.

18. 2 *TG* 35/15.

19. He wrote: 'Now let me relate to you another miracle that took place about that time. One Wednesday I drove to the business section of Los Angeles. Having finished my business quite late in the afternoon, and while walking across a street, I saw a woman driving toward me. But as I was almost to the middle of the street, I saw no danger for there was plenty of room for her to drive by. She nevertheless turned her car right square into me. Yes, she struck me from my left, and being overly excited she could not stop her car before she reached the middle of the block. And so she kept on going from the corner of the street to the middle of the alley. What happened to me when the car struck me? Did it lay me flat on the street, and did it run over me? No, this did not happen because something greater took place: An unseen hand carried me on ahead of the car, lightly sliding my feet on the pavement with my right side ahead, and my left side against the car's radiator! After having made about half the distance before the car stopped, something seated me on the bumper of the car, and I put my left arm around the car's left headlight! Then I said to myself, "Now lady you can keep on going if that is the best you can do." When she stopped, I put my feet on the ground and stepped away from the car. Just then I discovered that the pencil I had in my coat pocket had broken into half a dozen pieces from the impact, but my ribs were untouched.' 2 *TG* 35/21–2.

20. *History and Teachings*, 3.

21. Bailey and Darden, *Madman in Waco*, 18.

22. Victor Houteff, *Christ's Greetings* (1941), 44.

23. Ibid.

24. Ibid.

25. *The Shepherd's Rod*, vol. 1, was copyrighted in 1930, the second volume in 1932. Both were privately published and printed in the USA.

26. *The Great Controversy of the Shepherd's Rod*, 7.

27. Ibid. 5.

28. *History and Teachings*, 5, states: 'the leaders of the denomination were then exceedingly occupied with the services and the business of that great meeting [the General Conference meeting in San Francisco], and could not give to that document the immediate study and consideration that he [Houteff] demanded. Moreover, since the Houteff affair was at that time merely a local one, the matter was left to the local and the union conference concerned.'
29. Bailey and Darden, *Madman in Waco*, 18.
30. 'Laodiceans' here refers to the Seventh-day Adventists, who, Houteff argued, were the Laodicean Church of Rev. 3.14–22.
31. This was apparently not the same institution as Glendale Sanitarium, the general purpose health centre to which Houteff had been admitted several years earlier.
32. 2 *TG* 35/22–3.
33. *History and Teachings*, 5.
34. Ibid. 5–6.
35. Ibid. 6.
36. *The Great Controversy over the Shepherd's Rod*, 10. The letter is not dated, but elsewhere Houteff gives July 1931 as the date of the conversion of the first SDA medical doctor (Houteff, *Christ's Greetings*, 44).
37. See 1 *Symbolic Code* (hereinafter *SC*), 2, which states: 'Dr. W.S. Butterbaugh and Bro. W.A. Eckerman have recently taken full charge of the Treatment Rooms in Denver, Colorado, and their zeal in the message promises that this health center shall become the mother of many such institutions in the proclamation of the Third Angel's Message in the Loud Cry.'
38. 1 *SC* 1, 3.
39. See Victor Houteff, *Fundamental Beliefs and Directory of the Davidian Seventh-day Adventists* (1943), 20, which lists Butterbaugh as still living in Colorado.
40. *OM* 185.
41. 1 *SC* 4 (1934), 2.
42. Although strictly anachronistic, from this point on the term 'Davidian' will be used to refer to members of the Shepherd's Rod movement.
43. 1 *SC* 18 (1935), 3. This reference to the lost sheep of the house of Israel is theologically significant (quotation from Matt. 10.6). One cannot rule out, however, that as it is quoted here the text relates to the Davidian view that they must gather together the 144,000 individuals who, without knowing it, were literal descendants of the lost ten tribes of Israel.
44. 1 *SC* 18, 4.
45. 1 *SC* 17 (1935), 10.
46. 1 *SC* 14 (1935), 9.
47. 1 *SC* 17 (1935), 10.
48. The account of Smith's conversion is given in GSS2, 14–15.
49. On Wilson see *OM*, 184–5.
50. *The Great Controversy over the Shepherd's Rod*, 10.
51. 1 *SC* 5 (1934), 2.

52. For example, Glen Calkins to Victor Houteff, 15 Feb. 1934, letter published in *The Great Controversy over the Shepherd's Rod*, 17.

53. The members were A. G. Daniells (Chairman), W. G. Wirth (Secretary), G. A. Roberts, C. S. Prout, J. C. Stevens, H. M. S. Richards, Glenn Calkins, C. M. Sorenson, F. C. Gilbert, W. M. Adams, J. A. Burden, and O. J. Graf. See *History and Teachings*, 11, for details of the status in the denomination of most of these individuals.

54. See O. J. Graf and D. E. Robinson, 'The Shepherd's Rod: A Review' (1934). This is a later form of the original MS which has been added to by Robinson in an effort to cover further some of the issues with which Graf originally dealt. It was produced by the Elmshaven Office, St Helena, California. A copy is located in the Ellen G. White SDA Research Centre, Europe, at Newbold College, Bracknell, Berks. (Ref. DF 367a/4). Graf had apparently met Houteff on 11 Nov. 1932 (*History and Teachings*, 7).

55. Houteff, *The Great Controversy over the Shepherd's Rod*, 17–20.

56. According to Houteff, the subjects that were to have been considered were 'The Harvest', 'Ezekiel Nine', 'The Leopard-like Beast of Revelation 13', 'Hosea, chapters One and Two', and 'Matthew 20'; Houteff, *The Great Controversy over the Shepherd's Rod*, 22.

57. *History and Teachings*, 14; the response came in the form of a pamphlet, 'A Warning Against Error' (1934). This was expanded in *A Reply to the Shepherd's Rod* (1934).

58. See also R. L. Benton, 'Summary of an Address on the Shepherd's Rod given Sabbath, March 2, 1935 at Keene, Texas', unpublished MS (copy available through the Ellen G. White SDA Research Center ref. 367a/12). In this address Benton, who was president of the South-western Union Conference of Seventh-day Adventists, goes over some of the main doctrinal points of the Shepherd's Rod and seeks to refute them. The address seems to have been attended by Houteff himself—see 1 *SC* 14, 11; and W. N. Adams, 'A Challenge' (1936), unpublished MS available through the Ellen G. White SDA Research Centre ref. 367a/13.

59. Houteff, *Christ's Greetings*, 45.

60. Deeter was an early convert who was to remain central to the movement during the Houteff era. He was among those who first travelled to Waco to establish the Mt. Carmel centre, and became the Mt. Carmel chef. He is listed as a minister in the 1943 *Fundamental Beliefs and Directory*. Saether indicates further that Deeter was 'quite a leader and quite a talker' and that he had a great interest in snakes, a collection of which he kept on the Mt. Carmel property. He was married but his wife never joined the community; upon Deeter's death she came to take custody of their daughter Naoma (*OM* 189).

61. Mary Elizabeth Power, 'Mount Carmel Center', 18. Power does not give a specific source for this detail, but elsewhere says that most of the data upon which her thesis is based came from personal interviews with Mt. Carmel residents.

62. The Hermanson family were to play a central role in the development of Davidianism, not least through the substantial financial support that the family gave.

See further David G. Bromley and Edward D. Silver, 'The Davidian Tradition: From Patronal Clan to Prophetic Movement', in Wright, ed., *Armageddon in Waco*, 48–9.

63. Houteff, *Christ's Greetings*, 47.

64. *Mad Man in Waco*, 26 n. 9; the original plot of land was apparently purchased from one W. E. Darden (*Waco Tribune-Herald*, 27 Feb. 1955).

65. Houteff wrote, 'True we are establishing our headquarters on this mount that is found in prophecy, but our stay here shall be very, very short, for "He will finish the work, and cut it short in righteousness: because a short work will the Lord make upon the earth." (Rom. 9:28.)', 1 *SC* 14, 5.

66. The removal of the Branch Davidians to the 'new' Mt. Carmel is discussed in Chapter Five. By the early 1990s a remnant of the original Davidians re-established a presence at the 'old' Mt. Carmel by taking up residence on a small part of the old site. From there it now runs a literature evangelism programme and facilitates both regular weekly and annual meetings of Davidian Seventh-day Adventists. See further Appendix B.

67. Some reports indicate that they in fact met in Los Angeles. The reference to San Diego given here is from 1 *SC* 11–12 (1935), 1.

68. Ibid. 1.

69. *OM* 190–1 indicates that Wilson was married, but that his wife, a Seventh-day Adventist nurse, did not accept the Davidian message and they lived apart. Mrs Wilson did, however, eventually come to live at Mt. Carmel in order to work in the rest home. There was one son, who became a Davidian along with his wife. No names are given.

70. Mrs. Florence Floretta Charboneau (*neé* Gowell) was born 12 Dec. 1874 in Colfax Township, Oceana County, Michigan. She married Charles Edwin Charboneau on 27 May 1894. She had three stepchildren and one daughter. The daughter, Sophia, was to marry Oliver Hermanson and it was their daughter Florence who at the age of seventeen married Victor Houteff. Mrs Charboneau died on 2 Dec. 1935. (Details from obituary in 1 *SC* 18, 3.) *OM* 182 describes Mrs Charboneau as Houteff's 'right-hand man'.

71. *OM* 182 describes C. E. Charboneau as 'an older man and one of his arms was crippled, hurt in an accident. He wasn't a member of Brother Houteff's group. I mean by that he was not affiliated with them. Before he died he became a Christian in his very old age.'

72. Sophia Hermanson was the daughter of the Charboneaus and the mother of Florence and Oliver. She was married, but her husband became neither a Seventh-day Adventist nor a Davidian. There was one older child in addition to Oliver and Florence, but he stayed with his father and never joined the Mt. Carmel community (*OM* 189–90).

73. Oliver Hermanson was the brother of Florence, son of Sophia, and grandson of the Charboneaus.

74. *OM* 187 indicates that John Berolinger was a 'rough carpenter', that is, that he built bridges, but nothing 'fine'. He apparently took charge of the construction of

the Mt. Carmel centre and became very interested in health matters. His wife was disabled as a result of childhood polio. There were no children.

75. Saether estimates that Naoma (Naomi) Deeter was about 5 years old in 1935 (*OM* 183).

76. Saether says of Knipple, 'He was a believer but he was uneducated and he had two sons who became leaders but he never was really a leader.' Knipple was a widower who had either three or four sons in California, one of whom came to Mt. Carmel for a while (*OM* 183, 190).

77. Saether had a photograph of eleven of the twelve (Deeter apparently took the photograph and so does not appear in it) and was asked to name those in it by his interviewer. The names he gave were those listed here also (*OM* 182–7).

78. 1 *SC* 11–12, 1–2.

79. 1 *SC* 11–12, 2.

80. 2 *SC* 12, 32.

81. Mary Elizabeth Power, 'Mount Carmel Center', 24.

82. A picture of Victor and Florence Houteff is printed as plate one in this book.

83. 3 *SC* 2 (1937), 8; the date is confirmed in Houteff, *Christ's Greetings*, 47.

84. In common with the rest of the Seventh-day Adventist Church, the Davidians paid a tithe of their income to support the work of the Church. The Davidians were clear that this could be used only to support religious activities of the movement, that is the spreading of the message or the facilitation of worship.

85. The system is described in GSS1 44–7.

86. GSS1, 2, 3, 4 *passim*.

87. This detail is confirmed by Adair who recounts a story told to him about Houteff preaching one day on the subject of dress reform. A woman in the congregation complained, 'Brother Houteff, it's too hot here in Texas to dress like you're telling us', to which Houteff replied 'It's going to be a lot hotter where you're going if you don't change' (Adair, 'Interviews', 45).

88. The 1938 date is confirmed by Glenn Green (GSS4 19).

89. The Binghams were early converts to the Davidian cause, though not among the first to relocate to Mt. Carmel. Their role will be discussed further below.

90. Houteff lists 25 Oct. 1939 as the first 'day of days' in *Christ's Greetings*, 48. Sidney Smith also states that his wife has a photographic record of the history of the community almost from its beginnings, including 'All the weddings and all the feast days and the[,] you know, October 25's where they all gathered, and all the pictures of everything else' (GSS2 39). The tension that arose during Houteff's absence and the reconciliation that was eventually achieved is mentioned also by Green (GSS4 41–2). According to Green, 25 October was a 'high day' in the community and a special meal was prepared.

91. *OM* 137–8.

92. GSS1 47–8.

93. GSS4 38.

94. Adair, 'Interviews', 27.

95. Power, 'Mount Carmel Center', 27. Power gives some further details on the building programme during these early years. This includes the construction of two roads, a dam, and a sewage system (26–7).

96. Ibid. 25.

97. The eleventh-hour clock was designed by Houteff as a perpetual reminder of the nearness of the end. It was simply a clock set at 11.00. The clock has survived in its original setting, for this administration building now forms a part of the Vanguard School in Waco (Pitts, 'Davidians and Branch Davidians', 25, 39 n. 5).

98. Power, 'Mt. Carmel Center', 26; Houteff gives 1938 as the date that this road was constructed (Houteff, *Christ's Greetings*, 48).

99. According to Houteff, the telephone system was installed in June 1936 and the electricity supply was connected on 10 Sept. 1938 (Houteff, *Christ's Greetings*, 47–8).

100. *Christ's Greetings*, 44. Saether (*OM* 105–9) remembered getting a copy of this tract, though he was uncertain of the date ('1931, '32, '33, along there somewhere'). In the reprint form this tract is 56 pages.

101. Ibid. 45.

102. Ibid. (for dates and other details).

103. Power, 'Mt. Carmel Center', 34.

104. Ibid. 35: 'These Seventh-Day Adventists lay great stress upon their interpretation of the symbol of the two-horned beast of Revelation 13:11–18. They claim that this beast is the United States, and that soon we shall have here church and state united. The mark of the beast is Sunday-keeping.'

105. See further Newport, *Apocalypse and Millennium*, 172–96.

106. Power, 'Mt. Carmel Center', 1.

107. Ibid. 34.

108. Ibid. 65. Bonnie Smith (GSS3 12) drew attention to the Tuesday prayer meeting as an important part of life at Mt. Carmel. According to Adair ('Interviews' 27), there were study meetings also on Wednesday and Friday evenings.

109. Ibid. 59; *OM* 258.

110. Ibid. 41–2.

111. Ibid. 41.

112. The original date of this document is unclear; I have used the Universal Publishing Association facsimile reprint edition here which is dated 1992.

113. See further Adair, 'Interviews', 16–19. Adair mentions five of his class mates (apparently Houteff insisted that classes at the Academy should have at least six students): Dudley Goff, Harmon Springer, Stoy Proctor, Rod Winslow, and Brent DeGroat (neither Winslow nor DeGroat saw the course through).

114. Power, 'Mt. Carmel Center', 52. Don Adair's marriage also took place at Mt. Carmel (Adair, 'Interviews', 34).

115. Ibid. 69.

116. Pitts, 'Davidians and Branch Davidians', 27.

117. On the clock see above. An example of the currency has survived in TXC and is reproduced between pages 130 and 131 in Bailey and Darden, *Mad Man in Waco*.

118. See further Power, 'Mt. Carmel Center', 72–82.
119. Houteff, *Fundamental Beliefs and Directory*, 16.
120. The Binghams were early converts to the Davidian cause. Already by the time of the publication of 2 *SC* 5–6 (1936), Mrs Bingham had a letter published outlining a recent confrontation with a Seventh-day Adventist Church in California. She wrote: 'Sabbath morning, May 11, 1936, a group of us (teachers, parents, and students of the La Crescenta "Shepherd's Rod" Parochial Home School) presented ourselves at the Hawthorne S.D.A. Church for worship. Before reaching the church doors, we were met by an elder who hastily informed us that we were not welcome, and that if we persistently disregarded their wishes, they would be forced to take action by calling the police. We asked them for a reason for barring us from the church, but we received no answer save the usual retort. "The council has voted to keep you out. We just do not want you here." As it was useless to attempt to reason with them, we calmly stepped off the church steps, and stood in the parking strip in front of the church quietly studying our Bibles (2 *SC* 5–6, 4–5).'

   From this point on issues of the *Symbolic Code* contain reports of the Binghams' work in various parts of California. They apparently went to Mt. Carmel in 1936 (see 2 *SC* 7–8 (1936), 5). Don Adair reflected on his memory of Bingham and how, in Adair's view, Bingham was an educated man but went on rather too long in the pulpit (Adair, 'Interviews', 30). After the death of Houteff, Bingham emerged as a contender for the leadership of the group. His bid failed, and he and his 'Binghamites' went their separate ways, on which see further Chapter Five and Appendix B.
121. *History and Teachings*, 19 n. 46, which refers to 3 *SC* 2 (1937), 3, 8.
122. Pitts, 'Davidians and Branch Davidians', 29.
123. On the Davidians' views on war see especially *Military Stand of Davidian Seventh-day Adventists*. The original date of this publication is not clear. I have used the Universal Publishing Association facsimile reprint edition here which is dated 1992.
124. Houteff, *The Leviticus*, 3.
125. *OM* 264.
126. Adair, 'Interviews', 31–2, repeats the story of Bingham's adultery.
127. Each volume of *The Answerer* had an initial print run of *c*.30,000 (Houteff, *Christ's Greetings*, 47, gives precise details). Houteff's other publications include *Cookright Cookbook* (1947), *Reporting Un-Adventist Activities* (n.d.), *General Conference Special* (1950), *The White-House Recruiter* (1951), and *Jezreel Letters* (n.d., *c*.1953).
128. The distinction between the two phases and recollections of the implementation of the policy are clearly outlined by Bonnie Smith (GSS1 28–9).
129. Sidney Smith was sent to England with another hunter also called Smith (not his wife, who had stayed back in Waco to give birth to their son). He stayed only about six weeks and then got sick (because of the food he says). The other Smith stayed six months (GSS2 19).

130. Bailey and Darden, *Mad Man in Waco*, 35.
131. GSS1 19.
132. GSS2 19.
133. *OM* 322–6.
134. *OM* 322; Adair (*Davidian Testimony*, 202–3) says that a group gathered around Victor's bedside on the evening of 4 February. The subject of conversation was the forty-two months. See also Adair, 'Interviews', 48–9.
135. M. W. Wolfe is listed as a worker in the 1943 *Fundamental Beliefs and Directory*. Adair remembered Wolfe as being both his Bible teacher and work foreman at Mt. Carmel in 1952. According to Adair, Wolfe was one of the Davidians who left Mt. Carmel in the wake of April 1959 and joined with Herbert Armstrong (Adair, 'Interviews', 56). He was apparently blown off a building and died (Adair, *Davidian Testimony*, 19, 224).
136. [*Waco Times-Herald*] 6 and 7 Feb. 1955 (the actual title of the newspaper is a little unclear, the cuttings are found in TXC 2D212/8).
137. Smith (GSS2 36–7) described the funeral and indicated that many businessmen and officials from the city of Waco as well as a number of Seventh-day Adventists were in attendance. The figure of 10,000 that Smith gives as the number seems very unlikely, but it was clearly a major event.
138. [*Waco Times-Herald*] 6 Feb. 1955; the names are given as Nick, a resident of Milwaukee, and in Bulgaria Leo, Theodore, Marie (Starbovo), Anna (Demeter), and Famea (Gavrealeff). (The actual title of the newspaper is a little unclear, the cuttings are found in TXC 2D212/8).
139. The figure is a rough estimate, but probably not too wide of the mark. Sidney Smith arrived at Mt. Carmel some time in 1956 (he stated that it was about a year after the death of Houteff) and when he arrived, inhabitants numbered about seventy to eighty. Smith said that a number of persons left Mt. Carmel soon after Houteff's death (see GSS2 18).

4

'Thy Kingdom Come' (cf. Matthew 10.6): the Theology of Victor Houteff and the Davidian Seventh-day Adventists

The previous chapter gave an account of the career of Victor Houteff, and the progress of his Mt. Carmel centre up to his death in February 1955. In relating that story it was necessary to refer briefly to Houteff's theology.[1] For example, it was his view on the coming of the kingdom that led him to move his followers from California, to establish the centre in Waco in the first place, and to call it 'Mt. Carmel'. These were important aspects of Houteff's theological scheme, and the evidence is that they were beliefs that drove action, rather than being dreamed up as justification for actions already taken. Clearly, however, there is much more to be said with regard to Houteff's theological views, and that is the burden of this chapter.

The emphasis is upon eschatology. This reflects the substance of Houteff's writing, for while he did have things to say on a variety of theological topics, his interest in and preparation for events at the world's end held pride of place, and much of his writing is concerned with such matters. This eschatological emphasis remained central throughout his time as leader and carried on after his death. Koresh was later to be driven by it too.

Perhaps the most obvious thing to say about Houteff's theology is that it is extremely complex. This should not be underestimated. With Houteff (as indeed with his successors, including Koresh) one is not dealing with a simple-minded individual who simply grabs proof-texts at random to support theological views snatched out of the air. What one sees, rather, is a person with a detailed knowledge of the Bible, who has constructed in his own mind an extremely detailed mosaic of quite literally thousands of individual biblical passages. To him and also to his followers, this mosaic reveals the overall picture of what the last days will be like and the course they will take. It is all too easy to dismiss Houteff's almost impenetrable prose as the ravings of a madman (which is more or less how Koresh's views were later seen). But such a dismissal would be unfair—simply a failure on the part of the researcher to enter into Houteff's biblically saturated thought world.[2] One could argue of course that the results achieved are not worth the effort needed. Why bother, one may reasonably ask, to expend a considerable amount of time and energy seeking to understand the very strange world of the leader of a group whose numbers, at most, probably never went much over 1,000? That may be a valid question about Houteff. But he was Koresh's doctrinal grandfather, and a clearer picture of the thought world operating inside Mt. Carmel might just have helped the negotiators in the very difficult task they had to attempt. If nothing else, it could have been significant to appreciate the extent to which adherence to certain theological views, rather than a concern for personal survival, might dictate action on the part of the group members.

Houteff's theology owes much to that of the movement from which he came: Seventh-day Adventism. This is true of doctrines common to many Christian traditions, such as the inerrancy of scripture, and hence the ability of that scripture accurately to describe events yet future to the time of its composition. But it is true also of some more esoteric SDA doctrines such as the importance of the seventh-day Sabbath, the nearness of the end and the satanic role of the Roman Catholic Church. More important than these individual doctrines, however, is the basic method by which they are constructed and defended. Here again Houteff shared much with Seventh-day Adventism, for at the heart of both theologies lies a highly ingenious typological system of interpretation supported by explanatory statements from the writings of Ellen G. White.

A summary of the typological approach to scripture was given in Chapter Two. In very broad outline it is the method of reading scripture, most notably portions of the Old Testament, on the assumption that much of what it has to say points beyond itself and illustrates what is yet to come. Hence, for example, the Passover Lamb, while it fulfilled a function in its own context, was at the same time a type of Jesus, the true Passover Lamb (cf. John 1.29; 19.36 (cf. Exod. 12.46); 1 Cor. 5.7). As we have seen, the typological method has a distinguished pedigree and was important to Miller and to the early Seventh-day Adventists.

Houteff, however, took it a good deal further. Indeed, it became a principle of Davidian interpretation that 'where there is no type there is no truth'. Houteff wrote:

As fundamental to their structure of Scripture interpretation, the Davidians hold that 'the experiences of Israel were recorded for our instruction' (*Education*, p. 50); that indeed 'all these things happened unto them for ensamples: and ... are written for our admonition, upon whom the ends of the world are come' (1 Cor. 10:11); that, therefore, where there is not a basic type, there can not be and is not a basic truth, an antitype; and that, consequently, those who do not 'hear...Moses and the prophets, neither will they be persuaded, though one rose from the dead.' Luke 16:31.[3]

It was from just such a starting point that Houteff put together his under-standing of the revelation of God as foreshadowed in the Old Testament but coming to fruition only in the period of the New (that period extending to Houteff's own day).

In the context of the emerging Davidian tradition, perhaps the single most important aspect of this typology was Houteff's views about the king-dom of David. (This continued to be a theme right up to the 1993 fire; and '*Vernon*' Howell's change of name to '*David*' Koresh, and, it will be argued later, his active sex life, were due in part at least to his views on this subject.)

In the Old Testament 'the kingdom of David' is presented as a geographical and historical reality and a great deal is said about it. David became a shepherd, but was destined for greater things. First he served in the court of Israel's first king, Saul, but after defeating Goliath he became a hero of the people and eventually, despite Saul's efforts to kill him, ascended to the throne, first of Judah, then of all Israel. The best estimates are that he ruled from c.1004–965 BC. Details of his reign can be found in Deuteronomist historical sources such as 1 Samuel 16.14–2 Samuel 5.10, 1 Kings 1–2, etc. Davidians and Branch Davidians read these texts in a completely uncritical way.

For Houteff this biblical story of David and the kingdom over which he ruled was of far more than simply historical interest. In keeping with his view that 'the experiences of Israel were recorded for our instruction' and 'are written for our admonition, upon whom the ends of the world are come', he argued that the kingdom of David of old was in fact a type that pointed to a reality beyond itself. Its antitype was the eschatological 'kingdom of David' 'upon the throne of which Christ, "the son of David," ' is to sit.[4] This end-time kingdom, said Houteff, would be located first in literal Jerusalem and from there spread over the whole earth. This antitypical kingdom is symbol-ized in Daniel 2, where we read of a statue made up of four distinct parts, the feet being clay and iron mixed together. A stone 'cut without hands' smashes into the feet, bringing the entire statue to the ground. That same stone then grows to fill the whole earth. Daniel's interpretation of this part of the vision is given in 2.44–5:

And in the days of these kings shall the God of heaven set up a kingdom, which shall never be destroyed: and the kingdom shall not be left to other people, but it shall break in pieces and consume all these kingdoms, and it shall stand for ever. Forasmuch as thou sawest that the stone was cut out of the mountain without hands, and that it brake in pieces the iron, the brass, the clay, the silver, and the gold; the great God hath made known to the king what shall come to pass hereafter: and the dream is certain, and the interpretation thereof sure.

This kingdom is to be set up by God in the end times, but nevertheless 'in the days of' the kings represented in the statue. (Houteff was keen to point out that the kingdom was to come 'in' and not 'at the end of' those days.)[5] This, then, is a kingdom that will come into existence prior to the return of Christ. And in fact, argued Houteff, just as it would constitute the antitype of the kingdom of David of the Old Testament, so it would be ruled over by an antitypical king. By 1937 Houteff was arguing that this did not mean Christ himself, who would not return until some time after the kingdom had been set up. Rather there would be two kings—a spiritual and a literal. The spiritual was Christ and his rule would be invisible. But the antitypical David would rule physically, literally, and visibly:

Since therefore from the 'stem' of Jesse came the 'rod' (David), and from the rod sprang the Branch (Christ), David the visible king and Christ the invisible King of kings shall 'in that day'—in our time—constitute the 'ensign,' and 'to it shall the Gentiles seek: and His rest [or His resting place,—the location where the 'rod' or ensign stands—the kingdom] shall be glorious.' Yea 'I will make the place of My feet glorious' (Isa. 60:13), saith the Lord.

'And I will set up one shepherd over them, and he shall feed them, even My servant David; he shall feed them, and he shall be their shepherd. And I the Lord will be their God, and My servant David a prince among them; I the Lord have spoken it. And I will make with them a covenant of peace, and will cause the evil beasts to cease out of the land: and they shall dwell safely in the wilderness, and sleep in the woods.' Ezek. 34:23–25.[6]

The argument here seems to be that from Jesse there sprang two kings: a temporal and a spiritual (David and David's Son, Christ). So too, in antitype, there must be two kings: a temporal and a spiritual. Christ will hence rule over that end-time kingdom spiritually, while the antitypical king David (later to be identified as Houteff himself) will rule over it physically.[7] Ben Roden, the first leader of the 'Branch' Davidians, would later have himself crowned as that king, while Koresh thought that he was the chosen one. Houteff on the other hand seems to have been reluctant to state unequivocally that he was the one destined to sit upon the throne, a reluctance not shared by his wife or followers. What Houteff unquestionably did was introduce into the Davidian tradition (of which the Branch Davidians were heir) the expectation that in the last days prior to the setting up of the kingdom a great leader was to come who was to rule over them as David had ruled over Israel. The evidence is that those who died in the 1993 fire thought that the scrawny 'David' Koresh was he.

This anticipated, end-time 'kingdom of David', located physically in literal Jerusalem and ruled over by a visible king, was perhaps the most distinctive of

Houteff's doctrines. It was certainly the point at which even at an early stage of the development of the tradition he differed most obviously from his SDA mother faith. Quite when he began to teach the doctrine is not clear. The idea does not appear in *The Shepherd's Rod* volumes themselves (published in 1930 and 1932). What is envisaged there, it seems, is that following the gathering of the 144,000 and the cleansing of the SDA Church, the group will spread across the world to proclaim the gospel truth and hence call together the 'great multitude'. Nothing is said concerning the gathering of the saints into the restored kingdom of David in Jerusalem. Neither, it seems, does the doctrine appear in the first seven tracts (1933–1936), which echo the view put forward in *The Shepherd's Rod*. With the publication in 1937 of tract 8, *Mount Zion at the Eleventh Hour*, however, this changes and for the first time one finds a clear expectation that the 144,000 will gather together and inhabit one place, the literal kingdom of David, restored in Jerusalem.[8]

Mount Zion at the Eleventh Hour is not easy to read, being made up, like many of Houteff's publications, of lengthy Bible quotations placed one after each other in such a way as to prove a particular point that is itself not very clearly stated. As a result one can easily get lost among a mass of detail without catching clear sight of the main theme. However, in places Houteff's doctrine does come into somewhat better focus:

> The church of Christ's day was determined to have the kingdom set up then, when not all was yet ready for it; the church of today is determined not to have it now, when 'the end of all things is at hand' (1 Pet. 4:7)—when the time is fully come! The Jews wanted back the kingdom which they had lost—a kingdom of sin and sinners. They were eager to be freed from Roman bondage only, instead of from sin and sinners also. Consequently, when Christ said, 'My kingdom is not of this world' (John 18:36), they would not have it so; whereas the church today, blindly ignoring the scriptures which plainly declare that God is now to set up His spotless kingdom and is to free His people, not from Babylonish bondage only, but from sin and sinners also, is determined to put it off until after the millennium! Such is the ironic perversity of the natural heart.[9]

In later tracts and other publications Houteff is, thankfully, a good deal clearer in his exposition of arguably his most important doctrine. In 1953, for example, he again drew attention to what he saw as the irony that the Jews had been looking for a kingdom on earth when it was 2,000 years away, while the Seventh-day Adventists were looking for a kingdom in heaven when the earthly one was now imminent.[10] The kingdom, he stated unequivocally, would be set up in Jerusalem. He quoted Isaiah 2.1–2: 'The word that Isaiah the son of Amoz saw concerning Judah and Jerusalem. And it shall come to pass in the last days, that the mountain of the Lord's house shall be established in the top of the mountains, and shall be exalted above the hills; and all nations shall flow unto it.' And then commented: 'Not to Takoma Park,[11] not to Mt. Carmel Center, not to some other place, but to [the] house of Judah and Jerusalem shall the final converts from all nations flow. Isaiah you plainly see absolutely confirms that the gathering of the people shall be unto Judah. Do you?'[12] This concept of the antitypical kingdom was to dominate Houteff's message right up to his death and if anything his successors were even more focused upon it. In Waco, Salem, Exeter, and several other places where Houteff's vision today lives on, the coming of the literal kingdom is still awaited.[13]

It should be clear by now that whatever else one might say about Houteff's theology, one thing is for sure: he had a real concern to take the Bible seriously. In this context it is perhaps not surprising that, like so many others, he looked forward to the restoration of God's ancient people the Jews to their homeland. Numerous passages in the Bible speak of such a restoration and Houteff took them literally.[14] He was not the first Christian to do this, of course. Indeed, as early as St Paul the view had taken root in the Christian Church that the Jews had not lost their pride of place as God's people, and that the promises made to them would be fulfilled (Rom. 9–11). From then there have always been those in the Christian tradition who have looked for the restoration of the Jews as a precursor of the final events of this world's history. Indeed, such a view is very prominent in America today and, some have convincingly argued, may even have affected American foreign policy. (It is perhaps worth noting in passing that Ben Roden was later to get an audience with President Carter, whose help he sought to rebuild the Jerusalem temple.)

Houteff's theology was more imaginative on this point, however, than simply expressing the time-worn view that the Jews would be restored. What he said, in effect, was that 'the Jews' were now a much larger group than those who could be clearly identified as such by virtue of their traceable descent. The intermingling of Jews and Gentiles, a process that has been going on for millennia, means that it is no longer possible to say precisely who is a Jew and who is not; but God knows. The group that will inhabit the antitypical, end-time kingdom will in fact all have Jewish blood in their veins, even though they may not know it themselves. The gathering of this community will hence fulfil the prophecies of the Old Testament that predict the eschatological regathering of God's ancient people in their ancient homeland.

In later forms of Davidianism, principally the Branch Davidianism of Ben Roden, the anticipated return to Israel became accented even further, to the point where he actually moved a small band of believers to Israel as a sign of what was to come. Houteff never took that step, but neither did he abandon his belief in the inevitability of the group's eventual move. Of course if one reads the scriptures in the way that Houteff did one has to say that he did have an overwhelming body of evidence to support his views, for frequently in the Old Testament reference is indeed made to the restoration of God's kingdom and the rule over it by a 'Son of David'.[15] Other Christians, including the SDA Church, have dealt with such material by saying either that those promises of the kingdom are to be understood as a prophetic reference to the spiritual 'kingdom' of Christ, or else that those parts of the Old Testament will never be fulfilled, perhaps making the argument that they were conditional on Israel's acceptance of the Messiah (a standard SDA view).[16] Houteff would have none of this. God said it and it would happen.

For Houteff then the coming 'kingdom of God' was literal, and the expectation of that coming gave focus to his self-understanding. Indeed, among all the things he thought he had been called by God to do, the task of calling and then preparing the people of God for the establishment of the literal kingdom was the one that overarched all others, and defined the movement he established.

It is in this context that Houteff's view that he was both the antitypical Elijah and the antitypical John the Baptist is to be seen. These themes were evidently important both to Houteff himself and to the group he led. Again it is typology that lies at the heart of the system. Houteff's role as the antitypical John the Baptist is simple enough. In the New Testament John is seen as the precursor of the Messiah who cries out 'prepare the way of the Lord' and in other ways seeks to call the faithful in preparation for the coming of the Christ. So too Houteff, in Davidian theology, was the one who was preparing for the coming of Christ, for the setting up of the kingdom was a step paving the way for the second coming. Hence, as John the Baptist had announced the first coming of Christ, so Houteff was announcing the second. In this sense he was the antitypical John.

But the typology goes deeper still. Houteff also claimed to be the antitypical Elijah. Again he was concerned to anchor his views in the biblical text, and had no difficulty over the coming of an Elijah figure at the end of days. Indeed, as he was keen to point out, the promise that before the end an Elijah figure would warn of its near approach is found in the very last two verses of the Old Testament; in Malachi 4.5–6, we read, 'Behold, I will send you Elijah the prophet before the coming of the great and dreadful day of the Lord: And he shall turn the heart of the fathers to the children, and the heart of the children to their fathers, lest I come and smite the earth with a curse.' (Not unreasonably, Houteff took the view that God would not close the Old Testament with a couple of verses that were of no particular importance.) Here, it seems, was the promise of the coming of a figure of some significance, a last messenger who would warn of the 'dreadful day of the Lord'. In the New Testament this role of the latter-day Elijah is given to John the Baptist by no less authoritative a figure than Jesus himself (Matt. 17.12–13). According to Houteff's line of reasoning, however, the problem with this interpretation was that if John the Baptist had come to announce the 'dreadful day of the Lord' he was rather premature, for here they were more than 1,900 years on and that day had still not dawned. Houteff thus argued that while John may in some part have fulfilled the role of the antitypical Elijah, he did not complete the work. Another was still to come: Houteff himself. He was the one promised in Malachi 4.5–6. The great and dreadful day of the Lord was approaching and Houteff had come to warn the Seventh-day Adventists of it.

Much of this ground is gone over by Houteff in a special publication he wrote ahead of the meeting of the 1950 General Conference of Seventh-day Adventists, and there is no need to go into detail here.[17] Houteff's understanding of his own role as both the antitypical Elijah and the antitypical John the Baptist should not be underestimated. The SDA Church from which he had come saw and still see themselves collectively as fulfilling that role.[18] Houteff, for whatever reason, took the role exclusively to himself and in effect therefore transferred the title of 'God's chosen messenger' from an institution (the SDA Church) to an individual (himself).[19]

So here he was, the antitypical John the Baptist and the antitypical Elijah who had come to warn the world and to call the people of God to prepare for the coming (literal) kingdom. It was a bold, uncompromising vision argued on the basis of some pretty complex biblical exegesis and at times mind-boggling logic, but it nevertheless had absolute clarity of focus. But who was he to call? The answer, for Houteff, was plain enough: the 144,000 of Revelation 7.4–8 and 14.1–5. These passages were key to Houteff's thinking and to the self-understanding of the Davidian and Branch Davidian communities ever since. They read:

And I heard the number of them which were sealed: and there were sealed an hundred and forty and four thousand of all the tribes of the children of Israel. Of the tribe of Juda were sealed twelve thousand. Of the tribe of Reuben were sealed twelve thousand. Of the tribe of Gad were sealed twelve thousand. Of the tribe of Aser were sealed twelve thousand. Of the tribe of Nepthalim were sealed twelve thousand. Of the tribe of Manasses were sealed twelve thousand. Of the tribe of Simeon were sealed twelve thousand. Of the tribe of Levi were sealed twelve thousand. Of the tribe of Issachar were sealed twelve thousand. Of the tribe of Zabulon were sealed twelve thousand. Of the tribe of Joseph were sealed twelve thousand. Of the tribe of Benjamin were sealed twelve thousand (Rev. 7.4–8).

And I looked, and, lo, a Lamb stood on the Mount Zion, and with him an hundred forty and four thousand, having his Father's name written in their foreheads. And

I heard a voice from heaven, as the voice of many waters, and as the voice of a great thunder: and I heard the voice of harpers harping with their harps: And they sung as it were a new song before the throne, and before the four beasts, and the elders: and no man could learn that song but the hundred and forty and four thousand, which were redeemed from the earth. These are they which were not defiled with women; for they are virgins. These are they which follow the Lamb whithersoever he goeth. These were redeemed from among men, being the firstfruits unto God and to the Lamb. And in their mouth was found no guile: for they are without fault before the throne of God. (Rev 14.1–5)

The identity of this group was a matter of great concern to Houteff. It remained so right through the Davidian and into the Branch Davidian traditions. Just who are these 144,000 who seem to form a special group?

Among the kind of interpreters with whom we are dealing—biblically focused, apocalyptically orientated, and largely non-critical—the identity of the 144,000 and in particular their relationship with the 'great multitude' of Revelation 7.9 and 19.6 has always been an issue. Are they perhaps a part of the 'great multitude'? If so, why are they separated out for special comment? Are they perhaps an entirely separate group who have had a different experience from the larger number? And, importantly, is the '144,000' a literal or symbolic number, and what of the breakdown given in Revelation 7.4–8? Are these literal Jews, or 'spiritual' ones?

Houteff had clear enough answers. The 144,000 are those who would be the first to inhabit the restored kingdom of David in Israel. The 'great multitude' is a much more general group, the totality of all those who would one day be saved. The number '144,000' is literal and the breakdown into the twelve Jewish tribes is also literal: all the 144,000 would be Jews, though not necessarily commonly identifiable as such.[20] (This is another break with Seventh-day Adventism, which has generally argued that the number is symbolic rather than literal.)[21]

The 144,000 are also all Seventh-day Adventists and it is at this point that one finds the theoretical underpinning of Houteff's view that his mission was to that Church alone and not to the world in general. This relationship between Davidianism, Branch Davidianism, and the SDA Church has remained virtually intact ever since, and explains why almost all those at Mt. Carmel in 1993 were former Seventh-day Adventists. The few who were not were seen as a sign that the end was indeed very near and that even those on the 'highways' were now being invited to the wedding feast (cf. Matt. 22.9). This calling out of the faithful from the SDA Church ties in with the notion of the 'remnant' which, as we saw in Chapter Two, has always been central to SDA identity. Houteff is here building upon it (as in turn Roden was to do in arguing that the *Branch* Davidians were the remnant of the Davidians in general). Since the Reformation (at least), God has been calling his people out of a corrupted Church and truth has been progressively revealed. As part of this more general understanding, Houteff accepted the view that in 1844 the 2,300 days came to a close and God raised up the SDA Church to proclaim the three angels' messages to the world (cf. Rev. 14). But Houteff appeals further to Revelation 7.2: 'And I saw another angel ascending from the east, having the seal of the living God …' This 'other angel', argued Houteff, is seen ascending from the east at the same time as the three angels of Revelation 14 begin to sound, i.e. in 1844. He is 'ascending' but he has not yet come. This is a vision of one who is to come subsequent to 1844 who will have with him the seal of the living God. 'John prophesied of this movement and the scene of the angel ascending in the east (John's vision) became a reality in 1844, but the angel is in the east, and we must await his arrival, for when he arrives, the sealing begins.'[22]

Houteff then goes on to argue that while the observance of the Sabbath is a 'seal' by which God marks out his people, as Seventh-day Adventists had taught,[23] it is not the seal that is brought by the angel from the east. Only Sabbath-keepers, which for Houteff means members of the SDA Church, can receive this latter seal, but not all of them will do so.[24]

At this point Houteff draws attention to Ezekiel 9, which speaks of a group of people who are sealed by a man with an inkhorn. This chapter was absolutely central to Houteff's understanding of the purposes of God and is worth quoting in full at this point:

He cried also in mine ears with a loud voice, saying, Cause them that have charge over the city to draw near, even every man with his destroying weapon in his hand. And, behold, six men came from the way of the higher gate, which lieth toward the north, and every man a slaughter weapon in his hand; and one man among them was clothed with linen, with a writer's inkhorn by his side: and they went in, and stood beside the brazen altar. And the glory of the God of Israel was gone up from the cherub, whereupon he was, to the threshold of the house. And he called to the man clothed with linen, which had the writer's inkhorn by his side; And the Lord said unto him, Go through the midst of the city, through the midst of Jerusalem, and set a mark upon the foreheads of the men that sigh and that cry for all the abominations that be done in the midst thereof. And to the others he said in mine hearing, Go ye after him through the city, and smite: let not your eye spare, neither have ye pity: Slay utterly old and young, both maids, and little children, and women: but come not near any man upon whom is the mark; and begin at my sanctuary. Then they began at the ancient men which were before the house. And he said unto them, Defile the house, and fill the courts with the slain: go ye forth. And they went forth, and slew in the city. And it came to pass, while they were slaying them, and I was left, that I fell upon my face, and cried, and said, Ah Lord God! wilt thou destroy all the residue of Israel in thy pouring out of thy fury upon Jerusalem? Then said he unto me, The iniquity of the house of

Israel and Judah is exceeding great, and the land is full of blood, and the city full of perverseness: for they say, The Lord hath forsaken the earth, and the Lord seeth not. And as for me also, mine eye shall not spare, neither will I have pity, but I will recompense their way upon their head. And, behold, the man clothed with linen, which had the inkhorn by his side, reported the matter, saying, I have done as thou hast commanded me.

Houteff sees in this chapter a vision of his own sealing work. In essence he argues that the chapter is about the cleansing of the SDA Church (which in these latter days is the antitype of 'the city' and 'Jerusalem' in the chapter).[25] Houteff is the man with the inkhorn who will 'set a mark upon [the] foreheads' of those of Jerusalem that 'sigh and that cry for all the abomin-ations that be done in the midst thereof' (v. 4).[26] The ones with the mark will escape the slaughter. The rest will not.

What this means, Houteff says, is that Seventh-day Adventists who are distressed by the errors into which the Church has currently fallen and cry out in anguish receive the seal. They are the 144,000 and will respond to Houteff's call. As always Houteff is specific. Earlier he had produced a 'Partial List Of Abominations In The Church' concerning which those prophesied in Ezekiel 9 would sigh. The list includes such things as 'following the fashions of the world', selling denominational publications in churches and hence turning the house of God into a 'house of merchandise', 'disbelief in the Spirit of Proph-ecy', and failing to inform the church members of the Elijah message. This list of 'abominations' is punctuated throughout by references to the Bible and Ellen White.[27]

For all of these things and others, God, it was claimed, was calling the SDA Church to book through Houteff's message. Those who accept the rebuke and the new light that has come receive the seal and hence are numbered among the 144,000. They join the eschatological community, the final remnant who will soon inhabit the restored kingdom in Jerusalem and from there spread the message across the rest of the world.

It is unsurprising given such views that the group developed a somewhat antagonistic relationship with Seventh-day Adventism. Theologically the Seventh-day Adventists retained an important role in Davidian and later Branch Davidian thinking, but on a practical level the relationship has always been somewhat acrimonious. Some of this was explored in Chapter One, where note was taken of how keen the Seventh-day Adventists were to disavow any connection with the Waco group and the oftentimes forceful language they employed to do so.

Houteff did not shy away from the remainder of Ezekiel 9. The message of that chapter was seen by him as to some extent positive, in that there were some in 'Jerusalem' (the SDA Church) who cried out on account of the abominations within it, and as a result would receive the mark of the inkhorn (for Houteff the same as the seal of the living God mentioned in Revelation 7.2), but the majority did not, and would be slaughtered. And this, according to Houteff, is no spiritual event. Those who do not respond to his message will one day quite literally lie dead in their own blood.[28] The reference to the slaughter starting at 'my sanctuary' (Ezek. 9.6), says Houteff, is a reference to the fact that the leaders of antitypical Israel—SDA ministers—would be the first to feel the wrath of God.[29]

This is strong stuff and again one can see why the mainstream community would find the teachings of the Davidians not just erroneous, but offensive. This self-assured Church, which understands itself to be specifically mentioned in scripture as the remnant church of God, was being told by Houteff that in fact from them there would come another remnant while the majority would be literally and violently slaughtered in an eschatological cleansing of God's people. The very ones likely to be studying Houteff's message and giving a reply, the pastorate and the other professional Seventh-day Adventists, are singled out for particular condemnation. They are false rulers in Israel and as such they will be the first to feel the wrath of God that will come upon the church.

It is apparent then that apocalyptic violence has always been a feature of Davidian eschatology; the cleansing of the (SDA) Church would be a violent affair. This is no slaughter of error with truth, nor yet an abstract victory of light over darkness. This is about people being killed and lying in their own blood. It is important to note that as with so much of this sort of end-time rhetoric, the violence is God's, not humankind's. The anticipated slaughter would be the work of God, and the slayers heavenly beings not Davidians. As we shall see, the Branch Davidians under Koresh would introduce a variation on this theme. God would still be the key player; but according to Koresh's version of things the members of his own community would play some part in the blood-letting.

So far, then, we have seen how the Davidians under Houteff looked forward to the setting up of a literal kingdom in Jerusalem. It was he, many of his followers believed, who would be the antitypical King David who would rule over that kingdom, and it was he too who as the antitypical Elijah and John the Baptist was currently calling the 144,000 out of the SDA Church. As they learned the doctrines, practised holy living, and took the message to others, so they prepared themselves for entry into the kingdom. But entry into the kingdom would come only after further trial, for as the (144,000) Davidians now left behind their slain former co-religionists and began their journey 'home' (i.e. made their way to Jerusalem) the time of 'Jacob's trouble' would break out.[30] This, according to Houteff, was the time spoken of in Jeremiah 30.7.[31] This would be a time of persecution when none who did not worship the beast and its image could either buy or sell (cf. Rev. 13.15–17). But the faithful would 'be saved out of it'. The 144,000 would reach their homeland. The kingdom would be set up.

Houteff's views on what would happen after this were no less imaginative. The Church having now been cleansed and the 'first fruits' of the harvest (the 144,000) having been gathered, the harvesting in general may now begin. The 'loud cry' of Revelation 18.1 goes out from Jerusalem to the whole world. 'In response to this call', said Houteff, 'many nations will say: "Come, and let us go up to the mountain of the Lord, and to the house of the God of Jacob and He will teach us of His ways, and we will walk in His paths: for the law shall go forth of Zion, and the word of the Lord from Jerusalem." (Mic. 4:2).'[32] This, for Houteff, is the calling of the Great Multitude of Revelation 7.9 and 19.6. Those who respond to the call will flock to the kingdom; then will follow the dissolution of the worldwide organization of the image of the beast (Rev. 19.1–3), the close of the investigative judgment of the living (Rev. 15.5–8), the end of probationary time (Rev. 22.11), and the pouring out of the seven last plagues upon the wicked (Rev. 16).[33] During the seventh plague the armies of the wicked prepare for battle (the battle of Armageddon) against the armies of heaven. Christ appears and the wicked are slain. The righteous dead are resurrected and the millennium begins.

A distinctive feature of SDA eschatology in general is the expectation that the literal 1,000 year millennium is spent not on earth but in heaven.[34] Houteff too subscribed to this view. This ground is gone over thoroughly in *Behold I Make All Things New* (1940), where a fairly standard SDA scheme with regard to the millennial period is laid out. The main features are that upon the return of Christ, the living wicked are slain and the living saints transformed. The righteous dead are raised and they too meet with Christ 'in the air' (the influence of 1 Thess. 4 is apparent). The unrighteous dead meanwhile remain in their graves to await their final destruction, which will come about only after the millennial period. The saints return with Christ to heaven to reign with him for a thousand years, while the earth is left desolate. Only Satan inhabits the earth during this period; his fate is to wander across the globe unable to exercise his evil influence. Houteff wrote:

Decisively, therefore, the King of kings is to slay, just before the millennium, all except the righteous—except those who get 'the victory over the beast, and over his image, and over his mark, and over the number of his name.' Rev. 15:2. Then shall the righteous dead be raised, whereas the wicked dead remain in their graves and, along with the wicked living, all of whom are then slain by the Lord, live 'not again until the thousand years' are 'finished.' Rev. 20:5. Since, moreover, at the commencement of the millennium, when the wicked are slain, the heaven and the earth pass away, then, as a result, *the saints remove to another sphere.*

As The Revelation says that 'they lived and reigned *with* Christ a thousand years' (Rev. 20:4), Christ does not therefore, live with them on the earth, but rather they live with Him in 'the place' which He prepared for them, and of which John says (after seeing 'the first heaven and the first earth were passed away' and replaced with 'new heaven and a new earth'—Rev. 21:1): 'And I John saw the holy city, new Jerusalem, coming down from God out of heaven, prepared as a bride adorned for her husband.' Rev. 21:2.

The wicked being then hid in their graves, and the righteous being gone to live with Christ, hence *Satan is left alone.*

Wandering in the earth until the resurrection of the wicked (Rev. 20:13), Satan is confined to a thousand years of solitude! Bound by this chain of circumstances, he is unable to 'deceive the nations' (Rev. 20:3), till the dead who 'lived not again until the thousand years were finished,' arise to life, following the *judgment during the millennium.*[35]

What follows is also fairly standard SDA theology. During the thousand years in heaven, the saints will have the opportunity to examine the cases of all the wicked to see for themselves that God is a just God and that the sentence to be carried out upon the wicked at the end of the millennial period is just.[36] At the end of the thousand years the wicked dead (all those who have ever lived, including those slain by Christ at his appearing) are now raised to hear their final sentence. But (as in standard Seventh-day Adventism) their destruction is not immediate. There is one last period of rebellion (to account for Rev. 20:7–8); Satan has one last chance to defeat God. In Seventh-day Adventism the length of this post-millennial rebellion is left indefinite, but on the basis of Isaiah 65.17–20 Houteff argued that it would last for a hundred years.[37] At the conclusion of this period the wicked are finally and permanently destroyed by fire, 'whereupon all things shall be renewed, and God's original plan shall proceed to perfect fulfillment in an uninterrupted eternity of heavenly joy (Rev. 21:4)'.[38]

Such, then, in very broad outline is a summary of Houteff's eschatology. Some parts of it are highly distinctive, while others are common if not to millennial schemes in general, then at least to Seventh-day Adventism. As we shall see, what Houteff had to say on these matters laid the foundation of not just Davidian, but also Branch Davidian, theology. The Rodens introduced some important elements into it, Koresh took it in some new directions again, and all three had to adjust things so as to allow for their own singularly important role. But the vision remained largely intact at least until the period of the 'later' Koresh beginning in the early 1990s.

In more theoretical terms it is very difficult to place Houteff's eschatology on any spectrum of millennial belief. Formally he should be described as a pre-millennialist, since in his scheme the millennium does not occur until

Jesus returns, at which point the company of saints (both the 144,000 and the Great Multitude) journey to heaven, there to spend the next thousand years reassuring themselves of God's justice. As we have seen, however, this hardly accounts for the complexity of Houteff's scheme as a whole. In fact there are clear elements of post-millennialism also, for Jesus returns physically only once the 144,000 have been gathered and the kingdom has been set up. By the time he returns, then, the elect have been gathered and Jesus's pathways have been made straight. There is no rapture, but a time of tribulation, and saints will have to endure this on their way to the kingdom. Hence 'tribulationist pre-millennialist with elements of post-millennialism' is the nearest we can get in seeking to put a label on this group. In truth, however, the Davidians are *sui generis*.

Perhaps the most appealing feature of Houteff's scheme was its relative clarity, for despite being based upon a highly intricate reading of the Bible (including parts long forgotten by Christians in general) the end result had real substance and a focus able to give both a sense of identity to the movement and also a clear programme for action. The fact that the mission was only to Seventh-day Adventists was something of a limiting factor in terms of potential growth, though on the other hand any contacts made would have been meaningful. There was no need for the Davidians first to argue for such things as the typological interpretation of scripture, the prophetic status of Ellen G. White, or the general sense that the world was soon to come to an end. These and many other such things were already common to the potential convert and the one seeking to do the converting. Absolute pillars of the faith such as the sanctity and eschatological significance of the Sabbath, the need for health reform and the dependability of the Bible were also in place. Little wonder then that Houteff did meet with some success. When he died the number of his followers may have been in excess of 1,000: not a huge group admittedly, but not insignificant either. In fact on one major point at least Houteff was right. He thought that what he was doing was of supreme importance and that the group he had gathered would one day play a dramatic part on a world stage. In 1993 a remnant of them did, though not in the way Houteff had expected.

NOTES

1. The secondary literature on Houteff's theology is minimal. Adair, *Davidian Testimony*, is the best source, but brief comments are found also in Pitts, 'Davidians and Branch Davidians', 22–5; Bailey and Darden, *Mad Man in Waco*, 15–37; Tabor and Gallagher, *Why Waco*, 33–8.

2. Even Bailey and Darden, whose work on Houteff is considerably more balanced and certainly much better researched than most, refer to Roden as using 'the same virtually unfathomable logic used by Houteff' (*Mad Man in Waco*, 62).

3. Houteff, *The Leviticus*, 14. 'Education' is a reference to a book by Ellen G. White with that title, first published in 1903.

4. Ibid. 3.

5. See e.g. Houteff, *Behold I Make All Things New*, 42, where he wrote: '*In the days* of these kings [*not after*, but *in* the days of the kings who are symbolized by the feet and toes of the great image] "shall the God of heaven," says Daniel, calling attention to the kingdom at its beginning, "set up a kingdom, which shall never be destroyed: and the kingdom shall not be left to other people but it [the kingdom] shall break in pieces and consume all these kingdoms, and it shall stand for ever." Dan. 2:44. Thus we see that while the nations of our age (symbolized by the feet and toes of the great image of Daniel 2:41, 42) are yet in existence, the Lord will set up the kingdom with which He will overthrow them. Then it shall be said: "The kingdoms of this world are become the kingdoms of our Lord, and of His Christ; and He shall reign for ever and ever." Rev. 11:15.'

6. Houteff, *Mount Zion*, 47.

7. Elsewhere Houteff wrote: 'As ancient David is in his grave, the king here promised must be an antitypical David, just as the Elijah of Malachi 4:5 must be an antitypical Elijah. Otherwise, in order to fulfill the prophecies, ancient David must necessarily rise from his grave, and ancient Elijah descend from Heaven.' (*Behold I Make*, 43)

8. Adair, 'Interviews', 35, stated that the message of the kingdom was not one that appealed to all Davidians and that when *Mount Zion at the Eleventh Hour* was published a number left.

9. Houteff, *Mount Zion*, 73.

10. 1 *TG* 15/20.

11. The reference here is to the headquarters of the SDA Church in Takoma Park, Maryland.

12. 1 *TG* 15/7.

13. See Appendix B.

14. Among those Houteff was particularly keen on quoting were Ezek. 37.16–28 (2 *TG* 31/5); Mic. 3.12; 4.1 (2 *TG* 31/6) and especially Isa. 11.11–14, which reads: 'And it shall come to pass in that day, that the Lord shall set his hand again the second time to recover the remnant of his people, which shall be left, from Assyria, and from Egypt, and from Pathros, and from Cush, and from Elam, and from Shinar, and from Hamath, and from the islands of the sea. And he shall set up an ensign for the nations, and shall assemble the outcasts of Israel, and gather together the dispersed of Judah from the four corners of the earth (see 1 *TG* 31/5–6).

15. See e.g. Jer. 23.5; 30.9 (cf. 1 *TG* 30/18–19).

16. 'Conditionalism', as its name suggests, is the view that the promises made to Israel in the Old Testament were conditional upon Israel's obedience and, ultimately,

their acceptance of Jesus as the Messiah. God would have established Israel as a great and everlasting nation had they been faithful. But Israel was not, and hence what God said he would do did not come about, not as a result of any failing on God's part, but due to Israel's lack of faith. Such a view is found throughout SDA sources, but see especially Le Roy Edwin Froom, *The Conditionalist Faith of our Fathers* (Washington, DC: Review and Herald Publishing Association, 1963).

17. This is an interesting tract. It does not bear Houteff's name and begins very much as though it were a publication of the SDA Church itself. It refers to the 'Shepherd's Rod' as 'the prominent and most tormenting' of the offshoots currently troubling the Church (p. 3). However, the content of this tract is unquestionably Davidian in origin. It is attributed to Houteff by Adair (*Davidian Testimony*, 172).

18. Note e.g. *Seventh-day Adventists Believe*, 342: 'As John the Baptist prepared the way for Christ's first advent, so the Advent movement is preparing the way for His second advent—proclaiming the message of Rev 14.6–12, God's final call to get ready for the glorious return of the Saviour.'

19. For Houteff, Elijah was important too. It was he who had called Israel to account and as a part of that process had challenged the prophets of Baal and Asherah on old Mt. Carmel and defeated them (1 Kgs. 18). Houteff too, so he believed, was now calling antitypical Israel (the SDA Church) to account and was challenging their false prophets (i.e. their leaders).

20. Houteff's general views on this point have been noted above. On the 144,000 in particular he wrote, 'the 144,000 can be gathered from almost every nation, kindred, tongue and people, and yet be the sons of Jacob!' (*Mount Zion*, 10). He later referred to Ezek. 37.16–25, which speaks of a time when God will 'take the children of Israel from among the heathen, whither they be gone, and gather them together on every side and bring them to their own land: and I will make them one nation in the land upon the mountains of Israel; and one king shall be king to them all' (*Mount Zion*, 15–17). Tying in other passages of scripture, Houteff hence once again underscores his scheme. He, the latter-day Elijah, has come to call the 144,000, all of whom are of Jewish stock.

21. In SDA eschatology the 144,000 are those who are 'redeemed from the earth' (cf. Rev. 14.3), that is, they are those who have gone through the great tribulation at the end of time and who have not tasted death. The 'great multitude' on the other hand are all those who are saved—that is, all the righteous dead resurrected at the coming of Christ (*SDABC* 7/784–5).

22. Houteff, *The Shepherd's Rod*, 1/22.

23. The standard SDA doctrine is that 'the seal of the living God' mentioned in Rev. 7.2 is the observance of the seventh-day Sabbath, for it is the observance of this day that will mark out God's true remnant during the end times (see *SDABC* 7/782).

24. He wrote: 'This sealing of the 144,000 is not a Sabbath seal. However, those who are sealed must be Sabbath keepers. It is a seal, or mark, that separates the two classes in the church, and those who are sealed, or marked are not marked because

they keep Sabbath only, but because they sigh and cry for *all* the abominations that are done in the church.' (*Shepherd's Rod*, 1/29.)

See also Houteff, *The Answerer*, 2, 31–3.

25. *Shepherd's Rod*, 1/29.
26. See *Shepherd's Rod*, 1/51, where Houteff writes: 'The man with the writer's inkhorn of Ezekiel 9, is the one who performs the sealing of the 144,000 long before the close of probation.'
27. *Shepherd's Rod*, 1/34–5.
28. Question No. 25: 'The Shepherd's Rod teaches that the slaughter of Ezekiel 9 is literal. Could it not be a destruction such as is caused by so-called "acts of God"— earthquakes, famines, pestilences, the seven last plagues, or the like?'

Answer: 'The five agents that destroy the wicked in the church are not forces of nature but men with slaughter weapons in their hands. They are supernatural beings, not natural elements. Hence they cannot fittingly represent earthquakes, famines, or the like.

'Neither can they be the seven angels with the seven last plagues, for these angels are *seven* in number, not *five*. Furthermore, they do not have "slaughter weapons" in their hands, but vials. Still further, the plagues fall in Babylon (Rev. 18:4), whereas the slaughter of Ezekiel 9 takes place in Judah and Israel (Ezek. 9:9).

'Ezekiel 9, whether literal or figurative, effects a separation between the good and the bad, the tares and the wheat, in the church (Judah and Israel), just as the plagues finally do in Babylon (Rev. 18:4). And as the plagues are literal, then how can the slaughter be any less literal? The angel with the writer's inkhorn is to place a mark upon the foreheads of all who sigh and cry for the abominations, then the destroying angels are to slay both old and young (Ezek. 9:4–6).

' "The church—the Lord's sanctuary," is "the first to feel the stroke of the wrath of God. The ancient men, those to whom God had given great light, and who had stood as guardians, of the spiritual interests of the people, had betrayed their trust. They had taken the position that we need not look for miracles and the marked manifestations of God's power as in former days. Times have changed. These words strengthen their unbelief and they say, The Lord will not do good, neither will he do evil. He is too merciful to visit his people in judgment. Thus peace and safety is the cry from men who will never again lift up their voice like a trumpet to show God's people their transgressions and the house of Jacob their sins. These dumb dogs, that would not bark, are the ones who feel the just vengeance of an offended God. Men, maidens, and little children, all perish together."—*Testimonies*, Vol. 5, p. 211.

'As in *The Great Controversy*, p. 656, only an indirect parallel can be drawn between the slaughter of Ezekiel 9 and the falling of the plagues, because a common end (death) befalls both the wicked in the church of Laodicea and the wicked in the churches of Babylon. And only those who say, "We need not look for miracles and the marked manifestation of God's power as in former days," think the slaughter is not literal.'

The Answerer, 2, 42–4. See also *The Answerer*, 5, 56–7.

29. *Shepherd's Rod*, 2/278–9.

30. *Fundamental Beliefs and Directory*, 13.

31. According to the Seventh-day Adventists, just before the return of Christ, the Sabbath believers will go through a period of great persecution and the severest testing of their faith. This is referred to as the 'Time of Jacob's Trouble', since it is argued that Jacob's night of anguish (see Gen. 32.24–30) represents this end-time experience of the people of God. The influence of Jer. 30.7 is also significant: 'Alas! for that day is great, so that none is like it: it is even the time of Jacob's trouble, but he shall be saved out of it.' This understanding of things was embedded in Seventh-day Adventism long before Houteff picked it up. See e.g. Ellen White, *The Great Controversy between Christ and Satan* (Mountain View, California: Pacific Press Publishing Association, 1911), 615–16.

32. *Fundamental Beliefs and Directory*, 14.

33. Ibid.

34. Such a view is ubiquitous in SDA sources. See Kenneth G. C. Newport, 'The Heavenly Millennium of Seventh-day Adventism', in Stephen Hunt, ed., *Christian Millenarianism* (Bloomington, Ind.: Indiana University Press, 2001), 131–48.

35. Houteff, *Behold I Make*, 33–4 (for the sake of clarity, a few minor changes to the original format have been made).

36. The SDA view can be seen in *Seventh-day Adventists Believe*, 366–7.

37. *Behold I Make*, 37–8.

38. Houteff, *Fundamental Beliefs and Directory*, 15.

5

'But the End is Not Yet' (cf. Matthew 24.6): Florence Houteff and the End of the World

The death of Victor Houteff in 1955 was a serious blow to the community he had founded, and there ensued a period of crisis that almost saw the movement's total collapse. Problems came on several fronts. Not the least was the thorny question of why Victor had died, or, more precisely, how a dead person would be able to rule over a literal kingdom in Israel upon its expected and rapidly approaching establishment. The issue was very real. Adair indicates that the possibility of Houteff's death had been the subject of speculation beforehand, and while some said he would die, others had taken the opposite view. Houteff himself had got involved in the debate, and had at one point thrown out a challenge to his followers to prove from the Bible that he could not die (the implication being that he thought he could). Adair reported how Wolfe took up the challenge and preached a sermon on the issue, giving many references to the Bible, to Ellen White, and to the Shepherd's Rod material. So persuasive was the sermon, said Adair, that 'it led many at old Mt. Carmel and elsewhere to believe as [Wolfe] did'.[1] Saether also referred to this issue and stated that Houteff's death had been 'quite a shock to many of the Davidians' since 'some felt that he never would die, that he'd be the king in the new kingdom',[2] while Adair reported (though he was not present himself) that at Houteff's funeral there were people there who 'cried and weeped [sic] and wailed . . . and said that he was going to be resurrected in three days'.[3]

Theologically, then, the death of Houteff was a problem; but it was not insurmountable and various options were open to the community as they sought to come to terms with it. One was obvious: to posit the view that Houteff would be resurrected, and this appears to be what happened. Some had already evidently given voice to this view at the funeral, and quite soon the hope began to be more precisely formulated, backed up, of course, with biblical texts. Among those who took this view was Victor's widow, Florence. Soon after his death, she began to make a number of predictions about what the future would hold for the community, and the expectation that Victor would be raised was apparently one of them. Quite when this expectation was formulated is not clear and the surviving material is ambiguous. However, what is certain is that by April 1959 some Davidians at least were looking for Victor's resurrection later that month. That expectation continues to live on in the hopes of some Davidians today. Adair, for example, has argued the case at some length.[4]

Potentially much more damaging to the movement than the apparent disconfirmation of Davidian belief, however, was the danger that the Davidians would disintegrate as the result of the lack of clear leadership or through factional division. In the event it was the latter that proved to be the more serious threat.

Upon Houteff's death, at least four persons appear to have made some claim to the leadership of the movement: Bingham, Wolfe, Florence Houteff, and Ben Roden.[5] (Saether stated that he himself was seen by some as a successor, but that he did not wish to pursue the option.)[6] The struggle for leadership was long and messy, but Florence won the early victory and was to emerge as the leader. The leadership then stayed with her from February 1955 to her resignation in March 1962.

Even before Victor's death Florence had begun to position herself for the leadership of the community. As Victor's wife and also as a Hermanson, a family still very powerful at Mt. Carmel in 1955, she obviously had something of a start on the other contenders. This was increased significantly when she reported that on his deathbed Victor had told her that she should be the next leader, a claim no one else was really in a position to dispute.[7] Saether stated that after Houteff's death but before his burial Florence's brother, Oliver Hermanson, told him exactly the same thing; Florence had been nominated by Victor as the next leader of the movement. Her bid for the leadership had got quickly underway.[8]

What happened next is a little uncertain as the records have not survived. However, it seems fairly plain from Saether's account that upon Victor's death Florence immediately assumed the leadership role and presented her case, perhaps in written form, at meetings of the Executive Council. What we do know, since the minutes have survived, is that at a meeting of the Council held on 7 May the view was restated. Florence was in the chair and the question was raised by Wolfe: 'How can you prove that the President appointed you to be Vice-President?' to which she replied, 'I cannot prove it. I have nothing in writing. But since Brother Houteff did not appoint anyone else you are going to have to believe me when I tell you that he appointed me'.[9] It is unlikely that Wolfe was satisfied with this answer, but no further discussion is minuted. Actually, Florence appears to have sidetracked the issue by asking Wolfe, and by implication the other members of the Council, if they could prove that Houteff had appointed them as Council members, which they could not since it had all been done orally. Wolfe, then, had been silenced and the only other serious contender for the leadership at the time, M. J. Bingham, was in the Caribbean.[10] As yet Ben Roden, although he had leadership aspirations, had not reappeared on the scene. Florence was hence accepted as vice-president, the office of president being one to which one could not be voted, only appointed by God.[11]

The immediate danger that the group would disintegrate as a result of leadership squabbles had thus passed and to the outside observer at the time it must have seemed that the Waco Davidians could look forward to a return to their previous settled existence as members of an eschatological community patiently awaiting the setting up of God's kingdom and now, perhaps, the resurrection also of their dead prophet. There were, however, two other major storms brewing on the horizon that were yet to break, storms which the Davidians in the end did not survive intact.

One came in the form of Ben Roden. Roden had visited Mt. Carmel in *c.*1945 and had returned and stayed for several months in 1953. Perhaps fortunately for Florence, when Houteff died, the Rodens were in Israel and hence not in a position to make a determined quest for the leadership of the group. (In fact Ben did return to Texas in 1955 with this objective in mind, but by the time he arrived the battle had already been substantially won.)

The second 'storm' was the theologically almost suicidal decision of Florence to gamble on hitting the prophetic jackpot by predicting the precise date for the establishment of the kingdom, or at the very least the outbreak of the war in the Middle East that would immediately precede it. The date was given as 22 April 1959. The setting of so precise a date was dangerous. It would of course pay immediate dividends, since it gave the Davidians a real rallying call and focal point for evangelistic activity. But it was also open to being convincingly disproved and even though, as the date drew nearer, some flexibility was introduced into the prediction (on or about 22 April something significant but not very clearly defined would take place), a *terminus ad quem* for the movement had in effect been set. Again we know from other examples that it would have been possible for them to survive what to any outsider must have seemed like the inevitability of a crashing disappointment in April 1959; but it was a possibility and not a certainty and with hindsight it is plain that in setting the date Florence put in motion a process that in the end would lead to her movement's virtual collapse.

Like many other aspects of this story, the process by which the date of 22 April was arrived at is not completely clear, though some parts of the scheme are open to view. Certainly the key is the period of the forty-two months or 1,260 days mentioned in Revelation 11.2–3, a period which has long exercised prophetic interpreters. Florence's own views were novel to say the least.

Those views were put forward in the November 1955 issue of the *Symbolic Code*. By way of introduction it was stated that there had been many enquiries from Davidians regarding just what had been Brother Houteff's final prophetic message to the movement. In response Florence stated quite unequivocally that Victor's last concern of this sort related to the meaning of the forty-two months and other aspects of Revelation 11, and that he had come to the view that while they might have been fulfilled in type prior to his own day, they had not been fulfilled in antitype. The report reads:

During the last months of his life, Brother Houteff was engaged in studying *Timely Greetings*, Vol. 2, No. 15, preparatory to enlarging upon the subject matter therein for its reprint. At this time he expressed the definite conviction that the time prophecy of Revelation 11.2–12 and Daniel 12.6, 7 could have met their fulfillment *only in type* from 538 A.D. to 1798 A.D. and that they have a latter-day fulfillment.[12]

The article then argues that the forty-two months are a period without the 'latter rain' (i.e. a period when believers no longer have the gift of prophecy as manifest in the work of Victor Houteff) and that they end with the events of Ezekiel 9. No date is given for the termination of the period, but it is clearly stated that the time has already started. Towards the end of the article we read: 'As we approach the time of these events more can be said about them, but for now the important point to be emphasized is that it is clear that we have already entered the period of the forty-two months and that we have no time to lose in making every preparation for the day of our visitation.'[13] Whether this is actually what Victor himself had in mind as he lay dying we do not know. What is clear, however, is that something approaching this sort of interpretation had begun to be formulated by Florence fairly soon after Victor's death. Saether has an interesting recollection related to this point:

This was in 1955 and Mrs. Houteff cornered me one day in the office. We closed at noon on Friday so everybody could go home and get ready for Sabbath. She cornered me there and she talked all afternoon to me, trying to persuade me to her idea in Revelation 11. Well, one thing I could see and I acknowledged this right away. I told her, 'I can see you're right in this, that those days didn't take place back in the Dark Ages as the church had thought and as we thought, Brother Houteff thought and taught. We taught that those days were the days of papal supremacy and had to do with that. I could see that they don't. They're in present time. That they apply now in any definite way, you haven't shown it. You haven't got the proof, you haven't got the backing of it. Where is the proof of this?'[14]

The standard view in the SDA and then Davidian literature regarding this period of the forty-two months or 1,260 days is that they are to be taken as 1,260 literal years and relate to the period of papal supremacy, perhaps coming to an end during the French Revolution.[15] Clearly, however, Florence had departed from the tradition on this point and had come to the view that the period related to the present and/or future and not the past. She assured her readers of course that this was not her departure alone, but that it had been sanctioned by Victor, which might have been the case. Victor was, after all, near death and presumably knew himself to be so. Perhaps he indeed had a view on the period 'in the wilderness' that his followers were now about to enter, and had begun to picture this through, as always, a biblical lens.

Taking a more sceptical line, however, what might have happened is this: Florence took the view that the death of Victor was such a major event in the history of God's dealings with humankind that it must in some way be marked in scripture. Did not the Church in effect find itself in the wilderness now that Victor, the latter-day prophet, had died? Then perhaps this was the period spoken of in Revelation 11.3 and elsewhere during which time the Church was in the wilderness and being fed by God. (There is evidence that some at Mt. Carmel did come to this view. Adair said that Oliver Hermanson originally thought that the forty-two months were to be counted from the day after Victor's death.) Adding 1,260 days to the date of the death of Victor on 5 February 1955 one arrives at 19 July 1958. But the date set by Florence was not that but rather 22 April 1959. The reason for this postponement may well have been that, in 1959, 22 April was Passover. Passover had always been important in the Davidian tradition, as had the view that the SDA Church was in essence a 'spiritual' Egypt out of which God's people were to come prior to the slaughter that the rest of the Seventh-day Adventists were to face. This being the case, it may be that Florence simply considered the date upon which the 1,260 days were due to end must coincide with Passover.

Saether's further recollections are important here. On 9 November Florence published the view that 'We've now entered these [1260] days'. When he read the message, Saether said, he was dumbfounded and recalled that the meeting when he was 'cornered' by Florence was back in March or April: 'In March—it was in March that she told me this, or April, March, we'll say. April, May, June, July, August, September, October, November, eight months—not a word. Not a word was said. In the council or anywhere else. It was just kept q.t. Then, she come out and said we'd entered these days.'[16] So why had she kept quiet from March until November? Probably because by announcing it on 9 November and not soon after Houteff's death, the close of the 1,260 days would now fall on Passover.

This reconstruction is of course speculative, but it is not improbable. If this is what happened, Saether seems to have missed it. According to him a meeting of the Executive Council was called late in 1955 (after 9 November).[17] At this meeting the period of the 1,260 days was discussed.[18] The Council (and let us not forget that Florence was by now firmly ensconced as both chair of the Council and vice-president of the association) accepted the view Florence had put forward, that the community had indeed now entered the time period; the question was, when had it begun? There was discussion, and some argued for beginning the count from the day of Houteff's death. In the end, however, the view that won was that the period had begun on the day the message went out, i.e. 9 November. Quite by chance (says Saether) the end of the period hence came on Passover 1959.[19] At the very least this was a remarkable coincidence. To the Council members, however, who believed not in coincidence but providence, it must have seemed the confirmation of the view they had now taken regarding the starting date for the time proph-ecy. Indeed, Saether himself seems to have been impressed by the fact that when one adds the 1,260 days to the seemingly random date for the an-nouncement of the message one finds that the time period will end on Passover. Others of the group were also persuaded.[20]

By November 1955, then, the date of 22 April 1959 had been marked in the Davidian calendar as being particularly significant; at the very least they expected war in the Middle East to break out around that date. In the meantime, however, Florence applied herself to the very this-worldly task of selling up 'old' Mt. Carmel and looking for a new home. The sale of land at 'old' Mt. Carmel had begun three years earlier when funds were needed to finance the 'hunting' campaign, and was now accelerated. A report in the *Waco Tribune-Herald* for 27 February 1955 is interesting; it links the sale of the land with a need for funds to facilitate an unprecedented outreach, and specifically to urgent eschatological expectation on the part of the Davidians. Already by this date, scarcely more than three weeks after Victor had died, some 26 lots of an estimated 600 that had been put up for sale had been sold and indeed houses had begun to be built. The total sale was expected to raise in the order of $900,000.[21] Sales of the land continued apace so that by late 1957 all that was left was about 10 acres. Some parts of what was now becoming 'old' Mt. Carmel eventually passed into distinguished hands: in September 1973 several of the buildings and the associated land formed the basis of the now very prestigious Vanguard High School in Waco.[22] Houteff's original eleventh-hour clock remains in its original setting in the floor of the main building.[23] Similarly, to this day the streets in this now very well developed residential area of Waco continue to bear the names of the original Davidian settlers: Hermanson, Charboneau, Wilson, Deeter, Berlinger, and 'La Porte'. This latter example is a translation into French of the Bulgarian word 'Houteff' ('door'), which was considered too difficult to pronounce by the new inhabitants.[24]

To replace the 'old' Mt. Carmel a new site was chosen, a substantial parcel of land near Elk, about 12 miles from the centre of Waco. In December 1957 the Davidians purchased some 941 acres, costing $85,000, and the property was named by Mrs Houteff as the 'new' Mt. Carmel. The building programme started immediately and soon a church, a new headquarters, an office building, eighteen homes, and various farm buildings had been erected.[25] There was also a new printing press and this was soon put to use in the promoting of Florence's predictions for 1959.

Meanwhile, of course, 22 April 1959 itself moved ever closer. There is a great deal of speculation regarding just what the Davidians expected to happen on that day, including the suggestion that they were hoping for Victor's resurrection. In fact we do know in outline what they expected since some time shortly before then (note 'this Spring') the group put out a press release explaining just what they were anticipating.[26]

1. We expect that the world's religions are going to unite against Communism. This we have taught for the past 20 years. Our Biblical authority is found in Isaiah 8:9–13 and other prophecies. The World Conference on Religion which was held April 17 to 19 in Dallas reflects that the present thinking of the world's religions is travelling in this very direction.

Our stand on religious and national alliances is precisely what is given in Isaiah 8:11–13. By this scripture we understand that the Lord is not in such a confederation of churches and nations, and therefore God's people are to have no part in it. Since the Lord certainly is not in Communism either, therefore God's people must place their trust in the Lord alone. We expect this confederacy to form this Spring.

2. We believe also that sometime this Spring God will in a direct and terrible judgment as shown in Isaiah 66.15–20 and Ezekiel the ninth chapter, remove all the hypocrites from the Seventh-day Adventist denomination and also from among the Davidians.

3. We expect that sometime this Spring God will commence to set up His peaceful Kingdom in the Holy Land. Our biblical authority is found in Daniel 2:34, 35, 44, 45; Ezekiel 36; Isaiah 11 and many other prophecies.

4. We believe that the Holy Land will be prepared for the setting up of God's Kingdom by the war of Zechariah 14.

5. The April 22 date was calculated from the symbolic prophecy of the 1260 literal days of Revelation 11:3–6. Those days commenced November 9, 1955 and will end April 22, 1959. The events of verses 7–13 are to be fulfilled after April 22.

Unpacking this we get what is in fact a traditional Davidian scheme: war will break out in the Middle East, the land will become empty as a result, the kingdom will be set up and the Davidians will go to inhabit it. Running alongside these events will be the cleansing by slaughter of the SDA Church and the final gathering of the 144,000. There is no specific mention here of Houteff's resurrection, which, if it was looked for, is somewhat surprising. One should not overstress this point, however; perhaps the resurrection of Houteff was, for the Davidians, an integral part of the process of the setting up of the kingdom and while it is not specifically mentioned, it may well have been assumed. Certainly others expressed the view that the resurrection of Houteff was something that the Davidians were expecting to occur on the set date. For example the *Waco News Tribune* for 2 May 1959 gave a report on what the Davidians had been expecting, which includes the comment: 'The signal event believed to be the resurrection of the sect's founder, the late V. T. Houteff, was expected according to prophecy on or about the 22nd April'.[27] Similarly a report in the same newspaper for 23 April stated that [Dudley] Goff[28] had said in one meeting that the Davidians looked upon Houteff as the latter-day Elijah who would return just before the day of the Lord.[29] This may have been so, though it is not confirmed by material coming from the Davidians themselves. What is clear, however, is that they did look expectantly towards 22 April as marking at least the beginning of the end.

A little more regarding what it was the Davidians were anticipating can be found in other newspaper reports from the time (again with the possibility that the reporters did not fully understand Davidian theology). The reports appear to have been based on the content of meetings held at Mt. Carmel in the run-up to 22 April. On 22 April the paper ran a story which gave some details of what was being said at some of these meetings, and by whom. According to this report one of the speakers, Goff, had spoken at some length on the latter chapters of the book of Revelation. The reporter's published list of events that the Davidians were understood as expecting is very similar to the one found on the Davidians' own press release. There is one addition which may or may not be important: the separation of the wheat and tares (cf. Matt. 13.24–30) will be achieved 'with fire and the sword'.[30] This is the first explicit mention of fire in the context of the separation of the wicked and the righteous. It may simply be the influence of the language of Matt. 13.30.

On the previous day the same newspaper had run another story which also listed some of the Davidians' expectations. The report mentioned Goff and Wolfe as speakers, and noted that T. O. Hermanson was due to speak. 'Members of the sect', the report goes on, 'expect the following events to occur within the next few weeks: (1) outbreak of war in the Middle East, (2) purification of their church through the coming of the Lord—they say it possibly will not be visible—with fire and sword, (3) establishment of God's Kingdom in Jerusalem, and (4) purification of the remainder of the world's population.'[31]

In preparation for these grand events, a call was issued by Florence for the Davidians to assemble at Mt. Carmel. Quite when the call went out is unclear. However, it looks as though the gathering began to take place on Thursday 16 April. Two days before this date the *Waco Times-Herald* printed an article headed, 'Sect Gathers Here, Sees War, "Second Coming" '. There followed a news item indicating that 'this weekend' the Davidians will gather in Waco to prepare for events that will culminate in 'the Second Coming of Christ and the setting up of His physical kingdom in Jerusalem'. The Davidians would arrive on Thursday and the preparatory meetings would begin on Saturday.[32]

As the time drew closer, tension and expectation mounted. Saether reported how people began to arrive at Mt. Carmel in anticipation of the setting up of the kingdom.[33] The final estimate he gives is that about 1,000 people came.[34]

The people came and, I think possibly the most excited was Mrs. Houteff when she looked out and saw all those cars coming—a regular caravan—coming into the grounds. We could see them from the office. We were in the office looking out and we could see them coming up the road in trailers and cars and trucks and all coming there from all over the country.[35]

Numerous reports of the gathering appeared in the newspapers. The most detailed is in *The Waco Times-Herald*[36] for 21 April, which reported how many had come from all over the USA and Canada to be in attendance (it seems some who had thought of travelling from further afield still, Australia for example, were dissuaded from making the trip).[37] That report is worth quoting here in full.

'We were living in Narco, Calif., when we received the notice to assemble in Waco,' Tommy Thompson, a lean, weatherbeaten man in his 60's recalled[.] 'I owned a trenching machine business. After we received the notice, we sold the business, our house and furniture. We packed the rest of our belongings—our bedding and cooking utensils—in the car and a rented trailer and brought them with us'. Thompson and his wife are living in a tent at the Davidian world headquarters at Mt. Carmel Center nine miles east of Waco. 'We have no particular problems', Thompson said. 'We got what we asked for'. 'Of course,' Mrs Thompson added quickly, 'this mud has been worrisome. It seems like it's always underfoot.'

George Walton[38] brought his wife, son and 30 to 35 members to the centre when he came from California. And they, like the Thompsons, are living in a tent at the centre... 'We burned all our bridges behind us,' Walton said. 'We came prepared to meet whatever comes our way'. Walton was an employee of the city board of education at Los Angeles. He was also leader of the Davidian group in that area.

Mr. and Mrs. William Glynn of Bend, Ore., are luckier than most. They have two daughters living at the center. They invested part of their money in a house trailer before they came to the center. 'We came in a caravan,' they said. 'There were five cars in all when we started out, but we didn't all arrive at the same time. Some drove straight on through, but we stopped every night.'

Mr and Mrs. C. C. Lyons of Portland, Ore. were Bible workers and they said they 'were prepared for the call'. 'The Lord was with us,' Lyons said, 'we sold our home—signed the final papers and all—and moved out in the two weeks period between the time we received the call and the time we were supposed to arrive'... The Lyons are living in an apartment at the centre. 'We came prepared to camp out,' Lyons said, 'but Sister Houteff... wouldn't let us. [on account of Mr Lyons' heart problems, it seems.] She assigned us an apartment and that is where we are staying'.

Coming to Texas was a different kind of sacrifice for 20-year-old Richard Strutz, a member of the junior hockey team at Prince Albert in Saskatchewan, Canada. 'I'm sorry I have to give up hockey,' he said, 'but I'm glad to be here'. Young Strutz came to the center with his parents. His mother is still here, but his father flew back to Canada Saturday to make arrangements to sell the 640-acre Strutz farm in the heart of Canada's wheat belt.

Mr. and Mrs. J. D. Springer came to Waco from Yoder, Wyo., where they owned and operated a combination farm and rest home. 'We're still trying to sell our place', they said, 'but it's hard to do ...'

There are more than 600 people in Waco representing almost every state and Canada for the Davidian meetings. And according to Davidian Council member George Saether, most of them, like the Strutzes, the Lyons, the Glynns, the Waltons and the Thompsons have either sold their property or are trying to sell it.[39]

The meetings began on Saturday 18 April. They had been advertised as open to the public, but shortly before they began the decision was made to exclude outsiders. The reason given, and it was probably the real one, was that Mrs Houteff had become worried that proper Sabbath observance would prove impossible if Mt. Carmel were to be opened to the general public. The content of the meetings was, however, summarized and passed to journalists and other interested parties.[40] Regrettably, those press releases seem not to have survived. On 20 April the *Waco Times-Herald* ran a second piece giving more details of meetings that were taking place. According to this report there were some 600 Davidians in attendance. The speakers were Goff, G. Walton, and Wolfe; topics included, 'The First and Second Fruits of the Harvest', Daniel 2, and the beasts of Daniel 7 and Revelation 13. Saether had now informed the paper that the meetings were again open to members of the public.[41]

In the event 22 April came and went without incident. Unlike their spiritual and doctrinal grandfather William Miller, however, the Davidian Seventh-day Adventists had left themselves a little space for manoeuvre, since they had consistently said 'on or about the 22 April' and not specified what precisely the sequence of events was to be. They were expecting war in the Middle East, the cleansing of the SDA Church, and the gathering of the 144,000 into the literal kingdom in Israel; but when precisely these things would happen had been left slightly uncertain. However, 'on or about' 22 April clearly implied that it would be soon and it was not too long before the Davidians, like so many others who had gone before them, had to think of a way of coping with the stress of the apparent failure of the prediction. Already before 3 May some group members were talking of 'a feeling of desperation and panic', and there are reports that in the region of one third of the original gathered group had already left.[42]

But this was evidently not the experience of the group as a whole. Indeed, speaking of the period a week to ten days after 22 April, other reports indicate: 'if anything there are a few more tents on the grounds now than there were when the meetings first started.'[43] Certainly the group continued to exhibit confidence in the fulfilment soon of their predictions. Shortly afterwards a large advertisement appeared in one of the Waco newspapers indicating that 'because of the increasing, tremendous public interest in [the] Davidian's belief in the setting up of God's kingdom in Palestine a meeting will be held Sunday May 3 at 3.00 p.m. All are invited'.[44] The meeting took place as promised. Dudley Goff was again the main speaker. Much of the meeting was taken up with an explanation of Davidian beliefs, but it was also announced that the Davidians were expecting a massive influx of people to Mt. Carmel and had begun to make plans for their accommodation.[45] A few days later it was announced that as an immediate measure ten large barracks-type buildings were to be erected. Meetings had been cut back to one a day, possibly to give more time for the work of building the accommodation.[46]

These immediate actions of the Davidian Seventh-day Adventists are not at all out of keeping with the generally observed ways in which groups that have suffered a prophecy failure will respond to their disappointment. In some ways in fact the Davidians underscore the continued value of the old 'Festinger thesis', according to which when a prophecy fails those committed to it will become even more evangelistic than they were before. As more recent studies have shown, this is not the only way in which disappointed prophecy believers will react,[47] but it is one, and for a while at least the Davidians seem to have travelled down this track. Indeed, as scholars in this area know, there was no good reason why Mrs Houteff's group, now much expanded and living at the 'new' Mt. Carmel, should of necessity be facing a bleak future. Several strategies might have been employed to ensure the long-term viability of the movement.

It was at this time also that the official SDA Church made its most determined attempt to bring back its wayward child. SDA literature suggests that the invitation for talks came from the Davidians rather than the Church and there is no reason to doubt this.

On 20 June 1959 A. V. Olson, recently retired vice-president of the General Conference of Seventh-day Adventists,[48] preached in the Waco SDA church. The next day two Davidians (the report does not say who) asked Olson to come to Mt. Carmel and speak with the Executive Council. Following that meeting, he was invited to speak to the group as a whole, which he did several times from 24 June to 7 July. The report speaks of there being some 600 in attendance. A number of other SDA ministers joined Olson in these meetings; these included the pastor of the Waco SDA church, R. L. Winders, R. P. Montgomery from Cleburne, Texas, and R.L. Odom from the General Conference.[49] At the end of those meetings Florence read out a statement thanking Olson for the time and trouble that he had taken in addressing the Davidians. The document contained the following crucial statement:

Inasmuch as it has been the purpose and desire of our ministering brethren to see the Davidians and their mother denomination united in the truth, and as this is also our desire and purpose, we do not feel that our efforts to become united should end here in this meeting tonight... Therefore, Elder Olson, we propose at this time that a meeting be arranged for in the General Conference headquarters in Washington, D.C., at the earliest possible time with representatives of the Davidians and official representatives of the General Conference for the purpose of giving the teachings of *The Shepherd's Rod* a full and complete hearing.[50]

This well-mannered document did the trick. A series of meetings were accordingly arranged to be held at the Washington headquarters of the SDA Church between 27 July and 7 August 1959. Nineteen meetings of approximately two and a half hours each took place between these dates and a report was published by the Church in May 1960.[51] There were seven representatives from the SDA Church and seven Davidians.[52] These were, from the SDA Church, W. E. Murray, A. V. Olson, H. W. Lowe, L. C. Evans, A. C. Fearing, D. E. Neufeld, and R. L. Odom; and, from the Davidians, Florence Houteff, T. O. Hermanson, H. G. Warden, M. W. Wolfe,[53] J. D. Springer,[54] Dudley Goff, and Harmon Springer.[55]

The first ten sessions were taken up by a presentation of principal doctrines by the Davidians; in the next six the SDA ministers gave their reaction to what the Davidians had put forward. Meeting seventeen seems to have been abandoned as a result of the Davidians putting forward a proposal that the writings of Mrs White should be excluded from negotiations from that point on. Meetings eighteen and nineteen seem to have been given over to further discussion on this point, which in the end brought the sequence of meetings to an indefinite close. Needless to say, the SDA delegates took the request of the Davidians to eliminate the writings of Mrs White from further discussion as an indication that they had successfully shown that what the Davidians had to say was not in harmony with the writings of the prophetess.

The meetings hence broke up without resolution. The official report ended by stating that some Davidians had now rejoined the SDA fold. This may well have been the case. Certainly by this time the large number of people that had gathered at Mt. Carmel for the 22 April date was dwindling. The movement was in crisis.

The haemorrhaging got worse, it seems, when Mrs Houteff finally accepted that the events that had been expected 'on or about' 22 April had not happened and that there seemed no immediate possibility that this situation was going to change. A committee was set up to investigate and published its report in the September 1960 *Symbolic Code*.[56] There was a surprising conclusion: the kingdom had not been set up, so the report argued, partly because the Davidians had to date restricted their message to the Seventh-day Adventists only. In truth, it was proposed, the message was to go out to all Protestant Churches and not just to the Seventh-day Adventists (presumably Roman Catholics were thought to be too far gone in apostasy to have any hope). Consequently, in December 1960 a new programme of evangelism to all Protestant churches was launched and, it seems, gained the approval of the majority of those still in the movement.[57] The plan was put into action. Simplified forms of the Davidian tracts were published and sent out not just to Seventh-day Adventists but other Protestants as well. Dudley Goff was commissioned to undertake some radio evangelism through the reading of tracts on air.[58]

The heart of the movement was by now clearly in doctrinal turmoil as it sought to come to terms with the (non) events of April 1959 and, unsurprisingly perhaps, the disintegration continued. It was at this time that no less significant a person than M. W. Wolfe, who had long played a central and important role in the Davidian movement, defected and joined Armstrong's Church. (The only thing we know of him after this is that he died as a result of being blown off a roof—seen by some as a proper end for an apostate such as this).[59] Even more significant, however, was the decision of a number of Davidians to move from Mt. Carmel, elect a new Council, and establish a new headquarters for the work elsewhere. Consequently, some time in 1961 (the literature does not specify the month) a meeting was held in Los Angeles with this goal in mind and the result was the establishment of a publishing centre in Riverside, California. The meeting was not small—there may have been as many as one hundred in attendance.[60] In keeping with tradition no president of this association was elected, but the post of vice-president went to H. G. Warden with M. J. Bingham being appointed as the Director of Publications. (In 1962 this group suffered a further split when M. J. Bingham left to form his own faction.)[61] In 1970 the Riverside group moved to Salem, South Carolina, from where at the time of writing (2004) they still operate.[62]

The importance to the Davidian tradition of the 1961 meeting in Los Angeles should not be underestimated. It marks the point at which the original group effectively split in two, and although the process would not come to a head for some time, that split created the two main Davidian factions. The part of the group that stayed in Waco eventually became the Branch Davidians, although there were many defections before the transformation was complete. The Riverside group preserved the Houteff orthodoxy.

Houteff's original unified movement was hence by now all but dead. It probably could have survived had there been a leader at the helm strong enough to steer it through the difficult waters in which it now found itself; but Florence was not such a person and indeed had largely lost faith in the movement herself. On 1 March 1962, a little under three years after the 22 April date, Florence submitted her notice of resignation to the chairman and members of the General Association of Davidian Seventh-day Adventists. And it was not hers alone. There were seven signatories, the entire Executive Council. The document is addressed to 'the chairman and fellow members attending the Second Special Session of the General Association of Davidian Seventh-day Adventists' and then reads as follows:

For many years we of the Executive Council have whole-heartedly accepted and taught the teachings of 'The Shepherd's Rod' literature—the foundation upon which this organization was built. In 1955, at the death of V. T. Houteff, the administration of this Association fell completely into the hands of the Executive Council and the Association's remaining officers.

During the seven years that have since passed, we have directed and defended the Association with diligence according to our honest convictions of what constituted our duty. As long as we believed in all the teachings of the 'Rod' per se, we patiently bore the personal cost of being victimized by a constant stream of suspicion, slander, libel, and many other unpleasant experiences that came in the line of duty.

After our field of work broadened out to the inclusion of the Protestants, we set out to prepare the Davidians to teach from the only book Protestants will accept—the Bible. But in our thorough examination of the 'Rod' in the light of the Bible, we came upon the realization that adjustments in many of our doctrines were required if there was to be harmony between them and the Bible. For we discovered that some of our cardinal teachings were predicated on concepts Brother Houteff and/or Sister White expounded which the Bible actually does not support. This we say without attempting in the least to disparage their honesty and sincerity.

The dissertations covering related material in several chapters of Ezekiel as presented in the December 12, 1961 and January 16, 1962 open Newsletters to Davidians, is a partial presentation of the facts that came to light. Ezekiel chapters 4 and 9 were therein dealt with particularly as they were pre-eminently important in the founding and organizing of this Association and in defining its work, and also because they occupy so prominent a place all through 'The Shepherd's Rod' literature.

Due to the many inaccuracies that we found in the teachings concerning these chapters in Ezekiel and others that we have not discussed publicly, we must frankly state that we no longer are convinced that 'The Shepherd's Rod' is without error on consequential doctrines; neither are we convinced that our final authority in spiritual matters resides in the writings of Mrs. E.G. White from which 'The Shepherd's Rod' draws its conclusions on Ezekiel 9 and other doctrines and practices. It is our belief that the teachings of both Brother Houteff and Sister White have been used improperly in relation to the Bible, in that the Bible has been made subject to what they have said.

Yet we do not subscribe to the 'Rod's' claim that it contains either all Truth or no Truth. For much good has been brought to us from the writings of both authors. Especially are we appreciative of the enlightenment we received that led us to the truth of the Kingdom and related subjects. Nevertheless, if we would properly serve the interest of Truth all our beliefs and all that we would teach must be founded on the Bible. We submit, moreover, that if the Bible cannot be used as a reliable authority by which to examine and judge our claims of truth, then there is none. Davidians no more that others have the liberty to add teachings that are not in the Bible, regardless of who may have introduced them.

The Second Special Session of the Association has been called in order that we may resign from all our official positions in this Association and turn over to the session the full responsibility of replacing us, and of deciding all the issues before it. Under the circumstances it was impossible for us to appoint others to fill our vacancies.

There is no alternative open to us but to resign since, as we view it, so vital a change in the basic doctrines is involved that it leaves the Association without its declared prophetic commission. And, moreover, this Association was founded upon, and bound to, the teachings of the 'Rod' literature which has as a main feature a particularized application of Ezekiel 9 and 4 to the church today; but since we, the members of the Executive Council, do not now believe the Bible supports those teachings, we therefore are not qualified longer to head up the Association. The destiny of the Association rests entirely in the hands of the membership now.

As faithful stewards, we have taken care of all the business that needed attention, so that we are leaving our offices in good condition. A complete up-to-date inventory of all the assets and records plus the records themselves and all the financial reports are now ready to be officially turned over to the Chairman of this Session.

We would not fail to express our sincere appreciation to those who, by their faithful cooperation contributed their Christian part to make our tenor in office bearable as possible.

In a time like this we can ill afford to look only to the past; we must also look from the present into the future. As for ourselves, we are glad we can say that since our path of experience has brought us to a closer relationship to God and to a better understanding of the Bible than we have ever before had, we believe God has led us. Yet we have much more to learn. But as we conform our thinking more and more to what the Bible teaches we are confident that our understanding will proportionately increase. And so, as we tender this, our resignation, we leave ourselves in the hands of God and trust in him for the future.

This resignation is made by the following named persons from the positions which are also specified.

From the Executive Council

　Mrs. Florence Houteff

　J. O. Conrad

　Mrs. Mary Alen

　T. O. Hermanson

　M. W. Wolfe

　Mrs Sopha Hermanson

　J. R. Ouster, Alternate Member

From the Office of Vice-President: Mrs Florence Houteff

From the Office of Executive Secretary: J. O. Conrad

From the Office of Treasurer: Mrs. Sopha Hermanson

From the Office of Field Secretary: T. O. Hermanson

From the Board of Trustees: Mrs. Florence Houteff, J. O Conrad, Mrs Sopha Hermanson

Our resignation takes effect immediately at the reading of it in the Second Special Session of the Davidian Seventh-day Adventists, convened at Mt. Carmel Center beginning March 11, 1962. [signatures follow][63]

This document is surprisingly candid. It explains how the signatories have come to the conclusion that not all of the teachings of *The Shepherd's Rod* are in harmony with the Bible. Ellen White also, so the document states, was in error on several points. (The resignation of 1 March was not, it seems, the first time that such doubts had been expressed. An earlier statement to the same effect had appeared in an open letter dated 12 December 1961 with a second on 16 January 1962).[64] A point of no return had been reached. On 11 March a special session of the General Association was convened and to it was submitted a document entitled simply 'Resolution'. The document was clearly drawn up by a legal expert, presumably Tom Street who is named in the document itself as a trustee, and proposed 'that said General Association of Davidian Seventh-day Adventists be, and the same hereby is, dissolved, and shall henceforth cease to exist'.[65] The document then goes on to list in some considerable detail what is to happen to the property and other assets of the

Davidian community, and appoints McLennan attorney Tom Street as trustee, 'for the purpose of consummating liquidation and distribution ...' The document was signed by John P. Kelley.[66] The most important part of the agreement is that all the Davidian assets, including those from the sale of property, are to be distributed among the second tithers in proportion to what they had paid in.[67] Houteff's Mt. Carmel had come to an end. Well, not quite; for waiting in the wings was another person ready to take forward the vision leading the 144,000 into the kingdom: Ben Roden.[68]

NOTES

1. Adair, *Davidian Testimony*, 172; see also 'Interviews', 32–3.
2. *OM* 357. Saether also reported specifically on Wolfe's view that Houteff would not die and said that even when Houteff became very seriously ill, Wolfe maintained the view that he would recover (*OM* 326, 332).
3. Adair, 'Interviews', 36; Adair added that when this did not happen, a number of Davidians gave up their faith.
4. See Adair, *Davidian Testimony*, 277–8.
5. *OM* 327, 332. Mention was also made by Saether (*OM* 368–9) of 'a man by the name of Bashan' who left the group and went to Washington, DC. Saether thought that his full name was Alfred Bashan. One is tempted to think that Saether was getting a little confused here with the Bashan movement (on which see further Appendix B). However, he was very clear in what he said. According to him this Alfred Bashan had a small group of believers with him, mainly his family and a few others, and while in Waco lived on Hillcrest Drive. Saether described him as 'quite a sturdy little fellow. He's shorter than I am but heavyset. He's pretty strong looking'. Saether hence clearly had a definite person in mind.
6. *OM* 323, 330–1.
7. *OM* 323.
8. *OM* 336.
9. 'Minutes of the meeting of the Executive Council held in the office of the president at 7.45 p.m. May 7, 1955', 2 (TXC 2D212/3).
10. Saether says in fact that once Florence had been elected leader, Bingham refused to come to Mt. Carmel even when specifically asked to by her (*OM* 366). He appears to have gained the support also of Worden, though the two may later have parted company again, with Worden establishing a small group of Davidians in 'the East' (*OM* 368).
11. *OM* 343–5.
12. 2 *SC* 11/1 (November 1955), 3.
13. Ibid. 13.
14. *OM* 353–4

15. See further Newport, *Apocalypse and Millennium*, 176.

16. *OM* 356.

17. *OM* 384.

18. Saether (*OM* 385) actually said 'twenty-three hundred' days, but this seems to be a mistake. The 2,300 days are of course from Dan. 8.14, a key verse in SDA theology.

19. *OM* 385.

20. Ibid.

21. *Waco Tribune-Herald*, 27 Feb. 1955.

22. Bailey and Darden, *Mad Man in Waco*, 49 n. 13.

23. Pitts, 'Davidians and Branch Davidians', 25.

24. Ibid. 39 n. 6.

25. Bailey and Darden, *Mad Man in Waco*, 42.

26. 'Shepherd's Rod Press Release on Prophecy of April 22, 1959'; unpublished MS, a copy of which is in my possession. It may have been this press release that Saether was given to take into a local newspaper office (see *OM* 405).

27. *Waco News Tribune*, 2 May 1959.

28. Dudley Goff was a long-time Davidian who had joined the group some time prior to 1951. In this year he met Adair in Odessa and invited him to go to Mount Carmel to undertake training for the Davidian ministry (Adair, *Davidian Testimony*, 18). There is a picture of Goff in Bailey and Darden, *Mad Man in Waco*; it is the seventh plate, and Goff is seated to Houteff's right. Goff is not identified in the book, but Adair (*Davidian Testimony*, 223) supplies the detail. Goff played a key role during the years of Florence's Vice-Presidency, eventually becoming her radio evangelist. According to information supplied to me directly by Adair, Goff abandoned the Davidian movement some time in the mid-1960s saying that he would never again teach the Shepherd's Rod message.

29. It may be that this was just a misunderstanding on the reporter's part. The Davidians did think that Houteff was the latter-day Elijah and that his ministry from 1930 on was a fulfilment of biblical prophecy. In this sense the latter-day Elijah had already come.

30. *Waco Times-Herald*, 22 April 1959.

31. Ibid. 21 April 1959.

32. Bonnie Smith (GSS3 29) suggested that the gathering of the people was seen as the 'solemn assembly' of Joel 2.

33. *OM* 395.

34. *OM* 381.

35. *OM* 395.

36. The newspaper cuttings upon which some of this research is based do not carry the name of the newspaper. Most appear to be from the *Waco Times-Herald*, but some may be from the *Waco Times-Tribune* or the *Waco News Tribune*; complete accuracy of referencing is thus not possible. All cuttings are located in TXC.

37. Saether is quoted on this point in *The Waco Times-Herald*, 14 April 1959.

38. Don Adair remembers a 'G. Walton' being at Mt. Carmel when he (Adair) was also there, but remembers nothing further about him (e-mail from Don Adair to Kenneth Newport, 7 April 2004).

39. *Waco Times-Herald*, 21 April 1959.

40. Ibid. 19 April 1959.

41. Ibid. 20 April 1959.

42. *Waco Tribune-Herald*, 3 May 1959.

43. Ibid.

44. Which newspaper is not clear but it appears to be the *Waco News Tribune*; the date does not appear on the cutting.

45. *Waco News Tribune*, 4 May 1959.

46. Ibid. 9 May 1959.

47. See especially Stone, *Expecting Armageddon*.

48. Albert Victor Olson (1884–1963) was vice-president of the General Conference of Seventh-day Adventists from 1946 until his retirement in 1958 (information from *SDA Encyclopedia*, 2nd revised edition, 12 vols. (Hagerstown, Md.: Review and Herald Publishing Association, 1976–2000), 11.244).

49. *Report of a Meeting Between a Group of 'Shepherd's Rod' Leaders and a Group of General Conference Ministers, July 27–August 7, 1959, Takoma Park, Washington, DC* (Washington, DC: The Research Committee of the General Conference of Seventh-day Adventists, 1960); a copy is located in TXC 2D215.

50. 'A Statement Read at Waco, Texas, July 7, 1959' by Mrs V. T. Houteff. A copy of this document is in my possession.

51. *Report of a Meeting Between a Group of 'Shepherd's Rod' Leaders and a Group of General Conference Ministers*.

52. Ibid. 5.

53. This is given as 'N. W. Wolffe' in the document; 'Wolfe' is sometimes spelt 'Wolffe' in the literature. The 'N' in place of the 'M' seems to be a straightforward mistake.

54. J. D. Springer is listed as a Davidian minister in *Fundamental Beliefs and Directory* (1943) 17, 22; his address is given as in Nebraska. According to information supplied to me by Adair, J. D. Springer ran a rest home for Davidians in Yoder, Wyoming. Green (GSS4 43) also gives some of these details.

55. Don Adair has identified one of the figures in the seventh plate in *Mad Man in Waco* as Harmon Springer, the one on the right (Bailey and Darden suggest that this is Perry Jones, which is in error). Harmon was the son of J. D. Springer and, Adair states, was in the same class at Mt. Carmel as Adair and Dudley Goff. This would have been between January 1952 and December 1954. Adair spoke to Harmon Springer in 1989 and learned that he had left the Davidians and was now a member of a Sunday-keeping church; which one is not specified.

56. Adair, *Davidian Testimony*, 221.

57. Ibid. 223.

58. Ibid.

59. Ibid. 224; 'Interviews', 56.

60. The figure is arrived at on the basis of information given to me directly by Adair. In response to my enquiry regarding numbers, he stated: 'when I was there, I do not remember any report given about how many people were there. The church that was rented for our session was not small, so I would guess that there were between 75 to 100 Davidians'. However, in Adair's second interview he estimates that the number of people who made up the group in California was 60–80 ('Interviews', 61). This latter figure may be that of the number of persons who officially joined the group and were there at some point after the initial meeting. Adair published a photograph of some of the persons present (*Davidian Testimony*, 227), and although the quality of the photograph as printed is not good, at least 25–30 persons can be seen.

61. The theology and subsequent progress of Bingham's 'Bashan' movement is given in a little more detail in Appendix B.

62. The theology and subsequent theology of this group is given in more detail in Appendix B. At the time of writing the web site is found at www.davidian.org.

63. A copy of this document is in my possession.

64. These letters are referred to in Robert L. Odom, 'The Shepherd's Rod Organization Disbands', *Review and Herald*, 17 May 1962, 8.

65. TXC 2D215.

66. John Kelley was a convert to Davidianism who had moved to Mt. Carmel some time before 1952. He and his wife appear to have become very concerned with health reform and in particular with the evils of drinking milk. This led him into some dispute with Houteff and others and he was asked to leave. He and his wife would return periodically however to denounce milk drinking. (Adair reports that on one such occasion Kelley and his wife were escorted from the premises by Wolfe and as they walked away from Mt. Carmel they raised their hands in the air and shouted 'praise the Lord! We are being persecuted for Christ's sake'.) See further Adair, *Davidian Testimony*, 174–5, 238, and 'Interviews', 42–3.

67. Some payouts were clearly made. Green (GSS4 45) got $3,700 while Florence Houteff is rumoured to have received $20,000. But the agreement was never fully implemented, held back for the most part by Tom Street's difficulty in selling the land due to a constant barrage of legal challenges regarding who actually owned it. There is evidence too to indicate that some of those that had left Mt. Carmel before the formal appointment of Street simply took some of the money with them. According to Adair ('Interviews' 46–7) what happened was that those who had worked at Mt. Carmel calculated how many hours they had put in and then took the back wages they felt they were owed (above the 50 cents an hour they had been paid). According to Adair some ended up with tens of thousands of dollars.

68. Florence married again and became Florence Eaken (*OM* 191); 'Eaken' sometimes appears as 'Eakin' in the literature.

6

'Behold the Man whose Name is "The Branch" ' (cf. Zech. 6.12): Ben Roden and the Emergence of Branch Davidianism

The Davidian Seventh-day Adventists are a remarkable lesson in the resilience of religious movements. By March 1962 their days seemed well and truly numbered. Their founder prophet was dead, they had suffered the indignity of being proven unequivocally wrong in their predictions of the onset of the battle of Armageddon, and the entire Executive Council, including the vice-president, had resigned. Furthermore they had moved from their original home at 'old' Mt. Carmel, and now the new one they had purchased had been handed over to an attorney for disposal by sale. The future did not look bright.

They were nevertheless to survive, but that survival came only at the cost of fragmentation and transformation. By the end of 1961 the group that was eventually to settle in Salem, SC, under the leadership of Don Adair, had already gone their separate way.[1] Some others had simply drifted away from Mt. Carmel in the wake of the 1959 debacle, with yet more leaving once the Davidian Association was officially dissolved three years later.[2] By 1962, the once thriving 'new' Mt. Carmel property was in a sorry state and the small band of faithful Davidians who yet remained on the property were leaderless.

But for perhaps as much as seven years (i.e. since the death of Houteff) another potential leader had been waiting to take up what he considered to be his role in leading God's people as they prepared for the coming of the Davidic kingdom. That leader was Ben Roden, and his movement was called simply 'The Branch'.[3] They later became 'the Branch Seventh-day Adventists' but are more widely known by yet another name, 'the Branch Davidians'. It was this group that hit the headlines in 1993, and it was part of the 'new' Mt. Carmel property that the world saw in flames on 19 April. By then their leader was David Koresh, but he was not their original leader. He had taken up that role only in the mid 1980s. Before him the exceptionally dynamic and theologically imaginative Lois Roden (Ben's wife) had led the group for a number of years, while she in turn had become leader after the death of Roden himself.[4]

PLATE 3 Ben Roden, Founder of the Branch Davidians

In this chapter the emergence and development of the Branch Davidians under the leadership of Roden is described. The task of piecing this together has been problematic owing to the nature and relative scarcity of the sources that have survived. However, wherever possible the information given in this chapter has been cross-checked and precisely referenced. Again, materials in the TXC at Baylor University have proven central. While the focus of this chapter is on the events of Roden's life, and especially with his ultimately successful attempts to gain control of Mt. Carmel, some of his theology will have to be discussed for as ever it is theology that gives an overall framework to actions. The next chapter contains a more detailed account of Roden's system of belief.

Benjamin L. Roden was born on 5 January 1902 of Jewish stock in Bearden, Oklahoma, one of the six children of James Buchanan and Hattie Roden. Little is known about his childhood, other than that he grew up on a farm in his place of birth, graduated from high school there, and then attended a teacher's college. Following this, he spent a short time as a teacher in a county school. He then went into the oil business and spent a number of years working in the oil fields in Oklahoma, and then Odessa, Texas.[5]

On 12 February 1937 Roden married Lois I. Scott, a marriage which was to last until his death in 1978. There were six children: George,[6] Benjamin, jun.,[7] John, Jane, Sammy, and Rebecca.[8] The year 1937 was important in Ben's life in another way too, for in this year, so his obituary states, he joined 'the Christian Church'. It is impossible on the basis of the evidence that has survived to assess either the process by which he was 'converted' to the Christian faith or the extent of his previous adherence to Judaism.[9] What is relatively clear, however, is that like many other converted Jews (St Peter and St James perhaps being the best early examples), he carried with him into Christianity a good deal of his Jewishness. This is seen very clearly indeed in the theology he was later to develop, for example his concern for and practice of Jewish festivals long since abandoned by mainstream Christianity (Purim and Passover were particularly important to him).

In 1940 both Ben and Lois joined the SDA Church. Given Ben's own Jewishness, there would have been much about Seventh-day Adventism that he would have found attractive: the observance of the seventh-day Sabbath and adherence to the Old Testament food laws are two obvious examples. In fact the theological attraction may have gone a good deal deeper, for while Christianity has in general argued that the Old Testament is as much a revelation of God as the New, few traditions have sought as diligently as the Seventh-day Adventists to explain how this works in practice.[10]

According to the obituary and the address given at Ben's funeral, a tape recording of which has survived, part of the Rodens' decision to join the SDA

Church was a conviction regarding the importance of the seventh-day Sabbath, a point upon which Roden may have been culturally conditioned, but
which was brought home to him by his reading of the SDA book *Bible
Readings for the Home Circle* (1888).[11] This had been given to Ben and Lois
as a wedding present by Lois's mother.[12] (It is not known whether Lois's
mother was herself a Seventh-day Adventist or whether Lois had extensive
knowledge of the SDA Church during her childhood and teenage years. The
fact that *Bible Readings for the Home Circle* appeared as a wedding present
does surely indicate that Seventh-day Adventism was somewhere in the
family). By 1940 both Ben and Lois were members of the SDA Church in
Kilgore, Texas. They later moved to the SDA Church in Odessa, also in Texas,
where Ben became a head elder.

It cannot have been too long after their baptisms as Seventh-day Adventists
that Ben and Lois first came into contact with the Shepherd's Rod movement,
though again this aspect of the story is documented only poorly in the
surviving materials.[13] The obituary states that Ben accepted the Shepherd's
Rod message in 1946 (a date given also on the funeral tape), but it seems that
both he and Lois may already have been in contact with the movement at least
a couple of years prior to this. In fact the Roden family may have visited Mt.
Carmel perhaps as early as 1943 and probably no later than 1945 (Saether was
not certain of the precise date, but remembered their visiting Mt. Carmel
somewhere in the early to mid-1940s).[14] They stayed only a few days on this
first visit.

According to Saether it was at this time also (1945 at the latest) that the
Rodens were disfellowshipped at their local SDA church. They evidently did
not take the disfellowhipping well. Saether told how Roden felt he had the right
to go to the church, even though he had been disfellowshipped from it, since he
had helped finance the building. To gain access, said Saether, the Rodens had
removed the church door. Lois Roden, in what are clearly early signs of her
willingness to make a determined stand for what she considered right and her
flair for being in the thick of controversy, went into the baptistry and stayed
there for several days.[15] This is probably the same event to which Adair referred
when he told how Lois pushed her way into an SDA church after a meeting
had finished, having been barred at the door as the meeting began, and then
refused to move. According to Adair, Ben and son George soon turned up at the
same church with various supplies for Lois, who stayed in the church for a week
so as to be able to let the rest of her family in the next Sabbath. After this latter
church service, Ben took the doors of the church off their hinges and either he
or Lois called a local newspaper to come down and cover the story.[16]

One can only conjecture how this short but evidently intense relationship
with Seventh-day Adventism developed following this incident and how,

perhaps, it confirmed the view to which Ben and Lois had probably come, namely that the SDA Church was in a state of apostasy and was even now skulking in the shadows actively seeking to avoid coming into the light that had so graciously been given to it in the form of the Shepherd's Rod truth.

The events of the next few years of Ben's life are largely undocumented apart from a brief but important reference to Roden as the person who converted Don Adair to the Davidian faith in 1951. At that time the young Adair was working in Odessa and was approached by a woman who convinced him that Ellen White was a prophetess.[17] He wanted to know more, and was put in contact with Roden, who explained parts of the book of Revelation to the potential convert. Adair remained a student of Roden's for some time and accompanied him on evangelistic trips to SDA meetings.

It is apparent that from about 1945 onwards Roden was aware of the teachings of the Shepherd's Rod and had become convinced of their truth. In 1953 the Rodens returned to Mt. Carmel and this time stayed several months, setting up an organic garden on part of the property near the Lake (the date and the detail about the garden are agreed upon by Saether and the writer of the obituary).[18] In 1955, the year Houteff died, they were back again. Already Roden had his eye on the leadership of the movement, a fact testified to by Adair, who told of how he was visited by Ben and Lois and was told by them (actually it seems to have been Lois who took the lead) that Ben was now the new Elijah.[19] Roden's claim to the leadership of the Davidians was not accepted, the post going rather to Florence. Ben's failure to seize control was not through want of trying. Saether indicated that it was in 1955 that 'he [Roden] started his demands to take over Mt. Carmel'.[20] Similarly the obituary states that it was in 1955 that 'Brother Roden was endowed with the Prophetic Gift (Amos 3.7) to understand God's plan for the Davidian and SDA movements.' 'Thereafter' (states the writer) Roden 'laboured night and day to share with his brethren what God had revealed to him.'

In autumn 1955 Roden sent out a letter to Davidians asking them to congregate at Mt. Carmel, a call that would have overlapped chronologically with that of Florence Houteff and her claim that they had now entered the waiting period of 1,260 days. Speaking of this period and the influx to Mt. Carmel, Saether remembered that groups that began to congregate there at this time came in response not to Florence, but rather to Roden's call.[21] This is an interesting detail, and shows how he even at this early point had his supporters.

Some very specifically targeted work had evidently been done by Roden in issuing the 1955 call, probably facilitated by Perry Jones who, since he had previously worked in the Mt. Carmel office, had knowledge of the names and addresses of those to whom Roden's 'Branch' message might be of potential interest.[22] Already in1953, it seems, such names and addresses had been passed by Jones to Roden; it was in that year that Jones himself left Mt. Carmel, probably to be with Roden.[23]

The struggle for leadership continued with Florence refusing to give way. In September Roden began what turned out to be a sequence of seven letters to Florence in which he put forth his claim to leadership and an outline of his theology as it had by then developed.[24] As one might expect, this claim came in the form of a very complex argument based upon noting similarities and differences between passages of scripture that referred, among other things, to angels and other divine messengers. Using a logic that few outside the tradition would really be able to follow, Roden sought to show that Houteff, while very important, was not the final messenger who was to come.[25] Someone else was to follow to give the specific message about the timing of the judgement and the practices of the end-time community.

Some say that modern day Moses (V. T. Houteff) brought the truths that are to lead God's people out of all nations and interpreted Sister White's writings and the Bible on the subject of the purification of the church. Like Moses of old, the Lord did not see fit to use Brother Houteff to lead His people into the Kingdom. Instead, He will use another, Joshua, to first separate the thieves and idol worshippers from among His people, then take them to the Kingdom. 'Awake, O sword, against my shepherd, and against the man that is my fellow, saith the Lord of hosts: smite the shepherd, and the sheep will be scattered: and I will turn my hand upon the little ones' (Zech. 13.7).[26]

From this Roden went on to explain how his own work fitted into the divine plan. Houteff had been smitten (he had died), the sheep had been scattered, but the Lord would take care of those who were humble (that is, those who accepted Roden's message). Already in the first letter, Isaiah 11.1: 'there shall come forth a rod out of the stem of Jesse, and a Branch shall grow out of his roots' was in view. It is indicative of what was to come, also, that the letter is signed 'The Branch'. The message of the letters fell largely upon deaf ears. However, what is evident is that one way and another Roden had by this time already succeeded in gathering together a small band of followers, based in Odessa.[27]

On 10 October 1955 Roden came back to Mt. Carmel, but left again on the same day.[28] His arrival and departure should have been no surprise to the community there. In the letters to Florence, he had already identified 10 October as a very important day in the eschatological calendar. In the first letter he had suggested it as the day the fieldworkers could meet at Mt. Carmel to address the issues raised in the letter itself. In fact the letter ends with the words 'Let us know immediately if October 10th is satisfactory. If we do not get your answer by September 27th, we will conclude October 10th to be satisfactory. The invitation is for both workers and laymen.'[29] Initially, then, that was simply a suggested date upon which the Davidians could gather at Mt. Carmel and study together various Bible passages (including Isa. 11 and Rev. 7). However, it was soon to take on apocalyptic significance. In the second letter 'The Branch' said in effect that the first letter was the sounding of Joel's trumpet. A new movement began with the fast of Joel 1.14 'Sanctify ye a fast, call a solemn assembly, gather the elders and all the inhabitants of the land into the house of the Lord your God, and cry unto the Lord.' It appears now that the 'solemn assembly' mentioned in this verse was understood by Roden as the meeting that would to take place on 10 October: 'October 10 IS THE DATE SET for the solemn occasion. As in the days of Israel, all will want to be there that day. This, therefore, must be the first direct fulfillment of Joel's trumpet.'[30] Roden reasoned that since the children of Israel blew trumpets for ten days before the Day of Atonement, so the trumpet which is blown in Zion according to Joel 2.1 would sound for ten days. The trumpet sounds of that chapter are the letters he had sent and would send to the Davidians in the run-up to the 'solemn meeting'. By 7 October Roden's views had sharpened further. That letter began 'Dear Brethren: The Lord is coming in His Chariot October 10 to purify the Davidian camp. And they send a warning to all honest souls at Mt. Carmel to flee the Hill shortly after the meeting. For the Lord is going to rain terror on the Hill because of her sins.'[31] It ended with a further warning that those who did not come out of Sodom (by which he seems to mean Mt. Carmel under Florence Houteff's leadership) would have to suffer the same punishment as the people who remained in the city after Lot had left.[32]

Quite how this fits is not at all clear; the first letter was written on 23 September and Roden was probably working it out as he went along. The end date was, however, set, and when Roden and his followers arrived on the morning of 10 October his own view would have been that he was giving the last warning to a doomed community. If they did not repent and accept the 'Branch' light they were now being offered, they would have to face the consequences. The evidence is that on that day Roden told the Mt. Carmel Davidians about the 'new name' of Christ ('The Branch'). The message was rejected by the majority.[33]

On 10 October, then, Roden came and went and what happened next gives some further indication of what was going on in his mind. At about 2.30 a.m. on the morning of 11 October Saether answered the telephone. Perry Jones was on the other end and asked how things were at Mt. Carmel. Saether reported something of what Jones said, but unfortunately the transcriber has just 'unintelligible' at this point. What follows next is informative: 'Just like that, you know, and then he hung up. He actually thought—they actually thought the fire was going to come down. They were going to go so far away from it they couldn't see the glow of it even.'[34] This detail of not wanting even to see the glow of it may be related to the fate of Lot's wife who looked back at Sodom and Gomorrah as they burned and was turned to salt (Gen. 19.26). Roden in one place urged the Davidians to 'remember Lot's wife' (cf. Luke 17.32) and not look back when the Lord reigned fire on Mt. Carmel.[35]

It is probably this same expectation that Mt. Carmel was soon to be burned to which Don Adair later alluded in an interview with Dan McGee. Speaking of what appear to be parallel events, Adair stated:

So Ben came to Old Mount Carmel and tried to tell the people that he was the new prophet to take over, and of course, they didn't buy that story. So he told them, 'Because you've rejected me as Elijah, fire is going to come down and burn up Mount Carmel.' Now, I'm talking about Old Mount Carmel. And so a few of the Davidians were following him. One of his first loyal converts was Perry Jones. And so Perry Jones and all the rest of them ran home and turned on their TV and waited for the news to see Mount Carmel burn up.[36]

The fire did not come and the Rodens were back at Mt. Carmel again on 22 October. Again the visit should have been expected. Following the non-events of 10 October, Roden had written another letter to Florence and the Association in which he argued that the beginning of the 'ten days' during which the trumpets were to sound was on 10 October, since it was upon this day that the third letter had arrived at Mt. Carmel.[37] (Roden has plainly got himself into a bit of problem here since in letters 1–3 he quite unequivocally said that 10 October was the cut-off date and that Mt. Carmel would suffer fire and brimstone on that day.) He then argued that in fact 22 October would be 'the date of the showdown on Mt. Carmel', since it was the last day of the Jewish civil year and also the Day of Atonement. However, people would have to make up their minds by 20 October, the end of the ten-day period.[38] Again nothing happened, at least nothing very obvious, though Roden was later to argue that the date was the one upon which the Lord had begun to separate the wheat and the tares (cf. Matt. 13.30).[39]

Roden was back at the centre again on 25 October.[40] This date is particularly significant. As was noted above, in 1938, during a period of Houteff's absence from Mt. Carmel, there had been a rebellion led by Bingham against the regime of Elder Wilson. Upon his return Houteff had called the groups together and declared a 'day of reconciliation' among the various parties, a day when differences must be put aside and all Davidians come together to take forward the work. The day was 25 October, and thereafter, according to Saether, that became known as 'the day of days' in the tradition and was celebrated each year by the community in some style.[41] Roden may have been hoping that the spirit of concord to which the Davidian 'day of days' bore testimony might have inclined the Mt. Carmel residents to give him a hearing too. If so, he was wrong. No progress was made and the Rodens left yet again. The last few weeks had been depressingly uneventful.

Not easily discouraged, however, Roden was back at Mt. Carmel in 1956 and at this time told the residents that 'the King of Babylon came and sat down in the streets of Jerusalem':[42] odd words to an outsider's ears. However, a biblically informed community would not have missed the allusion to Jeremiah 39.1–3:

In the ninth year of Zedekiah king of Judah, in the tenth month, came Nebucha-drezzar king of Babylon and all his army against Jerusalem, and they besieged it. And in the eleventh year of Zedekiah, in the fourth month, the ninth day of the month, the city was broken up. And all the princes of the king of Babylon came in, and sat in the middle gate.

Roden was evidently still of the opinion that he was now the leader of the community and that the current leadership would be overthrown. As yet, however, this particular prophet was still without honour. His time had not yet come.

Still not to be dissuaded, however, Roden conceived of a very bold plan indeed that from this point on would consume a good deal of his interest and energy. He would go physically to Israel to prepare the way for the 144,00 by establishing a community there that would, as its numbers swelled, form the nucleus of those destined to inhabit the new Davidian kingdom once the Waco 'Jerusalem' (Mt. Carmel) had been stormed and its proper king en-throned. Both Victor and Florence Houteff had long dreamed of the time when all the Davidians would collectively make such a move; not content to wait for the missing tens of thousands, however, it was Roden who first sought to give the saints a physical foothold in the Holy Land.

In order to facilitate the setting up of such a community both Ben and Lois spent a great deal of time in Israel over the next several years. The obituary indicates that a particular high point came in 1958 when 'Elder Roden, his son George and wife, Carmen, and his son Benjamin II, went to Israel to prepare the way for the people to go to the Holy Land'. Fortunately, at this point the information gets better, for preserved in TXC archives are several documents relating to this period and to Roden's attempt to set up a base in the Holy Land that would be a foretaste of what was to come. It is clear in the documentation that Ben and Lois worked together on this; a good deal of it is addressed to Lois.

The first settlement was at Amirim in the Golan heights.[43] There were some problems. In a letter addressed simply 'to whom it may concern', Lois is direct in complaining about the way in which the group in Amirim have been treated.[44] They did not realize, she says, that they would be required to participate in joint ownership programmes of orchards and machinery and, since these were worked on the Sabbath, be in receipt of profits made by Sabbath breaking. The refusal to participate fully in such schemes caused friction with the other villagers and as a result the group agreed to move to a location in Jerusalem itself.[45]

While at Amirim the Rodens undertook a task similar to the one they had previously been engaged in at Mt. Carmel and established 'The Organic Agricultural Association in Israel'.[46] This organization expressed as its aims the desire to establish, improve and encourage the use of organic methods of agriculture. Lois was named as the director of the society, with George as the assistant director. Other members of the board were Joseph Parks (also an assistant director), Ben Roden (secretary), and Bonnie Gilham (honorary treasurer).[47]

By now the Branch Davidian Association (or something with a very similar name) had been formed, though trying to put a precise date on its coming into existence is difficult. The document relating to the regulations of the 'Organic Agricultural Society in Israel' carries the seal of 'The Branch Organic Agricultural Assoc—Israel' and there are a number of other documents from around this time that also give clear evidence that 'The Branch' had been institutionally formed. The most unequivocal of these is a letter dated 27 September 1962 headed 'The Branch Seventh-day Adventists',[48] a name that appears on some other undated publications.[49] However, the obituary implies that the formation of the 'Branch Davidian Seventh-day Adventist Association' was a good deal earlier than this, perhaps as early as 1955 when Roden was rejected as the leader of the Davidian Seventh-day Adventists.

It is doubtful that a formal 'Branch Seventh-day Adventist Association' had been established as early as the obituary suggests, but that things were moving in this direction even within a few months of Houteff's death is plain enough. Already in the seven letters to Florence 'the Branch' was being used by Roden as a name. Saether's evidence is again helpful. He remembered how Roden had come with a number of other people from Odessa in October 1955 and how they were all talking about 'The Branch', a term that these people had created to describe their movement.[50] He remembered also a letter signed simply from 'The Branch', and described how after a while the Mt. Carmel Davidians discovered that the author was in fact Roden.[51]

Over the course of the next several years the 'Branch' movement gained momentum and moved towards institutional foundation. Letters and studies from 1958 end with such greetings as 'yours to hear the "voice of the Lord" and with power to proclaim His glorious new (BRANCH) name'.[52] Particularly important in this context also is Roden's typescript study on 'The Stone', dated 24 November 1958.[53] This also gives as an institutional address: 'The Branch, Box 3088, Odessa, Texas'; Roden and 'The Branch' or 'The Branch Seventh-day Adventists' were to operate from this address for the next several years. Meanwhile Florence and the executive moved towards the 1959 date and then fell into turmoil. Roden waited for his chance.

In fact the final victory did not come until 1973, eighteen years after Victor Houteff's death. By this date 'new' Mt. Carmel had been in the hands of Tom Street for eleven years and it was his responsibility to act on behalf of the Davidians (now 'A Dissolved Association in Liquidation' as Street's headed paper put it).[54] The original plan had been to sell the property and divide the proceeds among those Davidians who had paid the 'second tithe', for the payment of the second tithe was taken to be a sign of true membership of the group. In accordance with this plan, most of the original 941 acre site at Elk had already been sold, along with the equipment and stock, but the remaining 77 acres were not so easy to deal with. These were the location of the bulk of the buildings, including the homes of some Davidians who had remained on the property even after the departure of Florence and the rest of the group. According to the original agreement, these Davidians had the absolute right to remain in their homes and to pay the current rent until 5 June 1962 and after that to be permitted to remain at the discretion of Tom Street and on terms seen fit by him.[55] One can imagine easily enough what happened. The bulk of the land was sold off, but the portion with the houses on it was kept and the properties were rented out. Thus while the 941 acres had now been reduced to 77, 'Mt. Carmel' continued to exist in some form at least, and Roden was still determined to take control if it.[56]

For ten years Roden went to and fro to between Israel, Odessa, and Mt. Carmel, never taking his eye off the task he felt called to undertake: gaining the leadership of the remnant people of God and preparing them for the move to Israel. The leadership remained with Florence, however, and the whole question was apparently rendered moot when the Association was dissolved in 1962. The issue came to a head once more in 1965 when the Rodens made a serious attempt to purchase the remaining Mt. Carmel property from Tom Street. Plans seem to have been in place early in the year. Roden was excited. On 10 March he issued a call to all believers to be at Mt. Carmel by 16 April so that the first Passover could be celebrated there. The address given for responses to the call is still the Odessa one, though given the content of the call Ben was clearly assuming that his movement would relocate in the very near future.[57] A newspaper report from this time similarly indicates that Roden was indeed at Mt. Carmel in April, presumably to celebrate the Passover, but it is not clear whether the move from Odessa was

PLATE 4 'New' Mt. Carmel much as it would have looked at the time when Koresh gained the leadership of the community

already complete.[58] Both Ben and Lois were certainly on the property by May 1965, though they did not as yet own it outright. A letter from Street indicates that they were still expected to pay rent on the property and indeed had to take responsibility for the payment of the rents on any homes rented out to persons they (the Rodens) invited to live on the Mt. Carmel site. (Street also wrote a letter in May 1965 indicating that if the Rodens did not stop the unauthorized use of water for gardening purposes, it would be cut off; Street was clearly still in control). From other documentation it seems that the sale had been agreed, but that Street maintained control until the full sum, which was to be paid in monthly instalments of $5,000, had been handed over for distribution among the second tithers.[59]

By 1965, then, Roden seemed close to realizing his dream and gaining control of the property. The payment of $5,000 per month was a serious issue, but at least it meant that the ownership of the Mt. Carmel property had become a practical matter rather than a legal one and Roden must have been confident that God could be called upon to provide the money. However, there were still problems ahead. In fact what happened next, as Bailey and Darden note, was a round of 'bewildering ... lawsuits, counterlawsuits and eviction hearings'.[60] These need not be unpacked fully here, but in essence what happened was as follows.

In September 1965 the Rodens wrote a letter to Street complaining that although they had agreed to purchase Mt. Carmel and were now seeking to meet the $5,000 a month payments, they were not able to use the rents from the homes to assist with the monthly payments (the rents presumably still going to Street); nor were they allowed to use the administration building, and this was holding up the work.[61] In the course of this correspondence the question was raised about a clear title to the property. The crux of the matter was whether Florence and the Executive Council of 1962 had the legal right to put the property in the hands of the receiver. Should Mt. Carmel not rather have passed to the remaining faithful Davidians, who, in Roden's eyes, were those who had accepted the 'Branch' light?

Unwittingly, perhaps, Roden had opened a can of worms, and soon after this first legal skirmish others entered the fray. A newly established group made up of a number of the original Davidians, now calling themselves 'The General Association of Davidian Seventh-day Adventists Inc.', also challenged the basic assumption that the Davidian Council of 1962 had the right to sell the property.[62] Florence Houteff (now Florence Eakin) fought the case, arguing that the decision to sell had been legal and that Street was indeed the proper trustee. Others too staked a legal claim. These included a group of seven Davidians from Colorado. Their case went to court and on 11 November 1965 the jury delivered a verdict in what was described as a 'complicated case'. Frustratingly, quite what that verdict was is not reported, but it is summarized as 'generally favouring the groups wanting to prevent the liquidation of the remaining church property'.[63] From this point the legal scuffle got even more complex. In March 1966 a decision was made that, as had originally been decided, the assets should be liquidated and Tom Street should act as receiver. The proceeds should be divided among the second tithers. This decision was appealed—successfully. In June 1968, however, an eviction order was served on the Rodens and a number of other (Branch) Davidians now living at Mt. Carmel. They failed to comply, and instead filed a counter-suit claiming that they were joint owners of the property since they were the proper heirs of the Davidian tradition. The court's view was that the Davidians had ceased to exist in 1962 and that the 'Branch Davidians' were a new movement in the court's eyes and hence had no claim to the property.

In the end Roden lost the legal battle. But he was nothing if not determined. A return was made to the original plan whereby he would purchase the property from the receiver. No clear documentation has survived explaining precisely how this took place, but what appears to have happened is that those

Branch Davidians who, as former second-tithe-paying Davidians, had a right to some of the proceeds from the sale of Mt. Carmel waived that right and in effect lowered the asking price.[64] The remainder of the money was raised and finally on 27 February 1973 Mt. Carmel was sold for $30,000 to 'Benjamin Roden, Lois Roden and George Roden, Trustees for the General Association of Branch Davidian Seventh-day Adventists'.[65] After a very long battle, Roden was finally in charge.

The efforts expended in these legal deliberations are somewhat surprising, given that Roden placed so much emphasis upon the move to Israel. He himself was thinking of returning there in 1965. It was in that year, however, that he apparently received a message from God regarding the importance of Waco in God's plans, and hence felt duty bound to fight to keep God's bit of real estate there. The vision is mentioned, but only in passing, in the obituary, and it is a pity that more is not known of his thoughts on this issue. In fact the 1965 vision was not the first he had received relating to Waco; during the various court cases that were fought over the property he had told the story of how he was once working underneath a car and heard God's voice saying 'Brother Ben, go to Waco and lead my people.'[66]

Another high point came on 14 June 1970. What happened on that day is remarkable; it represents not so much a break with, as a coming to fruition of, earlier Davidian thinking. Victor Houteff had looked for the coming of the antitypical king, as had Florence and others in the movement. On 14 June Roden took a step equal in confidence to the one he took when founding the community at Amirim: he was crowned at Mt. Carmel as 'Vicegerent of the Most High God'. There could be no further doubt. The kingdom could not be far distant— its king had now been crowned—not in Jerusalem but in Waco.[67]

The next few years at Mt. Carmel were very productive theologically and Roden produced a significant quantity of published and manuscript materials.[68] However, while the Mt. Carmel centre in Waco was now very much the focus of his activities, he never lost sight of the grander goal of moving to Israel and re-establishing the literal kingdom of God. In spring 1977 he was in Israel, and there received information from God on the rebuilding of the Temple, a task that was to occupy a central place in the thoughts of George Roden after his father's death. According to the report, Roden received very specific instructions on precisely where the Temple was to be built. It could not be on the old site, since this was too small. The Temple that Roden was to build, that outlined in Ezekiel 40–5, was on a much grander scale. Even the puzzle of precisely how big 'a cubit' was in Ezekiel's day was revealed to him.[69] In TXC two photographs of Roden are preserved from this period. These show him standing next to a small altar that he had presumably constructed himself, and then kneeling before it, arms raised high.[70] On the back of the photographs one reads 'at the Altar [on] Har Zaitem, Mt. of Olives, 1977'. Also in 1977 Roden published a pamphlet in which he called for the faithful to consider moving to Israel to help with the rebuilding plans. He wrote:

This year, 1977, further steps have been made in the clearing away of obstacles so that God's people can return to the land of Canaan. Are you interested in helping to rebuild the temple? This requires a major step of faith on the part of all Seventh-day Adventists. The Lord has told us to move, however inconvenient. Are you ready? Remember the Sunday blue laws are fast approaching.[71]

This call and the reference to the coming of the Sunday laws reflects Roden's by now well-developed view that the faithful would have to seek asylum in Israel in order to be able to keep the Sabbath during the period immediately preceding the cleansing of the SDA Church and the establishment of the kingdom. He had put forward such a view in a letter to Davidians and Branch Davidians as early as 1962, stating that only those who were faithful to God now (which meant keeping the feasts) would be able to get asylum in Israel in the future.[72] In September 1978, astonishingly, Ben and George Roden and George's first wife, Carmen, gained a personal audience with President Jimmy Carter at which they asked his assistance in the rebuilding plan.[73] Carter's apocalyptic views and his interest in the regathering of the Jews are now well known, but unfortunately his response to the request for assistance has not been recoverable. This was not the Rodens' first success in gaining the ear of the president of the United States. In 1974 Ben and George (and perhaps Lois too, but Ben does not say) attended a luncheon in Washington in honour of President Nixon. During the luncheon Ben gave a copy of a tract to Nixon and George gave the same to Mrs Nixon and their children. Which tract it was Ben did not say.[74]

Before he died Roden left instructions on how the work of the rebuilding of the Temple was to be divided among his four sons: George was to oversee the project, Benjamin II was responsible for the furnishings, John Scott was to be responsible for all work in precious metals and Samuel Shane was to be the construction supervisor.[75] Of the four brothers, George was the one who took his responsibilities most seriously.[76]

Running alongside this was another important development in the potential leadership of the group. Not to be outdone by the males of the family, by 1977 Ben's wife Lois had begun to make her own claim to prophetic office, and from then on her ministry became an important feature of life at Mt. Carmel. The ease with which she took over the leadership of the movement (other than a major dispute with George, concerning which more will be said in the next chapter), indicates that Lois was accepted by the Davidian believers. Ben, while not clearly endorsing Lois's prophetic claim, did not come out against it.

Roden died on 22 October 1978 at 4.30 p.m. in Temple, Texas. (Rather strangely, no one other than the writer of the obituary seems to have spotted that he died 134 years to the day after the Great Disappointment of 1844.) He was buried in Waco Memorial Park. Contrary to Luke 13.33 this prophet had died outside Jerusalem. However, thanks to the efforts of his wife he was at least buried there: in 1982 his grave in Waco was opened, his body disinterred and transported to Israel, and he was reburied on the Mount of Olives.

Such then was the life of Ben Roden. When he died he left behind a community that was a good deal more stable that it had been when he took over. The property was now secure, a clear message had been formulated and some success had been achieved in bringing in new members.[77] The leadership question had also been more or less settled, since Lois was already claiming the prophetic office. These were stabilizing features. However, one might think, the theological stability of the group must have been an issue since Roden, unlike Houteff before him, had proclaimed quite uncompromisingly the view that he was the antitypical King David who would lead the faithful into the kingdom. The latter-day Joshua, unlike his type, had gone to his grave without bringing the people into the promised land. The plan to rebuild the Temple also remained nothing but that: a plan. And there was much else that Roden had said that did not come to fruition. This is explored in the following chapter.

NOTES

1. See Appendix B.
2. According to Adair, some joined Herbert Armstrong's World-wide Church of God because they also kept the Sabbath ('Interviews', 56).
3. Zech. 6.12
4. The process by which Koresh became leader is complex. These issues are discussed more fully in Chapters 8–10.
5. The main sources for the life of Roden are found in two specific locations within TXC. These are a box of assorted items relating to Ben and Lois Roden (2D215), and some folders within the Mark Swett Collection. I have used those materials extensively in this chapter. Also useful is an audio tape of Roden's funeral, a copy of which is in my possession. The date of birth and most of the other basic factual information given here is taken from Roden's obituary published in the *Waco Tribune-Herald*, 30 Oct. 1978, a copy of which is in TXC (2D212/24). That folder also contains the impressive photograph of a young Roden that is published as plate three in this book.

6. George was probably born in *c.*1938 since it is widely reported that he was sixty when he died in December, 1998.
7. According to information found on a document issued by the American consulate in Haifa, Israel, in 1961 (TXC 2D212/23), Benjamin Lloyd Roden II was born on 8, July 1939 in Gladewater Texas.
8. See the photograph in Adair, *Davidian Testimony*, 13.
9. Roden's Jewishness is attested to by several of those who knew him; during the interviews, for example, Adair stated simply that 'they [the Rodens] were Jewish' ('Interviews', 19).
10. Some of this ground has been explored already in Chapter Two, where it was shown that Seventh-day Adventism has always placed great emphasis upon the antitypical interpretation of the Old Testament. Were it likely to yield results in terms of understanding Roden's thought processes, his motives, and/or his decision to join the SDA Church, other aspects of Seventh-day Adventism's approach to the Bible, e.g. its 'conditionalist' understanding of much Old Testament prophecy, could have been explored. However, since we know almost nothing regarding the process by which Roden became first a Christian in general and then a Seventh-day Adventist in particular, such discussion would be of only very limited value.
11. *Bible readings for the home circle: comprising one hundred and sixty-two readings for public and private study, in which are answered over twenty-eight hundred questions on religious topics* (Battle Creek, Mich.: Review and Herald Publishing House, 1888). This book is a classic in SDA literature and has gone through countless editions and translations.
12. Roden funeral tape.
13. Adair, who knew Roden as early as 1951, was asked specifically by his interviewer about the means by which Roden came into the Shepherd's Rod movement, but had nothing at all to offer on this point ('Interviews', 20).
14. Saether (*OM* 328, 336) was uncertain about the precise date that Roden first visited Mt. Carmel. He suggested 1945, but also gave 1943 and 1944 as possibilities. Lois was evidently with Ben on the visit, as Saether stated that Ben came with his family.
15. *OM* 327–30.
16. Adair, 'Interviews', 15–16.
17. Adair reports that the woman's name was 'Sister Ballew'. She appears not to have been a Davidian herself but a mainstream Seventh-day Adventist; she had introduced Adair to Roden, but evidently did not know that Roden was a Davidian. Adair continued the studies at Roden's house and eventually, not knowing the difference between what he was being taught by Roden and official SDA doctrine with which he had not before come into contact, applied to join the Odessa SDA Church. His association with Roden was quickly discovered and his application refused (Adair, 'Interviews', 9–13).
18. *OM* 327.
19. Adair, *Davidian Testimony*, 191.

20. *OM* 328.
21. *OM* 358–63.
22. There is a small amount of written material by Jones himself in TXC (Mark Swett Collection/Perry Jones). This is mostly in the form of letters to a Mr and Mrs Bunds but there are some more substantial items as well. From that material it is plain that Jones, who signed himself 'correspondence secretary', was given the task of dealing with incoming mail. Some of these letters include requests for literature; especially popular it seems was the tract *We're Fed Up with Catholics Crucifying Nixon*. There are also one or two items in which Jones sought to answer questions regarding the content of Branch literature.
23. *OM* 364–5.
24. Some of these letters are preserved in typescript in TXC. They were reprinted with slight augmentation under the title *Seven Letters and the Executive Council of the Davidian Seventh-day Adventist Association by The Branch* (Waco: The Universal Publishing Association, 1978); TXC 2D215/Roden Publications. References here are to that edition. The letters are dated 23 Sept., 3 Oct., 7 Oct., 18 Oct., and 15 Nov. 1955, and 3 Feb. and 12 Mar. 1956.
25. Roden's view on Houteff is found early in the sequence. In letter One he wrote, 'No greater message has ever come to this earth than came in 1929. At that time God sent Victor T. Houteff, a Seventh-day Adventist layman, with the message to save the 144,000.' (*Seven Letters*, 10).
26. *Seven Letters*, 57–8.
27. The size of that group is unknown, but it was probably quite small. Perry Jones was a member and Saether said that 'Nelda', Perry Jones's mother-in-law, was one of the early Roden converts (*OM* 374–5). A 'William Worrow' of Miami, Florida, appears in a photograph with Roden and Jones in an undated cutting from the *Waco News Tribune* (almost certainly April 1959). In a separate cutting (9 May 1959) three further persons are shown as they prepared for departure to Israel. These are named as W. N. Hixson, V. W. Johnson, and Ruby Olsen. The cutting is in TXC 2D212/24. Another early convert, much to Don Adair's distress, was his brother Dale Adair ('Interviews', 84).
28. *OM* 363.
29. Roden, *Seven Letters*, 15.
30. Ibid. 17 (emphasis original).
31. Ibid. 23.
32. Ibid. 24.
33. Ibid. 78.
34. *OM* 364, 369.
35. *Seven Letters*, 24.
36. Adair, 'Interviews', 84.
37. Roden, *Seven Letters*, 27.
38. Ibid. 28.
39. Ibid. 58.
40. *OM* 370–1.

41. *OM* 371.
42. *OM* 373.
43. Amirim is in the centre of Galilee, an hour or so from Nazareth and thirty minutes from the sea of Galilee. Numerous tourist-focused advertisements for it are currently found on the internet, its principal selling point, other than its location, being the fact the entire village is now vegetarian.
44. TXC 2D215/Lois Roden.
45. A letter dated 23 Oct. 1963 and sent to Lois Roden outlines the arrangements being made for the move of the families from Amirim to 'kilometer 21 near the water station'. Ten houses are being made available; TXC 2D215/Lois Roden.
46. This organization, or at least one very similar going by the name of the 'Branch Organic Agricultural Association', was evidently still in existence in 1985 since in a legal notice published in the *Waco Tribune-Herald* on 22 March 1985 George Roden is named as its president.
47. TXC 2D215/Lois Roden; the agreement was typed also in Hebrew and two copies are found in the TXC 2D215/Israel.
48. TXC 2D215/Roden MS.
49. These are *Revelation 14* and *The Mighty Angel*, TXC 2D215/The Branch Publications.
50. *OM* 363.
51. *OM* 360.
52. TXC 2D215/Roden MS.
53. Ibid.
54. TXC 2 D215/Tom Street (this file contains a number of documents relating to the Mt. Carmel property from 1962 until its eventual sale in 1973).
55. A copy of this document is held in the TXC 2D212/3.
56. A photograph giving some indication of what Mt. Carmel would have looked like around this date is printed as plate four in this book.
57. 'Calling all Davidians, Adventists and Reformers', unpublished typescript, 10 Mar. 1965. TXC 2D212/15.
58. *Waco Tribune-Herald*, November 1965 (day is unclear); copy TXC 2D212/24.
59. Letter of Ben and Lois Roden to Tom Street, 11 Sept. 1965; TXC 2D215/Tom Street.
60. *Mad Man in Waco*, 57.
61. Letter of Ben and Lois Roden to Tom Street, 11 Sept. 1965; TXC 2D215/Tom Street.
62. Some of the documentation has survived. It is now held in TXC, Mark Swett Collection/Roden 1.
63. *The Waco Times-Herald*, 12 Nov. 1965 (TXC 2D212/24).
64. Such arrangements were confirmed by Clive Doyle (interview, Nov. 2002, Waco, Texas). Some ill feeling on the issue was still evident. According to Doyle, 'we had to buy the property from ourselves'.
65. The receiver's deed has survived. A copy is held in the TXC 2D215/Tom Street.
66. *Mad Man in Waco*, 58.

67. *The Pentecost: What Is It?* (1973), 12–13; the date is also given in a letter Roden wrote on 2 Feb. 1978. The letter in TXC has been stamped 'copy', and the name of the person to whom it was addressed is omitted (TXC, Mark Swett Collection/ Roden 1).

68. Many of these are found in TXC 2D215. They include various volumes and numbers of *Branch Sabbath School Lessons* (n.d.); *The Man on the White Horse* (1965); *God's Holy Feasts* (1965); *The Flying Scroll: Zechariah 5* (1969); *The Leviticus of The Davidian Seventh-day Adventists: Branch Supplement* (1972); *Festival of the Purim* (1973); *The Pentecost* (1973); *The Daily: Part 1* (1976) and *The Daily: Part 2* (1978); *Tyre and Zidon* (reprint 1979); and several one-page evangelistic tracts. Unpublished at the time of writing, two separate sequences of seven letters are of prime importance to understanding Roden's theology. These are the *Seven Letters* to which extensive reference has already been made above, and *Seven Letters to Elder R.R. Figuhr* (originally written between Sept. 1956 and Feb. 1957; Waco: The Universal Publishing Association, 1976). Also of interest is a substantial sequence of letters from Roden, mostly to Mr and Mrs Bunds in California, dated 1970–1978 (Mark Swett Collection/Roden 1). There is little of real substance in these, but they give an interesting insight into the daily concerns of the movement under Ben's leadership. It is evident in the letters that the Bunds were supporting the work in a financial way, quite generously. Their support for the Branch Davidian cause would continue—later they purchased a house in California for Koresh.

69. See the letter of George Roden published in *Waco Tribune-Herald*, 13 Dec. 1978, where George explained how the size of a cubit was revealed by God to his father, who in turn passed the information on to him (copy in TXC 2D212/24).

70. TXC 2D212/23 has rather poor photocopies of the photographs.

71. Roden, *Deliverance In Mount Zion and in Jerusalem and in the Remnant: Whom the Lord Shall Call* (1977), 4.

72. Letter entitled 'The Atonement Day', 27 Sept. 1962. TXC 2D215.

73. Obituary.

74. See letter to Mr and Mrs Bunds, 20 June 1974 (TXC, Mark Swett Collection/ Roden 1).

75. These details are found in the obituary. The information on the Temple is given also by George Roden in the *Waco Tribune-Herald*, letter of 13 Dec. 1978. TXC 2D212/24.

76. According to Adair, who knew the Rodens well, it was really only George who accepted his father's beliefs; Adair, 'Interviews', 122.

77. Some evidence to this effect can be seen in Roden's letters. For example in a letter dated 12 Jan. 1976 he tells Mr and Mrs Bunds of several recent successes. Ben and Lois have been touring in the West for three months (mostly in Southern California) and have 'enjoyed meeting with many open-minded Seventh-day Adventists and Davidians'. Ben is pleased to report 'that there is a growing number of souls who desire to investigate The Branch for themselves'. A 'Jewish minister' is also interested in Roden's work on the feasts, while there have also

been some callers at Mt. Carmel. A 'Czechoslovakian Adventist brother' has been reading some of Roden's work in German translation, while a request has come in from Africa (no more precise details are given) for 400 copies of a recent issue of the Branch Sabbath School lessons. In another letter (21 Feb. 1975), Roden referred to a long-distance telephone call he has taken from a Seventh-day Adventist woman requesting 200 copies of a recent Roden publication. (Both letters are in TXC, Mark Swett Collection/Roden 1).

7

'The Branch He' (cf. Isaiah 11.1): Ben Roden and the Theology of Branch Davidianism

In the previous chapter it was necessary to refer to aspects of Ben Roden's system of belief. As we have seen, he was a man with a real sense of his own importance in God's plan for the world. It was his task to gather the 144,000 and prepare them for the kingdom. He was now God's vicegerent on earth and would soon be installed as the antitypical King David in literal Israel.

Despite such breathtaking claims (including it seems one to the effect that he would never die)[1] and the really quite exceptional determination that he could at times exhibit, there is some support for the view put forward by the author of his obituary that he was 'a quiet, unobtrusive, humble man'. Such evidence comes principally in the form of two surviving recordings of his teachings.[2] On these he comes across as remarkably quietly spoken and, in contrast to tapes of his wife, and even more so of David Koresh and Steven Schneider, as one whose style of teaching was anything but aggressive. The letters to Mr and Mrs Bunds, too, suggest that he could have a gentle, pastoral style in dealing with his followers.[3] The same disposition was not shown, however, towards those who rejected his message. Again the letters are helpful; when writing to the officers of the SDA Church he could be sharp and his tone hostile.[4] Catholics also came in for sharp attack.[5]

The one thing Roden did not lack was theological conviction, and in this chapter some of what he had to say regarding God and God's plans for the world will be outlined. The theology is not easy to grasp. Like Houteff, he was given in his writings to making extensive use of biblical quotations (and indeed quotations from the works of Houteff and White) without necessarily providing an analysis of how those quotations should, in his view, be understood. Nevertheless, as with the theology of Koresh, if one puts in the necessary mental energy it is possible at least to grasp the outline of what Roden had to say.

His starting point was his belief that God had called him as a prophet and given him the task of leading the remnant people into the kingdom.[6] Typically in the movement, while Roden did not shrink from claiming that God had revealed this to him directly (we may recall the story of the audible voice that came to him beneath a car), he worked out and defended the claim on the basis of the biblical text, with commentary passages from Houteff and White. An outline of Roden's thinking on this point is found in the letters to Florence Houteff discussed briefly in the preceding chapter. The rest of his writing allows some flesh to be put on those skeletal bones.

In essence what Roden argued was that the Old Testament account of the establishment of the people of God, their going into slavery in Egypt, their exodus, and the emergence of the kingdom of David, was all a type of the experience of the people of God in the latter days. Just as God called Abraham to be the (literal) father of the Jews, so God called Luther to be the (spiritual) father of his latter-day people.[7] (The anti-Catholicism is again obvious here). Roden dated this call of Luther to 1500 when he 'began the study of the Bible'.[8] In type, said Roden, it was 430 years from Abraham to Moses (the figure is presumably taken from Gal. 3.17, though he cited Ezek. 4 and Gen. 15.13)[9] and it was Moses who 'led ancient Israel under the *first* section of her deliverance'.[10] So too in antitype, for it was 430 years from Luther to the antitypical Moses, Victor Houteff, who in 1930 began the process of delivering the people of God from the bondage into which they had fallen. However, Roden was at pains to point out that it was not Moses but Joshua who eventually led the people into the promised land. Moses himself, though he began the process of liberation, did not live to see that process through. 'Joshua, not Moses, is the leader of the *second* section, the one that brings purification as Joshua, the type, did anciently'.[11] So too, in antitype, an antitypical Joshua had to come to complete the work of antitypical Moses—Roden himself. He would complete the work Houteff had begun.[12] It was hence important to Roden that just as Houteff had begun to announce his preparatory message in 1930, 430 years after Luther 'found' the Bible, so Roden's message began in 1955, 430 years after another key event in the life of Luther, that showed just how far from the Roman Catholic Church he had come: his marriage.[13]

According to Roden, then, 1955 saw the beginning of the work of the last messenger. The message to be delivered was multifaceted, but at its heart was a surprising claim: Jesus had changed his name to 'Branch'. His followers were therefore to change their name also. No longer should the remnant be called 'Christians' or 'Seventh-day Adventists'.[14] or even the 'Davidian Seventh-day Adventists', but rather 'The Branch'. Of particular importance to Roden was Revelation 3.12:

Him that overcometh will I make a pillar in the temple of my God, and he shall go no more out: and I will write upon him the name of my God, and the name of the city of my God, which is new Jerusalem, which cometh down out of heaven from my God: and I will write upon him my new name.

The change of name was hence of eschatological significance.[15] Important also was Isaiah 62.2: 'And the Gentiles shall see thy righteousness, and all kings thy glory: and thou shalt be called by a new name, which the mouth of the Lord shall name'. The 144,000 on Mt. Zion, then, would have a new name, and according to Roden that new name was 'Branch'. Part of the work of the last messenger was to reveal this new name, and this he did on 10 October 1955 when he (Roden) visited Mt. Carmel to let the inhabitants have the news. The revelation of Jesus's new name was the means by which God thrust the sickle into his remnant community and began to separate the wheat from the tares.[16]

The title 'Branch' is not as odd as it might at first sound to an ear unattuned to the echo of biblical references. There are several to be considered, and Roden spotted them all. Chief is Jeremiah 23.5 (cf. Jer. 33.15):

Behold, the days come, saith the Lord, that I will raise unto David a righteous Branch, and a King shall reign and prosper, and shall execute judgment and justice in the earth. In his days Judah shall be saved, and Israel shall dwell safely: and this is his name whereby she[17] shall be called, THE LORD OUR RIGHTEOUSNESS.

Roden argued that this text spoke of the end time and of two persons—'The Branch', the son of David, Christ, and 'a King' who would reign and prosper. The king in question was the antitypical King David, who would rule visibly in the kingdom as the 'under-leader' of The Branch.[18]

Also very important to Roden was Isaiah 11.1: 'And there shall come forth a rod out of the stem of Jesse, and a Branch shall grow out of his roots'; as with Jeremiah 23.5, the capitalization of 'Branch' is in the King James Version of the Bible (KJV). Roden argued that this had both typical and antitypical significance. In type the verse indicated that out of Jesse would come two rulers: King David and Christ. (Roden is working here with the view that Jesse was the father of David and also 'father' of Christ—cf. Matt. 1.6, 16). One was political, the other spiritual. David, 'the Rod', would rule over literal Israel and Christ (here called 'Branch') would rule over spiritual Israel. The process of founding the kingdom of God, then, began with Jesse, who fathered both the political and the spiritual ruler.

But Jesse was also, said Roden, a type of Seventh-day Adventism, in the sense that the work of bringing God's kingdom begins with the raising up of the SDA Church. Out of that foundation comes 'the Rod' (that is, the Shepherd's Rod movement) and out of that comes also 'the Branch' movement.[19] This is not Roden at his exegetical best, perhaps, but one can see at least how this part of his argument is developed.[20]

Other passages to which Roden drew attention included Zechariah 3.8 and Zechariah 6.12:

Hear now, O Joshua the high priest, thou, and thy fellows that sit before thee: for they are men wondered at: for, behold, I will bring forth my servant the Branch.

And speak unto him, saying, Thus speaketh the Lord of hosts, saying, Behold the man whose name is The Branch; and he shall grow up out of his place, and he shall build the temple of the Lord.

Again Roden saw these verses as referring to the end time. 'My servant the Branch' in the first text is a reference to Christ. However, 'the man whose name is The Branch' in the second is a reference both to Christ and to Roden himself, who, as one who had accepted the new name of Christ, also carried the name 'Branch' (just as 'Christians' carry the name of Christ). It was he who, directed by 'The Branch', would build the temple of the Lord.

By bringing these passages together Roden made his case that the Bible speaks of a time when a new name will be given to the people of God, and it will be the new name of Christ (Rev. 3.12 is really the lynchpin here). That new name would be revealed in due course and the message of it given to the people. That new name was 'Branch' or 'The Branch', a name or title used in several passages in the Old Testament to refer to the expected Messiah, the son of David.

The adoption of this name gives an indication of Roden's understanding of his own work and the importance of what he had been called to do. It gave a sense of eschatological urgency to the community, and was used by the members of that community to refer to themselves and to one another. Hence on surviving audio tapes both Lois Roden and Koresh can be heard using the term 'Branches' to refer to those to whom they were delivering a Bible study (rather as any Christian preacher might refer to the members of the congregation as 'Christians'). There is even some evidence to suggest that 'Branch' became used in the community in a similar way to the use of 'brother' or 'sister' by the Davidians, and indeed in many other Christian communities today.[21]

Building upon this Roden developed the view that acceptance of the Branch name was part of the process by which those destined for the kingdom could be 'sealed'. The notion of a sealing of the people of God is found within mainstream Seventh-day Adventism and also in the work of Houteff. In Seventh-day Adventism the seal of the living God referred to in Revelation 7.2 is said to be the observance of the seventh-day Sabbath; Houteff had also talked about the sealing work, linking it specifically to the mark made by the man with the inkhorn in Ezekiel 9.2, 3, and 11. Roden continued this line of thought, and identified three seals. The first had indeed come through the ministry of the SDA Church and its message of the Sabbath. Similarly, the second seal had been brought by Houteff—it was the message of the kingdom. The third seal, however, had become available, said Roden, only from the time of his own work. It was the seal of the 'new name' of Christ: 'the Branch'. The members of the Sabbath keeping, kingdom seeking remnant under Roden were sealed with this final seal. They accepted the new name of Christ and since they were his were also known by it. They were 'Branches' of Christ, 'the Branch'.[22]

As the last prophet, the antitypical Joshua—the one who would reveal the new name of Christ, rebuild the temple, and rule over the people as Christ's vicegerent—it is unsurprising that Roden saw himself clearly predicted in scripture and not just in the all important system of types and antitypes. Other passages, he said, pointed to him in no uncertain terms (Koresh would make the same uncompromising claim regarding his own prophetic role). Very important to Roden was Revelation 14. Seventh-day Adventists have long proclaimed that this chapter gives a summary of the work the remnant have to do on the earth, and the Church places great stress on the three angels' messages contained in it (Rev. 14.6–12 are in view). Roden, however, argued that these messages, so central to SDA eschatology, were only part of the whole, for in Revelation 14, he noted, there were not three angels, but five.[23] The first three of these angels (and their messages) are understood in a way substantially similar to that of Seventh-day Adventism. The first angel ('fear God, and give glory to him; for the hour of his judgment is come: and worship him that made heaven, and earth, and the sea, and the fountains of waters') warns that the time of God's judgment has come. Roden was insistent that this referred only to the first phase of the judgment—the judgment of those who had already died. The second message ('Babylon is fallen, is fallen, that great city, because she made all nations drink of the wine of the wrath of her fornication') calls for the gathering of God's people and their departure from fallen 'Babylon'. Roden agreed that this was a call to the people of God to come out of the apostate Churches and begin to form a new community of the faithful. Roden insisted that Miller had both these messages, a view in which he differed from mainstream Seventh-day Adventism. They were not the preserve of the post-disappointment SDA Church, though that Church is the end product of the call to 'come out of her my people'. The message of the third angel, however, is that of the Sabbath truth and the Sunday lie. This is the work of the Seventh-day Adventists, for it is they who, through Mrs White, have been proclaiming it since 1844.[24]

Thus far Roden was on relatively familiar SDA ground, though his insistence that it was Miller and not the SDA Church who first proclaimed the messages of angels one and two is something of a deviation. From this point on, however, Roden went his own way. In particular, he argued that the first three angels' messages came during the time of the judgment of the dead, but that the final two will come during the judgment of the living.

This division of time into the 'judgment of the dead' and the 'judgment of the living' is central to Roden's scheme and needs proper explanation at this point. It reflects broader SDA eschatology, though Roden introduced some new elements into it. The starting point is the SDA view that when Christ ascended into heaven he entered into the heavenly sanctuary. However, on 22 October 1844, so the argument runs, Christ's ministry in that heavenly sanctuary entered into a new and important phase, when he moved from the 'Holy Place' into the 'Most Holy Place' there to begin the work of judgment. The SDA Church was raised up to proclaim this message that the hour of judgment had come (cf. Rev. 14.7). Since then, the 'investigative' judgment has been taking place in the holy of holies. In SDA theology this investigative judgment is of one class of persons only—those who have professed faith in God. During the investigative judgment these claims are examined to see if profession and life are in agreement. (This is not a works' righteousness, though one could be forgiven for thinking that it comes close to it, and SDA theologians are sometimes hard pressed to explain how the 'imputed' and 'imparted' righteousness of Christ are mediated to the sinner solely on the basis of grace.) The cases of those who have not professed faith in God are not examined at this juncture, since the verdict is in any case not in doubt, though according to SDA theology all of the books will be open to view during the millennial period and all will be satisfied that God has in every single case acted in a fair and righteous way.

The investigative judgment begins with those who have died. Once all those cases have been heard, it turns to consider those of the living. This apparently obscure detail is in fact central to Roden's sense of call. At the close of this investigative judgment, when the cases of all professed believers have been heard, both those dead and those still alive, probation closes and the time of trouble begins. No further cases are heard after that event. Obviously, then, at some point between Christ's entry into the Holy Place in 1844 and this final close of probation a turning point must come. The cases of all those that have died will have been heard and it will be time to begin the judgment of the living. Just when that will be (or was) is unknown in mainstream SDA theology.[25] Roden, however, was much more confident. The judgment of the living was to begin in the autumn of 1964.[26]

Roden's logic here is pretty plain: the first three angels' messages go out during the judgment of the dead and are for the whole world. The last two angels' messages go out during the time of the judgment of the living and are for the SDA Church (the remnant) only. Roden then argued that the statement 'as it was in the days of Noe, so shall it be also in the days of the Son of Man' (Luke 17.26) means that the period of warning given to Noah's generation and to this one will be the same. Thus the message would cease to go to the world and start going to the Church after the same period. In the former case it was 120 years;[27] add 120 to 1844 and one arrives at 1964. 'Just what is to happen this Autumn, the end of the 120 years since the Atonement 1844', said Roden, 'we will not say'. He then made a link between the unknown event and the unexpected 'coming' of the Son of man mentioned in Luke 12.39, 40.

This coming is not Christ's coming in the clouds of heaven, for that coming will be *announced* to all the world. His coming as a thief is when our names come up in the judgment of the living (G.C. 483) when 'In the balances of the sanctuary the Seventh-day Adventist church is to be weighed ... For the time has come that judgment must begin at the house of God.' 1 Pet. 4:17[28]

With the call by God of Roden, then, the fourth and fifth angels' messages of Revelation 14 begin to sound. Since 1844 the messages of angels one, two, and three have gone out into the world to call the faithful into either mainstream Adventism or the purer form of it, Davidian Seventh-day Adventism. However, the world has now had its chance and God turns his attention away from that general call to the much more specific work of separating the sheep and goats within the remnant community. It is time for the purification of the people of God. Such a purification did not come with White or with Houteff, whose work it was only to call not to purify. This is not to deny the importance of their work but simply to state that what they accomplished was only preparatory to the fullness of the message that had now come. In fact, drawing on passages from Joel and Deuteronomy, Roden argued that it was Ellen White who brought the former rain and hence sowed the seeds of truth; Victor Houteff brought the latter rain that ripened the crop in preparation for the gathering in of the harvest. Under Roden himself the harvest actually takes place.[29]

In 1964, then, according to Roden, the judgment of the living was to begin. This signalled also the beginning of the purification of God's remnant, for God was no longer gathering the community from which the final remnant would be drawn, but rather was beginning the process of the actual purification of the 144,000 themselves. Hence while the messages of the first three angels have been sounding from 1844 to 1964, the message of the fourth angel begins in that latter year. The message is of the impending harvest.

And I looked, and behold a white cloud, and upon the cloud one sat like unto the Son of man, having on his head a golden crown, and in his hand a sharp sickle. And another angel came out of the temple, crying with a loud voice to him that sat on the cloud, Thrust in thy sickle, and reap: for the time is come for thee to reap; for the harvest of the earth is ripe. (Rev. 14.14–15.)

After quoting these verses, Roden commented:

The Fourth Angel's message is the same as the one bound in the Euphrates (Babylon) and is loosed *at a month*, (Rev 9:14, 15), it announces the purification of the church and setting up of the Kingdom of God—the Ark of safety for God's people as it was in Noah's day (Luke 17:26). A crown denotes a king and a kingdom and the sickle suggests a harvest—judgment.[30]

Roden saw this period in the history of salvation as the one during which the 144,000 would be gathered. This is not the time of slaughter—on that Roden is very plain and seemed particularly concerned to make the point. The slaughter would come only after the 144,000 had been called out and sealed.[31] These 144,000 were to come from two sources: the Seventh-day Adventists and the Davidian Seventh-day Adventists. The logic is that others must therefore be called, since their ears are stopped and their time is not yet. Like Koresh, who would also have to find a way around this part of the tradition, Roden seems not to have turned away potential converts who had not previously been Seventh-day Adventists or Davidian Seventh-day Adventists. In the letters to Mr and Mrs Bunds one occasionally finds references to people who are not Seventh-day Adventists but are being encouraged in their studies of Branch materials.

Roden's eschatology then reverts to a fairly standard Davidian form. Once the 144,000, the 'first fruits' of the great harvest, have been gathered, the rest of the SDA Church is (literally) slaughtered.[32] The 'kingdom' is now set up in Jerusalem and the saints are given the Holy Spirit at the antitypical Pentecost which enables them to take the message to the rest of the world. Roden links this to the 'Loud Cry' of Revelation 18.1ff.[33] As with Houteff's theology, Roden argued that the prophecies in the Old Testament that refer to the flocking of the Gentiles to the mountain of the Lord and the restoration of the kingdom of David found fulfilment in his own ministry. First he must call the 144,000, then they in turn (once the Church had been cleansed) would call the great multitude.

In explaining some of the detail of this scheme, Roden developed an argument based upon Ezekiel 37. That chapter, he argued, speaks of his own work in uniting the two 'kingdoms' of latter-day Israel and Judah. This is a type (and Roden, like Houteff, held that where there is no type there is no truth).[34] The latter-day kingdom of Judah is made up of the combined faithful from the SDA and Davidian traditions that come together in the Branch movement. These are the 144,000 so long at the centre of Houteff's concern. The latter-day Israel, however, are the people of God 'in the world'.

This is the great multitude that will come in once the kingdom has been established and the cleansing of the SDA Church has been done. Roden thought that this coming together of the 144,000 and the great multitude was symbolized in Ezekiel 37. Here, Roden noted, God tells the prophet to take two sticks in one hand, symbolizing how the two are reunited in the kingdom of the latter days. So too the two groups that make up the people of God will be reunited.

And say unto them, Thus saith the Lord God; Behold, I will take the children of Israel from among the heathen, whither they be gone, and will gather them on every side, and bring them into their own land: And I will make them one nation in the land upon the mountains of Israel; and one king shall be king to them all: and they shall be no more two nations, neither shall they be divided into two kingdoms any more at all... And David my servant shall be king over them; and they all shall have one shepherd: they shall also walk in my judgments, and observe my statutes, and do them (Ezek. 37.21–4).

References to this joining of the 'two sticks' (two classes of the saved) appear frequently in Roden's work, and it is plain that this chapter from Ezekiel was important to him. The title makes clear that he equated the work of joining the two sticks (kingdoms) with the opening of the first seal of Revelation 6.2.

Such, then, is an outline of Roden's thinking with regard to the process by which God's truth is brought to the world. He kept as close to the tradition as possible while finding a place for himself in the sequence of messengers. By this means he was able to accomplish a number of things. It was important, for example, that he did not alienate the existing members of the group by denying the centrality of those that they had already accepted as messengers of God (White and Houteff). By putting himself alongside these messengers he shared some of the esteem and respect in which they were already held, at the same time gaining some exegetical mastery over them. By defining himself as the last in a sequence he had the benefit not only of direct communication with God, but also of hindsight. Koresh would later go well beyond this and say in effect that all those who came before him were at best only hints of the real truth.

There can be little doubt that the heart of Roden's message was eschatological, and in his work the fundamental concerns of Houteff were continued. The role of the physical land of Israel was heightened even further in Roden's thinking while the role of the Jews (including himself of course) was maintained. However, while he did place great emphasis upon what, in his view, was soon to happen, he was also much concerned with the question of how the members of the eschatological community were to live as they prepared themselves for entry into the kingdom and the giving of the loud cry. Such concerns are common to eschatologically focused communities, but the detail of what Roden had to say on this issue is distinctive. He argued that the community was to live in accordance with the vision for it outlined in Ezekiel 37. In part this meant obeying God's statutes, for verse 24 of that chapter reads, 'And David my servant shall be king over them; and they all shall have one shepherd: they shall also walk in my judgments, and observe my statutes, and do them.' For Roden this included keeping God's feast days.[35]

Again Roden was able to appeal to his SDA and Davidian Seventh-day Adventist target group. Seventh-day Adventists have placed great stress upon the observance of the law; not just the 'new' law to love God and love your neighbour as yourself (cf. Matt. 22.36–40) but substantial parts of the Old Testament as well. The most obvious case is the observance of the Ten Commandments. Seventh-day Adventists argue that all of these, including the fourth, are still in force. But they go further than this, and also observe the food laws and abstain from unclean meats. They do not, however, practise circumcision or observe festivals such as Passover, Tabernacles, or Pentecost. In order to explain some of these inconsistencies the SDA Church appeals to a distinction between the 'moral' and the 'ceremonial' law; actually this is not too far from some of what is said by Paul and in the deutero-Pauline tradition (especially Colossians).

Roden, however, would have none of that. God had told his people to observe certain feasts, and it was as much incumbent upon them to do so now as it had been at any time in the past. The 'ceremonial' as well as the 'moral' law was, for him, an expression of the unchanging will of God and God's people must hence observe it. Only what he called the 'sacrificial' law had now passed, for in Christ that to which the sacrificial system had pointed had come. Christians need not, therefore, sacrifice animals. What Roden called the ceremonial law, however, was still in force. In fact the observance of this part of the law was, in his view, so important that it marked out the true remnant community and distinguished its members from those who only pretended to be so. It was nothing short of the 'testimony of Jesus' (cf. Rev. 19.10), the visible mark of the remnant.[36]

Returning to the all-important Revelation 14, Roden argued that the work of the final angel is to restore the proper observance of the feasts. Indeed he summed up the work of that being in the words, 'The Feast Laws in their true setting is the message of the 5th angel of Rev. 14:16, 17'.[37] He had a great deal more to say on this. Just as the true Sabbath was replaced in Christendom by the counterfeit Sunday, so too the biblical feast of Passover was replaced by Easter and, as the remnant in its SDA form had proclaimed the true Sabbath in these latter days, so the Branch now proclaimed the true Passover.

Pagan feasts (worshipping the created) have been substituted for God's Feast Days which point to the Creator of All things—Sunday, in honor of the Sun instead of the seventh-day Sabbath honoring the creator; Easter, honoring the Goddess of Spring instead of Passover which points to the sacrifice of the Lamb of God—all these are designed to take away the knowledge of creation and the redemption of man through the shed blood of the Son of God.[38]

This emphasis upon the way in which, in Roden's view, Passover points to the sacrifice of Christ is important to his understanding of the feast. He quoted with evident great approval some words of Ellen White to the same effect: 'The Passover was to be both *commemorative and typical*, not only pointing back to the deliverance from Egypt, but *forward* to the greater deliverance which Christ was to accomplish in freeing his people from the bondage of sin.'[39] Roden then went on to argue that the antitypical Passover is the Lord's Supper, which points forward to the deliverance of the people by The Branch. But he also took the view that (just as mainstream Seventh-day Adventism has always argued with respect to the Sabbath) it is not what you do but when you do it that is important. In a sense keeping the Sunday is really of no value, though God will respect a person's faithfulness so long as they are in ignorance. The true Sabbath, however, is from sundown on Friday to sundown on Saturday and getting the timing right is important. The hours are almost sacramental. They are qualitatively different to other hours in the week. Similarly Roden argued that the Passover should be kept according to the Jewish calendar, and the Lord's Supper should hence be celebrated but once a year, at Passover. To celebrate it at any other time is like celebrating God's resting from his work of creation on the first rather than the seventh day of the week.[40] Location in the proper time is as important as location in the proper place, and the proper time for the celebration of this feast is from the going down of the sun on the fourteenth day of the first month (cf. Ezek. 45.12), with the whole of the feast lasting a full seven days. During this time unleavened bread must be eaten.[41]

Roden is actually not too far here from the views of a number of other Christians who celebrate the Lord's Supper only once a year around Passover time. The Jehovah's Witnesses are an obvious example (though they tie it in with Easter rather than Passover and hold the service on the evening of Maundy Thursday). Such practice reflects the widespread view that Passover was a foreshadowing of the death of Christ and the new 'Exodus' (from sin) that the people of God can experience through that death. However, this is not the end of Roden's thinking. He also argued that the events of the first Passover were a type of things to come. Hence, the smiting of the firstborn in Egypt was a type of the events of Ezekiel 9 when God would smite those of antitypical Egypt, the unrepentant in the SDA Church. 'Passover in Egypt and the smiting of the first born is typical of the church *at the present time*: going out of Egypt—worldliness, purification, separation of the tares from the wheat, Ezek. 9 slaying.'[42] In Roden's view the feast of Passover is to be kept in conjunction with the wave-sheaf ceremony. Roden was here picking up the words of Levitius 23.9–12, which instructs the people to wave a sheaf of grain before the Lord as a sign of the first fruits of the harvest. The waving of the sheaf signified that the harvest was God's and the ceremony of the wave-sheaf was to take place, said Roden (using Ellen White for support), before the harvest itself began.[43]

True to form Roden, citing Houteff, saw all this as having antitypical significance. In the Davidian scheme of things two distinct harvests were anticipated: the harvest of the 144,000 and that of the great multitude. The harvest of the 144,000 was hence the harvest of the first fruits while the harvest of the great multitude would be a general harvest. Before the harvest of the first fruits could begin, however, there would have to be a preliminary gathering in of the wave-sheaf, the initial offering to be presented before the Lord in recognition that the harvest of the first fruits was his. The Branch Davidians under Roden, who numbered a good deal fewer than 144,000, were, he said, the antitypical wave-sheaf. This was a smart move. It gave the community a real sense of their own importance and effectively protected them from the worrying thought that they must be failing since their numbers were so few. It mattered not that the group did not (yet) number 144,000; their corporate importance in the sight of God was not shackled to the attainment of that number. They were already collectively important in God's sight since they were the wave-sheaf offering, a sign of what was to come but also important in its own right. Roden helped to give focus to this not only by coming up with a theological scheme that would support it, but also by introducing a ceremony of the wave-sheaf into the life of the community. In a densely packed (and awkwardly punctuated) paragraph Roden wrote:

Conclusively, then, since the wave-sheaf is barley, the first ripe grain, *first* of the first fruits (Ex, 23:19), and is offered at Passover which is at the *beginning* of the harvest of the first fruits; and since these *harvest rites are a figure of soul harvests*; and also since those that arose with Christ became a *typical* living wave-sheaf presented as trophies before the Father in heaven (3Tr 79:2); we conclude that since the mediatorial-judicial throne of Ezekiel 1 extends to the earthly sanctuary (church) (3Tr 46–47) *there must be an antitypical living wave-sheaf offered before God's traveling throne on earth at that time* (Passover).[44]

This concept of the wave-sheaf became important in Roden's Branch movement. One finds frequent reference to it in the works of Lois Roden[45] and in the teachings of Koresh and Schneider.

One needs to tread very carefully here. However, it would be remiss not to draw attention to the possibility (and perhaps that is all it is) that this emphasis upon the communal importance of the Branch Davidian community and their status as a wave-sheaf/wave 'offering' to be waved before the Lord at Passover time might in some way have been important in the context of the Waco fire. Here was a community that expected to be offered as a 'wave-sheaf' to the Lord ahead of the first harvest. Whether this actually filtered down to the rank and file of Koresh's Mt. Carmel must be questionable, but it cannot be ruled out altogether. Indeed, we do know that Koresh made reference to the community being offered as a 'wave sheaf' a week or so before the fire, and did so as in the context of anticipated communal death.[46]

The two other feasts to which Roden gave significant attention were Pentecost and Tabernacles, and as with Passover he invested them with great antitypical importance.

Roden associated the feast of Pentecost (feast of weeks) with the ceremony of the wave-loaves (cf. Exod. 34.22; Lev. 23.27), arguing that Pentecost marked the end of the first fruits harvest and that the wave-loaves that were offered to the Lord at the end of this harvest were a type of the first fruits of the eschatological harvest, that is, the community of the 144,000. However, the importance of Pentecost goes deeper still, for in the New Testament Pentecost was the point at which God poured out a measure of his Spirit upon the disciples so that they could begin the work of bringing in the harvest. Some 3,000 persons were added to the number of believers on that one day (Acts 2.41). Roden followed all this through. On the antitypical Pentecost God would send the fullness of his Spirit so that the relatively small band of believers (the 144,000) could bring in the rest of the world (the great multitude—the antitypical equivalent of the 3,000 of Acts 2.41).[47]

There is one further aspect to Roden's thinking on Pentecost that needs mention here. It was noted above that on 14 June 1970 Roden was crowned 'Vicegerent of the Most High God'. The day chosen was no coincidence. In 1970, it was the feast of Pentecost. The General Conference of Seventh-day Adventists had that same day called for another 'Pentecost', by which they meant a further outpouring of the Holy Spirit upon God's people that would enable them to finish the task of taking the message to the world. Roden, however, had a rather different view of things. What was really important about the first Christian Pentecost, he argued, was not what had happened on earth, but what had happened in heaven. In fact what had happened on earth (the giving of the Spirit to the disciples) was a result of what had happened in heaven, even if those celestial events had been hidden from mortal view. Roden quoted Ellen White on the issue. 'But after Christ's ascension His enthronement in His mediatorial kingdom was signalized by the outpouring of the Holy Spirit. On the day of Pentecost the Spirit was given'.[48] The chain of events was hence thus: Christ ascended into heaven, Christ was enthroned there as 'king', as a result of this the Spirit was given to the disciples to enable them to spread the message of Christ's kingdom. And all of this would have an eschatological counterpart that would contain the same elements: a coronation, an outpouring of the Spirit and the gathering in of the faithful. The coronation was that of Roden himself, who was now God's ruler on earth who 'received both the civil and religious crown'.[49] Christ's 'mediatorial' kingdom had become his literal kingdom as a theocracy had been set up on earth with Christ ruling through his 'under-ruler' or 'vicegerent' Ben Roden. Roden's coronation must be seen in this context.

The celebration of Pentecost helped the community keep all this in view. It reminded them of the time when the wave-loaves would be offered (that is the time when the first-fruit harvest of the 144,000 would be complete) and also of the great outpouring of the Spirit that would empower them to issue the loud cry to the nations of the world. It reminded them also that Christ's kingdom was coming. Indeed, the visible king of it had already been enthroned so the fullness of it could not be too far distant.

Finally there was Tabernacles. This was the feast that marked the end of the second harvest. The antitypical second harvest was the harvest of the nations of the world, to be accomplished through the giving of the loud cry. Roden went through the same steps as with Passover and Pentecost in arguing that Tabernacles, too, is a feast of the Lord and as such must be kept by those who wish to abide by the Lord's statutes (Ezek. 37.24). It reminded the community of the wilderness experience while at the same time pointing towards eventual deliverance.

The community under Roden was, then, an expectant community. For them the end was very close. As a means by which the mission of the Branch community could be kept constantly in mind, Roden reintroduced the observance of Passover (together with the ceremony of the wave-sheaf), Pentecost (with the ceremony of the wave-loaves), and Tabernacles. While even within the Branch community the importance of these feasts was not confined to eschatological matters, it was the work of harvesting the righteous that, for the Branch, really pulled the observance of the three feasts together. Passover reminded them of their deliverance from bondage and entry into the promised land. The associated ceremony of the wave-sheaf gave clear focus to their own role and status as, in Roden's words 'the first of the first fruits'. Pentecost reminded them of the time when the Spirit of God would be given to them to enable them to issue the loud cry, and the ceremony of the wave-loaves impressed upon them the goal that was in view: the gathering in of the 144,000. Tabernacles reminded them of the days when the second harvest would be complete and the great multitude gathered in. All gave confidence and must surely have been in their minds as they said, with the rest of Christendom but with a different focus, 'thy kingdom come'.

But the feasts were not just a means of teaching. Time and time again Roden emphasized that these feasts were instituted by God and that he expected his end-time community to keep them. The Passover seems to have particular significance in this regard since, said Roden, during the message of Sr White and Br Houteff no particular instruction seems to have been given with regard to the observance of the Lord's Supper. Now, however, such instruction had been given through the Branch message and the remnant knew that it was to be kept but once a year at Pentecost. This was very important to Roden who said that in fact by keeping the feasts, including the participation in the Lord's Supper, the Branch believers were circumventing death. After all, it says quite clearly in Romans 5.12 that 'the soul that sinneth, it shall die', and yet some sinful souls, the 144,000 that will stand on Mt. Zion with the Lamb, will not die. So Roden asked the question, 'What is the law that through faith the condemned sinner may receive everlasting life without passing through the grave?' To which he gave the answer, 'by keeping the feasts'.[50] The re-instituted feasts, especially the Lord's Passover Supper, had the power to cleanse God's people perfectly and save them from the law of sin and death. It was the means by which individuals who would not see death might in the present become pure and ready to enter the kingdom.

The Passover cleansed the church twice before; on that historical night in Egypt and again on that eventful night in Jerusalem when Judas separated himself from the church. The Lord's Passover Supper is again for the third and last time separating the wheat from the tares. Let all who will, be purified by the cleansing blood of the Passover Lamb.[51]

It is apparent, then, that Roden had some very distinctive views. He had a clear sense of his own importance and was willing to act upon it (witness his coronation). His message, as always in this tradition, was tied to the biblical text and what he had to say gave focus to the community he now led. Complexity ought not to be confused with woolliness. Roden was absolutely clear on his task and the status of the community. Here was a gathered remnant who now had been sealed with the new name of Christ (The Branch) and who were living in a potential state of perfection so long as they kept the feast laws. They might not be 144,000 in number, but that too could be explained. They were the 'wave sheaf' of the harvest, the first offering to God. As such they could be assured of his favour, so long, that is, as they kept the faith. Despite his expectations, Ben Roden was not to see the programme through. He died in October 1978. However, already standing in the wings as the next potential leader was an exceptionally impressive woman: Ben's wife, Lois.

NOTES

1. Adair, 'Interviews', 38, stated that one day while he was working in Waco, Ben Roden came straight up to him and said that he (Roden) was Elijah and would never die.
2. The two recordings are, 'The Assyrian' (parts one and two) and 'The Time of the Kingdom' (parts one and two). Both recordings, together with that of Roden's funeral, are preserved on one CD in TXC, Mark Swett Collection, Video and CD Box. (At the time of writing these materials had not been formally catalogued at Baylor). The Assyrian tape, a copy of which is on my possession, is dated 13 Aug. 1977.
3. TXC, Mark Swett Collection/Ben Roden, 1.
4. See e.g. the letter dated 2 Feb. 1978 (TXC, Mark Swett Collection/Ben Roden, 1), addressing an unnamed Elder who has apparently raised objections to the keeping of the feasts.
5. Roden's aggressive anti-Catholicism is apparent in much of what he writes; the clearest examples are the pamphlets *We're Fed up with Catholics Crucifying Nixon* (n.d.) and *Vatican Built Watergate Frame-Up* (n.d.).
6. A useful summary of Roden's understanding of his own role in the plans of God can be seen in a document written by Robert W. Olson in May 1967, a copy of which is in my possession. According to Olson, who was at the time attending the SDA church in Waco, some of Roden's followers had several times attended the church, disrupted the Sabbath School class and caused other offence by distributing literature to loyal church members. The document Olson produced is understandably critical, and allowance must be made for that. Nevertheless, some glimpse of Roden's self-understanding can be gleaned from it. In essence Olson said (and then refuted each point) that Roden believed himself to be a prophet who had a particular, indeed exclusive, mission to Seventh-day Adventists. Roden had no concern, said Olson, with the world in general. Olson also confirmed that Roden saw himself as the latter-day Joshua of Zechariah 3, a 'ruler' to lead the faithful to the kingdom in Palestine (he saw Houteff as the latter-day Moses). Olson indicated that Roden put great stress on the fact that in Hebrew, his name means, 'Ruler' and even referred to a statement from Ellen White regarding the coming of such a one, quoting her as saying 'I saw that God would raise up a Joshua that would lead us to the kingdom.' Roden gave a reference to the *Review and Herald*, 29 May 1860, in support of this claim; Olson said that there are no articles by White from 28 Apr. 1859 and 25 June 1861 in the *Review and Herald*. Investigation suggests that Olson was right.

7. Luther was important for Roden, who saw events in Luther's life as points from which to measure other eschatological events. For example, 1530 was the year the wound was inflicted upon the head of the beast by Luther; 430 years later, in 1960, that wound was healed when Kennedy, a Catholic, was elected president of the United States. (See also the MS, 'Revival and Reformation in the Light of the 430 years of Abraham and Ezekiel 4'; TXC, Mark Swett Collection/Ben Roden, 1, and the chart in the same location).

8. *The Man on the White Horse: Joining the Two Sticks* (1965), 21. This can also be seen clearly on a chart entitled *The Delivery of the Church from the Wilderness* (n.d.) that carries Roden's name as copyright holder. A copy is located at the Seventh-day Adventist Heritage Center, James White Library, Andrews University, Mich.

9. See e.g. *Seven Letters*, 29.

10. Roden, *Man on the White Horse*, 21.

11. Ibid. 21–2.

12. The view that Roden was the antitypical Joshua and Houteff the antitypical Moses must have been fairly high on the theological agenda of the early Branch Davidians; it is reported in a *Waco News Tribune* report, probably in April 1959. The report indicates that a 'third' splinter group (of the Davidians) known simply as 'the Branch' is 'headed by Benjamin L. Roden of Odessa, a man his followers believe is the modern-day counterpart of the biblical prophet Joshua'. Speaking of Houteff, one of the other Branch members is quoted as saying, 'we believe he was a combination of the modern counterparts of the Biblical prophet Moses ... and Elijah'.

13. Roden, *Seven Letters*, 105–6.

14. Roden, *Man on the White Horse*, 12.

15. Roden also argued that 'Branch' was the name written upon the stones mentioned in Rev. 2.17b 'To him that overcometh will I give to eat of the hidden manna, and will give him a white stone, and in the stone a new name written, which no man knoweth saving he that receiveth it' (*Seven Letters*, 113).

16. Roden, *Seven Letters*, 105. The importance of 10 Oct. 1955 evidently did not diminish with the passing of time. In an undated notebook (probably 1984) David Koresh was later to write that a particular message had come to the church on that date and that this marked 'the date of the beginning of the judgment of the living' (TXC, Mark Swett Collection/David Koresh).

17. The KJV has 'he' at this point, but Roden was insistent that it should be 'she'. The Hebrew text will allow Roden's translation, though if adopted the most natural interpretation would be that the 'she/it' in question was a city (a feminine word in Hebrew). For Roden, however, the 'she' here is a Church, which would carry the name 'The Branch Our Righteousness' (*Man on the White Horse*, 13, 22).

18. Roden, *Man on the White Horse*, 22.

19. Roden evidently even thought that the verse numbering of Isa. 11.1 was important; if one adds '111' to 1844 one arrives at 1955—the very year that the 'branch'

would shoot from the stem! MS study, 'The Branch: Rev. 18.1', TXC, Mark Swett Collection/Ben Roden, 2.

20. Roden, MS study, 'The Family Tree Isaiah 11.1'; TXC, Mark Swett Collection/Ben Roden, 2.

21. The evidence is not strong. In the letters of Roden to Mr and Mrs Bunds, for example, Roden continues to use 'Brother and Sister' rather than 'Branches' as a term expressive of their sense of Christian unity. However, in one much later document (date and origin uncertain, but after the end of the 1993 siege) the author's name is given as 'Branch Bill' (see further in Chapter Fourteen). The document is in TXC, Mark Swett Collection/Nancy and Chip Tatum.

22. There are numerous expressions of this in Roden's writings, e.g. his MSS 'The Family Tree' and 'The Marriage of the King's Son # 1: The Wedding Supper' (22 Feb. 1960); TXC, Mark Swett Collection/Ben Roden, 2.

23. A simple outline of this argument is found in the pamphlet *Can You Count to Five?* (1967).

24. *Revelation 14: The Harvest* (n.d., The Branch of Seventh-day Adventist (*sic*)). The address is given as Box 3088, Odessa, Texas, which indicates that the original publication was before the move to Waco in 1963.

25. This is a rather simplified view of the doctrine of the judgment in Seventh-day Adventism, but is all that is necessary to give the context of what Roden is saying here. See *Seventh-day Adventists Believe*, 312–3 for a rather fuller account.

26. Roden, *The Loud Cry: Rev 18:1* (published privately, 24 May 1964).

27. This is based upon a reading of Gen. 6.3 (cf. White, *Patriarchs and Prophets*, 93).

28. Roden, *The Loud Cry: Rev 18:1*, 4.

29. Roden, *The Pentecost* (1973), 11.

30. Roden, *The Loud Cry: Rev 18:1*, 5.

31. See e.g. *Seven Letters*, 81–2.

32. See e.g. Roden's MS study 'The New Name—Isaiah 62.2'; TXC, Mark Swett Collection/Ben Roden, 2. Here, as elsewhere in his writings, Roden argues that the revelation of Christ's new name comes before the events of Ezekiel 9 but that those who do not accept the new name will be eventually be slaughtered.

33. *The Loud Cry* ends with the words, 'Yours to stand on Mt. Zion with the Lamb, "girt for holy service", prepared for the Loud Cry' (Roden, *The Loud Cry*, 8). See also *The Mighty Angel of Revelation 18.1* (n.d., The Branch of Seventh-day Adventist [*sic*]), where the same points are made though in much less detail, and *The Final Atonement* (1962), which also goes over some of the ground.

34. Roden, *Seven Letters*, 19.

35. Some of this is found in Roden's second and third letters to Florence Houteff and elsewhere in the Roden literary corpus. The most precise formulation of the doctrine is found in *Man on the White Horse*. A summary account of Roden's view on the feasts is found in his publication *God's Holy Feasts: The Unrolling of the Scroll* (1965). The form of this publication used here is the reprint edition published by the Universal Publishing Association in 1974, a copy of which is in my possession. In it Roden went through the six feasts he found in Levitical law

which, he said, it is still God's will that true believers should observe today. As ever a great deal of use is made of typology. The six feasts are Sabbath, Passover, Pentecost, Day of Atonement, Tabernacles, and the Feast of New Moon.

36. Roden, *Man on the White Horse*, 25. The mainstream SDA view is that the 'testimony of Jesus is the Spirit of prophecy' (cf. Rev. 19.10), which in practical terms means the writings of Ellen G. White.
37. Roden, *The Loud Cry*, 6.
38. Roden, MS study 'Our Passover Lamb' (1 Mar. 1964), TXC, Mark Swett Collection/Ben Roden, 1.
39. Ben Roden, MS study 'The Feasts—No. 1' (27 Aug. 1959), ref. TXC, Mark Swett Collection/Ben Roden, 2. The quotation is from Ellen G. White, *Patriarchs and Prophets* (Oakland, Calif.: Pacific Press, c.1890), 277. Roden added the emphasis himself.
40. *The Final Atonement*, 6–7.
41. Roden, MS Study 'The Feasts no. 1'.
42. Ibid.
43. Ibid.
44. Ibid.
45. See e.g. MS letter dated 15 Dec. 1978, headed: 'A Prophetic View of the Wave-Sheaf, Wave-Loaves, Feast of Tabernacles'; another letter (dated 'Passover 1980') is signed by Lois 'sincerely yours to be a living wave-sheaf'; a third (28 Feb. 1984) begins, 'Dear Wave-Sheaf Candidate' (TXC, Mark Swett Collection/Lois Roden).
46. See page (Chapter 15, fos. 517–8)
47. Roden, *Seven Letters*, 86–7.
48. Roden, *The Pentecost: What is It?* (1973), 3.
49. Ibid. 12.
50. Roden, letter 'To Kingdom Bound Saints', TXC, Mark Swett Collection/Ben Roden, 2.
51. Ibid.

8

'The Branch She' (cf. Isaiah 11.1): Lois
Roden, *Shekinah,* and the Struggle for
Leadership

When Ben Roden died in 1978 the movement he had started, the Branch
Davidian Seventh-day Adventists, was in a relatively good position. Together
with Lois he had managed to secure ownership of the Mt. Carmel property.
The movement was, as far as we can tell, fairly stable; publications were in
good shape; and unlike the Davidians under Florence Houteff there was no
deadline for the end of the world. His sons, it is true, were expected to live to
see through the rebuilding of the Temple in Jerusalem, but this was a very
open-ended prophecy that was unlikely to cause a crisis. The question of
leadership ought not to have been a problem either. One prophet, Ben, had
died but there was already another poised to take over the mantle, and she had
been approved (by silence if not in word) by the one just deceased. This was
Ben's wife, Lois,[1] who by the time of his death had been claiming the
prophetic office for a year or more and had already gained a good measure
of acceptance by other members of the community. In reality, however,
the situation was rather more problematic, for while Lois had a clear claim
to the leadership, one major obstacle stood in the way: her son George.

George Roden was not a man to underestimate. Later he would stand for
President of the United States, engage in a gun battle with David Koresh,
invoke God to inflict herpes on a judge, kill the brother of Don Adair with an
axe, and finally (probably not before time) be sent to a mental institution. But
this was all still future. In 1978 he had just one thing on his mind, the
leadership of the Branch Davidians.

George's views on this were plain. As far as he was concerned, his father Ben
had appointed him to the principal role in the rebuilding of the Temple and
had told him that he was, thereby, 'the man whose name is the Branch' (Zech.
6.12: 'Thus speaketh the Lord of hosts, saying, Behold the man whose name is
The Branch; and he shall grow up out of his place, and he shall build the
temple of the Lord'). Accordingly, George was in the habit of signing his
letters 'the Man, the Branch' or 'the man whose name is The Branch'.[2] As the

PLATE 5 George Roden, son of Ben and Lois Roden

one entrusted with such an important task, George reasoned, he must now be the one to lead God's remnant people, the Branch Davidians.

George's mother did not agree, and a family feud was inevitable, though it did not break out immediately. Indeed for the first year or so following Ben's death things at Mt. Carmel remained fairly settled. Lois was now *de facto* the leader and prophet and no serious challenge to her position was made by George or anyone else. Beneath the surface, however, things were not so calm and in 1979 George succeeded in getting a leadership election called, with his mother and himself as the two candidates. Lois won. That ought to have settled it, but George did not bow out so easily. Hence began the long series of legal battles he was to have, first with his mother and then with Koresh.[3]

What happened, in brief, was this. Following Lois's victory in the election and the upholding of the result in a court of law to which George appealed for a ruling, George moved out of Mt. Carmel in August 1979—first to Bellmead, Texas, and later to California.[4] Over the next several years, despite being the subject of a restriction order taken out by his mother,[5] he continued to be a regular visitor to Mt. Carmel and to pursue the issue of who was the rightful leader of the group. As part of this process he began an active writing campaign, sending out in typescript exceptionally direct tracts and letters criticizing his mother's work and especially her 'illegal' leadership of the movement. Once the conflict with Koresh came into play, soon after Koresh's arrival at Mt. Carmel in 1981, he too was the object of George's acidic prose.[6] In early 1984 George called for another election, which he somehow managed to win. He moved quickly: the name of 'Mt. Carmel' was changed to 'Rodenville' and George was very much in control. On 22 March the *Waco Tribune-Herald* published a legal notice which began, 'Know all men by these presents: that George B. Roden was elected to the presidency of the Branch Davidian Seventh-day Adventist Association'. By now George's chief opponent was not his mother but Koresh. The dispute was to be bitter; it will be discussed further in Chapter Nine. Suffice it here to say that George was eventually arrested and imprisoned, during which absence Koresh secured the property and the leadership of the movement.

This struggle with her son regarding the leadership was a constant drain on Lois's energies, and presumably caused her some personal pain as well. However, if George was strong-willed, Lois was no less so, a trait evident throughout her very active life. That life began on 1 August 1916, when Lois I. Scott was born in Stone County, Montana.[7] Little further is known of her prior to her marriage to Ben Roden on 12 February 1937. She and Ben joined the SDA Church in 1940, and it was Lois who took the most dramatic stance against the leadership of the church in Odessa, when she and Ben were excluded from church membership. She and Ben were visitors to Mt. Carmel from perhaps as early as 1943, and certainly no later than 1945. They also moved together to and from Israel and it is evident that Lois was a central figure in developments in the Holy Land around the establishment of the community at Amirim and later in Jerusalem itself. Her name is found frequently on the documents from this period. She is, for example, named as the director of the 'Organic Agricultural Association in Israel', and when Ben made a move for the leadership of the Davidians after Victor Houteff's death, Lois was there too. Indeed according to Adair, it was Lois and not Ben who first put the case to him. He commented:

One hot day in 1955, while I was working on Freddie's house in Waco, Texas, who do you suppose came there and surprised me? It was my old friend Bro. Ben L. Roden and his wife Lois. I was quite happy to see them, because I had not seen them for such a long time. We did not, however, talk much about old times in Odessa, because his wife right away told me that since Bro. Houteff died, there must be another Elijah to take his place who would not die. And when I heard that, they surprised me the second time, because I knew that Elijah (V. T. Houteff) was the last prophet. And now for the first time I became very suspicious of them, and continued to listen apprehensively as she talked on about another prophet.

Finally, after hearing enough, I suddenly interrupted Sis. Roden and asked point blank, 'Who is this other Elijah?' My abrupt question must have caught her by surprise, because she hesitated and said, 'Well, er, my husband, he is the one'.[8]

Clearly already in 1955 Lois is arguing for her husband's role as leader of the movement. The picture one gets is of a strong-willed individual more than able to make her case and to do so, it seems, even though Ben is there with her.

Saether provides some further insight into Lois's character during these early years. Certainly Ben was theoretically in charge of things, but Lois was also a force to be reckoned with. As with Adair's account, the impression Saether gives is of a determined woman with a forceful presence. Speaking of the competing claims for the leadership of the Davidians in the wake of Victor's demise, he commented,

Well, there were upshoots or offshoots, I'll say, of our movement. Bingham was one of them. And [Ben] Roden was another and Bashan was there from Washington, DC, and who else? There were several there and the most aggravating was this man Roden. You see, he got these people out around Odessa to follow him and I think most of them liked Brother Roden. He was a pleasant sort of fellow. A big man. His wife was right with him in everything he did and I thought many times that she was the power behind the throne. What she decided, that's the way it went.[9]

Once the Rodens had gained control of the movement and of Mt. Carmel things became more settled. Indeed, in comparison with the hectic years of the late 1950s and early 1960s, the latter part of the 1960s, and early part of the 1970s were relatively uneventful. The emphasis was upon consolidation and publishing and in both Lois seems to have played an important part. In 1977, however, Lois experienced a vision, an event which was to change the course of her life and her perception of her own role within the Branch Davidian tradition. If the kind of evidence cited above is anything to go by, she had never exactly been in her husband's shadow, but following the vision her own sense of calling and prophetic importance became pronounced. From now on there would be not one, but two prophets at the Mt. Carmel centre.

Lois recounted the vision during an interview on the Paul Bryan Talk Show on WFAA Dallas, on 4 November 1980.[10] She stated:

It was at night, between 2 or 3 o'clock, that I saw this vision pass my window. It was of a silver angel, shimmering in the night. It was a feminine representation of this angel. I had been studying Revelation 18 and it said that this mighty angel was to come down to earth and that was my understanding. I had been studying about it.[11]

Lois went on to explain to the interviewer that the angel was not actually an angel at all, but a representation of God the Holy Spirit. The message she had hence been given, so Lois argued, was that the Holy Spirit was female.

This belief in the femininity of the Holy Spirit was a significant departure from standard Davidian and Branch Davidian thinking and it is not surprising that long-time member Perry Jones said that he could hardly sleep as a result of what he at first perceived to be blasphemy.[12] Other reports suggest that perhaps as many as one half of all the Branch Davidians left Mt. Carmel as a result of this disturbing message.[13] Undeterred, however, Lois spent a great deal of time seeking to promote her views. Indeed, it would not be an overstatement to say that it was this message of the femininity of the Spirit that occupied her time more than any other single doctrine; her efforts were considerable.

Most importantly, perhaps, Lois started the *Shekinah* magazine, the first edition of which appeared in 1980 (see plate six).[14] In all the issues, the name of the magazine is printed so as to emphasize the 'She' part of '*Shekinah*' and the publication is dominated throughout by Lois's concern to drive home her message of the feminine God. (The Hebrew word '*shekinah*' is that used for the presence of God in the Old Testament.)

Shekinah is a remarkable publication for its time and context. The material it contains has often been reprinted from other media and from those reprints it is evident that Lois had very considerable success in generating interest in her theology and getting people to report on it. The February 1981 issue, for example, reprinted an article first published in the *Toronto Sun* under the title 'Our Mother, who art in Heaven …', and the October issue reprinted a report with the same title from a San Bernardino newspaper. Much of the material in *Shekinah* is centrally concerned with the issue that was now dominating Lois's theological agenda. This said, however, one cannot but be impressed by the way in which the magazine gave voice to a spectrum of basically feminist issues. Articles deal with such things as the move towards inclusive language in Bible translations[15] and the ordination of women in the early church.[16] Much of the material is by respected and established scholars and it is impressive that Lois managed to gain their permission, or that of the publishers (if in fact she did), to reprint the articles.[17]

Lois was herself ordained in 1977, though by whom has not been ascertained.[18] This is another break with both the Davidians and Branch Davidians traditions, and also with the wider SDA movement in general, which, despite being prophetically led for several decades by Ellen G. White, does not sanction the ordination of women. From this point on Lois's message took on its own name, 'The Living Waters Branch', and several publications appear with that imprint.[19]

The year 1977 was, then, very significant in the development of the Branch Davidians and of Lois's perception of her own role within the movement. With the coming of the message regarding the Holy Spirit, she argued, and the

FEBRUARY SHEKINAH **1981**

P.O. Box 4098   Waco, Texas 76705   Telephone 1-817-863-5325

A non-sectarian, non profit publication. Subscription is free.

The Toronto Sun, Wednesday February 4, 1981

Our Mother, who art in Heaven. . .

MARK BONOKOSKI

It has been written that when Lois Roden first started preaching that the Holy Spirit is a woman, she nearly lost half her flock of Seventh-Day Adventists — the male half.

Blasphemy was all it was. Pure and simple blasphemy, the evil work of the Devil himself — himself, not herself.

Roden, however, does not look like the Devil's hand. She looks more like a little, 64-year-old granny from Waco, Tex. Which she is.

But she is also a grandmother who believes the Holy Trinity — the Father, Son and Holy Spirit — is actually Father, Son, and Mother.

Hebrew word for God

She points to "Elohim," the Hebrew word for God. *Eloh*, she says, is feminine, and the suffix *im* is both masculine and plural. Elohim, therefore, is a combination of a woman and two men.

It all began one day back in 1977, when at 2 a.m., as she was studying Revelations 18:1, Roden looked out her bedroom window and saw, as she describes, a "vision of a shining, silver angel flying by.

"Nothing was said. But I knew right there the angel represented the Holy Spirit Mother.

"It was feminine in form," she explained. "Until that moment, I had always thought the Holy Spirit was masculine."

See Page 3

LOIS Roden: Holy Spirit is a woman.

PLATE 6 Cover of an issue of Lois Roden's *Shekinah* magazine

consequent joining together of the 'Branch He' message (that of Ben Roden) with the 'Branch She' (her own), a turning point had been reached. By 29 May 1978 at the latest Lois was proclaiming this clearly, arguing that in the previous year the dawn had broken of the seventh and final stage in the reforming work, and that the reformation of the Church that had been going on since the time of Luther was now nearing completion.[20]

In the summer of 1981 the young Vernon Howell, later to be known as David Koresh, arrived at Mt. Carmel and almost from the beginning was to occupy a central place in Lois's life. It appears from the surviving materials and eye-witness accounts that Lois had a particular regard for him; she was impressed with his ability as a handyman and also with his knowledge of the Bible. It is generally reported that the relationship between them was a good deal more than platonic. One account reports how Koresh went to Lois and on the basis of Isaiah 8.3 ('I went to the prophetess, and she conceived') suggested that they begin a physical relationship. Lois would have been in her late sixties at the time, but certainly the weight of evidence supports the view that the two were indeed sleeping together.[21] This is confirmed by Breault,[22] and was not denied by Koresh. If the reports are accurate, what might be seen here is an early expression of Koresh's later very well developed view that his literal children were destined to become central to the setting up of the new kingdom.

Lois's travels continued through the early 1980s, as is evidenced by the reprints of articles relating to her in issues of the *Shekinah* magazine and occasional references from other sources. During 1980, Adair reports, Lois together with Perry Jones and 'Kay' Matteson visited the Davidians in Salem 'to promote her Holy-Spirit-Feminine doctrine'.[23] In 1981 she was in Toronto,[24] and in Kingston, Ontario,[25] in February, and in San Bernardino in September.[26] By July 1982 she was addressing the fourth international prayer congress in the Philippines and now referring to herself as 'Bishop Lois Roden'.[27] In October she was in Oshawa and Toronto, again making reference to herself as 'Bishop' Lois Roden and claiming that her 'Living Waters Branch' was 'an interdenominational church group' whose numbers were in the tens of thousands. In the same year we read in *Shekinah* of how a congress has been planned for Detroit and that Lois was seeking an audience with the Pope.[28]

In November Lois was in Israel seeing to the reburial of her husband, Ben. He had been disinterred from his temporary resting place in the Waco Memorial Park and his remains were taken via New York to Israel and re-interred on the Mount of Olives. This reburial was quite a feat for Lois to have accomplished; one Rabbi is reported as saying, 'I really do not know how difficult it is [to arrange a burial on the Mount of Olives], but it is not easy ... you can't just buy a plot. You have to get permission from the government. You have to be screened by a special committee.'[29]

In February 1983 'Bishop Roden' was in Brockville, Canada, and telling reporters that she was planning to see the Pope during his forthcoming visit to America and convince him to change his mind on the ordination of women.[30] The same article reports that Lois travelled to Israel two or three times a year.[31] Thus the story continued as Lois travelled the world proclaiming the message of the femininity of the Holy Spirit.

From this period come the bulk of the audio tapes left behind by Lois. What emerges as one listens to that material is that Lois was a very clear-minded person who was totally convinced of the truth of what she had to teach. There is not a hint of hesitation in anything she says. Her style is authoritarian and she dominates the teaching sessions. Her practice seems to have been basically to lecture to those assembled and to intersperse what she had to say with questions to the group. The questions are not designed to elicit contributions, but to make sure that the students have got the right answers. Many of the questions come in the form of unfinished sentences which the students are asked to complete, and if the students give the wrong answer or make no response, Lois is quick to correct them. Koresh must have attended many such studies under Lois. Indeed, on one of the tapes he can be heard reading passages from the Bible in response to Lois's request that he do so. He developed the same teaching style, which may in part have been due to Lois's influence.

Lois died on 10 November 1986 and was apparently transported to Jerusalem for burial alongside her husband.[32] The cause of death is unknown, though according to George's second wife, Amo, she had been diagnosed with breast cancer.[33] Her burial in Israel had clearly been something for which she had been planning. There is a letter to her dated 7 February 1983 from the Maalin Bakodesh Society Inc., based in Brooklyn, New York, a company that, according to its stationery, arranged 'burial services in all cemeteries throughout Israel'. It informed her that the price of $4,100 quoted for a cemetery plot in Israel would be increased unless payment for the full amount was sent by return of post.[34] The money must presumably have been paid. So now she and Ben lay resting in the Holy Land. Neither had lived to see the establishment of the Davidian kingdom, and the movement had now lost yet another prophet. But this time there was another one waiting not just in the wings, but centre stage: Koresh.

From this brief account of Lois's life, it is clear that she was centrally concerned with the Branch Davidian cause. She was no pale shadow of her husband, but an equal with him, and developed her own very distinctive message. This message, so clearly put forward in the Living Waters Branch publications, including *Shekinah* magazine, did concentrate upon the issue of the gender of the Holy Spirit, but as one reads through those publications it is evident that this is but the tip of what was clearly a much larger feminist-theological iceberg. Let us now examine that theology in a little more detail.

Lois's views on the Holy Spirit are reasonably easy to discern. In outline what she argued was that within the Trinity there are both a male and a female part. Her reasoning was simplistic, but gained strength in the eyes of many on that very account. She drew attention in particular to Genesis 1.26–7.

So when I went back to Genesis 1:26, 27, I understood that it said, 'Let *us* make man in *our* image, male and *female*.' And because Adam and Eve were both made in the image of the Godhead I saw that Eve was not made in the image of the Father or the Son, but in the image of a feminine person of the Godhead. So, at least two persons said, 'let us make man in *our image*, male and *female*'. That was the key that I had gotten.[35]

Lois appealed to this basic argument elsewhere: God said let us make man in *our* image and the created beings were both male and female. Hence, so she argued, God too is both male and female. In another publication she said that the creation of Eve was a higher act of creation than that of Adam, for whereas Adam was formed out of dust, Eve was formed out of flesh and blood. Further, Adam was a type of Christ, a male, and Eve was a type of the Spirit, the 'other' comforter spoken of in John 14.26, a female.[36]

While Lois's views on the femininity of the Holy Spirit and the related matter of the ordination of women were without precedent in the tradition, other aspects of her theology were built upon an easily recognizable Davidian/Branch Davidian foundation. Like Ben and others before her in the tradition, Lois too looked forward to the coming of the antitypical kingdom of David. To this end, she said, the Church had been undergoing a process of reform. Such a view comes across on a relatively early tape recording of Lois speaking to the Davidians at their regular 9.00 a.m. gathering (the Davidians met at 9.00 and 3.00 for the 'daily' (cf. Dan. 8.14), which they understood as the proclamation of the truth). On 29 May 1978 she ran through the standard Davidian view that since the time of Luther, the Church had been undergoing a process of reform.[37] There were, she said, seven steps in the process. The first six were the reforms under Luther, Knox, Wesley, Campbell, Miller, and Ellen White. The seventh step had not as yet been taken, but the message needed for its completion had been given, for it was the 'Branch message'.[38] This seventh step was the message of the angel of Revelation 18.1 ff.—that is, the proclamation that Babylon was fallen and the cry 'come out' of her. This was also, she said, the fulfilment of Isaiah 52.1–2, when the Church becomes pure and undefiled.

There is not much here that is new to the Davidian way of seeing things; Lois's contribution was the extent to which she saw her own message as being part of the process, for, she said, the final step in the giving of the Branch message began in 1977 with the message of the 'Branch She'—that is, her own message regarding the nature of the Holy Spirit. In 1977, then, the collective message of Victor Houteff, Ben Roden, and Lois herself came to completion and the stage was set for the coming of the kingdom.

This idea of what one might call 'progressive revelation' is a commonplace in Branch Davidianism, as indeed it is in Davidianism and Seventh-day Adventism. Joined with it is the concept of 'the remnant', that is, the view that in every time God has preserved a faithful few who will carry the flame of truth in an otherwise dark world. Seventh-day Adventists have traditionally believed that they have been called out of apostate Christianity; Houteff thought he had been called out of apostate Seventh-day Adventism and Roden that he had been chosen to call out from the Davidians those who were faithful and would respond to the call of 'the Branch'. Lois was clearly buying into this paradigm. She was now leading the faithful community and it was her task to announce the seventh and last step in the proclamation of the truth. Half of the membership might have defected upon hearing the news that the Holy Spirit was feminine, but this was just part of the winnowing process and the purification of the true remnant people of God.

It seems, however, that not even Lois's feminism was able to bring her to being able to proclaim that she was the one who would lead the people into the kingdom. That was the job of her dead husband. Before his death, it seems, she had come to the conclusion that he was the second latter-day Elijah (the first being Victor Houteff) and that he would not die. However, the plain fact was that Ben had died, so the thinking had to be adjusted. What she said following his death was that at this point the seventh seal of Revelation 8.1 was opened.[39] The end was therefore certainly very near: by 1980 she was confidently proclaiming that the revelation given to her regarding the femininity of the Holy Spirit was 'in preparation of the end of the world ... which will come within the lifetime of people now living on earth'.[40] In another tape she explained that the end was very near since the latter rain, the outpouring of the Holy Spirit, had come upon the Church to prepare the faithful for the work of taking the message to the world and also to keep them safe during the time of trouble. On this tape she adopted an almost Joachite view regarding the three stages of the world's history—the age of the Father, the age of the Son, and the age of the Holy Spirit. In the 'Branch-She' message the end has drawn very close indeed.[41]

This 'end of the world' was conceived by Lois in fairly standard Davidian and Branch Davidian terms. Before the coming of Christ there would be a war in the Middle East between the Jews and the Arabs. America and Russia would also be drawn into this war, and, surprisingly, Israel and their American backers would lose. As a result the Jewish presence in the Middle East, particularly in Palestine, would be ended. At this point, said Lois, here following Houteff, God would intervene and destroy the Arabs as well, and hence the region would be left empty. Not for long, however. Lois, in common with the tradition to which she belonged, argued that the land would be re-inhabited by the 144,000. The kingdom would hence be set up, the nations would have their opportunity to enter it, and, finally, Jesus would return.

Such was the basic outline, but to it Lois added many details. For example, she argued that in 1960 with the coming of the Branch He (Ben) someone had begun 'standing in his lot'.[42] This is a reference to Daniel 12.13, where it is promised that although Daniel must seal his book for now, he will neverthe-less 'stand in his lot' at the end of days. Lois linked this to the message of the seven thunders of Revelation 10.3–4, which were also a message of the end time. In 1960, she said, the judgment of the living began, when Ben arose to give the Branch message. This is not quite what Ben had said. According to him the judgment of the living began in 1964. Both Ben and Lois were working within the overall framework of standard SDA thinking regarding the 'investigative judgment', and the end point of Lois's argument was the same: the end is very near. What Ben had not originally understood (accord-ing to Lois) was the need for his message to be completed by someone other than himself. This completion came with the message of the Branch She in 1977. Lois wrote:

In 1977 ANOTHER comforter OF the same NAME (John 14:26; 16:7–13) the Branch SHE, the Lord our righteousness, Jer 33:15, 16, as announced to JOIN the Branch He in the most Holy Place of the Heavenly Sanctuary for the Living, to finish the atonement for the church and the world—to determine those worthy to have a part in establishing God's kingdom on the earth.[43]

The work was hence progressing. Lois had very clearly in view the point at which the kingdom would be established. In a tape from 1982 she spoke about the return of Christ to the Mount of Olives, a return which, she insisted, would be premillennial: 'I think that we can logically conclude that the return of Christ to the Mount of Olives is a different coming than the second coming and is for the establishment of his kingdom.'

At first sight this is somewhat confusing; however, what Lois was saying here fits in well enough within the wider Davidian tradition, in which it was taught that Christ would rule, invisibly, in the new kingdom alongside his visible counterpart the antitypical King David.[44] In support of this view Lois applied various biblical texts and passages from Ellen White.

In a tape recorded on 28 November 1982 Lois examined in some detail the nature of the resurrection.[45] In essence she agreed with her SDA predecessors in arguing that the dead know nothing. The death of the body brings the death of the spirit as well, for the two are inseparable. The idea that one continues to live 'in heaven' after death, says Lois, is 'the great lie' that was introduced by Satan in the garden of Eden when he told Eve, 'ye shall not surely die' (Gen. 3.4).

Other aspects of Lois's theology could be sketched in easily enough, but that seems hardly necessary. Already a picture has emerged of her main concerns and interests. In essence she followed in the footsteps of Houteff and Ben on most major points, but on the question of the nature of the Holy Spirit (and by extension that of the nature of God) she went in a very distinctive direction. To this was joined a host of basically feminist concerns relating to the place of women in the church, in both a contemporary and a historical setting, and, of course, her own importance as a latter-day prophetess.

There is, however, one particular aspect of Lois's theology that calls for further attention at this point: her apparent expectation that before the setting up of the kingdom, the remnant would be baptized by fire. This baptism, she said, would be literal and 'by immersion'. On one tape in particular she had a great deal to say on this issue.[46] What she said in outline, several times, was that according to her reading of Houteff, the baptism of which John spoke in Matthew 3.11—a baptism with the Holy Ghost and with fire—was not to be accomplished by Jesus: he only baptized with water. She quoted the passage: 'I indeed baptize you with water unto repentance: but he that cometh after me is mightier than I, whose shoes I am not worthy to bear: he shall baptize you with the Holy Ghost, and with fire'. On the tape Lois then went on to say that this baptism by fire would come at the end of the age when God would cleanse Jerusalem. 'And where is Jerusalem now?' she then asked her students, to which came the answer, 'here, Mt. Carmel'. She agreed and then stated that this Jerusalem must be cleansed by fire and that this was the 'gateway' into the new kingdom. The people who wished to enter that kingdom would hence need to go through that cleansing fire. The baptism by fire, she said, like baptism by water, must be by total immersion and not by sprinkling (as was the case at the first Pentecost, which was a type of what was to come). The fire, while purifying the righteous, would at the same time burn the chaff. For more than forty-five minutes she continued with this basic thought.

In a 1983 publication she seemed to return to this kind of thinking, though the pamphlet is terse and not easy to understand fully without the benefit of knowing the broader context, which is not now reconstructable.[47] In this publication Lois reminded her readers of the 'signal fire' that God gave as he led his people out of Egypt—the pillar of fire and the pillar of smoke that went before the people by day and by night respectively (Exod. 13.21). She linked this with the words of Isaiah 14.31: 'Howl, O gate; cry, O city; thou, whole

Palestina, art dissolved: for there shall come from the north a smoke, and none shall be alone in his appointed times.' This 'smoke from the north', she said, was a signal fire calling together the people of God, assembling them 'for a forward march out of Egypt'. Lois then went on: 'As the almighty used *Moses* and the *rod of power in the prophetic office* to deliver ancient Israel as symbolized by the *pillar of fire by night* and *a cloud by day* (a signal fire), just so, shall their descendents be preserved and delivered in the final restoration of the land to them.'[48]

It would be foolish indeed to argue that any of this proves that the Branch Davidians set fire to Mt. Carmel on 19 April 1993 in an effort to bring on the cleansing or to call the people of God to assemble. Such an argument would be far too simple, and is not proposed here. However, as a broader context for what others were later to say (Steve Schneider in particular), Lois's views might be helpful. As will be made clear in later chapters, at least some of the Branch Davidians under Koresh were expecting that the events of the Apocalypse would include their own deaths (to be followed soon after by their resurrections), and it seems to have been anticipated that fire would play its part in that process.

Lois Roden, then, is an important figure in seeking to understand the broader context out of which Koresh himself was to emerge. It was she who nurtured him and prepared him for leadership of the movement. According to Bailey and Darden she even anointed Koresh as the next leader as early as 1983; this has not been possible to check.[49] Her influence upon Koresh was significant. It is true of course that he could have picked up a lot of what he learned from Lois elsewhere in the tradition, but the simple fact was that it was Lois who thought so well of him and who, as his immediate predecessor, prepared much of the ground that he was later to cultivate.

And Lois is perhaps important in another way too: she provides an example of how a leader, even one as strong as she, will not necessarily leave his or her stamp on the movement once the leadership changes hands. There can be no doubt that Lois was committed to the basic eschatological message of the Davidian and Branch Davidian traditions to which she belonged; she may even have heightened significantly some individual points. However, the surviving primary materials unequivocally indicate that her overriding passion was with feminist issues rather than straightforwardly eschatological ones. When one moves into the period of Koresh however, such concerns disappear virtually without trace. The most one finds is an occasional reference to the Holy Spirit being female. (This doctrine was later used by Schneider in an aggressively homophobic argument about the workings of the Trinity, the 'family in heaven', and how his God 'is not a queer'.)[50] In this respect Lois was swimming against the tide. The very essence of the

Davidianism of Houteff and the Branch Davidianism of Ben Roden was eschatological. Lois had other interests as well and for a while the movement appears to have taken them on board and worked tirelessly to see them served. When she died, however, her non-eschatological concerns went with her to the grave and the movement returned once more to the path that it had previously been treading. And it would tread this path for several more years until it was stopped in its tracks by the events that overtook it from 28 February to 19 April 1993.

NOTES

1. Sources on the life of Lois are not abundant and those that do exist can rarely be cross-checked. By far the best collection of material is located in TXC (mainly Saether and various materials in box 2D212), but even that material is thin on details of Lois's life. The material in the Mark Swett archive at Baylor is also valuable, but more so for Lois's theology than her life. Complete accuracy is not therefore claimed for the following account and there unfortunately are gaps. One may be more confident about Lois's theology, where sources are much more plentiful. They include various occasional publications by Lois, materials found in her magazine *Shekinah*, and a set of some twenty-six audio tapes in my possession. J. J. Robertson, *Beyond the Flames* (San Diego, California: ProMotion Publishing, 1996), 87–122, has some material based mainly on the sources he has now deposited in TXC.

2. Examples are a letter to Brother Bingham (TXC 2D216/George Roden) and a typescript on 'Female Dominance' (an answer to Lois Roden's publication *In Her Image*, TXC 2D212/17).

3. See further Bailey and Darden, *Mad Man in Waco*, 68–70, where there is an excellent summary of these developments. There are three principal folders containing the legal materials in TXC. These are found in boxes 2D213 and 2D216.

4. Exactly when he moved to California is unclear; however, one document in the archive, which looks like the first of a series of typescript tracts called 'Rough Wind', is dated 22 Dec. 1983 and gives the address as 'Garden Grove, California'.

5. In Sept. 1988 George was jailed for ninety days for breaking this order.

6. The most sustained attack comes in the 'Rough Wind' series of tracts, which pulls no punches in attempting to deal with his mother's perceived errors. There are a number of other tracts such as 'The Fall of the Jericho in Antitype', 'The Demise of Antitypical Lucifer in the Branch Kingdom', 'Events of the Opening of the Seventh Trumpet', and 'The Red Heifer'. All of these are in TXC 2D216, 2D212, and 2D213.

7. Obituary notice, *Waco Tribune-Herald*, 12 Nov. 1986.

8. Adair, *Davidian Testimony*, 191, and 'Interviews', 37–8.

9. *OM* 414–15. Saether also stated that Lois was the sharper of the two. On the visit Lois and Ben made to Mt. Carmel on 25 Oct. 1955 Ben spoke about a letter he had sent to Mt. Carmel from Springfield, Missouri, allegedly from a group in Missouri (though now it turned out that Roden had written it) saying that the group intended to come to Mt. Carmel in the near future. 'He thought this was quite a joke', said Saether, 'he's not as keen as his wife. She was sharp ... He let the cat out of the bag. I know his wife would not have done that.' *OM* 373.

10. A transcription of the interview appears in *Shekinah*, Dec. 1980, 8–14, 17. See also Bailey and Darden, 65.

11. *Shekinah*, Dec. 1980, 8.

12. Adair, *Davidian Testimony*, 295.

13. Bailey and Darden, *Mad Man in Waco*, 65.

14. A run of *Shekinah* magazine from 1980 to 1983 is located in TXC, Baylor University.

15. *Shekinah*, Feb. 1981, 13.

16. *Shekinah*, Apr. 1981, 1–5.

17. See e.g. Richard Mansfield, 'Women as God's Agents', *Shekinah*, July–Dec. 1983: 25–7, and George M. Lamsa, 'An Introduction to the Peshitta: The Authorized Bible of the Church of the East', *Shekinah*, Oct. 1981, 4–8.

18. Bailey and Darden, *Mad Man in Waco*, 65.

19. Those so far been identified are *Christ and the Holy Spirit*, 2 parts (1978); *A Master Plan for America* (1979); *Behold Thy Mother*, 3 parts (1980); *As an Eagle* (1981); *In Her Image* (1981); *Merkabah*, 3 parts (1983–4); *The Bride of Christ* (1986)—this was apparently planned as a five-part tract, but only parts 1–3 and part 5 appear actually to have been completed (they were reprinted in one booklet in 1992); *In Their Image* (n.d.); *By His Spirit* (n.d.); *A Story of Shavuot* (n.d.); *Balancing out the Trinity* (n.d.)—a reprint of an article by John Dart, and not Lois's own work. Copies of all of the above are located in TXC 2D215/Lois Roden Publications and TXC 2D215/Living Waters Branch. Other tracts listed elsewhere but not identified in this research include: *In Her Image* (n.d.) and *The Wife of God* (n.d.).

20. Lois Roden, 29 May 1978; the same point is made clearly on several other tapes, for example Lois Roden, 3–4 July 1978, where Lois states that the year 1977 saw for the first time the existence of two distinct messengers with two complementary messages. This marks the final stage in the revelation of God in preparation for the perfection of the Church and the establishment of the kingdom. Copies of both tapes are in my possession.

21. See further Tabor and Gallagher, *Why Waco?*, 41 which outlines further evidence that Koresh and Lois had a sexual relationship. Part is the testimony of Teresa Moore, a close friend of Lois, who claimed in a telephone conversation with Philip Arnn that Lois and Koresh had been married in a private, non-legal ceremony before a trip to Israel in 1983 (Philip Arnn, 'The Rod and the Branch: From Victor Houteff to David Koresh', *The Watchman Expositor*, 11 (1994), 21–2).

22. King and Breault, *Preacher of Death*, 41–2.

23. Adair, *A Davidian Testimony*, 296.

24. *Shekinah*, Feb. 1981, 3.

25. *Shekinah*, Apr. 1981, 6.

26. *Shekinah*, Oct. 1981, 9–10.

27. *Shekinah*, July–Sept., 1982.

28. *Shekinah*, Oct.–Dec. 1982, 23.

29. Information comes from an article in the *Waco Tribune-Herald*, reprinted in *Shekinah*, Oct.–Dec. 1982, 20–1.

30. This was not the first time Lois had dogged the Pope's steps. In a report dated 1 Oct. 1979 Lois reported how she and a number of other Branch members had gone to New York on 29 Sept. ahead of the Pope's visit, due to begin on 1 Oct. On the day the Pope arrived Lois and company were on Boston common 'to protest the coming of the Pope and the ever increasing aims of the papacy to control America, by distributing thousands of Branch leaflets'; TXC, Mark Swett Collection/Lois Roden.

31. *Shekinah* Jan.–June 1983, 16–18.

32. Bailey and Darden, *Mad Man in Waco*, 80; Lois's obituary appeared in the *Waco Tribune-Herald*, 12 Nov. 1986.

33. Ibid. 80.

34. TXC 2D215/Lois Roden.

35. *Shekinah*, Dec. 1980, 8.

36. Lois Roden, *In Their Image*, 6.

37. Lois Roden, 29 May 1978. A copy is in my possession.

38. Roden is quite clear that this seventh message did not come with Houteff, but through the revelation through the Branch.

39. Pitts, 'Davidians and Branch Davidians', 36.

40. *Shekinah*, Dec. 1980, 3.

41. Lois Roden, tape of a meeting recorded at Mt. Carmel on 28 Oct. 1978. A copy is in my possession.

42. Monthly Field Letters, Nov.–Dec. 1985, 5.

43. Ibid.

44. Just before this, Lois argues on the tape that when Jesus was raised from the dead he gained the ability to be invisible.

45. A copy is in my possession.

46. The tape was recorded on 21 Mar. 1978 at the Mt. Carmel centre. A copy is in my possession.

47. Lois Roden, *Merkabah, Part 2: Chariots of Fire* (Waco, Tex.: Living Waters Branch, 1983).

48. Lois Roden, *Chariots of Fire*, 8.

49. Bailey and Darden, *Mad Man in Waco*, 72.

50. This remark is found on the Manchester tapes, where Schneider also develops the notion of the femininity of the Holy Spirit more generally.

9

'A Pale Rider' (cf. Revelation 6.8): Vernon Howell and the Branch Davidians, 1959–1985

So far in this book an account has been given of the historical and theological development of Branch Davidianism up to and including the leadership of Lois Roden. We have noted how this group, like so many others before it, relied heavily upon an imaginative reading of prophetic parts of the biblical text to provide a sense of purpose, urgency, and particularity to a specific eschatological task. Hence while Miller laid the foundation for Seventh-day Adventism's view of its own eschatological importance, Houteff sharpened that sense further by arguing that even the remnant church had in effect become the church of Laodicea and now itself needed reform. The dark night of the soul experienced by the movement in 1959 was followed by a much brighter dawn. To be sure there was fragmentation, but for the Branch Davidians at least the light that came with Ben Roden brought with it the promise of rejuvenation. His leadership was rather uneventful, but it had the effect of bringing stability to a group that might easily have become extinct had it not been for his steadying hand. Lois Roden, to be sure, was a much more colourful figure and under her the movement flourished. Houteff's original theology was adapted to suit the needs of the new community; never, however, did the group lose sight of the central Davidian and Branch Davidian doctrine of the coming of a literal, end-time kingdom to be established in Israel.

This history and theology of the Davidians from Houteff to Lois Roden has been examined before, though in general rather briefly. The material in this book to this point, then, is substantially new, though the prior work of Bailey, Darden, and Pitts is acknowledged. Now the focus turns to a period in the history of this religious trajectory that has been subjected to much more detailed analysis: that under the leadership of David Koresh. As we saw in Chapter One, Koresh has had a good deal of negative publicity, being categorized as 'mad' and/or 'bad'. He may have been neither, either or both. We will not know, however, unless we make a proper attempt to understand what he had to say and to appreciate the context in which he said it. That attempt is made here.

For the sake of clarity the dealings with Koresh are divided into two parts. This and the next chapter discusses his life (and with it, where appropriate, the progress of his Branch Davidian movement), whereas in Chapter Eleven the focus turns to his theology. As ever when dealing with this tradition, the two cannot be disentangled completely, and there will inevitably be some overlap. Both of these sections need to be substantial; although a good deal of attention has been paid to Koresh's involvement with the people at Mt. Carmel, much of what has been written to date has been only poorly documented and often comparatively thin. These three chapters will hence provide the most substantial account to date of the life and theology of a man whose impact on American religious and political life has been profound.

Vernon Wayne Howell[1] was born in Houston, Texas, on 17 August 1959 to Bonnie Clark, a young unmarried mother of fourteen or fifteen years old.[2] His father was twenty-year-old Bobby Howell, a carpenter and mechanic.[3] For the first two years of his life Vernon lived with his natural mother and father in Houston. During this time he earned the nickname 'Sputnik' on account of his apparent hyperactivity.[4] The relationship between Clark and Howell did not last. They separated, and Clark, who had never married Howell, married another man.[5] That marriage soon went the way of the previous relationship and shortly afterwards Vernon was placed in the care of his maternal grandmother, Earline Clark, and his aunt. In time he came to believe that his aunt was in fact his mother, and that the 'aunt Bonnie' who came to visit from time to time, who was of course his real mother, was his aunt. This continued for three years.

In 1964 Bonnie Clark married Roy Haldeman, a former merchant marine who now worked as a carpenter. The child was taken back by his mother and the three went to live on Haldemann's farm in the Dallas-Fort Worth area.[6] The family soon grew to include Roger, Howell's half-brother.[7] (It is perhaps interesting to note that, like Jesus, Howell was born out of wedlock to a very young mother and was the stepson of a carpenter and that like Jesus, according to at least one main school of thought, he was thirty-three when he died.[8] Such details were not lost on later Davidian apologists).

According to later testimony, Howell lived rather in the shadow of his brother and it was Roger, so Howell later said, who was the favourite.[9] (One ought to remember how selective memory can be when it comes to sibling rivalries.) Breault and Reavis suggest that other evidence indicates that, like many of his fellow Texans, Howell was severely and physically punished as a child.[10] He was later to claim also that he had been sexually abused as a child by a group of older boys,[11] and that his mother worked as a prostitute (a claim denied by Bonnie Haldemann herself). Reavis also states that Howell's stepfather had a rather dubious background and that his (Howell's) half-brother was to spend time in prison for burglary and drug offences.[12] On balance, then, Reavis's conclusion seems justified: 'The household that produced Vernon Howell was not a model of the virtues of family life'.[13]

Howell's mother had been raised as a Seventh-day Adventist and Vernon attended the SDA church as a child; his grandmother took him to the local SDA church during the years he spent in her household, and on moving to the Dallas-Fort Worth area his association continued. Indeed, he was initially sent to the Dallas SDA Academy, but transferred to state school in subsequent years.

Life at school was not easy. It is said that Howell had a learning disorder, perhaps dyslexia, though there was no diagnosis at the time. He was also bullied and on account of his apparent slowness became known as 'Mr Retardo'. The pain inflicted at school as a result of his 'special' status clearly stayed with him. On one of the negotiation tapes (i.e. the tapes of the FBI–Branch Davidian negotiations during the 1993 siege), he remembers being in a special class with a small number of other students: it is break time and he and the other 'special' children make a dash for the swings. As they race out of one of the side doors, the other children are already in the playground and on seeing the 'specials' shout 'here come the retards'. Koresh comments: And it's like I, I just stopped in my tracks. It's like the sun went down over my world … I couldn't function and that day was the longest day in my life. I mean I stood over by the swing set, you know, and I'm like a third grader, right?[14]

Howell did have learning difficulties and according to close associates he remained a poor speller and writer throughout his life.[15] This is why, perhaps, he wrote down so little, preferring to transmit his message by audio tape. Even the letters he signed (sometimes in Hebrew as 'Yahweh Koresh') show traces of his use of an amanuensis. The letter to Dick DeGuerin dated 14 April 1993, for example, is very accurately punctuated throughout, including the proper use of colons and semi-colons.[16] This is not the natural writing style of someone unable to grasp even the alphabet properly. He excelled at school in sports, but in his academic work his progress was disappointing and by eleventh grade he was forced to drop out.[17]

It would be easy, then, to paint a picture of Howell as a high-school drop out of questionable intellectual ability. To anyone who has studied his interpretation of the Bible, however, such a portrait will not be convincing. Certainly there are few who would think that he was 'right' in what he had to say about the scriptures. His understanding of some parts of the Bible was highly idiosyncratic and in many cases what he had to say about its interpretation was, at best, rather strange. However, no one who has looked into the matter could fail to be impressed by both the extent to which he had huge portions of the Bible memorized, and the exceptionally complex web of interpretation that he placed upon it. That interpretation is highly imaginative and very complex, and requires one to be able to hold in the mind a huge amount of text in order to be able to see connections. As one listens to the tapes or reads the transcripts one can hardly fail to be struck by the extent to which the speaker was able to think creatively and laterally about what he found in the Bible. He may have had difficulties at school, but the later evidence suggests that he was not lacking in sheer intelligence. It does not take a child psychologist to note a pattern here: a hyperactive child who, despite an apparently high IQ, has learning difficulties and fits in very poorly with those with whom he comes into contact. If he were a child at school today he would probably be assessed for Attention Deficit Hyperactivity Disorder.

When he was fourteen it was decided that Howell should return to live with his grandmother, who by this time had moved to Ardmore Avenue in Tyler.[18] Despite the fact that there was room in the house, he decided to live in a shed in the garden, which he quickly patched up and made into something like a home for himself. Reports suggest that this was one of his happier times as a child and young adolescent, but it was not to last. His grandfather eventually became exasperated by his grandson's presence and he was sent back to live with his mother and stepfather.

In 1977, when Howell was eighteen, he met a sixteen-year-old girl. By now he was working as a carpenter for the H. T. Ground Construction Company in Dallas,[19] but evidently spent time in the evenings at an arcade in Richardson, where the couple met.[20] During the siege Koresh spoke affectionately about his relationship with this young girl, 'his first love',[21] and also about her father, 'Dick'.[22] In fact during the siege one of the taped cassette messages that the FBI allowed into Mt. Carmel was from her. His response to the message can be heard on one of the bug tapes.[23] She also appears to have called the FBI and left a message for Koresh on or before 21 March.[24]

The relationship quickly became intense. One evening after giving the girl a lift home Howell was invited into the house, an offer he did not refuse. On the negotiation tapes he states that when he discovered that her father was already in bed, he said: 'Well, look, I better get out of here. And she says, well, no, we can just talk a bit. So, we ended up talking and stuff like that and everything. And one thing led to another and I tell you what, you know. There should be a law against it but you know how humanity is.'[25] Guilt set in almost immediately; Howell went round the next day to apologize, but ended up doing the same thing again. Soon after he left Dallas and went to Tyler, apparently to escape the temptations that Dallas had sent his way.[26] Not too long afterwards, however, Howell returned and the relationship restarted, and soon he had moved into the house to live with her. Before long she was pregnant, an event which resulted in his being thrown out of the house by the girl's father and the relationship came to an end. A child was born, however; Shayna Cull.[27] She was the first of Koresh's many children, though he was never to see her.[28]

Evicted from the house Howell spent a couple of months living in his pick-up truck. It was during this time that he first began formally to associate as an adult with a religious group, choosing the Southern Baptists.[29] His association with them did not last very long. In 1979 he returned to the faith in which he had been brought up, and was baptized in the Tyler SDA church. The members of the church were evidently pleased to have among them this sincere young man who had a passion for the Bible, especially so perhaps as he was evidently a sinner who had repented and returned to the Church upon which he had previously turned his back. A married couple at the church, Bob and Maggie Bockmann, even provided him with somewhere to live in return for work on their farm.[30]

However, while a member of the Tyler church, Howell was again to run into trouble. He was, like many young men at the age of twenty, somewhat obsessed by sexual matters, but unlike the majority he did not keep his thoughts to himself. Things reached a crisis point when he claimed to have had a vision in which he was told that God wanted him to take the pastor's daughter as his wife. According to King and Breault (presumably based upon a conversation on the subject between Koresh and Breault at some point) Howell was praying, when he experienced himself drifting in the clouds. He saw the pastor's daughter in the middle of the clouds and was told by God that she was to be his wife. The pastor was not impressed and banned Howell from seeing her. Nevertheless, so Koresh, according to Breault and King, later claimed, he continued his relationship with the girl, which again resulted in two pregnancies, both of which miscarried.[31]

This was not the first vision Howell claimed to have had. Earlier, while living in his truck after being evicted from the home of his first girlfriend, he seems to have had another; at least that is his later recollection. Again the negotiation tapes are of help. Speaking to Henry Garcia on 4 April he stated that on one occasion while he was praying in a field 'expressing my emotional patterns to, to this God',

This presence enshrouds me … and I'm talking about [how] its authority encompasses me. And here I am zeroed in and all of a sudden I start shaking and I'm scared to death. I mean, you would be scared if you was out in the field and all of a sudden two black guys came at you, wouldn't you? And, all of a sudden, this zero, zeroed in on me. And here I am looking at the sky, but all of a sudden it's like, it's like I'm being watched from every angle. And there's this, there's this being confronting me and it's like I have no place to run, Henry .... No place to run. And it is—one part of me is terrified and the other part of me is awed. Like, you're real? You know, it's kind of like, you're real? Really? Re—you know. And there's this, there's this voice says to me, it says—it's not a voice such as, see, when I'm talking to you ... It's a voice that imparted a picture completely perfect in my mind ... It, it overruled all my perception banks and, and it sort of like jammed m—any kind of perception except what it wanted me to know. And he says, you're really hurt, aren't you? And, and, you know, 19 years of life flash in front of me, just like on a film. The whole d—aura of being. Everything ... And then a voice all of a sudden—it, it re—it, it reviewed to me all of these weird and strange and unique and enstrengthening experiences throughout my whole childhood and life. And it says, don't you know that for 19 years I've loved you and for 19 years you've turned your back on me and rejected me? And all of a sudden everything is like bang. It hit me all at once. Ah. What an ability to forget the reasons and the purposes of life. So, from that point I had this, you know, knowledge of what the next phase that I had to experience and to do. Because, see, Linda, she's a part of my life and my experience.[32]

The powerful experience underscored a simple message: just as Howell had felt rejected by his girlfriend, so God had felt rejected by Howell.

Another particularly important vision to Howell's sense of his own mission also comes from around this period. Howell recounted it to David Thibodeau.[33] Again he was praying when suddenly, so the report goes, he felt that he was being taken up an elevator shaft and after the ascent saw two gigantic walls, one of which had 'law' written on it, the other 'prophecy'. Howell then told how he saw God himself, who had in one hand a book, while holding out the other to Howell, who reached forward for it. What happened next is not described, but if we were able to follow this up, one suspects that we would find that this was seen by Howell as a call to open the book that God had in his hand—his 'anointing' perhaps as a chosen one: a Christ. Later visions include one in Jerusalem in 1985, about which more is said below. Here, then, even at this early stage of his life, is an individual who has an intense religious experience to the extent that he even believes himself to be in direct communication with God though visions. During the siege Koresh's belief that he was in direct communication with God was to take on particular importance, for it was the lack of a clear directive from the Divine that he interpreted as meaning that he and the other Branch Davidians ought not to leave the Mt. Carmel centre.

Howell's life as a Seventh-day Adventist was, then, somewhat problematic. His interest in the pastor's daughter coupled with his claim to be the recipient of direct messages from God could not but lead to tension. In April 1981 he was formally disfellowshipped from the Tyler congregation.[34] However, be-fore that date he had attended a series of evangelistic meetings held by the SDA Church led by Jim Gilley of Arlington, Texas. These featured the standard SDA evangelistic package which goes under the title of 'Revelation Seminars', seminars still used in the Church today.[35] They cover standard SDA doctrine relating to the last days and the interpretation of the book of Revelation. As such they are filled with dramatic images of Revelation's beasts and replete with accounts of earthquakes and other natural disasters and the terrifying ordeal through which God's people must go in the last days. Jim Gilley, by all accounts an excellent preacher, made the seminars even more dramatic than they already were. Howell was captivated and clearly took the message to heart. But even at this early stage he was not entirely satisfied by what he heard. He offered to assist Gilley in rearranging the material; the offer was rejected. Howell also reported to his aunt Sharron that there was something missing from the scenario Gilley had outlined: the seventh seal. Further, so Howell claimed, the interpretation of this part of Revelation could not be understood until a new prophet had come. Whether Howell had already at this time come to the view that he was that figure is unclear, but it seems that he might have been toying with the idea.[36]

By 1981, then, Howell had been through some traumatic experiences. As a child he had been rejected by his natural father and grandfather, apparently beaten by his first stepfather, left by his mother with his aunt to the point where he thought that the aunt was actually his mother, only to be told a few years later that she was not. At school he had been known as 'Mr Retardo' and there is evidence of other physical and perhaps even sexual abuse by older boys being a factor in his childhood.[37] But he was also now in direct communication with God. These two, probably symbiotic, aspects of his life need to be noted carefully. Others may wish to draw conclusions regarding the relationship between Howell's early life and his evolution into David Koresh, but such would be beyond the scope of this study. What is clear, however, is that when he was disfellowshipped from the SDA Church he had already come to the view that he had a direct line of communication to God and an understanding of the truth that even seasoned SDA evangelists like Jim Gilley could not match. He may not as yet have come to the firm conclusion that he was a prophet, but he soon would, and his experience so far in the SDA Church must surely have suggested something further: that he was not about to be honoured in his own country.

The recently disfellowhipped Howell visited Mt. Carmel in the summer of 1981.[38] The reason seems to have been a report he received (from whom is not clear) to the effect that the community was led by a living prophet who received messages direct from God.[39] This 'living prophet' was at this time

Lois Roden. On that first visit Howell stayed only a few hours; when questioned directly on the matter of Koresh's first visit to Mt. Carmel, Doyle remembered being asked to put together a package of literature for him to take away.

From this point on, Howell returned to Mt. Carmel several times, on each occasion staying a little longer and engaging in Bible studies.[40] At first he was treated as a very junior member (which he was) and given the lower jobs including the washing of dishes. Breault quoted him as saying later of this period, 'I washed enough dishes to last me a lifetime. Everyone looked down on me. I was just the camp bum, the loser that did all the dirty jobs, the things nobody else wanted to do. It was always "Vernon do this, Vernon do that".'[41]

However, Howell's undoubted skills as a handyman and mechanic were soon put to good use and it was this very practical usefulness that appears first to have led to a more enthusiastic acceptance. Certainly his status grew. Others have painted a picture of him as a domineering individual who thought little of using others in order to get his own way. There may be something in this; but what is certain at this point is that he was a very determined young man who had shown throughout his somewhat troubled life that he had a real, single-minded quest for God and 'the truth'. One might disagree with the direction it took, but few could doubt the intensity or sincerity of the religious quest. The fact that he had also gained a very impressive command of the scriptures (his mother once said that he had a good part of the New Testament memorized by the time he was thirteen)[42] must also have been a plus in the text-focused community he had now joined. Similarly, though he could not write at all well, anyone who has listened to his taped messages would find it difficult to deny that he was an impressive speaker. (Even when one is not quite sure what he has said, one has the overriding impression that whatever it was, he said it very well.) Not all will be drawn to the very black and white conceptual world in which he lived and few indeed would have much sympathy for his interpretation of the biblical texts. To those who shared some of his basic presuppositions, however, he must have seemed nothing short of inspirational—indeed, inspired.

Howell was fairly quickly seen by Lois Roden as her natural successor and it is plain that he also had the support of others in the Branch Davidian movement from an early stage. The key point of transition came in the autumn of 1983 when, at Lois's suggestion (it is difficult to see how he could have gained a hearing without her support), he presented a series of eight meetings at which he explained those things he felt God had revealed to him.[43] Those meetings became known as 'the Serpent's Root' studies and marked the point at which he began the transformation from the community's handyman to its undisputed prophet and leader. After hearing what he had to say, the majority of the group accepted that he had a message and that he was indeed a prophet of God. Lois was among those who gave their support. Around the same time as the Serpent's Root studies (September and/or October 1983), he made his first of an eventual three trips to Israel, accompanied by Lois.

On 18 January 1984 Howell legally married Rachel Jones, who was then fourteen.[44] She was the eldest daughter of long-time Branch Davidian Perry Jones. Three of his sixteen children were born of this marriage—Cyrus, Star, and Bobbie Lane. All three died in the fire.[45]

By the beginning of 1984, then, the young Vernon Howell stood poised to take over the leadership of the group; he had been accepted by the membership as a prophet, had the support of the current leader, and was now the son-in-law of Perry Jones, who was arguably the second-in-command at Mt. Carmel. Ben and Lois Roden had shared the prophetic office for the last year or so of Ben's life, and it hence ought to have been possible for Lois and Howell to share the same office while Lois was still living. There was, however, one major obstacle standing between Howell and the leadership: Lois's son George.

George Roden had never adjusted to the fact that it was his mother and not he who had taken the leadership after Ben's death. But Lois was herself now beginning to age, and the thought must have been in George's mind that gaining the leadership was only a matter of time. (The events here described were marginally before George's victory in the early 1984 Branch Davidian Leadership election discussed briefly in Chapter Eight.) Vernon Howell did not fit in well with these plans and, predictably, tension between the two was the result. For a while the two factions existed side by side, helped by the fact that George was not on the Mt. Carmel property; but it could not last. The issue came to a head when Lois visited her daughter in California. George was there too, seeking to promote his chances of being elected President of the United States of America. It was at this time that the nature of the relationship between Howell and Lois Roden became known to her family and George was particularly upset. On hearing that Howell and Lois were now sleeping in the same bed, George quickly returned to Waco. On the morning of 13 January 1984 he heard Howell preach some new doctrines at a morning meeting and noted how 'it seemed like the whole group there was taking it in, hook, line, and sinker'.[46] That night the truth about Howell and Lois's relationship was confirmed. Howell's own recollection of George's reaction was that he (George) 'came in and he's waving around a .357 Reuger, a Nighthawk or a Magnum. And he was telling people he was going to blow my balls off and he was going to, you know, all this kind of stuff'.[47] Wisely, in the light of what we know about George's rather volatile temperament, Howell soon fled Mt. Carmel; on

28 January he wrote a letter to George which includes the statement, 'I miss Mt. Carmel so much', so he had, then, clearly left.[48]

The letter Howell wrote to George is important on several fronts. Some of the theology implied is examined later, but we may note here in passing that it is clear that by now Howell's understanding of his own role during these end times had become focused. Hence in one place he said, 'You also know that the angel of Revelation 14.17 is what I claim to be'. That verse reads, 'And another angel came out of the temple which is in heaven, he also having a sharp sickle.' The work of the angel is not described in detail, though in a Branch Davidian context it would be fair to assume that the figure, clearly one involved in 'the harvest', was to gather the 144,000 and lead them to Mt. Zion. This was actually quite a major step for Howell to have taken; Ben Roden had claimed the role of this sickle-wielding angel, and indeed it had formed a central part of Roden's message. Howell must by now have felt very confident that he had the status required to usurp the position Roden had so clearly claimed.

Hence Howell had a problem on his hands. Just as his own sense of prophetic office was becoming clear, he had become physically separated from those to whom he felt it his duty to preach. However, though he had lost (temporarily) his foothold on the Mt. Carmel property, he had done enough during the time he had been there to ensure that he had a significant following, and his work came to fruition when they too left Mt. Carmel to be with him.[49] The group, which appears to have been about forty in number, moved first back into Waco itself, and then to the Texas town of Mexia for about a month.[50] Finally they set up a more stable, but still temporary, base on a 40 acre site in Palestine, Texas, about 90 miles from Waco. Facilities were largely non-existent, with no running water, electricity, or, to begin with, toilet facilities. The accommodation seems to have been largely in the form of semi-converted buses.[51] Howell was now firmly in charge of this group and from this point on he went from strength to strength.[52]

In 1985 Howell and his wife went to Israel, possibly in an attempt to ensure that their first child, Cyrus, was born in the Holy Land (in the event he was not, for by the time of his birth both parents were back in Texas). It was during this trip to Israel that Howell had an experience that was to change his life.

The impact of that experience, whatever it was, should not be underestimated. As the letter to George indicates, even before his trip to Israel Howell had come to the view that he was the angel of Revelation 14.17. In the same letter, however, he also expressed more than a passing interest in the identity of the angel of Revelation 10.7.[53] During the days of the voice of this latter figure, 'when he shall begin to sound', so the text of Revelation states, 'the

PLATE 7 One of the buildings at Palestine, Texas, where Koresh and his followers lived prior to gaining control of Mt. Carmel

mystery of God should be finished, as he hath declared to his servants the prophets'.[54] It would appear that during his time in Israel, Howell came to the view that he was this other angel too. Not only that, the content of that 'mystery of God' had been revealed to him. It was his task to communicate this to others, that is, he must unpack the full revelation of God as it had already been given in the Bible.

This new-found sense of his own identity appears to have come through a visionary experience, which, as we have seen, was not the first such experience to which he laid claim. The precise shape of that vision is difficult, perhaps impossible, to piece together, but there are some relevant passages in the surviving materials. The most extended reference comes as a part of the negotiations. On 8 April 1993 the following is heard:

KORESH: ... so there's only one acid test for anybody that claims to be enlightened in regards to the knowledge of God—show me the seals—and if they can't then they have to wait until somebody can.

FBI: David? How did you get the point where you can interpret the seals?

KORESH: Well—in 1985 I was in Israel. And ah—there was ah—there was these Russian cosmonauts that were—ah ... The reason I am telling you about this is 'cause we got two—we got two witnesses to this. The Russian cosmonauts gave the report that they saw seven angelic beings flying towards earth with the wings the size of a jumbo jet. OK. So what happened was in 1985 when I was in Israel I met up with those people; seriously.

FBI:	You met up with who now? The seven? The two cosmonauts?

KORESH:	No. No. No. See—the Russian cosmonauts were in their space station.

FBI:	Right.

KORESH:	And they radioed down to their headquarters. They were terrified.

FBI:	Right. I can understand …

KORESH:	That they saw seven angelic beings …

FBI:	Um-hm.

KORESH:	… moving towards the earth.

FBI:	OK. And you met these seven angelic beings.

KORESH:	Exactly.

FBI:	Where?

KORESH:	In Israel.

FBI:	Yeah. But where in Israel?

KORESH:	(laughing) On Mt. Zion over in Israel.

FBI:	Oh. OK.

KORESH:	OK. Let me tell you something. It's awesome. Angels don't really have wings. But what they have is called a Merk—a Merkhavah.

FBI:	A what?

KORESH:	A Merkhavah.

FBI:	Which is?

KORESH:	It's a—it's a spaceship.

FBI:	A spaceship?

KORESH:	It's—it's—it's a vehicle. I mean—it—it travels by light …

FBI:	OK.

KORESH:	… the refraction of light. You know how the rainbow and all that.

FBI:	You know this sounds—are you familiar with Eric ah—oh well. Eric Von Daniken?

KORESH:	Who's that?

FBI:	Chariot of the Gods?

KORESH:	Yeah. Well see—I got that film in 1986 or '87 because I was looking for—for documentation to try and explain to my students just exactly when—how I got this knowledge of the seals.

FBI:	Um-hm.

KORESH:	So what happened to me—literally happened to me didn't just happen to me so I could say, 'Wow man. I was taken up to—past Orion and it was—wow—and I saw this and …'

FBI: Was there anyone with you when this happened, David?

KORESH: Absolutely not!

FBI: And you were just on top of this mountain and this happened?

KORESH: Well see—Mt. Zion is really—is where the city is. It's where the—ah—the old city is.

FBI: OK.[55]

Of course this conversation took place eight years after the events being recalled, but it at least gives an indication of how Koresh saw things looking back.[56] He was in Israel, on Mt. Zion, and he was visited by seven angelic beings who explained to him the secrets of the seven seals. (The reference to the Russian cosmonauts is interesting; several newspapers and magazines from 1985–6 contain this peculiar report of the sighting of the seven angels—precisely where Koresh got the story is not clear.)[57] Whatever one makes of the claim, one thing seems reasonably certain: Howell did come to some sort of much more focused self-understanding while in Israel. Things were moving in this direction already, and had been doing so for at least a couple of years (i.e. since the Serpent's Root studies), but it was in Israel that it seems to have fallen into place for him. Tabor reports that surviving Branch Davidians who remembered him before and after the trip to Israel spoke of his coming back to Waco with a renewed sense of purpose and much clearer view of things.[58] Tabor suggests that one can detect this in the tapes by comparing the style and content of the message before and after the Jerusalem experience, a judgement that seems sound enough.

On another tape Koresh also mentioned the Israel experience. This was the tape of his interview with talk-show host Charlie Serafin on the KRLD radio station on the night of 28 February.[59] Here he was asked specifically about the change of his name from his birth name to 'David Koresh'. In response he said:

OK my natural name is Vernon Howell, that's what my mother named me. I'm from the—my father's name is Bobby Howell, from Houston, Texas, they never got married. But the thing of it was that she later on married Roy Haldemann which basically raised me; OK. Now in 1985 when I was in Israel I had an encounter and I was instructed by this encounter with regards to the seven seals. And so the thing of it is that with this light that was given to me I was also given a name, a name that would represent my position according to the prophetic writings. All the prophets talk about David, the son of David, Christ; Revelation 1 says that I am the root and offspring of David, the bright morning star. Peter says that prophecy is a light that shines in the dark places until the day-spring, day-star arises in your heart. So you see Christ is this great light. I am the light of the world.

Unfortunately Koresh was interrupted by the interviewer at this point and never returned to the subject of his name change. However, the basic point he was making is plain enough. In 1985 he was given the task of taking the truth of the seven seals to the world. Along with the commission came a change of name (biblical precedent may have been an influence here).[60]

It was this instantaneous coming to the knowledge of the seven seals that he was probably talking about also at one point on a tape recorded on 24 August 1987

And because I've got the football I get tackled. That's all there is to it. I'm no different from you except one thing—the Lord's given me His eternal word. That's all. I didn't learn from the school Steve learned from. I learned like that [at this point on the tape Koresh can be heard snapping his finger].[61]

Interestingly, one tape from this period in Jerusalem has survived. This is, 'The Loud Cry', which begins with the words, 'This is the first month, the thirtieth day, 1985 and here we are in Jerusalem, Israel.'[62] This is a special study, says Howell, that concerns the subject of 'the Loud Cry' (the influence of Revelation 14.8 seems obvious here). The opening story seems to be significant. Here Howell tells how he visited the Knapp family and had dinner with them.[63] During dinner the Bible came under discussion and 'eventually—you know—it was made known that—uh—the seventh angel's message was not being taught'. Some members of the Knapp family had drawn out some of Houteff's charts and Howell took the opportunity to explain how these charts were inspired. However, while the Knapps were already acquainted with 'the sixth angel's message' they did not know that of the seventh. Howell asked them if they wanted to have some studies of the seventh angel's message, but they declined even though he warned them that this was the last chance they would have. Prior to the start of the Sabbath, however, a 'big, beautiful full-coloured rainbow was all around Jerusalem' and there was an earthquake. 'Now,' says Howell, 'Branches can take this as they will'. The way he understood it is plain: on the tape he links it directly to Revelation 10: 'And I saw another mighty angel come down from heaven, clothed with a cloud: and a rainbow was upon his head, and his face was as it were the sun, and his feet as pillars of fire.' 'The earthquake' to which Howell referred (actual or not) is presumably the earthquake of Revelation 16.18; indeed he also referred to 'voices, thunders and lightnings' which are also mentioned in Revelation 16.18. Elsewhere on the tape he stated very clearly that Houteff was the fifth angel's message and that Ben Roden was 'the same voice'. However, when Ben Roden died, the sixth angel's message was already on the ground, namely Lois Roden. The implication that he [Koresh] was the seventh angel is plain. His work had begun.[64]

Howell's view that he was now the one chosen by God to lead the remnant people was uncompromising. Lois and Ben Roden may have been able to live with the view that there were two living prophets and a dual leadership, but he was not. In 1985 he began to distance himself from Lois Roden and indeed to question her status and authority. By now she was not in any case the legal leader of the Branch; that post had gone to George. Her previous credentials must still have given her some continued status, at least with those who had been with her for some time, people like Perry Jones and Clive Doyle. Koresh's willingness to question the role of Lois was hence a gamble, though in the end it was one that paid off.

The clearest evidence of this change in direction is found on the 'Seven Eyes' tape. The date of this tape is not clear.[65] However, there is a clear indication that Howell and Lois had a major dispute as a result of Lois's decision to go to the 1985 General Conference Session (of the SDA Church) and present some literature to all who would take it.[66] Howell was deeply unhappy about this for some reason; the reason is not made plain but it may have been the content of the literature rather than Lois's decision to distribute it *per se*. At one point Howell talked of Lois 'singing like a harlot' and of her refusing to take his views into account. A power struggle was in full swing and it seems from the circumstantial evidence that Koresh won it hands down.

The transformation of Mr Retardo into a powerful leader of a highly committed religious group was by now more or less complete. Howell's own sense of commission and calling had taken several years to come to fruition, but by 1985 it was there for all to see. Here was a man chosen by God to reveal to the world the secrets of the end times: a man who could tell those who would listen just what that 'mystery of God' was that had been revealed to 'his servants the prophets', a man who had been predicted by the very texts he had come to interpret. The 'young man' of Zechariah 2.4,[67] the 'mighty angel' of Revelation 10.1, the angel with the loud cry of Revelation 14.6, had come. So powerful had Howell become that he was able even to eclipse the work of Lois Roden. There was just one final obstacle to be overcome, but that was a big one: George Roden.

NOTES

1. The convention in other chapters of referring to him as Koresh regardless of the date is set aside here. He is Howell until the change of name was at least an element in his mind, and Koresh thereafter.

2. The main sources of information on Howell's early life are the accounts re-searched and published during and shortly after the siege. These were based largely upon interviews with those who knew him at the time. In addition to the works of Breault and King, Thibodeau and Reavis (esp. 23–30), such sources include William Clairborne and Jim McGee, 'The Making of David Koresh', in *Spectrum*, 23/1(May 1993), 18–25. This was edited in an article by the same authors under the title, 'The Transformation of the Waco "Messiah" ', in *Washington Post*, 9 May 1993. References here are to the article as it appeared in *Spectrum*. See also Brian Harper, 'God, Guns and Rock and Roll: David Koresh as seen from the Church Pews and Bar Stools of Downtown Waco', *Spectrum* 23/1 (May 1993), 26–29. Haus and Hamblin, *In the Wake of Waco*, 37–44, also give information relating to this part of Howell's life, but it seems to be based upon a somewhat imaginative reading of the sources listed above. The most reliable information is probably that found sporadically on the negotiation tapes. These tapes (hereinafter 'NT'), which number over 200, are the recordings of the discussions between the FBI negotiators and the Branch Davidians during the siege. A near full set of these tapes is in my possession, as are transcripts of some.
3. That Bobby Howell was a carpenter is stated clearly by Clairborne and McGee, 'Making of Koresh', 22. The source seems to have been Jean Holub, his mother.
4. Reavis, *Ashes of Waco*, 23.
5. Clairborne and McGee, 'Making of Koresh', 19.
6. Koresh made a few brief remarks regarding his father on NT 87.
7. Brief mention is made of Roger Haldemann on NT 48, NT 87.
8. Luke states that Jesus was 'about thirty' when he was baptized (Luke 3.23), and John's gospel seems to suggest a ministry that lasted three years.
9. King and Breault, *Preacher of Death*, 28.
10. Reavis, *Ashes of Waco*, 24; King and Breault, *Preacher of Death*, 28–9.
11. King and Breault, *Preacher of Death*, 29–30.
12. Reavis, *Ashes of Waco*, 23–25.
13. Ibid.
14. NT 45.
15. See Reavis, *Ashes of Waco*, 25–6, for the testimony of those associates. The best example of his handwriting and English skills is found in a sequence of three fairly substantial notebooks located in TXC (Mark Swett Collection/David Koresh). There are many errors in language throughout.
16. Note for example the following extract: 'Dear Dick, As far as our progress is concerned, here is where we stand: I have related two messages, from God, to the FBI; one of which concerns present danger to people here in Waco.' A copy of this letter is in my possession.
17. It is widely reported that Koresh dropped out in the ninth grade, but this seems to be in error. See further Reavis, *Ashes of Waco*, 26.
18. Clairborne and McGee, 'Making of Koresh', 19. The information is from an interview with Earline Clark and hence seems secure.

19. NT 45; elsewhere Koresh says that he was a 'finish carpenter' and used to do trim work (e.g. NT 56).
20. NT 45.
21. On the KRLD tape of 28 February (see further Chapter Twelve) Koresh says to the interviewer (Charlie Serafin, vice-president and station manager for KRLD), 'Would you do something me a favour … would you tell Linda Campion—Linda Campion that I still love her and I'm gonna be back, OK? … and also tell Sandy, tell Sandy Berlin that I'll be back and I still love her too.'
22. NT 45; on the KRLD tape Koresh mentions Linda's father, a man he clearly holds in very high regard.
23. These are discussed more fully in Chapter Thirteen. Koresh says, in effect, that Linda did not listen to him and must now, sadly, face the consequences. FBI bug tape 16, March 1993, SA66–1.
24. NT 149.
25. NT 45.
26. It was at this point, it seems, that he began dating another girl, Debbie Owens, a sixteen-year-old waitress. Clairborne and McGee interviewed her, and she apparently told them, rather interestingly, that during the seven months or so that she and Koresh were going out with one another he never once mentioned the Bible or religion ('Making of Koresh', 21).
27. NT 46; see also Reavis, *Ashes of Waco*, 29.
28. See King and Breault, *Preacher of Death*, 33. On the KRLD tape Koresh seems to refer to his child by Linda Campion when he says 'and tell Linda [to]—keep my little girl, you know I've let her do what she had to do but I still love her OK'. There is a scribbled note preserved in TXC 2D216, 'Miscellaneous box 2', that begins 'Dear Linda, how's my favorite person doing? Well I am going to get straight to the point … Will you marry me'; this may have been written by Koresh.
29. This detail emerges in the course of a speech at the Hawaiian Diamond Head Seventh-day Adventist Church meeting that expelled a number of members on account of their association with the Branch Davidians. The meeting was held on 27 June 1987 and was taped; a copy is in my possession.
30. Clairborne and McGee, 'Making of Koresh', 22 (the authors have evidently interviewed the Bockmanns).
31. King and Breault, *Preacher of Death*, 35. No further evidence has been found in support of this story.
32. NT 46; see also Reavis, *Ashes of Waco*, 29–30.
33. Thibodeau, *A Place Called Waco*, 42.
34. Clairborne and McGee, 'Making of Koresh', 18 (the authors evidently interviewed Hardy Tapp, an elder at the church, and hence the date seems reasonably secure). See also King and Breault, *Preacher of Death*, 35.
35. Evidence can be found in plentiful supply by typing 'Revelation Seminar Adventist Church' into almost any web search engine.
36. Clairborne and McGee, 'Making of Koresh', 23.

37. For example, Maggie Bockmann said that while Koresh was living with them he would tell her sometimes of physical abuse he had suffered as a child (from what source is not stated). He even revealed a physical scar on one occasion which, he said, has been caused by being forced to kneel on a heat register (Clairborne and McGee, 'Making of Koresh', 23).

38. Adair, 'Interviews', 94, stated that Koresh visited him in his home in Salem in 'the late seventies'. If so, this would mean that Howell had an interest in Davidianism before his first visit to Mt. Carmel in 1981. However, Adair seems in error on this point, for he also stated that Koresh's visit was 'after he got control of new Mount Carmel'.

39. There is an alternative account of how Howell became involved with the Branch Davidians in Roberts, *Beyond the Flames*, 99. According to that account, which Roberts said was given to him by George Roden, it was Howell's mother who first became interested in Lois's message, and hence it was through this contact that Koresh became acquainted with the tradition. Roberts also has the more widely known account, which, he says, was given to him by Branch Davidian Sheila Martin (*Beyond the Flames*, 100).

40. The main source of information is a personal interview I conducted with Clive Doyle in Waco on 18 Nov. 2002.

41. King and Breault, *Preacher of Death*, 38.

42. Bailey and Darden, *Mad Man in Waco*, 71.

43. Doyle said that these studies were given in Sept. 1983.

44. Bailey and Darden, *Mad Man in Waco*, 73.

45. The other children who died were Serenity and twins Chica and Latwan (born to Michele Jones, Rachel's sister), Dayland and Paige (born to Nicole Gent), Chanel (born to Katherine Andrade), Startle (born to Aisha Gyarfas), Mayanah (born to Judy Schneider), and Hollywood (born to Lorraine Sylvia). Three children had left Mt. Carmel prior to the raid—Shaun (born to Robyn Bunds) and Sky and Scooter (born to Dana Okimoto). The count also includes Shayna Cull, the daughter born before Koresh joined the Branch Davidians, but not the two unborn children who died *in utero* during the fire. See further Tabor and Gallagher, *Why Waco?*, 231 n. 22.

46. Bailey and Darden, *Mad Man in Waco*, 74.

47. NT 7.

48. The letter is headed, 'points for George'. A copy is located in TXC 2D216.

49. The last 'Howellites' left Mt. Carmel on 17 Mar. 1985; *Mad Man in Waco*, 77 (the source used by Bailey and Darden here is George's typescript 'The Red Heifer', 5, located in TXC 2D212/17).

50. The period of time is given in *Mad Man in Waco*, 78. Mexia is in Limestone County, about 35 miles from Waco.

51. See the short account of life at Palestine provided by Elizabeth Baranyai in King and Breault, *Preacher of Death*, 60–1 and the photographs of the encampment in Bailey and Darden, *Mad Man in Waco*, 130–1. Some further photographs are

found in an album in TXC 2D218 and TXC 2D218, one of which is produced as plate seven in this book.

52. There is one letter from this period in Palestine, Texas, which unfortunately is not dated. It begins: 'Brothers and Sisters at Campmeeting [presumably an SDA camp meeting] The Lord is very angry because your leaders have rejected the fourth, fifth, and sixth angel's messages of Revelation 14:14–18, which came in 1929, 1955, and 1977. The seventh angel's message, Revelation 10:7, 14:17, and 18:1, HAS ARRIVED and once again they have turned aside and ignored this FINAL MESSAGE from heaven.' It is signed 'The Seventh Angel'. The letter is probably to be dated after the trip to Israel in 1985 and is located in the TXC, Mark Sweet Collection/David Koresh.

53. See also *Why Waco?*, 59.

54. The words 'as he hath declared to his servants the prophets' were particularly important to Howell. It was his view that the work of the seventh angel was not to reveal new truth as such, but rather to unpack what was already there in the writings of 'his [God's] servants the prophets', i.e. in the Old Testament. This will be explored in detail in Chapter Eleven.

55. NT 198; see also NT 7; NT 9; NT 21; NT 46; NT 57 *et passim* where Koresh repeats some of these details, emphasizing that it was in 1985 that he began his work, and explaining further that while he was in Israel he had been given 'additional laws' which he then came back to Waco to pass on the community. On NT 134 Koresh says, '. . . in '85, like I say, you know, when I was in Israel, that's, that's exactly what got this whole thing started'.

56. A very brief reference to some sort of experience in Israel in 1985 is found also during the course of a video tape recorded in Los Angeles in 1987. Here Koresh said simply that he had 'an experience' while he was in Israel and that he was instructed to teach people the prophecies. A copy of this video is in TXC (Mark Swett collection video box). It is dated 28 Feb. 1987.

57. The only one it has been possible to trace to date is in *Parade* magazine; an undated photocopy of the relevant pages is in my possession. According to this source, six Soviet cosmonauts said that they witnessed the most awe-inspiring spectacle ever encountered in space—a band of glowing angels with wings as big as jumbo jets. According to the Weekly World News, presumably the source of the magazine article, cosmonauts Vladimir Solevev, Oleg Atkov, and Leonid Kizim said they first saw the celestial beings last July during their 155th day aboard the orbiting Salyut7 space station. ' "What we saw", they said, "were seven giant figures in the form of humans, but with wings and mistlike halos, as in the classic depiction of angels. Their faces were round with cherubic smiles." Twelve days later, the figures were seen by three other Soviet scientists, including woman cosmonaut Svetlana Savitskaya. "They were smiling," she said, "as though they shared in a glorious secret" '.

58. Tabor and Gallagher, *Why Waco?*, 59.

59. Koresh had evidently telephoned into the show and can be heard very clearly on it. The quality of the recording is naturally very good given that it was professional.

What Koresh says is quite extensive and also very interesting as it captures his mood on the night of the siege. Further remarks on the content of the tape, a copy which is in my possession, are found in Chapters Eleven, Twelve, Thirteen, Fifteen, and Sixteen.

60. Hence, according to Gen. 17.5, 'Abram' became 'Abraham' and 'Simon' was renamed by Jesus as 'Cephas/Peter' in Mark 3.16 ('Cephas' is the Aramaic word for 'rock', which, when translated into Greek, becomes 'Petros').

61. Wisconsin Tape, 24 Aug. 1987.

62. A copy of this tape is in my possession. The quality is patchy. Most of side one is audible, though one section is so faint as to make it virtually impossible to hear. Side two is very faint indeed.

63. The Knapps are probably Ruth and Harold Knapp. According to Paul Lippi, pastor of the SDA congregation in Jerusalem, the Knapps attended the congregation in Rehov, Lincoln, and in fact had donated and installed a new carpet in the church (email from Paul Lippi to Kenneth G. C. Newport, 21 Jan. 2001). It is evident from what Howell said that the Knapps were known well before his arrival in Israel as supporters of the Branch Davidian cause.

64. Some further insight into the centrality of the events in Israel can be found on the recording of the Diamond Head SDA church meeting. Here Howell talked about his trip to Israel in 1985 and said that while he was there he was 'shown the whole Bible'. He then went on to link in Zech. 2.4 and stated unequivocally that he was the 'young man' mentioned in that verse. He continued: 'And so in 1985 a young man comes back from Israel saying 'listen!'; and not one scholar or theologian has been able to gainsay the mass of information and the combining of all the prophets for the first time in the history of the world and making all the stories very clear and very plain.'

65. The date written on the tape box itself is '2/4/85', but this is almost certainly wrong since the tape strongly implied that Lois is already dead (she died Oct. 1986).

66. There is a General Conference Session every five years. In 1985 it was in New Orleans and met from 27 June to 6 July.

67. NT 75.

10

'And Death Shall Follow in His Wake' (cf. Revelation 6.8): Vernon Howell, David Koresh, and the Branch Davidians, 1986–1993

George Roden was not a man to be underestimated, and Koresh was wise not to make that mistake. Rather than forcing the formal leadership question at this juncture Koresh[1] was to spend the next two years in fairly intensive evangelistic activity, both inside and outside the USA. In this he was assisted at first by his father-in-law, Perry Jones, and later by others of his early converts. The recruitments went well, and with every new recruit Koresh's influence, power, and sense of divine favour must surely have increased.

One of the earliest converts was also one of the most important: Marc Breault. Breault, a native of Hawaii, was a Seventh-day Adventist who had studied for an undergraduate degree in theology at the SDA Pacific Union College in Angwin, California. Upon completing his studies, he was deeply disappointed not to be offered the chance by the SDA Church to become a pastor, a decision which he rightly or wrongly put down to the fact that he was all but blind. In January 1986, after what he considered to be a divine instruction to that effect, he began studying for a postgraduate degree at Loma Linda University in California (also an SDA institution). It was at this time that he came into contact with the Branch Davidians.[2] According to his own testimony, he was in a supermarket when he was approached by Perry Jones. They got talking about the book of Revelation and Jones told Breault that he thought Koresh, his son-in-law, was a prophet. 'I figured God would send some prophets eventually,' stated Breault, 'so I was open to listening.'[3] Within a few days Jones had introduced Breault to Koresh himself. With regard to this early encounter Breault wrote:

I was impressed by Vernon. He was straightforward, sure of what he believed, and had a wealth of biblical knowledge within the conservative SDA context. In those days, the BDs were extremely conservative. I did not join the group at once. I took my time making up my mind and Vernon was happy to give me whatever time I needed.[4]

But Breault did make up his mind and about three months later joined the Branch Davidians, though apparently staying at Loma Linda to complete his studies before moving to Waco.[5] He was to play a central role in Branch Davidian history from this point, first as an able evangelist and firm supporter of, and confidant to, Koresh, and later a vociferous ex-member who did all he could to bring Koresh to the attention of both the SDA Church and the USA government authorities.

In January 1986, then, Koresh was in California, where he met Breault, but his efforts to spread the word that God's mystery was now being revealed were not confined to the USA. In February 1986 he arrived in Australia.[6] With him was Clive Doyle, a native Australian who had been at Mt. Carmel since 1966 and was well placed to advise Koresh on tactics.[7] Not only was Doyle on the Australian SDA network, but he also had a good knowledge of the Seventh-day Adventists in Australia who were interested in specifically Branch publications. For years he had played a key role in Lois Roden's Branch Davidianism, had served as editor of *Shekinah,* and had other significant responsibilities with regard to the publishing work.

Prior to his visit to Australia, Koresh had evidently sought to prepare the ground to some extent by sending ahead audio tapes of his message. These were mailed to those in Australia already known to have an interest in or commitment to Branch Davidianism. However, according to Breault those studies had received only limited attention.[8] One person who was interested was Elizabeth Baranyai, later to become Breault's wife.[9] She convinced other Australian Branch Davidians that they should at least give Koresh a hearing, a process which led to the visit. Baranyai met Koresh at Tullamarine Airport in Melbourne and facilitated his meetings with other interested Branch Davidians and Seventh-day Adventists. He met with some of these, and following this and later meetings a number of Australian Branch Davidians accepted his message. It was at this time, for example, that the Gent family became involved with Koresh. The conversions were not instantaneous, nor did they all occur during this first visit. In the end, however, all four of the Gents (twins Peter and Nicole and parents Bruce and Lisa) became followers.[10] Jean Smith was also recruited at this time.[11]

This was not the only trip Koresh was to make to Australia. He was evidently there again in 1988 and in February 1990.[12] 'Pastor Whelan' (then pastor of one of the Melbourne SDA churches) spoke of this last trip when he recorded that he had attended a Branch Davidian recruitment meeting with another SDA pastor, Pawel Cieslar.[13] The total number in attendance is not given by Whelan, but he noted that about twenty of his own church members were there.[14] Other Australians who accepted the Branch Davidian message and were at Waco at the time of the siege include Oliver[15] and Aisha Gyarfas[16] and Graeme Craddock.[17]

It is not clear how long Koresh's 1986 visit to Australia lasted. However, by the summer of that year he was in Hawaii. Again the trip was well planned. During the first months of 1986 the newly converted Breault, himself a native of Hawaii, had sent a number of letters to his friends back home telling them of his new-found faith in the message of Koresh.[18] It was Breault who first contacted Steve Schneider,[19] an individual who was to play an absolutely key role in later Branch Davidian recruitment trips, especially in England. (It was Schneider too who took the lead role in the negotiations during the stand-off;[20] he also, in all probability, was responsible for the single shot to the head that brought Koresh's life to an end on 19 April).[21] Schneider was no fool. He had studied for the SDA ministry at Newbold College, but in February 1973 had been asked to leave following a bout of drunkenness.[22] He also had an MA degree in Comparative Religion from the University of Hawaii and according to some sources taught a module there in the subject.[23] In 1986 he was a deacon and a Sabbath School leader in the SDA Church.[24] It was Breault, too, who recruited the wealthy businessman Paul Fatta, who was later to be centrally involved in Branch Davidian business concerns, including the trading of survival equipment.[25]

The recruitment in Hawaii was a considerable success. A core group of interested persons was formed under the guidance of Breault and Schneider. According to Breault, that group included Margaret Lawson,[26] Gertude and Henry Chun, Dana Okimoto,[27] the Wendell family,[28] the Vaega family,[29] Peter Hipsman,[30] and Paul Fatta. The group grew with the later additions of Greg Summers,[31] Sherri Jewell,[32] and Karl Henning.[33] Koresh arrived in August 1986 and soon a number of other Hawaiian Seventh-day Adventists had also become convinced of his message. Some of the core group seem in the end to have rejected the message, or at least not taken up the challenge of moving to Waco, while others who were not part of the original group came in. In the end there were eighteen solid converts from Hawaii. These were Breault himself, Paul Fatta, Peter Hipsman, Sherri Jewell, Andre Kale,[34] Margaret Lawson, Jeff Little,[35] Dana Okimoto, Judy Schneider,[36] Steve Schneider, Fioracita Sonobe,[37] Scott Sonobe,[38] Greg Summers, Margarida Vaega, Neil Vaega, Jaydean Wendell, Mark Wendell, and Kevin Whitecliff.[39] As one might expect the interaction between Breault, Koresh, and the Hawaiian SDA Church was far from smooth, and in the end fourteen members were disfellowshipped.[40]

It was not long before other possible targets for evangelism were marked out. Steve and Judy Schneider were originally from Wisconsin and hence it was probably at their suggestion that Breault went to Wisconsin to spread the news there too. Schneider himself remained in Hawaii to take care of the work there. This was in July 1986, still a month or so before Koresh himself arrived.

In December 1986 both Schneider and Koresh joined Breault in Wisconsin prior to the move back to Palestine, Texas. About a year later Schneider returned to Wisconsin in a second attempt to further the work there.[41] The work in Wisconsin did not go well. There was some initial interest and even some visits to Texas, but in the end there were no firm conversions. Schneider's sister, it seems, was instrumental in persuading others in Wisconsin that her brother, Breault, and Koresh were wrong.[42]

During 1987 Koresh was also active in other parts of the United States. Don Adair remembered that Koresh once stopped at Salem. The year appears to be 1987, but the precise date is not given. Adair stated:

He [Koresh] was going around to all the Davidians, trying to get converts. And he came here, and stood at this blackboard and drew some things up there. And I had the students with me, and we all listened for a while, about an hour or so. And he was so mixed up that I finally told him that we didn't want to hear any more, and he left, and we never heard from him again.[43]

A visit of Koresh to a Los Angeles SDA Church was videotaped; the date is given as 28 February 1987.[44] On the video we see a heavily bearded Koresh who lacks, at least at the start of the tape, some of the powerful self-confidence that later sources clearly indicate he had.

This meeting in California was not the only time that Koresh was in that state. In fact during this period he moved between Texas and California very frequently. In substantial part this was through contact with and the support of long-time Branch Davidians, the Bunds family. It has been noted above that Donald and Jeannine were firm supporters of Ben Roden and contributed financially to the movement; Roden wrote to them frequently. They supported Koresh too. They paid for two houses, one in Pomona[45] and the other in La Verne,[46] and these, together with a rented house in Los Angeles,[47] formed a physical HQ for the Branch Davidians in California. Koresh was there frequently. (On one of the negotiation tapes, Schneider says of the house in Pomona, 'we, of course, spent a lot of time there, a lot of people, from about the time of 87'.)[48] The Bunds' two children, David and Robyn, were also Branch Davidians. The whole family later defected and became vociferous in their opposition to Koresh.[49]

The influx of new converts from these evangelistic campaigns must have given Koresh and the rest of the Branch members back in Texas considerable cause for celebration. But a strange situation had developed. Koresh had the people, George Roden, on the other hand, still had the property and, officially, the leadership of the group. This situation was eventually changed through a chain of events that must surely be among the strangest even in the oftentimes odd world of religious movements.

It was George Roden who threw down the gauntlet. Sometime in October 1987 he decided to settle matters once and for all by challenging Koresh to a contest which would, surely, put the issue to rest. George sent word to Koresh that he had dug up a body and placed it in the chapel. Whoever could raise the person from the dead would be acknowledged as the rightful leader of the movement. The body was that of Anna Hughes, who had died some twenty years earlier.[50]

Koresh was not going to be drawn into such a contest, but saw another way to sort the issue out. He visited the sheriff's office and made a charge of corpse abuse against George. The authorities said they would need evidence before the matter could be taken further. In an effort to supply such evidence, Koresh and a few of his followers went to Mt. Carmel with the intention of taking photographs, and were successful. When questioned, Doyle remembered the photographs of the coffin, noting that it was still covered in mud and somewhat rusty in places. An Israeli flag was draped over it.[51] This evidence was not enough, however, and the authorities asked for a clear indication that the coffin actually contained a body. Undeterred, on the night of 2 November Koresh and seven of his followers went back to attempt to secure a more precise photographic record of what was going on in the chapel. The seven were Paul Fatta, Peter Hipsman, Floyd Houtman,[52] David Jones, James Riddle,[53] Gregory Summers, and Stan Sylvia.[54] It was night and Koresh, very wisely given that he was dealing with George, was armed. The coffin had gone.

According to Doyle, the group then spent the entire night hiding in a ditch waiting for sunrise and the opportunity to search the Mt. Carmel site for the missing coffin; this was a rash move given George's propensity for violence, but in the end it paid off. They began their search by going door-to-door and asking for information. Unsurprisingly, it was not long before George was alerted and he reacted in a way that could have been predicted. A gun battle ensued between George, who was apparently in possession of an Uzi machine gun, and the group, armed with semi-automatics.[55] Eventually George was pinned by Koresh behind a tree, being shot at if he tried to escape from either one side or the other. Even in a relatively isolated place such as Mt. Carmel, such activity could not go unnoticed for long and soon law enforcement officers arrived and both the Koresh group and George were arrested. Charges of attempted murder were brought against Koresh and the other members of the group. The trial was reported extensively in the local papers and also in the *Dallas Morning* News.[56] Within three days Koresh had posted the $50,000 bail. The other seven accused remained in prison,[57] but all eventually met the bail terms.

George had opposed the release of Koresh and his followers on the grounds that they would come back to the property and finish the job they had started.

Not known for his diplomacy, George then began a campaign of lodging motions with the court written in his usual style. A page of one of those motions is found in the archives. Part of it reads (George's spelling corrected): 'If you think you're God then God would have taken the poor into account. But you sons of bitches have your goddam clique to take care of don't you? You can't afford to allow the poor to get any benefit or you might lose your ass in the process. You fucking son[s] of bitches . . .'[58] The paper then predicts (in even more intemperate language) that the judges will probably get herpes and AIDS as part of the seven last plagues.

Not surprisingly the court asked George to cease this onslaught. He did not—a big mistake which lost him 'Rodenville' as a result. On 22 March 1988 Judge Walter S. Smith (who was to play an important role in later developments in the tragedy) found Roden in contempt of court and jailed him for six months. The next day about forty people returned from Palestine and walked onto the Mt. Carmel property. According to a newspaper report the group was led by Perry Jones, which suggests that Koresh himself was not present. Amo Roden, George's wife, protested, but was ignored.[59] Koresh's group was back at Mt. Carmel and would remain there until the fire.

The trial of Koresh and his followers took place in April 1988. The proceedings lasted ten days and in the end, on 25 April, a verdict of not guilty was returned on all defendants other than Koresh. The jury was unable to come to a decision on him, and the judge declared a mistrial. After a few weeks the charges against Koresh were dropped and no retrial ever took place.[60]

By April 1988, then, Koresh and his followers were in a good position: George was in jail for contempt of court, and Mt. Carmel was vacant. The next move Koresh made was a very smart one: he raised some $62,000 of back taxes that were owing on the property, and paid the bill off. By the end of April the entire group had moved from Palestine back to Waco.[61] Anna Hughes was still resting in her coffin in a shed. She was eventually reburied in the Mt. Carmel graveyard on 4 May. Koresh spoke a few words at her graveside on the afternoon of her reburial; David Jones, who as a boy of thirteen had helped lower Hughes into the ground the first time she had been buried, fulfilled the same duty again.[62] George was finally released on 22 December 1988; at the conclusion of his six-month term for contempt of court he was sentenced to a further thirty days for previously violating the restraining order that his mother had taken out against him in 1979.[63] He continued his campaign against Koresh until on 18 October 1989 he was charged by the Odessa police with killing Dale Adair, the brother of Don Adair.[64] George was judged to be insane and sent to a mental institution, where he died in 1998.

PLATE 8 Early photograph of David Koresh

Koresh was now firmly in charge and was able once again to turn his mind to recruitment. Later in 1988 the very able Steve Schneider arrived in England to make the first concerted attempt to bring the message to the SDA churches there.[65] He headed for Newbold College, the SDA training institution about thirty miles from London (not, as is widely stated in some secondary literature, near Nottingham). Schneider already knew the college since he had been a student there fifteen or so years before; a request was made that the college provide space for meetings to take place, but the request was denied. Schneider then conducted meetings in the house of one of the college's staff members. Precisely how many meetings took place is not clear, but notes from one of them at least have been preserved. These are dated 20 September 1988.[66]

Three key converts were made at Newbold—Livingstone Fagan, John McBean,[67] and Cliff Sellors.[68] The latter two died in the fire. Fagan left Mt. Carmel during the siege and was given a forty-year prison sentence, later reduced to fifteen years, for his part in the 28 February shoot-out. He was to play a major role in post-1993 Branch Davidianism and his contribution is assessed in greater detail in Chapter Sixteen.

From Newbold the evangelistic work spread to several other parts of the UK. Fagan was active in Nottingham, where he was a ministerial intern. McBean worked in Manchester and further work was undertaken in London. A number of further recruits were won. These included, from London, Leslie Lewis,[69] Bernadette Monbelly,[70] and Teresa Norbrega.[71] Renos Avraam[72] also came into the movement around this time. Following a visit in late 1988 or possibly early 1989 by Koresh himself[73] and another visit by Schneider in 1990 a further substantial number of converts were made.[74] Twenty-three of those who died on 19 April were British and a further six Britons left Mt. Carmel during the siege.[75] Britain, then, was a major recruitment ground.

But the work continued back in the USA as well. Waco itself was hardly the best of recruitment grounds, but the foothold the Branch Davidians had in California was more promising; it is clear that Koresh and other members of the group spent a good deal of time in California even after gaining legal ownership of Mt. Carmel. Koresh came into contact at this time with David Thibodeau. Thibodeau, originally from Maine, had gone to Los Angeles in February 1989 to attend the Musicians' Institute there. In early 1990 he was in a music shop on Sunset Boulevard purchasing some drumsticks when he noticed two other men, who turned out to be Steve Schneider and David Koresh. Schneider told Thibodeau that they were looking for a drummer for their band and handed him the 'Messiah Productions' business card. A few days later Thibodeau called Schneider and was taken out to the Pomona house (a 45 minute drive). Shortly after this he was visited by Schneider and some of the other Branch Davidians (but not Koresh) in his apartment for a pre-arranged Bible study. A number of Thibodeau's fellow lodgers were there. Schneider led the Bible study, on Isaiah. Over the next few weeks this pattern of music sessions and Bible studies continued. In September Thibodeau was invited to visit Waco for the Day of Atonement celebrations, an offer he accepted.[76] After about two weeks Koresh told Thibodeau to go home to Maine to think things over before making a decision on whether or not he wanted to join the Mt. Carmel community. If he did decide to join, however, Koresh said, his commitment must be total.[77] Thibodeau duly went back to Maine, made his decision, and returned to Los Angeles to meet again with Koresh.

It is plain, then, that the house in Pomona, and the rented property in Los Angeles, were used for recruitment and as a base for the Branch Davidians in California. The house in La Verne, however, seems to have been used for another purpose. From fairly early in his prophetic career Koresh came to the view that it was his right, indeed his duty, to have numerous children. He was probably aiming for twenty-four, the number of the elders seated around the throne in Revelation 4.4, 10 *et passim*. Clearly if he was to do this he would need more than one partner. Once he was in control of the group he quickly set about taking what he considered his right, namely sexual access to the women of the community. This came in two stages: first, to unmarried Branch Davidian women, and then, in 1989, to all the women of the community, including those already married. This latter phase was introduced as the so-called 'new light' doctrine. The house in La Verne seems to have been the place where Koresh often engaged in this activity, especially before 1989. It was where his harem sometimes lived.[78]

Tales of Koresh's sexual exploits abound in the literature and there can be no doubt that he did engage in significant sexual activity, some with very young girls.[79] Probably the youngest of these was Michele Jones, the younger sister of Koresh's legal wife Rachel. She later became Thibodeau's wife; when he met her she was fifteen.[80]

Thibodeau's link with Michele Jones led him to make some enquiries regarding her association with Koresh. Thibodeau, one must remember, was and is sympathetic to Koresh's vision of things. With regard to Koresh's sexual conduct Thibodeau is clear: Koresh did have sex with Michele Jones.[81] The first time was in early 1987 and Jones was twelve at the time. Two years later Jones had a child by Koresh, Serenity. It must not be forgotten that by the time Thibodeau wrote, Jones was his now-dead wife. This being so, what he has to say about Koresh's sexual exploits can be taken as being pretty near the truth of the matter. (If you are sympathetic to a person and want to invent something to say about him, saying he had sex with your now deceased wife when she was hardly pubescent is not the kind of story you would be most likely to come up with).

In fact Koresh's interest in Michele seems to have begun even earlier. On his return from Israel in 1985 Koresh announced that he had received a command from God that he should have a child with Michele. She would have been only ten or eleven at the time. There is no suggestion that he actually then engaged in sex with Michele, but he was clearly thinking about it. This instruction to have a child with Michele was evidently discussed with the community in general and with Rachel Jones in particular, who was 'devastated' by the news. Discussions continued for some considerable time—a couple of years, in fact. However, in the end Rachel cleared the way by reporting that she had had a dream in which she was shown that Koresh might be destroyed by God if he failed to carry out God's orders. It was at this point that he began to have sex with the under-age Michele.

Once this line had been crossed, things developed quickly. In the same year, 1987, Koresh began sexual relations with a number of other women in the community. These included Robyn Bunds,[82] the daughter of Donald and Jeannine Bunds; Dana Okimoto; and in the following year he 'married' nineteen-year-old Nicole Gent.

Several of the younger women with whom Koresh was engaging in sexual activity were married off to other members of the community (Robyn Bunds to Cliff Sellors, Michele Jones to David Thibodeau). It may be that Koresh encouraged some of these marriages to head off possible investigation by immigration authorities (though some of those married were already US citizens). If so, they had the further (perhaps unintended) benefit of heading off possible suspicion that statutory rape was taking place. The legal age of consent in Texas is seventeen, but marriage is permitted at the age of fourteen (with parental consent) and sex may occur within that marriage. Hence while the pregnancy of girls between the ages of fourteen and seventeen might have raised questions on the part of the authorities, if the girls were married the assumption would have been that the child's father was the husband and hence that the sexual activity was legal. However, if an unmarried fourteen-to-seventeen-year-old were seen to be pregnant, then statutory rape must necessarily have been involved. None of this counts in the case of Michele Jones, who was under fourteen when she fell pregnant. Indeed, since she was under fourteen the crime was a first-degree felony (the rape of a girl over fourteen would be a second-degree felony). In having sex with Michele, Koresh was risking ninety-nine years in prison.

Koresh, then, had an extremely active sex life at this time. However, more was to follow. In 1989 he began to teach the 'new light' doctrine, which brought to the community new stresses but also an even greater sense of single purpose. According to this doctrine, Koresh was the only male at Mt. Carmel permitted to have sex, and he was permitted, in fact commanded by God, to have sex with the wives of the other Branch Davidian men, not just those who were in marriages of convenience, but those who had married even before coming to Mt. Carmel. Consequently in the same year he began sleeping with a number of married women. These included Jeannine Bunds, Judy Schneider, Lorraine Sylvia,[83] and Jaydean Wendell.[84] This was a bold move on Koresh's part and he was taking a big risk. So dramatic and direct an attempt to divide husband from wife and reorder the sexual patterns of the group could easily have gone badly wrong. It is surely a measure of the loyalty those at Mt. Carmel felt towards Koresh that in fact this 'new light' was accepted. There may have been some dissent and it must have been very difficult. However, in general it seems that the group accepted that Koresh as leader ought to have exclusive sexual access to the women. This was agreed by both the women and the men concerned. Such radical adjustments of social structures within the context of a high-commitment group is not unique, but it is only at the extreme end of the scale that one is likely to meet it. Such doctrines can bring an even greater sense of cohesion to any group that espouses them, for it is only the very committed who can make the necessary mental and spiritual adjustments to accommodate them. Some of the weaker members of the group may be lost, but those who remain will be strong and will be aware that their investment in the group has gone far beyond mere money. They are now investing even their most treasured personal relationships in pursuit of the common (in this case millennial) goal.

From 1985 on, then, Koresh pursued an aggressively sexual agenda and was highly successful not only in persuading women to sleep with him, but also in convincing the husbands, mothers, and fathers of those women that it was all part of God's plan. The end result is difficult to ascertain, since for obvious reasons the paternity of the children born at Mt. Carmel was not always made clear in the registration documentation. However, Thibodeau's summary seems about right (if anything, perhaps, a little conservative): 'By April 1993, David had had sexual relations with a total of fifteen women, including Rachel Jones and Linda Campion . . . and had fathered seventeen children with eleven of them'.[85]

It was not all plain sailing, however. In July 1989 Koresh lost one of his most loyal converts: Marc Breault. Breault had evidently been having some serious doubts about Koresh for some time, but in July 1989 matters came to a head. As Breault told the story he was working on a computer one evening when he saw Aisha Gyarfas go up to Koresh's room. Breault stayed at the computer all night and awaited Aisha's return, which occurred at about 5.00 a.m. and Breault took both the fact and the length of the young girl's stay in Koresh's room (Aisha Gyarfas would have been about thirteen at the time) as an indication of sexual activity. Breault later said that it was at this point that he decided to leave the Branch Davidians. His way out was to persuade Koresh that they needed to go to California to buy some musical equipment. While there, Breault telephoned his wife in Australia and asked her to send him money for his airfare, which she did. On 29 September 1989 he left the house in Pomona and caught a flight to Melbourne. It was a major defection and would have serious consequences.[86] Soon after Koresh would give a message that surely ranks as one of the most forceful to survive. In that message he warned of the dire consequences of rejecting his revelation, for if one rejected that (as Breault had now done) one rejected also the one who sent the message and the one through whom the message came.[87]

Koresh had stepped over the line in the case of Michele Jones and had committed statutory rape, though in the end the crime was not taken up by the authorities. But another alleged offence was, that Koresh had attempted some sort of sexual relationship with Kiri Jewell. It was Breault who sought to bring that relationship to the attention of those outside the community: in the first instance the attention of the girl's father, and then the law-enforcement authorities. Kiri Jewell was the daughter of Sherri Jewell (one of the Hawaiian converts) and David Jewell, who was never a member of the Branch Davidian movement. David Jewell and his wife Sherri had divorced in 1982, at which time Sherri moved back to her native Hawaii, where she came into contact with the Branch Davidians.[88] In October 1991 Marc Breault telephoned David Jewell, then living in Michigan, and informed him that his daughter Kiri was destined for 'the house of David', that is, that she would soon be one of Koresh's wives.[89] This story was later backed up by a number of others, all of whom said that they had heard Koresh speak about the time when Kiri would be in his 'house'. No actual case of abuse was alleged, but the possibility that such a crime might occur in the near future was clearly raised. Startled by this thought, David Jewell immediately sought custody of his child and the case went to a Michigan court. Marc Breault, Elizabeth Baranyai, and Jean Smith flew from Australia to testify in the case and provided the court with graphic details of Koresh's sex life.[90] Sherri Jewell did not testify. In the end David Jewell was awarded sole custody, though Sherri was awarded visitation rights.

Koresh's opponents had, then, won something of a victory not only in this particular case, but in general, in that they had brought Koresh squarely to the attention of the authorities. Encouraged by this, on 26 February 1992, Jewell and Breault contacted the Texas Department of Human Services and made further charges of actual or potential child abuse at Mt. Carmel. The next day Joyce Sparks from the Child Protective Services Department visited

Mt. Carmel to investigate the report. This visit is referred to in the affidavit filed in support of the request for the search-and-arrest warrants. According to that source Sparks, two other people from the Department of Human Services and two McLennan County sheriff's deputies visited Mt. Carmel, but Koresh was not there. However, Koresh went to see Sparks in her office in early March to discuss the charges and she returned to Mt. Carmel on 6 April and again on 30 April.[91] No evidence of child abuse was found during these visits, and the case was closed.

This was not the end of the story, however. According to the 1993 *Report*, Sparks interviewed 'a young girl...a former compound resident' on 22 February 1993 (the *Report* includes an extract from an interview conducted with Sparks). Sparks said that the young girl explained how Koresh had abused her in a hotel room.[92] No charges were brought against Koresh on this count, but it does seem to have been a factor in the issue of the search and arrest warrants. (This ought not to have been the case, since the jurisdiction of the ATF did not extent to such matters.)

It is certain, then, that Koresh did have sex with a significant number of the female members of the community. While this was in general consensual sex with adults, it seems certain too that he was guilty of the statutory rape of Michele Jones. Whether he also abused the unnamed girl interviewed by Sparks is not clear.

Why did he do it? Perhaps the most obvious possibility is that he did it for sheer selfish sexual gratification, and the sense of power that he got over the whole group by virtue of having exclusive sexual access to the women of the community. According to this theory his excessive sexual activity was the result of his selfish manipulation of the community and the abuse of the power the Branch Davidians had afforded him. This is possible. However, the model that such an interpretation reflects, namely that such communities are composed of a company of duped followers who are either too stupid or too brainwashed to see through the manipulative tactics of their egocentric leader, seems less than satisfactory in the case of the Branch Davidians. Under Koresh they were committed, serious, spiritual individuals, some of whom had razor-sharp minds. In putting their trust in Koresh the other members of the community may have been mistaken, as Koresh may have been mistaken in thinking of himself in the way that he did. But being mistaken is not the same as being fooled. Indeed, some might want to argue that the whole community, including Koresh, saw the procreation of the 'twenty-four children of David' as central to their communal goals. The women saw it as an honour to bear Koresh's children; the men saw it as a sacrifice that had to be made, tough as it was. Koresh may have got the better deal. He may have experienced significant physical pleasure and probably did get a huge ego boost from the whole experience. But this does not mean, necessarily, that he, unlike the rest of the group, did not actually believe in the goal towards which the Branch Davidians were corporately working. In fact, as we shall see, it is at this point that the FBI negotiators may later have made a fundamental mistake in seeking to deal with the Branch Davidians during the siege: the social unit that made up 'the Mt. Carmel Branch Davidians' was cohesive. It was not a flock of dazed sheep led to the slaughter by a predatory wolf. In communities of all kinds individual self-interest must be balanced with collective goals and at Mt. Carmel the balance come down heavily in favour of the latter.

There is one other possibility too. It will become apparent later that Koresh did have something of a death wish and was, despite vociferous claims to the contrary made by his supporters, looking for a fight with the authorities. How conscious he himself would have been of this is not known; perhaps, however, like the early Christian saint Justin Martyr, he openly courted death at the hands of the authorities in an effort to win favour with God. This is guesswork of course, though there is some evidence to support it. In a relatively early tape, 'The Bird' (August 1987), Koresh made it unambiguously clear that because of his wives 'the Bird' (himself) would be put to death by the authorities. Perhaps he was being overly negative here, thinking through the results of the actions he had already begun and seeing what their consequences might be. But it is strange that he said that he would be 'killed' as a result of what he was doing. Having sex with lots of women, providing they are of the age of consent, may be morally suspect but it is not a capital offence. Perhaps, then, this was a determined plan on the part of Koresh to bring on the showdown. He knew that having sex with someone under fourteen would result in his arrest for a first-degree felony. Was this, as Thibodeau himself hints, all part of Koresh's plan to bring on the end times?[93] Was Michele the means—the red rag—that Koresh needed to attract the attention of the American bull?

Since the days of Houteff, the Davidians and Branch Davidians had been very much a community gathered around a prophetic leader. There can be no doubt, however, that under Koresh the importance and status of that leader increased significantly. Indeed by 1993 Koresh himself had a near divine status in the eyes of many in the community. The theological underpinning of such views is taken up further in the next chapter, but here we note in passing at least one particular visible sign of the increasingly exalted status Koresh came to hold: his change of name. On 15 May 1990 Vernon Howell filed a petition in the California State Superior Court in Pomona requesting that his name be changed to David Koresh. The petition was granted by judge Robert Martinez on 28 August.[94] The reasons put forward in support of the change of name were centred upon Koresh's musical career, but the real reasons were theological. They will be discussed in some depth in the next chapter.

From 1990 to his death in 1993 Koresh stayed mainly at Mt. Carmel, with some trips to other parts of the United States. The community he had gathered was a loyal one and together its members lived at the centre, seeking to know God's plans for the future and making ready for the coming of the kingdom. Some insight into the nature of that community may be seen in the account by Derek Lovelock of the time he spent there (see Appendix A). Life was not easy, and the Branch Davidians worked physically very hard to revamp their property and construct the set of buildings that became so familiar to TV viewers around the world in March–April 1993. In 1992 Koresh put out a call for all the Branch Davidians to gather at Mt. Carmel for Passover; Doyle remembered that the numbers at the centre were, as a result, swelled to about 150.[95] About 130 of these were still there on the morning of the ATF raid some ten months later. Eighty of them were to die.

NOTES

1. The change of name did not legally take place until 1990, but it was clearly linked to the 1985 experience in Jerusalem. The new name is used from now on.
2. On this Breault stated: 'I met Koresh in January of 1986 in somewhat bizarre circumstances. Those circumstances were that in 1985, prior to having met or heard of either the Shepherd's Rod or the Branch Davidians, I had a dream out of the blue in which an angel bade me go to Loma Linda where I would meet seven people involved in a musical group. These seven people would help me see because I was blind spiritually. The angel said my physical eyesight, which is poor, mirrored my spiritual one. I did not have the money to follow these instructions so I was about to settle down to passing this off as just some weird experience, when out of the blue, the center for the blind in Hawaii where I lived offered to pay my full tuition for my master's program, pay for all of my books, and give me two thousand dollars toward the purchase of a new computer. Stunned, I decided to go to Loma Linda. Perry Jones and his daughter Rachel (Vernon's wife) were two of the seven people in my dream. When I saw Perry and Rachel, I recognized them instantly.' (E-mail to Kenneth Newport, 25 May 2003.)
3. E-mail to Kenneth Newport, 25 May 2003.
4. Ibid.
5. Dalton Baldwin, 'Experiences at Loma Linda', *Adventism Today*, 1 (May–June 1993). Baldwin was apparently one of Breault's teachers and remembered Breault asking permission to miss class for a week while he travelled to Waco to celebrate Passover.
6. Breault and King, *Preacher of Death*, 52.

7. Clive Doyle was born in 1941 in Melbourne, Australia. His first religious attach-
ment was to the Baptist Church, but some time before 1966 he came into contact
with the Branch Davidian message and accepted it. He moved to the USA in 1966.
(Information from Civil Trial Transcripts, 1081–1083.)

8. E-mail to Kenneth Newport, 25 May 2003.

9. Elizabeth Baranyai was born of a German mother and a Hungarian father. She has
a brother John, who had no interest in Koresh's message. Although she spent time
at Mt. Carmel she had defected from the movement several years before the siege.

10. Both Bruce and Lisa defected prior to the siege. Peter and Nicole Gent, the
children of Bruce Gent and step children of Lisa, accepted the message and
both died in Waco—Peter on 28 February and Nicole on 19 April. Nicole was
heavily pregnant when she died, and it is generally assumed that the child was
fathered by Koresh. There were two other children in the Gent family, Michelle
and Ian Manning, Lisa Gent's children of a previous marriage. Michelle Manning
became Michelle Tom and she and her husband James spent time at Mt. Carmel.
Ian Manning became a Branch Davidian together with his wife, Allison, and spent
time at Mt. Carmel. Ian Manning later defected and became a vociferous opponent of Koresh. For example, both he and Allison were involved in the Kiri Jewell
custody case, which will be discussed later (extracts of the relevant affidavits are
found in the *Treasury Report*, 224–5). Further, in a letter Ian Manning wrote to Dr
Gilbert Valentine, then pastor of the Newbold College Church, he stated, 'I first
met Howell in 1987 and listened to his teachings until about May of 1990. At this
time I was shown by others who had left Howell's following where his teachings
were wrong. During three years I listened to Howell's interpretations of the Bible
[and] I made a total of three visits to the United States; I might add that these
trips were made at considerable expense in terms of finance and time.' Ian
Manning to Gilbert Valentine, 20 May 1991. The letter then goes on to warn
Valentine about Koresh and asks for Valentine's help in locating Britons known to
be under Koresh's influence. A copy of the letter is in my possession.

11. In March 1986 (very shortly after his first visit) Koresh sent a tape-recorded letter
to Jean Smith expressing his pleasure at having met her and the other 'branches'
in Australia. Koresh then went over some fairly standard material (from his point
of view) on the coming of an end-time messenger who would 'seal' the people of
God. Smith did travel to the USA, though it is not clear how often, if at all, she
went to Waco. What is certain is that she did stay at the Branch Davidian house in
La Verne, California. She too evidently defected from the group some time before
1992, since it was in that year that she, with Marc Breault and Elizabeth Baranyai,
flew from Australia to California to testify against Koresh in the Jewell custody
hearing. Smith was seventy-two at the time (*Waco Tribune-Herald*, 'The Sinful
Messiah', part 7).

12. This date is given in *The [Australian] Record*, 98, no. 11.

13. The report (published in 1993) actually says 'about three years ago'.

14. *The [Australian] Record*, 98, no. 17.

15. Oliver Gyarfas was nineteen at the time of the fire. He was at Mt. Carmel on the day of the ATF raid, but exited on the evening of 14 March (Thibodeau, *Place Called Waco*, 172–3, says he was with Gyarfas during the first stages of the events of 28 February and gave an outline of their actions). Gyarfas was held without bond as a material witness, but was not charged with any offence.
16. Aisha Gyarfas was seventeen at the time of the fire and was the legal wife of Greg Summers. She died on 19 April from a gunshot wound. She was nearly nine months pregnant; it is generally assumed that Koresh was the father of the child.
17. Graeme Craddock was born on 29 Nov. 1961, and escaped the Waco fire. He is described as an engineer and at his trial said that it was his responsibility to keep the physical lines of communication between the Davidians and the FBI open. In 1994 he was jailed for forty years, a term later reduced to fifteen years.
18. There are two main sources of information on the progress of Koresh's evangelistic endeavours in Hawaii. These are an interview with the then pastor of the Diamond Head Seventh-day Adventist church, Charlie Liu (published in *Adventism Today*, 1 (May–June 1993)) and tape recordings of the disfellowship meeting that took place in Hawaii on 27 June 1987 (a copy of those tape recordings is in my possession).
19. Born 16 Oct. 1949, died 19 Apr. 1993. Schneider will appear frequently from this point on so no attempt is made to summarize his association with the Branch Davidians.
20. According to Tabor and Arnold (*Why Waco?*, 216, n. 14, quoting from the *Department of Justice Report*), 96 hours were spent by the FBI negotiators talking to Schneider and 60 hours talking to Koresh.
21. This is discussed in Chapter Fifteen.
22. Waite, 'The British Connection', 113. In the article Waite, who was a lecturer at Newbold College at the time, gave some further details regarding Schneider that appear to be based on Schneider's college files.
23. King and Breault, *Preacher of Death*, 67.
24. See Joel Sandefur and Charles Liu, 'Apocalypse in Diamond Head', *Spectrum*, 23/1 (May 1993), 30. Liu was pastor of the church in 1986.
25. That Breault was the one who converted Paul Fatta is clearly stated on the tape of the Diamond Head SDA church meeting held on 27 June 1987. Paul Fatta was born 28 Feb. 1958. He and his son Kalani were outside Mt. Carmel on 28 February attending a gun show; nevertheless he was jailed for fifteen years.
26. Margaret Lawson is reported as being either seventy-five or seventy-six at the time of the siege. She left Mt. Carmel on 2 March.
27. Dana Okimoto, a Hawaiian of Japanese extraction, was later to bear two sons for Koresh (Sky and Scooter). She left the community a few months before the siege began (see further Thibodeau, *A Place Called Waco*, 111).
28. The family consisted of Mark and Jaydean Wendell and four children, Tamara, Landon, Juanessa, and Patron. Jaydean was a police officer in Hawaii before her recruitment. She was killed during the initial raid on Mt. Carmel on 28 February, and her husband died in the fire. All four children left Mt. Carmel on 1 March.

29. Neil and his wife Margarida, along with their daughter Joann, moved to Mt. Carmel from Hawaii, where they had owned and operated a bakery. Joann was released to the FBI in early March and now lives with her sister Ursula. Both her parents died in the fire (information from www.members.aol.com/karenwmp/waco/neil.htm).

30. Peter Hipsman was a native of upstate New York (Thibodeau, *A Place Called Waco*, 76). He was either twenty-seven or twenty-eight at the time of his death. He was shot during the initial ATF raid on 28 February, and died from two further shots to the head, fired at close range in what was clearly a mercy killing. (Thibodeau, *A Place Called Waco*, 177–8.)

31. Sometimes spelt 'Sommers' in the literature. He was twenty-eight when he died in the fire. He was married to Aisha Gyarfas, but lived a celibate life (Thibodeau, *A Place Called Waco*, 84).

32. Sherri Jewell, her husband David, and their daughter Kiri were to play an important part in the development of the authorities' views on Koresh, as will be discussed later. Sherri died of smoke inhalation during the fire.

33. Karl Henning appears originally to have been from British Columbia and worked as a teacher. His association with the Branch Davidians was relatively short-lived. In the 'Sinful Messiah' series (part one) Henning (spelt 'Hennig' in the article) is said to have studied with the group 'for two months in 1987', which suggests that he never actually joined the Branch Davidians or visited Mt. Carmel.

34. Andre Kale attended the Diamond Head SDA church and joined the Branch Davidians after listening to some lectures by Breault in June 1986. He met Koresh in Hawaii in August that year and moved to Palestine, Texas, in December. According to Breault, Kale had AIDS by the time he joined the movement and on account of this was treated with some caution by others. Kale eventually left the group because of doctrinal disagreement (though there was some tension between Kale and Perry Jones, who was in charge when Koresh was away). Kale died about six months later.

35. Jeff Little attended the University of Hawaii and while in Waco worked as a computer programmer outside Mt. Carmel. He was married to Nicole Gent and died in the fire at the age of thirty-two.

36. Judy Schneider (*neé* Judy Peterson) was from Wisconsin and married Steve Schneider in 1981 (Thibodeau, *A Place Called Waco*, 19). She was forty-one when she died in the fire. She had one child with Koresh, a daughter, Mayanah.

37. Floracita Sonobe died in the fire aged thirty-four.

38. Scott Kijoro Sonobe, of Japanese extraction, was born in Berkeley, California (NT 228). He was seriously injured in the initial shootout on 28 February and died in the fire at the age of thirty-five.

39. Kevin Whitecliff was born on 23 June 1961. He worked as a prison guard in Hawaii (Thibodeau, *A Place Called Waco*, 186). Whitecliff left Mt. Carmel on 19 March (Thibodeau says Whitecliff and Brad Branch were 'banished' for sneaking shots of whisky—*A Place Called Waco*, 221) and was sentenced to forty years (later reduced to fifteen) in prison.

40. Some of the story can be reconstructed from Diamond Head recordings. There was a period of 'discussion and dispute' in Aug./Sept. 1986, and then on 3 Jan. 1987 an open church meeting was held where members were invited to share their concerns. On 27 Jan. 1987 the church board sent a letter to those in the 'study group' asking them for their position on the 'new movement'. On 18 Feb. 1987 the church board met to discuss the response. Ten days later a decision was taken to place the members of the study group under a thirty-day censure period. The crunch came on 31 March when the board met and unanimously recommended that fourteen members of the Diamond Head SDA church be disfellowshipped. After some difficulty in arrangements a meeting of the church session took place on 27 June to discuss the recommendation of the board. On 3 Sept. 1987 a meeting took place under the chairmanship of Pastor Liu; a number of Branch Davidians spoke at this meeting, including Breault, Schneider, and Koresh. The meeting lasted for three hours and was followed by a secret ballot of church members, and the fourteen were disfellowshipped.
41. Schneider evidently took with him a tape that Koresh had made, in which he said it had been about a year since 'we' were with you. The tape goes over some familiar ground with regard to the importance of the 'seventh angel' and other matters relating to Koresh's role as a messenger for these last days. A copy is in my possession.
42. Marc Breault, E-mail to Kenneth Newport, 29 May 2003.
43. Adair, 'Interviews', 94.
44. A copy is held in TXC, Mark Swett Collection, video box 1.
45. On one of the negotiation tapes Schneider gives the address as '178 East Arrow Highway in Pomona, California' (NT 105). It was known by the Branch Davidians as 'The Rock House' since it was built of stone.
46. The house in La Verne was on 'White Avenue' (NT 114).
47. The house was on Melrose Avenue; Thibodeau, *A Place Called Waco*, 67.
48. NT 105. Thibodeau said that when he was first taken to the house in Pomona he met Jaime Castillo, Greg Summers, Mike Schroeder, Scott Sonobe, and Paul Fatta (*A Place Called Waco*, 20).
49. The dispute between the Bundses and Koresh appears to have come to a head in June 1990, when David Bunds and his wife were expelled from Mt. Carmel for breaking dietary rules (Thibodeau, *A Place Called Waco*, 109). Robyn Bunds defected a few weeks later, and Donald and Jeannine Bunds left in September 1991 (King and Breault, *Preacher of Death*, 371–2). The departure of Robyn and her son Shaun led to a custody battle with Koresh, which Robyn won. She was later to testify to an ATF agent as he began to gather the evidence in support of the ATF request for the Feb. 1993 search and arrest warrants. It is clear, however (*Civil Trial*, 1810ff.), that Donald Bunds returned to Mt Carmel even after this date and sometimes stayed a few months at a time. He was there on the morning of 28 February, when he was arrested outside the complex.
50. Hughes had died in 1968, having apparently come from California that year to live at Mt. Carmel. *Waco Tribune-Herald*, 5 May 1988.

51. Interview with Clive Doyle, Waco, November 2002.
52. Floyd Houtmann died at the age of sixty-one on 19 Apr. 1993.
53. James Riddle died of a gunshot wound on 19 Apr. 1993 at the age of thirty-two.
54. Stan Sylvia was the husband of Lorraine and the father of Joshua, who left Mt. Carmel on 1 Mar. 1993 when he was seven years old, and Rachel. On 19 April Sylvia was in California and watched on television as Mt. Carmel burnt, with his wife and daughter (aged twelve) inside. He was apparently interviewed by Reavis who stated that in 1995 Sylvia was maintaining a Branch Davidian faith (Reavis, *Ashes of Waco*, 112).
55. *The Waco Tribune-Herald*, 6 Nov. 1987 reports that tests done by the McLennan County sheriff's department and the ATF show that the rifles confiscated from the men were 'semi-automatic'. This was Koresh's first brush with the ATF; the next one would be fatal.
56. TXC 2D212/24.
57. *Waco Tribune-Herald*, 6 Nov. 1987.
58. TXC 2D212/24.
59. *Waco Tribune-Herald*, 24 Mar. 1988.
60. Bailey and Darden, *Mad Man in Waco*, 94.
61. Reavis, *Ashes of Waco*, 81.
62. *Waco Tribune-Herald*, 15 May 1988.
63. Ibid., 9 Dec. 1988.
64. The events leading up to the death of Dale Adair are not entirely clear. Breault (*Inside the Cult*, 107) said that Dale, who had been converted by Ben Roden some thirty years earlier (Adair, *Davidian Testimony*, 192), had turned up at Mt. Carmel some time during the summer of 1988. Dale had drifted away from the faith, but now wished to return. During a private Bible study at which only Koresh, Breault, and Dale Adair were present, Dale suddenly looked up to heaven and said, 'My God, my God. After all these years I understand. I'm the Messiah. I'm the David.' He then left Mt. Carmel. Where he went is not clear, but by 16 Oct. 1989 he was staying at the Roden's house in Odessa and told George Roden he (Dale) was the Messiah. At this point George became enraged and killed him. The forensic evidence suggests that George killed Dale with an axe, shot the mutilated body afterwards in order to claim that he had shot Dale in self-defence, and then chopped the body up in a fit of rage. See further Adair, *Davidian Testimony*, 305–6. Some further detail is found in Adair, 'Interviews', 96–8, which confirms the evidence from Breault regarding the place where Dale Adair was killed.
65. On the British converts see especially Albert Waite and Laura Osei, 'The British Connection', *Spectrum*, 23/1 (May 1993), 34–8.
66. Apparently written by Peter Van Bemmelen, then a lecturer at the college. A copy is in my possession.
67. John McBean died on 19 April at the age of twenty-seven.
68. Prior to his move to Waco, Sellors was a ministerial student at Newbold College. He was a highly talented artist whose ability was put to work by Koresh; among

other things he decorated a number of Koresh's guitars. He died from smoke inhalation on 19 Apr. at the age of thirty-three.

69. Leslie Lewis died on 19 April. Her body was one of those not specifically identified at post mortem.

70. Bernadette Monbelly died on 19 April at the age of thirty-one.

71. Teresa Norbrega died on 19 April at the age of forty-eight.

72. Renos Avraam was a Greek businessman from London. He survived the fire but was later jailed for forty years (reduced to fifteen). Some time fairly soon after the fire, Avraam came to the conclusion that he was the 'chosen vessel' whose job it was to complete the message of the seven seals. See further Chapter Sixteen below.

73. Breault is very clear that Koresh did visit the UK in either 1988 or 1989. He wrote, 'Vernon definitely went to England before 1990. I don't remember exactly when it was, but it was before I left the group, and it was before Passover of 1989. I believe it was later in the year, around November, of 1988, although it could have been early in 1989.' (E-mail to Kenneth Newport, 4 June 2003).

74. Part of that evangelistic campaign has survived on a series of nine audio tapes, copies of which are in my possession. They were recorded in Cheetham Hill, Manchester, in Jan. 1990. McBean can clearly be heard on the tapes and frequent reference is made by Schneider to other persons by name.

75. See Appendix D for details.

76. The outline given above is based upon Thibodeau, *A Place Called Waco*, 9–24.

77. Ibid. 61.

78. Jean Smith was later to testify that the La Verne house was ordinarily out of bounds to Branch Davidian men and that 'The women in any of those rooms could be called by Vernon at that stage' (*Waco Tribune-Herald*, 'The Sinful Messiah', part 7).

79. Thibodeau, *A Place Called Waco*, 107–23, contains what appears to be fairly solid information on this issue written by an insider. The chapter of the book to which these pages belong begins, 'My [Thibodeau's] link with Michele provoked me to discover more about her relationship with David and also about his sexual connection with underage girls in general' (107).

80. Ibid. 31–2.

81. Ibid. 107–9.

82. Robyn and Jeannine Bunds later appeared on the Oprah Winfrey Show, when Robyn said that she and Koresh began having sex when she was fifteen and that he took her as a wife when she was seventeen. A transcript of that show is in my possession

83. Lorraine Sylvia was the wife of Stan Sylvia and the mother of three children, including Hollywood, generally assumed to be by Koresh. She died in the fire.

84. See further Thibodeau, *A Place Called Waco* 107–11. Jeannine and Robyn Bunds' later appearance on the Oprah Winfrey Show is also illuminating in this regard. A transcript of that show is in my possession.

85. Ibid. 110–11. Thibodeau has probably omitted Lois Roden from the count.

86. Details of Breault's departure from the group are taken from *Preacher of Death*, 195–204.
87. Koresh, 'Foundation' (audio tape); this is in my possession.
88. Donahue Show, 10 Mar. 1993.
89. John R. Hall, 'Public Narratives and the Apocalyptic Sect' in Wright, *Armageddon at Waco*, 216.
90. Breault and King, *Preacher of Death*, 271–9, contains Breault's own account.
91. Hall in Lewis, ed., *Armageddon in Waco*, 217.
92. *Report*, 219–20.
93. Thibodeau, *A Place Called Waco*, 114–16.
94. Tabor and Gallagher, *Why Waco?*, 58; Bailey and Darden, *Madman in Waco*, 95.
95. Clive Doyle, interview with Kenneth G. C. Newport, Waco, Texas, Nov. 2002.

11

'The Seventh Angel': David Koresh and the Mystery of God

But in the days of the voice of the seventh angel, when he shall begin to sound, the mystery of God should be finished, as he hath declared to his servants the prophets.

(Revelation 10.7)

Koresh was nothing if not self assured. From his rather unpromising start in life as 'Mr Retardo', by the age of thirty-three he had somehow managed to become the undisputed leader of the Branch Davidian community. His prophetic, nearly godly, status was accepted by a substantial number, including some who by contrast had spent years (not to mention vast sums of money) in the tertiary educational system. He had got the better of George Roden (no mean feat) and had even managed to eclipse Lois for the last year or so of her life. The undisputed control of the Mt. Carmel property, which he had rescued from the hands of receivers by paying tens of thousands of dollars in back taxes, was his. In addition he had amassed significant personal property including cars, trucks, guns, and, most of all, musical instruments. Some very beautiful women dreamed of the day when they would be allowed to sleep with him, while the men of the community looked to him for leadership and direction even to the point of giving up their own conjugal rights and accepting that it was Koresh and not they who must co-create children with their wives. Whatever else one might wish to say about Koresh, this is not the profile of an idiot.

It was theology that had brought about the change in Koresh's fortunes, for although he could not write very well, he had a knowledge of the Bible that few could match and his ability to stitch together passages from that sacred text was nothing short of awe-inspiring. It may have been misguided, but it was impressive and it is not at all surprising that individuals such as Fagan and Schneider were attracted to it. Here was one who seemed to have the whole Bible in his head, and could at last make sense of all those odd bits in

Zechariah, Amos, Malachi, Ezekiel, and so on. Here was one who spoke from the Bible and almost from the Bible only, except when a previous inspired interpreter of the text was used to explain the book itself. The Branch Davidians under Koresh lived and breathed theology. The status they afforded their leader was dependent upon his ability to supply them with it, and he did not disappoint them. This chapter gives an outline of what that theology looked like.

Perhaps the first thing to note about Koresh's theology is that it was not static. What he said in 1983 (the date of the 'Serpent's Root' studies, which launched his theological career) was not necessarily what he might have said in 1993. However, after 1985 and the experience in Israel, at least the core of what he had to say seems to have been in place, and while complete consistency in detail is not to be expected, a relatively stable outline does seem reconstructable. It was added to and expanded rather than fundamentally changed. Even such hard doctrines as that of the 'new light' may be seen in this way; not so much a radical break with the Koreshian tradition as a significant extension of it.

It is also important to recognize at this early stage just how complicated Koresh's theology could at times be, despite constant references on the surviving tapes to its being 'plain', 'obvious', or 'simple'.[1] This complexity is often the result of Koresh's developing a theological point by creating a long chain of biblical texts stitched together by overlapping words or phrases. As one listens to Koresh's tapes it is immediately apparent that this interpretative strategy above all others gave a basic system to what he had to say. It is not always easy to follow. To be sure, there is often an unequivocal inter-textual echo to be heard as Koresh assembles his various biblical passages, but often this echo takes on some of the characteristics of a game of Chinese whispers, with the later passages in the sequence bearing little or no resemblance to those considered earlier.

An example will best illustrate the point. According to Koresh the figure on the white horse in Revelation 19.11 is a figure of the end time (himself) who is to come to destroy the wicked. But that figure is similar to the figure on the white horse who rides out at the opening of the first seal (Rev. 6.2), so in Koresh's reasoning these two riders are the same. The figure in Revelation 6.2 holds a bow. Now if he has a bow, reasons Koresh, he must have some arrows; there is a figure (a king) shooting arrows in Psalm 45.5; therefore, so argues Koresh, the rider in Psalm 45 is the same as the one in Revelation 6 who is the same as the one in Revelation 19. However, reading on in Psalm 45 we hear that this king is to have children who are to be princes in the earth (Psalm 45.16). From this Koresh concludes that he, the rider on the horse in Revelation 19.11, is to have children who will be princes in the new kingdom.

Such reasoning leaves the majority of people either amused or confused, but for Branch Davidians it all made good sense. In such communities the Bible is not seen as sixty-six separate books written in their own contexts and reflecting the concerns of the times in which they were individually written. It is seen as a unified revelation of God's past, present, and future dealings with humankind. Koresh's great appeal was his ability to construct these complex exegetical webs linking Bible passages together. We are not dealing with someone only able to engage in apocalyptic rants (though on occasion this could happen).[2] There is a system to what he had to say, though not one that is easily discernible at the outset.

There is one other major point to be made clear, very much linked to the one above. According to Koresh the book of Revelation was a summary of prophecy, a sort of coded shorthand to the rest of scripture. 'All the books of the Bible end and meet there,' he once said of Revelation (following the SDA prophetess Ellen White).[3] By this he seems to have meant that, in his view, the book of Revelation brings together and presents an overview of all the other prophetic books. Hence, as Koresh read Revelation he discovered the verbal clues that led him to Old Testament passages. Those Old Testament passages led to other Old Testament passages and so on. Hence, the book of Revelation is really the tip of the prophetic iceberg: the bulk lies beneath the surface in places like Isaiah, Jeremiah, Zechariah, Daniel, Nahum, Amos, and so on (Koresh had great regard for the 'minor prophets', as scholars call them).

In this same context Koresh placed great emphasis upon the words of Revelation 10.7: 'But in the days of the voice of the seventh angel, when he shall begin to sound, the mystery of God should be finished, as he hath declared to his servants the prophets.' Koresh thought he was that seventh angel, and he had come to sound. However, he said repeatedly that what he has to say as the seventh angel was not brand new. He had had dreams and visions, he said, but these were not what mattered, and in fact he barely talked about them.[4] He was about interpreting the scriptures already in existence. His interpretation of what 'he [God] hath revealed to his servants the prophets' was the heart of his message. This bibliocentrism appealed to Seventh-day Adventists, for even if some might have disagreed vehemently when it came to what Koresh made of the scriptures, his claim that they were the only sure rule of doctrine would have been accepted without question by his SDA potential converts.

Seeking to understand Koresh's teaching, then, means trying to read Revelation as he read it, looking for the points at which the book links to an Old Testament passage (which is almost everywhere, in fact) and then following Koresh down the line of literary exploration and theological analysis. The task is time-consuming and not easy, but from it some sense of where Koresh and the Branch Davidians under his leadership were coming from begins to emerge.

Perhaps the most obvious place to start on Koresh's theology is with a look at his own self-understanding, which was really at the core of what he had to say. In this, as with all other aspects of his theological system, he was centrally concerned with the biblical text and the way in which, so he said, the text pointed to him and to the work he was to accomplish in these last days. In a Davidian/Branch Davidian context, of course, there was nothing particularly unusual about such a claim and in fact a number of the passages Koresh saw as central in this context had been important in the Davidian tradition since Houteff, who similarly thought that he and his work were predicted in scripture. However, Koresh went further. Not only was he more confident than Houteff or Roden that such texts did apply to him as opposed to some other leader yet to come (though Roden's self-coronation should not be forgotten), but he widened considerably the number and variety of the texts in this category.

There is of course one very visible fact about Koresh that gives an indication of how he viewed himself and provides a way into his thinking: his change of name. While this did not formally take place until the summer of 1990, it is clear that the theology symbolized by the change was being formed well before the legal move. Both new names have considerable theological significance, and will be examined in some detail.

The change from 'Vernon' to 'David' is simple enough. Koresh thought he was the antitypical King David who had come to rule in the new kingdom. The expectation that such a figure would come to rule in a premillennial kingdom had been part of the 'Davidian' tradition since its inception, hence the movement's name, and Koresh was here treading a well-worn path. Like Houteff and Roden before him, he was able to appeal to numerous Old Testament passages that indicate that the kingdom of David would one day be restored and a king would come to reign over it. Koresh was just as confident as Roden here. The latter had had himself crowned; Koresh changed his name.[5]

Koresh, then, made the claim that he was the antitypical leader of God's people, the end-time King David; nothing very new about that in a Davidian/ Branch Davidian context. Where he differed from those who had gone before him was in the complexity and detail of the work that he as the end-time leader had to do. The book of Revelation was important in this context, but the book of Psalms no less so. After all, Koresh reasoned, the Psalms are 'the Psalms of David'. Though he probably would not have had the grammar to express it, Koresh took this to be an objective rather than subjective genitive, that is, they are Psalms about David and not necessarily Psalms by David.

Koresh as the end-time David was hence the object of these Psalms. They speak of him. They are prophecy, which for Koresh meant that they speak of events later than the time they were composed. In fact, he argued, they speak of his life and the experience of the community under him.

Koresh seems to have divided the Psalms into two distinct groups. Psalms 1–18 were about the experiences he and the community would have to go through in the last days, while 19–150 were more generally about his person and work. This basic conviction is seen throughout his interpretation of the texts, beginning with the very first two verses of Psalm 1: 'Blessed is the man that walketh not in the counsel of the ungodly, nor standeth in the way of sinners, nor sitteth in the seat of the scornful. But his delight is in the law of the Lord; and in his law doth he meditate day and night.'

Koresh took these verses as a reference to himself (perhaps together with his followers); he is the specific 'man that walketh not in the counsel of the ungodly' and who meditates upon the law of God day and night. The Psalm goes on to say that the wicked will be blown away like chaff in the wind, a reference to the fate of those who opposed Koresh and the community.[6]

Psalm 2 was of particular interest to Koresh and comes up very frequently. He took the Psalm as referring to the opposition that the Lamb (himself) would face during his ministry: 'Why do the heathen rage, and the people imagine a vain thing? The kings of the earth set themselves, and the rulers take counsel together, against the Lord, and against his anointed, saying, Let us break their bands asunder, and cast away their cords from us.'

During the siege itself these words from Psalm 2 took on particular significance for the community. This is seen clearly and often in the negotiation tapes, where numerous references are made by Koresh and other Branch Davidians to this passage. The Psalm describes prophetically the reaction to Koresh and his message by the wider world. The 'bands' spoken of in the Psalm, according to Koresh, are the messages of the seven seals. The 'bands' are the 'seals' around the sealed book of Revelation 5.1ff.

One example of this will suffice: in conversation with one of the FBI negotiators on 1 March, Koresh stated

But Zechariah and the other prophets say that the world will not regard these messages of mercy. They have no interest in being instructed by anyone but themselves. Now, they say, let us break his bands asunder, let us cast his cords away from us. But scripture says, which is taking place right now, it says that he that sits in the heavens—That's the Father, you see?—shall laugh, for the Lord shall have them, the heathen, in confusion. See, the heathen don't know what they're doing. And this time they can't be forgiven because this time they wilfully reject the subject which so plainly has been laid in the Book of Revelation, a subject which everyone is to be very familiarized with for the latter days.[7]

How this sounded to the ears of the FBI can only be guessed.[8]

While Psalm 2 became an important text for the besieged community, it is quite evident that Koresh had already adopted such a reading before the crisis began. In a video tape of his preaching, recorded as part of the Australian documentary *A Current Affair*, Koresh can clearly be heard interpreting the second Psalm in this way.[9] This is potentially important, for it indicates that his interpretation of the Psalms was not simply the result of the crisis brought on by the initial raid and subsequent siege. Well before the actual confrontation began, he was already expecting opposition and anticipating some sort of showdown with those who would seek to 'break his bands asunder'.

The basic pattern of arguing that these Psalms refer to an end-time confrontation between himself and those in opposition to him continues through Psalms 3–17 and the first part of Psalm 18. Throughout this material, according to Koresh, the psalmist laments the way in which the 'man who walketh not in the counsel of the ungodly' (i.e. Koresh and his community) is received by those to whom he has been sent as the messenger of the end times, and expresses that figure's own cries as he experiences this rejection.

It is not all lament, however, for interspersed throughout are references to the vengeance the Lord will one day exact. For example in Psalm 3.7 we read, 'Arise, O Lord; save me, O my God: for thou hast smitten all mine enemies upon the cheek bone; thou hast broken the teeth of the ungodly.' And in

PLATE 9 Photograph of 'Ranch Apocalypse', a painting by Cliff Sellors. The horses are those described under seals 1–4 of the book of Revelation (cf. Revelation 6.1–8).

Psalm 18.7ff. the material changes direction dramatically. In the first part of the Psalm, the psalmist cries out to the Lord in his distress. The cries are heard, and then:

Then the earth shook and trembled; the foundations also of the hills moved and were shaken, because he was wroth. There went up a smoke out of his nostrils, and fire out of his mouth devoured: coals were kindled by it. He bowed the heavens also, and came down: and darkness was under his feet. And he rode upon a cherub, and did fly: yea, he did fly upon the wings of the wind. He made darkness his secret place; his pavilion round about him were dark waters and thick clouds of the skies. At the brightness that was before him his thick clouds passed, hail stones and coals of fire. The Lord also thundered in the heavens, and the Highest gave his voice; hail stones and coals of fire (Psalm 18.7–13).

Again this Psalm is quoted more than once on the negotiation transcripts. For example, on 7 March Koresh refers to it as he talks to the negotiator about how God is going to make an example of the belligerent power (the USA/FBI) by bringing it to an end. God would hear the cries of his people and would act. The mountains would tremble and the earth rock; smoke would go up from the Lord's nostrils and fire from his mouth.[10] The potential significance of this scheme is important. Koresh thought the Psalms were about him and the community in the last days. Psalm 2 said that the wicked will rage against them and seek to break Koresh's 'bands' asunder. However, Psalm 18 said that God will hear the cries of his people and come to their aid. Given this understanding of the prophetic text, which predated the actual crisis, Koresh was probably not inclined simply to walk out of the door of Mt. Carmel. The Lord would come, the earth would reel and rock. Smoke would ascend from the nostrils of the Lord and fire from his mouth and the world would be laid bare at his rebuke.

As Koresh read the book of Psalms, then, he found that they spoke of himself and his community. There is little point in giving further detail here. However, one Psalm was particularly important to Koresh and crops up time and time again both in what he said about himself and in what other Branch Davidians have had to say about him. It is Psalm 45. There we read of a figure who is called 'the king', who is blessed by God, teaches the truth, and is anointed with the oil of gladness above all others. The arrows of this figure are 'sharp in the heart of the king's enemies' and the people fall as a result. He has 'honourable women' who enter his palace, his children are to be princes over all the earth, and the name of the king is remembered for ever.

This figure of Psalm 45 was seen by Koresh as himself. This comes across numerous times on the negotiation tapes and elsewhere in the surviving material. For example, on 6 March he is recorded as saying, 'The same king in Psalms 2 is the same one in Psalms 45', which, when seen in context, is plain enough.[11] Further, in a letter that Koresh wrote to the FBI on 11 April, he warned them of the importance of what was happening, and in particular drew attention to his real identity as one who held a very important and special place in the plans of God. To the letter Koresh attached the text of Psalm 45.[12] The implication is clear, though as often in Koresh's materials it is not spelt out.

The rider on the horse in Psalm 45 shoots arrows into the enemies of the king, that is, Koresh slays his enemies by revealing the truth of the seven seals. The arrows of Psalm 45.5 are hence first and foremost 'arrows of truth'.[13] However, the reference to the women and to the children 'whom thou mayest make princes in all the earth' was taken very literally. According to Koresh this is a reference to his own duty to raise up a significant number of children. Other materials indicate that the precise number of these children was known to him; it was twenty-four—the number, that is, of the elders around the throne in Revelation 4.4 etc.[14] In the new kingdom Koresh would rule as king and his literal children as princes. As he is heard to say on another tape, 'Only the Lamb is to be given the job to raise up the seed of the house of David isn't he? Isn't he? You know that in the prophecies, Psalms 45'.[15] It is little wonder then that Koresh had such direct things to say to the FBI about his children and the important role they were yet to play in the plans of God. It is little wonder too that none of those in Mt. Carmel came out when the raid took place. Koresh was determined to keep them with him. They were 'different' from the others.[16] They were special and different, of course, because they were his own flesh and blood; any father could be expected to hold his own offspring apart from children in general. However, Koresh's paternal instinct, like every other instinct he had, was channelled into a theological formulation.

It is hence plain that Koresh saw himself as the antitypical David not just in very general terms, but in some significant detail. He was to rule in the new Kingdom and his 'princes' would be his children. Before that could happen the events spoken of in the Psalms would have to come about. Opposition was to be faced as the wicked sought to break his bands asunder. But God would hear the cries of his people and intervene. And when he did, the earth would indeed tremble.

Returning to the issue of his changed name, Koresh went beyond the familiar link with David. Not only did he change 'Vernon' to 'David' but he changed 'Howell' to 'Koresh'. 'Koresh' is the Hebrew form of 'Cyrus'. This Old Testament figure appealed to Howell for a number of reasons, not least, in all probability, because according to the book of Ezra it was Cyrus who issued a decree that set free the people of Israel and called for the rebuilding of the temple in Jerusalem (Ezra 1.1–2). However, Howell was attracted to the figure of Cyrus also because it was Cyrus who became known as the one who overthrew Babylon.

The overthrow of Babylon is the subject of Daniel 5. According to this, God's wrath came upon Babylon as a result of the desecration of the vessels taken from the temple in Jerusalem (Dan. 5.2–4). The announcement of judgment came through a hand which wrote upon the wall the words 'Mene, Mene, Tekel, Upharsin' (Dan. 5.25). Daniel was then called in to interpret the words and deciphered them as 'God hath numbered thy [the king of Babylon's] kingdom, and finished it. Thou art weighed in the balances, and art found wanting. Thy kingdom is divided, and given to the Medes and Persians' (Dan. 5.26–8). That very night Babylon fell.[17]

Cyrus was hence an instrument in God's hands and it comes as no surprise that he is described in Isaiah 44.28 as a 'shepherd' of the Lord—that is, we presume, one who looks after the Lord's sheep. In the following verse, Isaiah 45.1, Cyrus is called the Lord's 'anointed', for it is he, who, despite not being a Jew himself, brings deliverance of God's people, their return from exile, and the rebuilding of the temple. This description is important. To be 'anointed' means to be set aside for a particular purpose. 'An anointed one' would be expressed in Hebrew as a 'messiah' and in Greek as a 'Christ', and in fact in Isaiah 45.1 the Hebrew word that is used is indeed 'messiah'. Given Christian sensitivities, however, Isaiah 45.1 is usually translated so as not to call the uniqueness of Jesus into question. The KJV, for example, has 'Thus saith the Lord to his anointed, to Cyrus, whose right hand I have holden …', whereas the NRSV has, 'Thus says the LORD to his anointed, to Cyrus, whose right hand I have grasped …' However, on the basis of the Hebrew, 'Thus says the Lord to his Messiah, to Cyrus, whose right hand I have grasped …' would be perfectly acceptable. The Old Testament (typical) Cyrus had destroyed Babylon, freed God's people, and rebuilt the temple. According to Howell, the eschatological (antitypical) Cyrus would do the same.

Precisely when Howell came to the view that he was the antitypical Cyrus is not clear, but a letter to the SDA Church (which appears as an appendix to this chapter) indicates that by the time he wrote it (the date is uncertain) the view had already become firmly fixed in his mind. 'My Name is Cyrus,' he writes there, 'and I Am here to destroy Babylon (Rev. 9.14)'. The question is then, what did Koresh understand as now constituting Babylon?

Some indication of Koresh's thinking on this point can be gained from the negotiation tapes, where Koresh refers to 'Babylon' numerous times. For example, on 6 March he is engaged in a conversation with a negotiator, John Cox, and quotes extensively from Revelation 18:

Babylon the Great is fallen, is fallen. And has become the habitation of devils and the hold of every foul spirit in the cage of every unclean and hateful bird. For all nations have drunk of the wine of the wrath of her fornication. And the kings of the earth have committed fornication with her. And the merchants of the earth are waxed rich through the abundance of her delicacies.[18]

Picking up (it seems) from the end of this quotation, the conversation then continues:

KORESH: If it wasn't for this nation in the latter days whose expenditure is so great and national deficit is so great, if it wasn't for this nation who above all nations is blessed with toys and things and springs and—you know what I'm talking about...

JOHN COX: ...Um-hum.

KORESH: then the rest of the world would not be as drunk. And everybody likes to come to America, don't they?

JOHN COX: Well, if they ...

KORESH: There is ...

JOHN COX: ... don't, they should.

KORESH: Oh, yeah, exactly. There's no greater nation.

JOHN COX: No.

KORESH: But God doesn't speak too highly of it. And I heard another voice from heaven saying ...

JOHN COX: God doesn't speak too highly of America?

KORESH: Right. He doesn't.

JOHN COX: Why do you say that?

KORESH: Well, God calls it Babylon.

JOHN COX: Why do you say that?

KORESH: Well, because you've got to find out why in Revelation 13 ...

JOHN COX: How can, how can you say that God describing Babylon is talking about America?

KORESH: What does Babylon mean?

JOHN COX: He could be talking about Yugoslavia.

KORESH: Uh-uh-uh. No one ...

JOHN COX: Why not?

KORESH: ... has...nobody has merchandise in Yugoslavia that makes all the nations of the earth drunk.[19]

This seems pretty clear. Koresh certainly shared the more general view that the term 'Babylon' could be used to refer to false religion, but he did apply it also directly to America. America (antitypical Babylon) was here and Koresh (the antitypical Cyrus) would destroy it. Just how this destruction would take place is not always plain. Some of the things Koresh said are fairly innocuous. For example, later in this tape he refers to the fact that there is doctrinal confusion in Babylon/America and that it is his task to sort this out. Even potentially violent references on the tapes might actually be meant in a spiritual sense—for example, in the following quotation the reference at the end to the seven seals seems to imply that the 'bringing down' is a spiritual humiliation rather than a physical one:

For he bringeth down them that dwell on high. That's you guys. The lofty city he bringeth, layeth it low, layeth it low, even to the ground; he bringeth it even to the dust. That's the fall of Babylon. The foot shall tread it down, even the feet of the poor, and the steps of the needy. Now the way of the just is uprightness: thou, most upright, which is the Father who sits on the throne, dost weigh the paths of the just. That's the seven seals.[20]

However, in other places the language seems less ambiguous. On 31 March, Koresh is again talking about Babylon and says to the negotiator:

Have you ever heard of Babylon the Great? ...Yeah, that's what this prophecy is talking about. 'Behold, I am against thee, saith the Lord of hosts, and I will discover thy skirts upon my face, and I will show the nations thy nakedness and the kingdoms thy shame'. You know, there's no nation that's been given greater privileges than the United States of America. It's supposed to protect its people. It's supposed to have an ear to listen and to learn. It's supposed to have freedoms to be able to know the word of God and what God states. You know, In God We Trust, it says on the currency, doesn't it?[21]

The conversation then continues for a while before Koresh says:

Behold, thy people in the midst of thee are women, and the gates of thy land shall be set wide open unto thine enemies, the fire shall devour thy bars. You know who brings that fire, don't you? God does. Remember in Psalms 18 where it talked about Messiah saying that his enemies were too strong for him? ...They start—they, they, they destroy him. And it says that they prevented me the day of my calamity. And it says, the heavens depart and God comes down and hits them with fire and brimstone... But that's not the end of the world, though. It takes place before the end of the world. Draw thee waters for the siege, fortify thy strongholds, go into the clay and tread the mortar, make strong thy brick-kiln. There shall the fire devour thee, the sword shall cut thee off.

There is violence here. Regarding the timing of this Koresh later said 'in the days of the—that's when Babylon is going to fall'. It is very probable that what he meant was 'in the days of the voice of the seventh angel', a phrase that he uses frequently elsewhere. In other words, the destruction of Babylon/

American is at hand. It will be accomplished in his own ministry, although, as the longer quotation above makes clear, 'they [the forces of Babylon] destroy him' first.[22] Koresh, then, saw his task as including the destruction of anti-typical Babylon. He would destroy America and false religion spiritually and then physically.

As we have seen, in the Old Testament Cyrus is called the Lord's 'anointed' one—that is, who had a special task to complete. Koresh also took such a view of his own place in the plans of God. He too was 'a' messiah. He too had been anointed by God for a special purpose. Part of this was to destroy Babylon, but his destruction of Babylon was but a part of an even greater task, namely the revelation of the seven seals to the faithful.

Central here is Koresh's view that he was identified in scripture as an angel of the Lord (a view which he shared, of course, with Houteff and the Rodens). He was particularly interested in the angelic figure of Revelation 10. Here we read of a 'seventh angel' to come who will fulfil the mystery of God:

And I saw another mighty angel come down from heaven ... And he had in his hand a little book open: and he set his right foot upon the sea, and his left foot on the earth, And cried with a loud voice, as when a lion roareth: and when he had cried, seven thunders uttered their voices. And when the seven thunders had uttered their voices, I was about to write: and I heard a voice from heaven saying unto me, Seal up those things which the seven thunders uttered, and write them not. And the angel which I saw stand upon the sea and upon the earth lifted up his hand to heaven, And sware by him that liveth for ever and ever ... that there should be time no longer: But in the days of the voice of the seventh angel, when he shall begin to sound, the mystery of God should be finished, as he hath declared to his servants the prophets. (Rev. 10.1–7).

Koresh seems to have come to the view that he was this angelic messenger as early as 1985 and by 1987 was proclaiming it quite openly. Reference has already been made in Chapter Ten to a heavily bearded Koresh teaching in Los Angeles in that year.[23] On that video he is heard to quote: ' "in the days of the voice of the seventh angel, when he shall begin to sound, the mystery of God should be finished, as he hath declared to his servants the prophets" '. He then says very clearly, 'My job, my responsibility [to] God, is to simply open up all that the prophets have written—to harmonize them'. Whether the people in the room were actually aware of the magnitude of what Koresh was claiming is not clear, but when the tape is viewed within its wider context there seems no doubt: Koresh is here claiming to be the angel of Revelation 10; he has come to explain 'the mystery of God'.

On the Los Angeles video Koresh spends a good deal of his available teaching time claiming to be the one who could reveal the truth. Other sources, such as those already surveyed in this chapter, similarly indicate that he was more concerned with this point than with any other. By contrast, in the sources that have survived, he says comparatively little about what 'the truth' actually is. In effect, above all he reveals that he is the revealer. As a result, listening to the tapes can be very frustrating; time and again Koresh comes back to this theme and it often dominates, almost to the exclusion of anything else he has to say. On the 'Foundation' tape, for example, he manages to keep going for the best part of seventy-five minutes without actually saying anything other than that he is the lamb of Revelation 5 who has come to reveal the book; he is the rider on the horse in Psalm 45 whose arrows (of truth) are sharp in the enemies of the king, and his work is summed up in the image of the first seal. The same is true of much of the other material. On the taped message 'The Bird' (1987), he can again be heard engaging in conversation with several other people, including Steve Schneider, about 'the Bird' mentioned in Isaiah 46.11 who is called from the east.[24] 'The Bird' is Koresh himself, with a message for the end times.

It is obvious that Koresh had a high regard for himself as an end-time messenger of God, who had come to reveal the truth perfectly. In this sense he was 'a' messiah, sent by God to undertake a very special and particular task. However, his sense of his own messianic status probably went well beyond this. There is reasonably clear, though slight, evidence to suggest that he thought he was in some way ontologically related to Jesus. Perhaps clearest of all is what he is heard to say at the meeting in the Diamond Head SDA church on 3 September 1987. Towards the end of that meeting Koresh is speaking. He refers to the mainstream SDA sanctuary doctrine, saying that according to his reading of Ellen White there will come a time when Christ leaves the heavenly sanctuary and comes to earth with a message of truth.[25] This is not the second coming, but, said Koresh, the coming of Christ to chastise the unfaithful shepherds in the [SDA] Church.[26] He refers also to the prophecy of Daniel 12.1, which speaks of how Michael will 'stand up',[27] and to Zechariah 2.13, which says, 'Be silent O all flesh, before the Lord: for he is raised up out of his holy habitation.'[28] Koresh then says, 'and I can sit up here—stand up here—and quote a hundred other texts from the Old Testament prophecies about Christ raising up out of his mediatorial work'.[29] What Koresh seems to be saying here is that there will come a time when Christ, Michael,[30] will leave his 'holy habitation' (the most holy place) and 'stand up' among his people on earth.[31]

Koresh seems to have taken the view that he himself was that appearance of Christ. There are several strands of evidence that point in this direction. For example, near the beginning of the KRLD tape[32] Koresh refers to Psalm 2. The figure mentioned, said Koresh, is Christ, for Christ is the anointed one. He then goes on to argue that that figure is able to take off the 'bands' or 'seals' of the book of Revelation and make the book known. The only one who can do this, said Koresh, is 'Christ', and in fact the book of Revelation was to remain sealed 'until Christ comes again'. The logic then is plain, although as usual Koresh does not spell it out step by step. He is the figure of Psalm 2;[33] he is the one who hence takes off the 'bands' that seal the book of Revelation. Only Christ can take the bands off Revelation, therefore Koresh is Christ.

But it gets clearer still. A little later on the tape Koresh is still talking about how during the end times Christ will be revealed. Talking about the coming of the Son of man he asks if, when that figure comes, he will find any faith upon the earth (cf. Luke 18.8) and then suddenly refers to the events described in Matthew 24. He is then heard to state (and the tape is 100 per cent clear at this point), 'that's why in Matthew 24 when I told my disciples that where the carcase would be—you Gentiles have been worse than the Jews'. Despite the broken sentence, the claim here is unmistakeable: Koresh 'told his disciples' the things attributed to Jesus in Matthew 24. He is claiming some sort of direct equivalence with Jesus here. What is more, immediately after this he refers to how Moses struck the rock not once but twice (Numbers 20.11). Although, again, Koresh does not spell it out, what is going on in his mind seems clear. In 1 Corinthians 10.4 Paul says explicitly that the rock Moses struck was 'Christ'. The fact that this rock is struck twice is taken up by Koresh as meaning that Christ will be smitten twice, once by the Jews and once by the Gentiles. What he is actually heard to say on the tape is: 'Why do you think that Moses struck the rock twice for? Christ should not have to die again, no he shouldn't, but how come the Jews killed Christ? They didn't know what they were doing.' Unfortunately the conversation takes a different track just after this and Koresh does not complete his line of reasoning. However, it is probably important that earlier on the tape one can hear him saying, 'God bless these guys, they are doing the best they can; I don't condemn them for they don't know what they do.' The implication is again plain: Koresh is Christ and just as he was killed before by the Jews 'who knew not what they were doing' (cf. Luke 23.34), so he will be killed again now, and this time by the Gentiles who again 'don't know what they do'. This was all foretold long ago in the symbolic action of Moses striking the rock not once but twice.[34]

Later in the tape a further claim is made. Koresh has been given the opportunity to give out a message live on air (in return for the release of two children). The message is typical Koresh with numerous references to Old Testament prophecies, the book of Revelation, the seals on the book, his status as the one who can unseal the book, and so on. However, there is one claim that is not typical, at least not in the direct way he said it. He is talking about how the events taking place are those described under the fifth seal (which is ominous enough); the next events will be the darkening of the sun and stars just as it says in Joel 2 and in the other prophets. This is not to be in literal Jerusalem now, but elsewhere (this is also a major shift); Koresh then can be clearly heard to say (it should be remembered that this is a recording of a telephone call into a radio station and the sound quality is good):

Jerusalem today is not Jerusalem, just like I said to the woman at the well; I told her in the New Testament, 'woman, the day is coming and now is when they that worship the father will not worship him in Jerusalem or on the Mount of Samaria for God is a Spirit and those that worship him must worship him in spirit and in truth'.

This is plain enough: again Koresh is claiming some connection to Jesus, for the conversation with 'the woman at the well' is plainly that recorded in John 4.[35]

While Koresh then did unambiguously make the claim to be in some way equivalent to the Jesus of the New Testament, precisely how he would have explained this is not at all clear. Since he could say such things as 'as I told my disciples' and 'as I said to the woman at the well', he must have had some view on the matter but what it was cannot be ascertained. It seems reasonably certain, however, that he did not see himself as identical to Jesus Christ. This was not a simple matter of the reappearance of the man who had been crucified almost 2,000 years ago. After all, Jesus had been a 'sinless Messiah', but Koresh was to be the 'sinful' one. They were not the same being.

Conversations with other Branch Davidians, however, suggest that Koresh was a dynamic monarchian, that is he believed in the existence of a 'Christ Spirit' independent of the persons of Jesus of Nazareth and of himself.[36] Dynamic monarchian Christology has been around almost as long as Christianity itself and was condemned as heretical from a very early date. In it this 'Christ spirit' empowered the person of Jesus of Nazareth, into whom the Spirit entered at his baptism. If Koresh was of this persuasion, it seems reasonably plain that he did not see the 'Christ Spirit' in impersonal terms but thought rather that there was a personal being of some sort constituting the 'Christ Spirit'. In a sense, then, he might have taken the view that there were two persons inhabiting one physical space: the Christ Spirit and the (human) Koresh.

So far things have been reasonably plain. Koresh was clear on his own importance and it is not at all difficult to get in view an outline of what he thought the content of that importance was. Seeking to identify a wider theological framework within which he worked is, however, much more difficult, perhaps even impossible. This may be partly because so little material has survived. From all accounts Koresh must have spent literally thousands of hours preaching and teaching his version of the Branch Davidian message, especially in the later 1980s and early 1990s, but very little indeed of what he said remains available to the researcher. At the most generous count there are perhaps forty tapes (not all of which are very audible),[37] a small number of videos,[38] and some written documents.[39] The paucity of material is even more problematic because there is next to nothing from the period from 1989, which was a key time, until we get to the negotiation tapes, which are fairly substantial. Somewhat surprisingly, an analysis of this material reveals relatively little of what Koresh taught beyond that he was the one who had come to reveal the truth for the last days. That he did have other major things to say is clear from what is found on the Schneider tapes, which are much more detailed. These again have mainly to do with eschatological matters and the way in which the kingdom will come, but there are other concerns evident there (such as the femininity of the Holy Spirit). In the primary Koresh material itself, however, there is relatively little.

   This said, there are some points that can be picked up. Unsurprisingly most of these have to do with eschatology. For example, while much on the taped 'Letter to Steve Schneider and the Brethren in Wisconsin'[40] is entirely predictable as Koresh goes again over his main theme that he can reveal the truth, one can pick up at least an outline of what he had to say on such important Davidian/Branch Davidian matters as the coming of the kingdom. What he said is in keeping with the basics he had no doubt picked up from Lois Roden and others who had been Davidians/Branch Davidians before him, though like Houteff and the Rodens Koresh had to adjust the tradition so that his own perceived place in the purposes of God could be accommodated. Similarly on 'the Bird' tape Koresh is likewise primarily concerned with the claim that he is the messenger; however, here again it is also possible to discern something of his wider eschatology. Unpacking that eschatology reveals that it is somewhat unimaginative when seen in the context in which it was formulated: the remnant will one day inhabit the Holy Land and 'the nations' will flock to it. Other tapes indicate that Koresh shared the common Davidian/Branch Davidian view that God's purposes can be seen in the way in which truth has been revealed in the past, but that it has always become corrupted. Hence Wesley had some light, but it became corrupted and the movement he started failed to move on. The same is true, said Koresh, of the movements that began under Miller and White. Truth is given, but at once becomes entombed in the mausoleum of tradition (not Koresh's phrase).[41] There are even some tapes that seem to say nothing at all of any significance. For example, the first half of the 'Jonah' tape (April 1989) is little more than a paraphrase of the book with a few very obvious remarks about how the text of Jonah might be relevant to the present day. This is followed by a more general discussion on eschatological matters that includes some discussion of 'the Ravenous Bird from the East'.

There is hence little to be gained from further summary of the taped material. Already the main themes are clear and what has been given above is an accurate reflection of what is found in the corpus as a whole. In summary, Koresh accepted the basic outline of Davidian and Branch Davidian theology as it had developed since the time of Houteff himself. He looked for the dawn of the new, pre-millennial, kingdom that would be established and be ruled over by a literal king. Koresh's view that he was that king comes across very strongly, and his view also that he must prepare for the coming of the kingdom is underscored. As part of that preparation the twenty-four elders needed to be brought into existence—these were to be the 'princes' mentioned in Psalm 45, the literal children of the king.

Koresh must have taught more than this, but it has gone with him to the grave, except where it can be reconstructed from secondary sources such as the work of Schneider and the reflections of surviving Branch Davidians such as Castillo and Fagan. However, unless the portion of Koresh's work that has survived is hopelessly skewed, which seems unlikely given that it was this material which was recorded in the first place and which others in the tradition have seen fit to preserve and distribute ever since, the picture is of one primarily, almost exclusively, concerned with his own role in the end times. This itself is an indication of his desire to be accepted as important both to his fellow believers and to God. One may wish to reflect on how this relates to the rather sorry start he had in life.

Appendix: Koresh's Letter to the Seventh-day Adventist Church[42]

Dear Brethren in the Seventh-day Adventist Church:

I am the Son of God. You do not know Me nor My name. I have been raised up from the north, and My travels are from the rising of the sun.

All the prophets of the Bible speak of Me. I Am The Branch, Isaiah 4:2; The Serpent, Isaiah 5:26; The Immanuel, Isaiah 7:14; the Root, Isaiah 11:10; The Holy One, Isaiah 12:6; The Voice, Isaiah 13:2; The Fiery Flying Serpent, Isaiah 14:29; The Lamb, Isaiah 16:1; The Stammerer, Isaiah 28:11; The King, Isaiah 32:1; The Righteous Man from the East, Isaiah 41:2; The Elect, Isaiah 42:1; The Ravenous Bird, Isaiah 46:11; The Loved One, Isaiah 48:14; The Sharp Sword, Isaiah 49:2; The Learned, Isaiah 50:4; The Arm, Isaiah 51:9; The Servant, Isaiah 52:13; and David, Isaiah 55:3, 4.

I have been rejected in the person of My prophets over and over. I have seven eyes and seven horns. My Name is the Word of God and I ride on a white horse (Rev. 19:11). I Am here on earth to give you the Seventh Angel's Message (Rev. 10:7).

I Am the prophets: all of them. I want to invite you to My marriage supper. The invitation is in Psalm 45. Read it and confess that you do not know Me. I Am the Word of God. The key of David is in My hand. I only can open up the prophecies of David and Solomon. I have ascended from the east with the seal of the living God. My Name is Cyrus, and I Am here to destroy Babylon (Rev. 9:14). I have come in a way that is contrary to your preconceived ideas. I will reprove you for your world loving. I will scold your daughters for their nakedness and pride that they parade in My Father's house, and by My angels I will strip them naked before all eyes because of their foolish pride. Read Isaiah 3:13–26.

The young men will abuse My kindness. They will take My life, but I will arise and take theirs forever more.

You ministers will lament your foolishness. Your lost flock will tear you to pieces.

I Am the Word and you do not know Me. I ride on a white horse and My Name is secret. Psalm 45 is My invitation to you for extended mercy. I will visit you at your unholy feast. Isaiah 3:13; 12:6; Daniel 2:44; Hosea 2:21; 2:5; 4:6; Joel 3:16, 17; Amos 1:2; 8:2; Obadiah 1:21; Habakkuk 3:13; Zephaniah 3:5; Zechariah 2:13; Malachi 1:11; 4:4; Testimonies, vol. 2, pp. 190, 191.

PREPARE TO MEET THY GOD

NOTES

1. For example, on the tape concerning Revelation 13, Koresh is explaining his thinking on the Lamb-like Beast. At one point he appears to bang his hand down on the book, saying, 'see how *clear* it is!' A minute or two later he says, 'Isn't that simple?', and then, 'simple isn't it?' Anyone listening to the tape might well come to the conclusion that it was not simple at all.
2. The best example of this is the 'Foundation' tape, where Koresh gets so worked up that he starts shouting quite abusively and begins making some quite threatening statements. The tape is not typical; in general Koresh is calm and collected and seeks to build up a case piece by piece, moving through various biblical texts that, according to him, are linked to and explain others. A copy of this tape is in my possession.
3. The remark is found near the beginning of the tape, 'Judge What I Say' (1985); the Ellen White quotation is from *The Acts of the Apostles* (Mountain View, Calif.: Pacific Press, *c*.1911), 585.
4. This general point is clearly expounded by Koresh in a talk in October 1989, an audio copy of which is in my possession. Koresh says on the tape that he has had various visions over the course of the past five years but has hardly mentioned them to anyone. He then says, with obvious emphasis, that the message he has to give is 'strictly biblical' and is not taken from his visions. He seems to have followed this through to the point where even his 'new light' doctrine (i.e. that God had decided that Koresh should father many children by the women of the community) was argued in the context of Old Testament polygamy.
5. Koresh's explicit claim to be the 'David' who was to come is found in many places in his work and there is no need to list them here; one example will suffice. In a letter he sent to the SDA Church, he first makes the claim that he is 'David' and then draws attention to Isa. 55.3–4: 'Incline your ear, and come unto me: hear, and

your soul shall live; and I will make an everlasting covenant with you, even the sure mercies of David. Behold, I have given him for a witness to the people, a leader and commander to the people.' The rest of the letter is a catena of Koresh's claims regarding himself. It is reproduced as an appendix to this chapter.

6. Such a view is attributed to Koresh by Castillo (Letter of Jaime Castillo to Kenneth G. C. Newport, 10 Apr. 2001) and it can be seen in the negotiation tapes, *passim*.

7. NT 10A.

8. See also letter of Koresh to FBI, 10 April, where Koresh told the FBI to read Psalm 2 as a way of interpreting what is happening at Mt. Carmel. This letter, like that of the next day, was signed by Koresh in Hebrew, 'Yahweh Koresh' (though in fact he writes the Hebrew words, but not the letters, left to right; so what he wrote, if it is read as Hebrew, is 'Koresh Yahweh'). However, the contents of the letter, with its references to 'my servant David', make it plain that Koresh saw himself as a prophet who was speaking for God in a 'thus saith the Lord' sense, rather than actually being God himself. A copy of the letter is found in Appendix E of *Report*.

9. The finished documentary did not include this part of the recording, but it is on a tape clearly made by King and his crew which is now in TXC, Mark Swett Collection/video box.

10. NT 75.

11. NT 71.

12. A copy of the letter is found in appendix E of *Report*.

13. Koresh seems also to have seen these arrows of Psalm 45.5 as symbols of his own children who would one day rule the earth (cf. Psalm 127.4, 'As arrows are in the hand of a mighty man; so are children of the youth. Happy is the man that hath his quiver full of them: they shall not be ashamed, but they shall speak with the enemies in the gate.') See e.g. NT 10A where he comes very close to saying this.

14. See further Tabor and Gallagher, *Why Waco?*, 72–5.

15. 'Foundation' tape.

16. NT 57.

17. The book of Daniel says at this point that Daniel prospered in the reign of Darius (the Mede) and Cyrus (the Persian). While it is Darius and not Cyrus who is specifically mentioned as the conqueror (Dan. 5.31), the assumption is that Cyrus was also involved in the conquest; and we know from other sources that it was indeed Cyrus who conquered Babylon in 539 BC.

18. NT 71.

19. NT 71.

20. NT 80.

21. NT 29.

22. It was Koresh's doctrine that he would be killed and shortly thereafter return to wreak vengeance upon the wicked. This important point will be discussed further in Chapters Fourteen and Fifteen.

23. This video is dated 28 Feb. 1987. Some of what was originally on it has been lost (the tape suddenly switches to a home movie of a wedding). The second video is undated, but was surely taken by the crew that filmed for King's *Current Affair*

programme and hence may be dated 1992 (King himself appears at one point on the tape). Most of the tape is of Koresh preaching to the assembled Branch Davidians. However, the last few minutes contain footage of Mt. Carmel residents. The interviewer (King) is heard to ask two persons (one aged sixteen) if they are afraid of Koresh, to which comes the answer 'no'; 'is anyone here afraid of him?' King asks; again the answer is 'no'. The whole tape is approximately twenty-six minutes long. There is little on this second video that cannot be found in other sources, but it is very interesting to see Koresh in action. His style is dynamic; he makes much use of gesticulation and intonation and frequently asks his audience to complete his sentences.

24. A copy of this tape is in my possession.
25. Recording of the meeting at the Diamond Head SDA church, a copy of which is in my possession.
26. Ibid.
27. Koresh actually says Daniel 11; this is a rare example of his getting a reference wrong.
28. Recording of the meeting at the Diamond Head SDA church, a copy of which is in my possession.
29. Ibid.
30. According to Seventh-day Adventists, 'Michael' is in fact Christ himself. This is a vestige of an angel-Christology found in some earlier SDA theologians. See further Kenneth G. C. Newport, 'Seventh-day Adventism—Jesus Christ in the Theology of', in J. L. Houlden, ed., *Jesus in History, Culture and Thought*, 2 vols. (Oxford and Santa Barbara: ABC Clio, 2003), 789–95.
31. In this context it is interesting that Pastor Liu, who had evidently spent several hours at least talking to Koresh and others before the meeting took place, began the meeting by drawing attention to some of the discrepancies between SDA doctrine and the teachings of the Branch Davidians. One of these is that whereas Adventists teach that Christ is in the heavenly sanctuary, the Branch Davidians teach that he is on earth. The statement is found on the recording of the meeting at the Diamond Head SDA church, a copy of which is in my possession.
32. I.e. the tape recording of Koresh's remarks made live on KRLD radio station on 28 February.
33. Note further that later on this tape Koresh refers again to Psalm 2 and to the way in which the 'rulers take counsel together against ... the anointed'. He is then asked directly, 'do you think that is what is happening here?', to which he replies, 'oh definitely, I am the anointed one'.
34. Others in the movement took this view of Koresh too. Exactly the same scheme is proposed by Livingstone Fagan who, writing after the death of Koresh, referred back to the Numbers passage and to the striking of the rock/Christ twice.
35. When explaining his change of name to Koresh on the KRLD tape, Koresh also states: 'I was also given a name, a name that would represent my position according to the prophetic writings. All the prophets talk about David the son of David, Christ. In Revelation I say that I am the root and offspring of David the

bright and morning star. Peter says prophecy is a light that shines in a dark place until the day spring, day star, arises in your heart. So, you see Christ is this great light—I have the light of the world.' And there is more still on the negotiation tapes, though it is unnecessary to unpack it all here. One example will suffice. On NT 76 Koresh makes a number of statements of potential importance to the issue being discussed here. A good example is fairly near the beginning of the tape: '... but of course, like I say, I'm the Dayspring in the clay. I'm hiding. I look like a person. Which I am a person. And I am a person. I've been here for thirty-three years, but there's something a little more deeper under the skin.'

36. For example, such a view came across in a conversation with Derek Lovelock (interview with Kenneth G. C. Newport, Manchester, Nov. 2002)

37. There are thirty-five tapes in my personal collection, but there are a number of others whose existence is known that I have not been able to access. Some of these are recent arrivals in TXC.

38. The main video evidence is found on the Los Angeles video and the material shot for the Current Affair documentary.

39. Several of Koresh's letters are reproduced in *Report*, Appendix E. In addition TXC holds a number of other written items, some quite substantial (TXC, Mark Swett Collection box 2). Some of the material consists of what appear to be notes that Koresh has taken at Bible studies with Lois Roden. There are also some letters. There is little of value in these in seeking to reconstruct Koresh's theology. The material is not at all systematic and, as so often with Branch Davidian writings, makes extensive use of long quotations from the Bible and Ellen G. White. The TXC material also appears to be early, before 1985.

40. The tape was recorded in 1987; a copy is in TXC, Mark Swett Collection.

41. Such a view is expressed on a taped message concerned with the interpretation of Revelation 13 (1987), a copy of which is in my personal possession.

42. The letter is undated, but was transcribed by Marc Breault and is widely available on the internet. I have used the form prepared for web publication by Mark Swett.

12

<hr>

'A Lamb-Like Beast' (cf. Revelation 13.11–18): the Branch Davidians and the ATF

The Seventh-day Adventist, Davidian, and Branch Davidian traditions have always expected that the present age would pass into the age to come only by means of a violent rite of passage. Quite what form that would take has been a matter of some discussion, and the three groups have taken rather different views. One particular point has been agreed upon by all, however: America would play a key role in the final drama, not just as a location, but also as an agent. In short it was America who, perhaps in conjunction with the Roman Catholic Church,[1] would act in the last days as the great instrument of Satan in enforcing a Sunday law which would have flush out Sabbath-keepers. These Sabbath-keepers, it was argued, are those that 'keep the commandments of God' (Rev. 12.17), and hence are the true remnant. This expectation goes back a long way in the SDA tradition and has continued right up to the present day.[2]

The biblical framing of this belief can be seen in the way in which Seventh-day Adventists have interpreted Revelation 13, an interpretative tradition that the Davidians and Branch Davidians inherited. In that chapter the career of two beasts is outlined. The first arises from the sea, the second from the land. The second beast is particularly deceptive, since although it 'speaks like a dragon' in appearance it is 'lamb-like' (Rev. 13.11). Together the beasts blaspheme the name of God and deceive the people of the earth, causing them to engage in false worship.

In SDA literature these two beasts are seen as symbols of literal powers to come—the first of papal Rome, the second, the 'lamb-like' beast, of end-time America. It is end-time America that will seek to destroy the remnant of God and enforce false worship. Naturally the beasts must be resisted and in particular the 'Mark of the Beast' must not be taken. There is a call for 'the patience and the faith of the saints' (Rev. 13.10).

Traditional Seventh-day Adventists, then, and their denominational offspring, the Davidians and Branch Davidians, have been constantly on guard, watching for the time when America would turn belligerent and align itself with Satan and his Church (Rome) in an effort to drive truth from the earth. At various times throughout this trajectory some thought they spotted the Beast lurking somewhere in the shadows, but none had as yet looked it squarely in the eye.[3] On 28 February 1993, however, that was to change when the Beast, unmasked and not looking like a lamb at all, thundered up Mt. Carmel's driveway.

In SDA depictions of the 'Lamb-like Beast' it is often the 'beastly' rather than the 'lamb-like' qualities that are underscored; the result is often an image of a bull or a bison which is clearly a beast, but has two small horns like a lamb.[4] Given this bovine iconography, it was perhaps particularly ironic that the form the Beast took on this cold Texan Sunday morning was of two cattle trailers. As the eighty[5] or so heavily armed, black-uniformed ATF officers poured out of the backs of these trucks, any biblically informed onlooker might have been visually reminded too of the eruption of the locusts from the bottomless pit in Revelation 9. To those inside Mt. Carmel what was happening must have seemed clear: their worst fears, but also, given the eschatological context, their fondest hopes, were now about to be realized. The Beast had come to make war on the Saints (Rev. 13.7).

PLATE 10 ATF agent seeks to enter Mt. Carmel via a first-storey window

The initial decision by the ATF to enter Mt. Carmel by force, and to do so using a strategic 'dynamic entry' procedure, has been the focus of considerable criticism. This is a complex issue and one ought not to run the risk of oversimplifying, but in essence there are three basic questions that do need to be addressed. First, was the initial decision to serve a search and arrest warrant on the Branch Davidians justified? Was there in fact probable cause to believe that crimes had been committed at Mt. Carmel? Second, if that decision was justified (and it will be argued here that it was), was the decision to serve those warrants through the means of a 'dynamic entry' into the Mt. Carmel property also justified? Would it not have been better, many have asked, to have picked Koresh up outside the Mt. Carmel complex, perhaps on one of his fairly frequent visits into town? Third, and in some ways most important, was it wise for the ATF to stick with the course of action upon which they had decided once the element of surprise had been lost (as it clearly had on the morning of 28 February)? These issues cannot be dealt with here in anything like the detail that they deserve. Fortunately, however, this is one part of the Waco story that has received fairly extended treatment elsewhere, and that extensive literature is readily available.[6] In this chapter, then, only a brief overview need be presented.

Formally the assault of 28 February was made to execute two warrants issued on 25 February by Magistrate Judge Dennis Green. An arrest warrant authorized the arrest of David Koresh on suspicion of the illegal possession of a destructive device '... in violation of 26 United States code, section 5845(f)',[7] while a search warrant authorized the search of Mt. Carmel for unregistered machine guns and 'destructive devices'.[8] A further warrant authorized the search of the 'Mag Bag', a garage about four miles from Mt. Carmel that the Branch Davidians were renting and from which they operated an auto repair business.[9] The 'destructive devices' mentioned in the warrants could have been any number of items defined as such under US law.[10] In this instance, however, Koresh's alleged possession of grenades seems most obviously to have been in view. There were other issues raised in the affidavit, but these do not appear seriously to have affected the decision to search Mt. Carmel and arrest Koresh.[11]

In the affidavit, ATF special agent Davy Aguilera gives some indication of how the Branch Davidians first came to the attention of the authorities. According to Aguilera, some time in June 1992 Larry Gilbreath, the driver of a UPS delivery truck, had delivered 90 lb of powdered aluminium metal to the 'Mag Bag'. In itself the delivery might have gone without further note, had it not been that Gilbreath had earlier indicated that in May 1992 he had delivered two cases of inert hand grenades and a quantity of black gunpowder (40–50 lb) to the same address. Gilbreath also stated that on his visits to

Mt. Carmel to make deliveries he saw 'several manned observation posts, and believed that the observers were armed'. This and other similar information was originally passed by Gilbreath to Lt Barber of the McLennan County sheriff's department, and from Barber to Aguilera. In January 1993 Aguilera interviewed Gilbreath himself, and the reports originally given to Barber were confirmed.

None of the materials Gilbreath reported delivering was illegal at the time and the simple possession of them did not constitute an offence. Only if it could be shown that there were reasonable grounds to suspect that Koresh was using, or intending to use, these materials for illegal purposes would there be reason to issue a warrant for his arrest.

The grounds to suspect that the materials were indeed intended for illegal use were supplied mainly by ex-Branch Davidians, not an independent source of information one suspects, but not one that could simply be ignored either. For example, the affidavit indicates that on 25 January 1993 Aguilera had interviewed ex-Branch Davidian David Block[12] in Los Angeles, California. Block stated that he had been a member of the Mt. Carmel community from March until June 1992. (Block had been 'deprogrammed' by Rick Ross some time in 1992; it may well have been Ross who originally suggested that the ATF agents speak to Block.)[13] Aguilera stated in the affidavit:

During his time at the Mt. Carmel Center, Mr. Block was present on several occasions when Howell would ask if anyone had any knowledge about making hand grenades or converting semi-automatic rifles to machine guns. At one point he also heard discussion about a shipment of inert hand grenades and Howell's intent to reactivate them. Mr. Block stated that he observed at the compound published magazines such as 'The Shotgun News' and other related clandestine magazines. He heard extensive talk of the existence of the 'Anarchist's Cookbook'.

According to Aguilera, other ex-members said similar things. Breault said that Koresh had once told him he wanted to obtain and/or manufacture machine guns, grenades, and explosive devices, while Jeannine Bunds said she had seen pineapple-type hand grenades at Mt. Carmel. There were also reports from a Robert Cervenka, a Mt. Carmel neighbour, who said he had heard explosions on the Mt. Carmel site.

Scholars of religious movements might well have cautioned Aguilera against accepting uncritically the testimony of ex-community members, while the explosions that Cervenka heard may have been, as was later claimed, dynamite being used as part of the building activities of the Mt. Carmel residents.[14] However, once the information had come to the ATF's attention it could not just be ignored. There was good solid evidence that materials had been delivered to Mt. Carmel that could be used to manufacture illegal

PLATE 11 A sample of weapons found at Mt. Carmel following the fire

weapons. A number of people in a position to know quoted Koresh as indicating that he planned to use such materials to manufacture explosive devices. Aguilera had hence built up something of a case in the affidavit and one can see why Judge Green was prepared to act upon the basis of it. After all, he was not required to come to the conclusion that explosive devices were being manufactured at Mt. Carmel, only that there was 'probable cause' to think that they might be—as there was.

In addition to the possible production of the 'destructive devices' there was also the issue of the guns. This is more complex. It is often claimed in the literature dealing with Waco that the Branch Davidians were running a perfectly legitimate weapons and survival gear business, and this business is often given as the reason for the presence of so many guns and associated paraphernalia at Mt. Carmel.[15] This argument certainly has some substance to it, though it is easy to confuse the issues involved. Even in Texas there is a difference between buying and selling guns/other weapons and buying and selling 'associated paraphernalia'. With regard to the latter it is undoubtedly the case that the Branch Davidians under Koresh did trade in such items for profit. They were bought and sold under the umbrella of the 'David Koresh survival wear' company. Activities included trade in ammunitions, gas masks, gun grips, MREs (meals-ready-to-eat), and the like. The group also manufactured and sold hunting jackets adorned with dummy grenades. The key player here, in addition to Koresh himself, was Hawaiian business man and Branch Davidian convert Paul Fatta.

To trade legally in guns, however, one needs a gun dealer's licence, which the Branch Davidians never obtained. Instead, some time in either 1991 or 1992 they entered into partnership with licensed Texas gun dealer Henry McMahon, who operated under the name of 'Hewitt Handguns'.[16] This is often understood to have been a simple buy-and-sell business. However, there is a problem here. We know that the Branch Davidians bought a lot of guns, since the documentation of their purchase has survived. What is not at all clear is whether they actually sold more than just a handful of them. It is safe to assume that very few, if any, could have been sold at gun shows, since they had no licence. The most obvious way for them to have sold guns, then, would have been through McMahon, and here there are some interesting statistics. It has emerged that McMahon sold 223 weapons to Koresh, but sold for him only a total of seven. This leaves a balance of 216 guns; in the absence of any evidence to the contrary it must be assumed that the vast majority of these were still at Mt. Carmel. This was in about September 1992.[17] It seems unlikely, and there is no evidence to support the view, that Koresh and the Branch Davidians suddenly engaged in a mass selling of guns from this point on. In February 1993, then, most if not all these guns would have been on the premises.

In addition, however, it is equally clear that the Branch Davidians were manufacturing guns as well. Again in association with McMahon, they had purchased the parts necessary to assemble AR-15 semi-automatic rifles. On 30 July 1992, for example, ATF agents Davy Aguilera and Jim Skinner visited the registered offices of Hewitt Handguns (McMahon's home) to check on trading records. The books revealed that some sixty-five of the 100 or so AR-15 lower receivers the company had purchased were unaccounted for. These items, so McMahon informed the agents, were with the Branch Davidians. According to Reavis, McMahon stated that this was only for safekeeping. However, as Reavis himself goes on to document, it is clear that by this time Koresh was purchasing parts from McMahon and assembling guns at Mt. Carmel.[18]

The Branch Davidians may have been acting illegally in assembling the AR-15s, but if so it was only because they may have manufactured more than fifty of them. According to federal law, Skinner informed McMahon, those who manufacture such weapons on that scale must pay an 11 per cent federal excise tax.[19] No other aspect of this operation seems to have been illegal, and in fact there was no real proof that any part was. The receivers may have been still at Mt. Carmel in the form in which McMahon had supplied them—that is, not as yet assembled with the other parts to make the gun.

There was suspicion, if not proof, then, that the Branch Davidians might be in the process of manufacturing in the region of sixty-five AR-15s. Further investigations revealed that during 1992 they had purchased a large quantity of other firearms and related materials. This included 104 upper receivers for AR-15s, ammunition for the same, ammunition for AK-47s, a grenade-launcher, and a number of hand guns.[20] Again none of this was in itself illegal, but the scale combined with the testimony of Block and others made it a worrying discovery. A further question with regard to the guns was whether the Branch Davidians were in fact converting legally held (even if illegally manufactured) AR-15s, which, being semi-automatic, fire only one shot per pull of the trigger, to fully automatic M-16s, which can fire continuously. The requirement was that such weapons had to be registered and the appropriate $200 fee paid. If the fee was paid the weapon could be held legally.[21] The main evidence that fully automatic weapons were indeed being manufactured at Mt. Carmel comes from the same two sources as those who gave Aguilera cause to suspect that explosive devices were being manufactured there: ex-Branch Davidians and Robert Cervenka. The latter indicated to Aguilera that during January and February 1992 he had heard fully automatic fire on the Mt. Carmel property, while, as has been noted, both Block and Breault said they had heard Koresh express an interest in the production of fully automatic weapons. It is important to remember that all that was needed at this stage was sufficient evidence to give 'probable cause' to suspect that such activity was going on, not incontrovertible hard evidence that it was; though it is worth pointing out that the on-site post-fire scene reports indicate that such hard evidence did in fact exist, even if it was not available before 28 February. This latter point ought not to be underestimated. The ATF suspected that Koresh and the Branch Davidians had built up an arsenal and events proved them right. Investigations on the scene after the fire revealed that the weaponry amassed at Mt. Carmel was nothing short of awe-inspiring. Even in Texas the inventory would raise eyebrows. The full list may now never be known, but among the 300 or so rifles and shotguns recovered, forty-six had been converted to fully automatic. The full list included two .50 caliber BGM rifles, thirty-four AR-15 assault rifles, sixty-one M-16 assault rifles, sixty-one AK-47 rifles, and five M-15 rifles. Additionally, the rangers recovered sixty assorted pistols and thousands of pounds of live and spent ammunition, twenty-one sound suppressors/silencers, a number of hand grenades (some of which were inert, though others live and many showed signs of attempted modification), numerous parts for the assembly of guns, and other weaponry.[22]

There is reason to think that Koresh's interest in guns, explosive devices, and associated paraphernalia was not simply commercial. Koresh, it seemed, was also preparing for some sort of battle during which significant fire power would be needed. While his apocalyptic framework could not have been known in full to the ATF, they might well have suspected at least some of what was later to emerge more fully from reports given to Aguilera from a number of sources. One such source was Joyce Sparks, from the Texas Child Protective Services Department. As discussed in Chapter Ten, she had visited Mt. Carmel on two occasions to investigate allegations of child abuse; Aguilera indicated that she told him that on the second of her visits to Mt. Carmel, Koresh told her that:

he was the 'Messenger' from God, that the world was coming to an end, and that when he 'reveals' himself the riots in Los Angeles would pale in comparison to what was going to happen in Waco, Texas. Koresh stated that it would be a 'military type operation' and that all the 'non-believers' would have to suffer.

A second source was Robyn Bunds. Again the affidavit indicates that Bunds told Aguilera that she and other members had watched a number of violent war films, which Koresh referred to as 'training movies'. Again, one might well suspect that this evidence ought to be taken with at least some caution; allowance must be made for the fact that it is coming from someone who had reason to wish to paint a picture of Koresh that was not favourable. Sparks's evidence is more robust.

For these and a number of other reasons, then, the ATF might well have had 'probable cause' for concern. In the event the concern was well founded. Although his statements came only after the initial raid, on at least one occasion Koresh was explicit on the question of just why there were so many weapons at Mt. Carmel. That evidence comes on the KRLD tape. At one point Koresh is asked specifically about the guns, and in answer says:

Look let me explain the weapons in the beginning; OK. The weapons were bought originally because—you know—in the prophecies we understand that as it was...I know this is going to sound weird to you, you don't know, you don't—Nahum, you don't know Micah, you don't know Zephaniah—but any way 2000 years ago Christ tried three and a half years to present the gospel right...and the night of his crucifixion he told his servants, he says 'before I sent you out without cloak nor purse nor sword, so now I say unto you, if you do not have a sword go sell your cloak and buy one'. The Christian church is not to stand idly by and be slaughtered. The importance of truth is so that men may hear the truth and be convicted by reasoning that the words of God do harmonise, they are in perfect harmony and that they are the truth. Now if people come along and just nab and grab and push people around no one gets to say anything. So my hope was that these agents would have backed up …

At this point Koresh is distracted by a report that 'great big army trucks or something' are coming onto the Mt. Carmel property and the conversation is broken. However, the interviewer returns to the question, saying 'well you were explaining about the necessity in your mind for the collection of the weaponry that you have there'. Koresh continues 'So that we could show uh— a force—so they would stay away... so that we could speak and try to explain our position from the Bible'.

This is an interesting unguarded response to the question of what Koresh was intending to do with the weapons amassed at Mt. Carmel. Of course, he may just simply be being a bit bullish here; the adrenalin that had built up during that day might not have worn off. Nonetheless, it is possibly informative that when asked about the presence of weapons at Mt. Carmel Koresh did not seek to explain them as being part of a legitimate business, but (as always) looked to the Bible to provide the key statements, including Jesus's instruction: 'if you do not have a sword go sell your cloak and buy one'. Koresh seems to have carried much of the Bible in his mind, and it is possible that this text might have sprung to him instantly as soon as he was questioned about the guns. It is perhaps more plausible, however, that the appeal to Luke 22.36 was not a response on the spur of the moment, but a much more carefully thought out policy. In short, in addition to any legitimate gun dealing business that might have been going on at Mt. Carmel, Koresh does seem to have been preparing for battle.

The answer to the first question set out above, then, 'was the initial decision to serve a search and arrest warrant on the Branch Davidians justified?', seems to be in the affirmative. Once the Branch Davidians had come to the attention of ATF it would have been improper for the authorities not to take things further. It was certain that raw materials had been delivered to Mt. Carmel that could be used for highly dangerous ends, and a number of people had supplied testimony that those ends were indeed in mind. Further, there was the issue of straightforward illegal activity. The evidence suggested that the Branch Davidians might be manufacturing explosive devices, assembling more than the permitted number of semi-automatics, and converting semi-automatics into fully automatics. Something needed to be done. The question was, 'What?' The issuing of the search and arrest warrants was the first step of the response.[23]

Warrants were thus in place for the arrest of David Koresh and the search of the Mt. Carmel/Mag Bag property. In deciding to do the two things at the same time, and to do them by means of dynamic entry into Mt. Carmel, the

ATF were putting into practice a tactical decision made several weeks earlier. Dynamic entry must have been on the agenda at least since 21 January, when a letter was drafted for the signature of the ATF's chief of special operations to the Army regional logistics support office in El Paso, Texas, requesting the use of the Fort Hood facility for training exercises and the loan of seven Bradley fighting vehicles and driver training and maintenance support for the Bradleys.[24] The request was initially refused, but following further requests (and the dropping of the request for the Bradleys) ATF agents did receive some training at Fort Hood and also the use of helicopters from the Texas national guard, these to be used as decoys during the raid.[25] The date of the proposed raid was set for Sunday 28 February.

The use of military personnel and/or equipment in actions against US citizens is a serious business; indeed it is prohibited by the *Posse Comitatus Act* of 1878. However, in 1981 and 1989 exceptions to the Act were made which allowed the military occasionally to be directly involved, and more frequently to be indirectly involved (as training agents), where the actions to be taken were part of the national 'war' on drugs.[26] It was to this that the ATF appealed, claiming that Mt. Carmel was the site of a methamphetamine laboratory. Actually, they did have something to go on here. Some years before, George Roden had permitted the use of Mt. Carmel's property by two drug dealers/manufacturers.[27] However, these two had vacated Mt. Carmel when Koresh took over, and Koresh himself had brought to the attention of the authorities what had been going on there, a fact not taken into consideration, it seems, by ATF.[28] It was further alleged that a number of those in Mt. Carmel had drug convictions. The case for asking for military assistance was hence perhaps rather weak, but technically justified. However, the end result was that ATF agents received significant training at Fort Hood, and perhaps more importantly could rely on helicopters acting as decoys, as they prepared to enter Mt. Carmel.

The more general question of whether the decision to enter Mt. Carmel 'dynamically' was justified is an important one and is much debated.[29] One ought not to forget the context. The intelligence so far had indicated that Koresh and the Branch Davidians had already amassed a sizeable arsenal which included 'explosive devices', semi-, and possibly fully-, automatic firearms. It had also been reported that the Mt. Carmel residents did have some extremist views and were looking for a showdown with the authorities. Koresh was known to have a propensity to violence and the use of firearms as his shootout with George Roden had demonstrated. There was hence good reason to suspect that an unannounced visit by law enforcement authorities would not go unchallenged.[30] There was at least the real possibility of danger and the ATF might well have taken the view that it was better to err on the side of caution. (This is put rather more directly in the *Treasury Report*, which states that 'the ATF planners reasonably concluded that a polite request to search the Compound without readiness to use force would have been foolhardy and irresponsible'.)[31]

Neither was the possibility of arresting Koresh while he was away from the premises without problems. In fact, the ATF planners seem to have been of the opinion that Koresh rarely left Mt. Carmel, though the basis upon which this assumption is made is not at all clear. If this was their view, it represents (as, to its credit, the *Treasury Report* makes clear) a serious breakdown in intelligence on the ATF's part. But if this was the intelligence supplied to the planners it perhaps explains why it was that the option of arresting Koresh outside Mt. Carmel appears not to have been explored very fully. Additionally, it must have been a factor that the warrants were both for the arrest of Koresh and the search of Mt. Carmel. Both needed to be done. Had word of Koresh's arrest seeped back to Mt. Carmel prior to the arrival of the search party, the weapons might have been concealed. And in any case, as is argued here at length, Koresh, while a strong leader in Mt. Carmel, was not the only one capable of taking control. To arrest Koresh away from Mt. Carmel would not guarantee that a subsequent approach by ATF agents would be any the less dangerous.

The plan that was drawn up was, then, quite an understandable one. Had it gone according to expectation it would have overcome all of the problems associated with the alternatives. The plan was to go in hard while the men were working away from the main building, secure the arsenal, and arrest Koresh. It proved not to be that simple.

As it turned out, on the morning of 28 February there was already great excitement in the Branch Davidian complex. The day before, the *Waco Tribune-Herald* had published the first in what was to become a seven-part series on Koresh under the title 'The Sinful Messiah', and this had sparked some serious reflection. Thibodeau's account of his own frame of mind the day before the raid shows what was already being anticipated:

That Saturday seemed to go on forever...I watched the rainy Texas sunset that evening and felt I was living in a highly symbolic moment—the end of our world, if not the end of the whole world. I was simultaneously exhilarated and terrified. I didn't want to die, but I was now so identified with the community that the prospect of sharing its biblical destiny made my heart thump with excitement. It troubled me, though, that I might never see my family again, especially my mother, who, by the light of our faith, would be damned.[32]

If Thibodeau is remembering correctly, there was excitement and anticipation at Mt. Carmel in part generated by the attention the group was receiving from the *Waco Tribune-Herald*. Even on the day before the raid the community were already thinking in terms of the coming of 'the end' (whatever that meant in the context), which might well, so Thibodeau believed, involve individual and communal death.

On the Sunday morning itself, two people (David Jones and Donald Bunds) left the centre to buy copies of the newspaper. They took different directions in an effort to find stores that still had the now day-old newspaper (the Branch Davidians would not have purchased the paper the previous day since it was the Sabbath). Donald Bunds was taken into custody, but was never charged with any crime. David Jones drove a little way before meeting a camera crew who appeared to be lost. He offered assistance and was asked for directions to Mt. Carmel, because the ATF were to launch a raid on the property that morning and the crew wanted to cover the story. On hearing this, Jones drove immediately to a place to call back to Mt. Carmel to alert the group that the ATF were on their way.[33]

The question of how and why the camera crew knew about the proposed raid is much debated. One view is that the ATF were desperate for some good publicity ahead of major funding decisions regarding the agency and tipped off the media in an effort to make sure the raid was covered on local, and perhaps national, TV.[34] Another (not mutually exclusive) view is that the media learned of the raid from an employee of an ambulance firm that the ATF had contracted to accompany them to Mt. Carmel in case of injury.[35]

Again it has to be said that in much of the literature dealing with this part of the Waco story there is something of a lack of clarity: the general assumption is that since ATF took care to see that the events of 28 February were on film, this must have been central to the decision to go at the Branch Davidians in the first place and go at them hard. According to this view, it was not just the management of the media coverage of the events of 28 February, but the actual events themselves that were determined by external factors and the need for a media 'splash'.

There are, however, two related but not inextricable questions here and they need to be separated. First, was the initial decision on the part of ATF— to use 'dynamic entry' as the means by which the search and arrest warrants would be served—determined in whole or in part by a desire to make a big media impression ahead of funding decisions? (That such funding decisions were on the agenda is not actually in dispute.) If the argument is going to be made that it was, some substantial hard evidence will need to be produced. However, in the literature such evidence is lacking. Rather the situation is, to repeat, read backwards. There are variations on it of course, but the basic argument is: the ATF needed good publicity and hence sought to make the most out of the raid in terms of its potential for boosting its public image (which may or may not have included the tipping off of TV stations). Therefore the decision to use dynamic entry itself was also driven by public image concerns. This is clearly a *non-sequitur.*

In fact, as has already been argued above, there was good cause for the ATF to believe (rightly or wrongly) that the heavily armed Branch Davidians did present a real potential threat and that dynamic entry was the best way to serve the warrants and secure the property. That decision may very well have been taken without any thought to funding problems, potential mergers with the FBI, or anything else. It may simply have been a decision taken on the basis of the best intelligence available and to date no one has produced any hard evidence (as opposed to perhaps reasonable speculation) that this was not precisely the case.

Whether the ATF then decided that given the political situation they were in they might as well make sure that the importance of their work was brought squarely to the attention of the American people is quite another issue. To exploit a given situation for media gain is not the same as creating it. Hence, while one reading of the decision making process leading up to the events of 28 February might be that the raid was a publicity stunt and that the decision to use dynamic entry was the same, another equally plausible reading would be to argue that in fact the decision to use 'dynamic entry' was quite properly arrived at on other grounds but that the ATF then decided it would be expedient to make sure that it was taped and shown on news bulletins. If the ATF did tip off the media (and it is not absolutely certain that they did) this does not mean that the whole event was staged.

The debate on this issue will no doubt continue: what is certain, however, is that for whatever reason the media did know, and they inadvertently alerted those inside Mt. Carmel that a raid was about to take place. It was a very unfortunate slip which was to have disastrous consequences.

For some time the ATF had had an agent inside Mt. Carmel: Robert Rodriguez (or Robert 'Gonzalez' as he was known the Branch Davidians). On 10 January 1993 he had moved into a house directly opposite the Mt. Carmel property, and from there he and a number of others were watching Koresh and the other Branch Davidians across the road.[36] The Mt. Carmel residents knew they were there and feared that they were being watched by the immigration service. Rodriguez began making visits to Mt. Carmel, sat through a number of Koresh's Bible studies, and took part in some target practice with Koresh.[37] On the morning of the 28th Rodriguez was on site.[38] He was there to make sure that it was safe for the ATF raid to begin. When Koresh was given the news by Perry Jones, who had taken the telephone call from his son, that ATF were on their way, he returned to where Rodriguez was and announced that the ATF and the national guard were coming. Rodriguez left the house promptly (this was at approximately 9.05 a.m.), making the excuse that he had to meet with someone for breakfast, and made an urgent call to raid commanders Philip Chojnacki, Chuck Sarabyn, and the special agent in charge Ted Royster to tell them that the Branch Davidians knew the ATF raid was about to take place.[39] There was then a difficult decision to make.[40] Was the raid to be called off, thereby 'wasting' all the time and money that had been put into it, or was it to proceed even though the Branch Davidians were aware of the plans? The decision was taken to proceed. It would be another forty minutes before the cattle trailers drove up the driveway of Mt. Carmel. The Branch Davidians had plenty of time to prepare.

The decision to go ahead with the raid even knowing that the element of surprise had been lost needs some explanation. From a distance the decision looks highly questionable. After all the ATF case was built upon the argument that Koresh and the Branch Davidians might well have a considerable stock-pile of firearms and perhaps other weaponry, which makes it surprising that the decision was made to go head-on against such a potentially deadly opponent. Planning to catch the group unawares was one thing; planning to take on a heavily armed apocalyptic group who had had a good forty minutes to prepare for confrontation was quite something else. It is difficult not to conclude that this was a huge error on the ATF's part.

The trucks rolled. At approximately 09.45 a.m. the cattle trailers entered Mt. Carmel's driveway. At the same time three national guard helicopters also arrived; these had long been planned as a diversionary tactic and agents Chojnacki and Royster were among their passengers.[41] According to the Danforth *Final Report* no shots were fired from these helicopters, though the Branch Davidians tell a different story.[42]

As had been planned, the agents rushed the front of the complex and put into action what they had practised at Fort Hood. As is always the case in this story, the understanding of what happened next depends upon which side you are listening to. According to the Branch Davidians, Koresh was waiting, unarmed, near the front entrance. The entrance was by a set of two doors and Koresh opened one of them. Seeing the agents rushing towards him he shouted, 'What's going on? There are women and children in here.'[43] The agents shouted back 'Police, search warrant, get down' and aimed their weapons at Koresh.[44] He backed away, slamming the front door shut as he did so. A hail of bullets came through the door hitting at least two persons (Koresh and Perry Jones) in the process. According to Reavis, Dick DeGuerin, and Jack Zimmerman, who gained access to Mt. Carmel during the siege, they inspected the doors and confirmed that most of the bullet holes that could be seen were the result of bullets passing into Mt. Carmel rather than passing out.[45]

The ATF account is somewhat different. According to Agent Ballesteros, who was running towards Mt. Carmel's front door as it closed, a number of rounds were fired through the door from inside;[46] the Branch Davidians and not the ATF fired first.[47]

There has been a huge amount of discussion regarding these two accounts and in particular with regard to a 'missing' door. As can be seen on video footage and photographs of Mt. Carmel taken during the siege, the two double doors that formed the entrance to the main building were intact, if damaged, after the events of 28 February. After the fire, one of those doors was discovered among the rubble, the other was not. There quickly arose questions about this 'missing' door and suspicions were raised that it had somehow been taken away to avoid inspection of potentially incriminating evidence.[48] In fact, this is perhaps the best example (together with Michael Schroeder's cap—on which see more below) of how a conspiracy theory can easily grow from the absence of evidence. 'Missing' evidence is assumed to support the Branch Davidian case in a way that would counterbalance the actual evidence available. As can also be seen on a mass of video and photographic evidence from Mt. Carmel both the right-hand and left-hand doors had bullet holes in them. It was the left-hand door, and it alone, that was found after the siege. The door was badly warped either from the heat or from being run over by a vehicle but otherwise intact. Agents later claimed that the right-hand door had melted in the heat.[49]

The disappearance of the door is an issue, but not one that can be solved here. Perhaps government agents did take it away to prevent inspection. If they did, however, they must have been very short-sighted. It would surely have been an act of almost unbelievable stupidity on the part of a would-be tamperer with the evidence to take one side of the door but leave behind the other, hoping that later investigators would believe that one side of the double door had been destroyed in the fire or had in some other way simply vanished from the scene. And one should not shirk from considering what would need to be the case here: some persons would have needed to conspire with other persons to remove a substantial (and heavy) piece of physical evidence from the scene. They would have needed to plan for removing a door to prevent its inspection, and made arrangements to retrieve the door and transport it to another location, presumably for destruction. During the planning of this attempt to remove incriminating evidence it presumably dawned upon no one that the fact that only one door of a pair had disappeared would be as potentially incriminating as the door itself (presuming that it did show evidence of bullets being fired into Mt. Carmel). All this is possible, but it would mean that the evidence-manipulators were probably of well below average intelligence. On the other hand it is also difficult to believe that the fire consumed one door completely but left the other intact. At least as plausible, perhaps, is the possibility that the door was dragged away by one of the assault vehicles on 19 April and somehow got lost amid the general rubble. This is not a view that can be argued here; it is based on little more than speculation—as is the theory that the door was whisked away by the FBI; but it is worth considering.

But actually it probably matters not at all that the door went missing. What, after all, could it have proved that was not already known? It is not actually in dispute that some of the bullets that passed through the doors of Mt. Carmel that morning went from the outside in. The surviving door proves that; at the June 2000 civil trial the door was produced and a government agent stated that 'there were bullet holes going both directions'.[50] Even if the other door exhibited holes showing that the bullets went through it were all from the outside, nothing more would be known. In particular it could not in any way help with the really crucial question of 'who fired first?' The only way this could be answered categorically would be if all the bullets fired through the doors came from one direction. However, to repeat, the surviving door makes it clear that this was not the case and no one claims that it was.

As noted briefly above, the other really major contentious issue raised by the differing reports of what occurred during the first few hours of the stand-off is whether ATF agents fired on the Branch Davidians from helicopters. Again, this cannot be discussed in detail here, and need not be, for there is already a wealth of literature on the topic elsewhere.[51]

The initial assault resulted in four ATF deaths: agents Conway LaBleu (30), Todd McKeehan (28), Robert Williams (26), and Steve Willis (32). All died from gunshot wounds. Precisely who shot whom has never been settled, but on 26 February 1994 five Branch Davidians—Renos Avraam, Brad Branch, Livingstone Fagan, Jamie Castillo, and Kevin Whitecliff—were all found guilty of aiding and abetting manslaughter.[52] Kathy Schroeder had earlier pleaded guilty to one count of armed resistance.[53]

The raid also resulted in the deaths of six Branch Davidians. (Koresh originally claimed that a two-year-old child was also killed, but this was almost certainly not true. He may simply have been playing for public sympathy at this point.)[54] Those deaths have been the subject of great debate elsewhere and little purpose would be served here in going once again over all of the evidence.[55] Nevertheless, a brief account does seem proper.

The cause of Perry Jones's death is in dispute.[56] The Branch Davidian account, supported by Thibodeau and Kathy Schroeder, is that on 28 February Jones suffered significant injuries and Koresh gave someone, perhaps Neil Vaega, permission to put him out of his agony by 'mercy' killing him, which he subsequently did.[57] The autopsy report indicates that Jones was killed by a single shot to the roof of the mouth. This could have been self-administered, and in fact would fit in with the apparent preferred method of suicide taught by Koresh, but it might also have been administered by someone else.[58] However, the autopsy report also states strongly that there were no other injuries to Jones and hence brings into question the view that he was 'finished off' as an act of mercy. Indeed, reading the autopsy one would be much more likely to conclude that Jones had committed suicide. There seems little chance of moving this debate on given the directly conflicting evidence and no further time will be spent on it here. In either case Jones was dead probably within hours of the initial raid. He was buried in a grave inside the concrete tornado shelter at Mt. Carmel and his body was thus preserved from the worst effects of the fire.[59]

Certainly killed that day was Jaydean Wendell. Moore has claimed that Wendell was asleep when she was killed, but it seems much more probable that she was shooting at the ATF; this is the explicit testimony of Victorine (Vickie) Hollingsworth and Thibodeau who (unlike Moore) were there at the time.[60] The single low velocity hydra-shock bullet that hit her killed her instantly. Who fired that shot has not been ascertained. Wendell was buried in the grave in the tornado shelter; her body was exhumed after the fire.

Peter Hipsman suffered four gunshot wounds. Two of these were apparently administered by fellow Branch Davidian Neil Vaega who, according to Kathy Schroeder, stated that it took two shots to finish him off.[61] The origin of the other two shots is in dispute. According to the Branch Davidians the shots were fired from a helicopter, a claim disputed by government accounts.

Peter Gent was working inside a water tower when the events took off. There is no disputing that he was shot dead by ATF agents. There is dispute over whether he was armed, and again whether the shots that killed him were fired from a helicopter. At the civil trial evidence was brought forward to indicate that Ofeila Santoya, a Branch Davidian who exited Mt. Carmel on 21 March,[62] had seen Gent carrying a gun on the morning of 28 February.[63] Thibodeau, however, claimed that Gent was unarmed when he was shot. According to him, Gent may have been shot from a helicopter, though he states also that a sniper might have been responsible.[64]

The death of Winston Blake is even more contentious. Blake was killed by a single shot behind the right ear. The USA autopsy stated clearly enough that the shot was administered at close range, and pointed to the presence of soot in the wound (though not on the outer skin, which had decomposed). The bullet was identified as coming from a .223 high-velocity rifle. This could have been self-administered, but not easily. The implication is, then, that Blake was shot at close range by one of his co-religionists. Why this would have been the case is not at all clear since there were no other apparent injuries.

Blake's remains were repatriated to the UK, where they were re-examined. The report of this examination was rather different.[65] According to this document the wound sustained by Blake was consistent with a shot being fired from a distance and passing through some other structure (the walls of Mt. Carmel for example) before entering Blake's head (the entry wound was reported to be jagged, indicating that the bullet was not flying true when it struck but was wobbling somewhat). To this must be added the testimony of both Clive Doyle and Derek Lovelock, both of whom have confirmed that Blake was dead when he was found (Lovelock said in fact that it was he who first came across Blake's body).[66] Of course, it could be that unknown to Doyle or Lovelock another Branch Davidian had shot Blake and then made an exit before the body was discovered. This seems unlikely. On the other hand, the *Final Report* is absolutely clear: 'the range of fire is very close/near contact' and 'soot/gunpowder is present in the dermis, in the subcutaneous tissue and on the underlying bone at the entry site'.[67]

The sixth Branch Davidian to die on 28 February was Michael Schroeder.[68] He was working in the Mag Bag that morning along with two other Branch Davidians, Woodrow Kendrick, and Norman Allison.[69] Much later in the day all three sought to return to the community and approached Mt. Carmel from the north-west. Precisely what happened as they drew near to the property is in dispute. According to one account the three came across ATF agents and a gun battle ensued. The 1993 *Report* suggested that all three tried to 'shoot their way into' Mt. Carmel.[70] However, it was later claimed by ATF officers that in fact only Schroeder had fired a weapon.[71] Fire was returned and Schroeder was hit six times. Kendrick fled and Allison was arrested.[72] What is clear from these reports is that at least Schroeder had fired at the agents and that he was killed in self defence.[73]

Needless to say this is not the only account on offer. According to Moore (who, we must recall, is coming at this question from a very particular point of view): 'troubling evidence suggests that angry BATF agents may have shot an unarmed Schroeder, assassinated the wounded man, planted a gun and shells around his body, and impeded the Texas Rangers' investigation in order to cover up their crime.'[74]

These are serious charges and it has to be said that Moore's account of things does not bolster confidence in the suggestions she is making. Her narrative is, to say the least, somewhat speculative. However, no attempt can be made here to enter fully into the discussion that surrounds Moore's remarks. Suffice it to say that there has been significant debate on the issue. Reavis in particular has constructed a narrative of events that, as with Moore, raises some issues with regard to the 'official' account, even if it does not overturn it. Perhaps the most significant is the fact that of the six wounds, two were to the head. The question hence arises as to how, even if Schroeder managed to remain standing after being shot four times in the body (one shot was a graze, but one punctured a lung and another severed an artery) he managed to remain on his feet having been shot in the head twice. One could argue of course that Schroeder was felled by any one of the shots, and then shot up to five more times as he lay either dead or dying on the ground. The autopsy report is not out of keeping with such a view.

There might of course be an explanation that would fit with the 'official' account of what happened that evening. However, it did cause people to question whether in fact something more sinister happened. Perhaps, some surmised, Schroeder was felled by one or more of the body shots but 'finished off' at close range with the two shots to the head. The *Final Report* is clear that there is no ballistic evidence to support this theory: 'there is no evidence to indicate any of the gunshot wounds were contact, close or medium range'.[75] That seems plain enough and unless one is prepared to argue that this is a fabrication one must go with it.

There is a further complication, however. Some argue that there is evidence that Schroeder was wearing a cap the day he died and that any gunpowder or soot deposits that would have been left had the shooting been at closer range would have been not on Schroeder's skin but on the cap. The cap itself was not among the evidence logged by investigators. For many years it was claimed that the cap (like the right-hand door) had somehow gone missing, with the fairly clear implication that something underhand had taken place.[76] However, it was eventually discovered in Waco evidence lockers in Austin, Texas, by film maker Mike McNulty in 1999.[77] The 'missing cap' now looks to be more the result of a mistake than a conspiracy. If one is going to make a piece of evidence 'disappear' one place not to hide it, we presume, would be in evidence lockers. No tests have been carried out upon the cap to date, and until they are suspicion is bound to remain.

The crisis begun about 09.45 a.m. was hence quick to develop, and soon a number of persons had lost their lives. What had been planned as a quick, dynamic entry into Mt. Carmel to be followed by the securing of the arsenal and the arrest of David Koresh turned out to be far from that. At approximately 9.47 Branch Davidian Wayne Martin called 911 and was put through to the McLennan County deputy sheriff, Larry Lynch. One can clearly hear shots as Martin talked to Lynch and it is evident that Martin was in a state of real distress as he called out on the phone, 'There's about seventy-five men around our building and they're shooting . . . tell them there are women and children in here and to call it off . . . call it off!'[78] Martin then hung up. Fifteen minutes or so later, with the crisis now in full flow, Lynch called Martin and began an extensive conversation that eventually resulted in a ceasefire some two hours later.[79] Those two hours saw a frenzy of activity as amid the chaos some on both sides sought to calm the situation down.

The 911 tapes give a dramatic, often chilling, insight into what was going on inside Mt. Carmel during the period, and also some of the frustrations Lynch faced as he tried to relate the message to ATF that he had a line into Mt. Carmel. These and other audio recordings indicate further the impression on both sides of what firepower they were facing. Martin clearly thought that he was being fired on from helicopters, while ATF agents can be heard to shout, in what is clearly a reference to what they feared was being fired at them, 'fucking machine gun'.[80] Reports came in that ATF agents were being shot and killed, while there were reports inside Mt. Carmel of injuries and fatalities.

By the time the ceasefire was in place, the FBI were on the scene.[81] The initial assault on Mt. Carmel had been a disaster. The ATF had not achieved its goals and in the process had lost four of its officers. For their part the Branch Davidians had also suffered fatalities. And now the battle lines had quite literally been drawn. A heavily armed religious group that had long expected to be set upon by the agents of Satan shortly before their passing into glory were pointing some ferocious weaponry out of the windows of their home at those they considered to be an end-time foe. A number of their colleagues lay dead and their leader lay wounded. The ATF had suffered a humiliation and, more importantly, had seen four of its colleagues gunned down by a group of, as they would have seen it, religious fanatics led by a maniacal leader. The FBI hence walked into a crisis not of their own making.

The crucial question was whether this now dire situation could be turned around. There were some early successes and signs for hope especially in the first few days as a number of children left the centre. However, it is likely that even within a few hours of the initial ATF actions the Branch Davidians, or at least Koresh, had decided that the end had come. That night Koresh spoke to the KRLD radio station and gave some general indication of how he now viewed the situation. What had happened that day, he clearly thought, was the fulfilment of Psalm 2; the heathen had come 'to break [Koresh's] bands asunder'. Now was also the time when the sun and moon were to be darkened (cf. Joel 2.10). Koresh talked about how Moses struck the rock twice (Num. 20.11) and clearly implied that this was a sign that Christ must die twice (cf. 1 Cor. 10.4). Then, rather ominously, he said very clearly, 'you see now people are going to lose their lives over this. Now the next event . . . we are in the fifth seal right now . . . the next event to take place is that the sun and the moon and the stars will be darkened just like Joel 2 and all the prophets teach.' Koresh continued with this for some time and was then interrupted by Charlie Serafin, the talk-show host, who encouraged Koresh to seek medical help so that he could continue his ministry. As Serafin was talking, Koresh broke in with some very chilling words indeed: 'I am going home, I am going back to my father and we have...like I say the next thing you are going to see according to Matthew 24 is that you will see the Son of Man coming in the clouds with great glory and power.'[82] One must remember that as yet very little could have been known by the FBI or indeed anyone else on the scene about the theology of this group; so it is unsurprising that these indications of what was going on in Koresh's head on the night of the raid seem to have been missed. However, with hindsight it is plain: he expected to die.

It might be argued that this is not to be taken too seriously. Perhaps Koresh was simply feeling suicidal following the events of the day. Perhaps, like Paul who, when sat in a cold dark jail, thought that it would be better for him to depart and be with Christ (cf. Phil. 1.23), Koresh too considered his death and departure to be preferable over what he was now facing. There is a difference though: unlike Paul, Koresh thought he was a manifestation of (or at least possessed by) the Christ spirit (it is on this very tape that he said, 'as I said to my disciples' and 'as I told the woman at the well'). And Koresh thought too that he was 'coming back'; he said further on this tape, 'tell Linda Campion, Linda Campion that I still love her and I'm gonna be back OK...and also tell Sandy, Sandy Berlin that I'll be back and I still love her too'. Putting this together it is difficult not to conclude that Koresh had already come to a clear understanding of what the immediate future held. The heathen had come to break the bands of the king asunder. The fifth seal was being fulfilled (and hence the souls must go under the altar). But the sixth was also about to break: the sun and moon were to be darkened, an earthquake was soon to come.[83] And then would come the great day of the wrath of the Lamb. Koresh was 'going home', going back to his Father, but, as he assured Linda Campion and Sandy Berlin, he would be back. This all fits in theologically with Koreshian Branch Davidian theology. Seen in this context it is reasonably plain that the KRLD tape does not contain the ranting of a wounded man shocked by the events that had come upon him and his community. It is, rather, the reiteration of some long-standing Davidian and Branch Davidian hopes. The Apocalypse was about to break.

NOTES

1. Thus the paradigm; Koresh seems to have dropped this aspect from his thinking.
2. For a full discussion see Newport, *Apocalypse and Millennium*, 172–96.
3. From time to time some Seventh-day Adventists will put forward the view that a particular act on the part of the American government is evidence that the Lamb-like

beast is about to take on its eschatological role and that as a consequence the Sunday laws will soon be in force. Contemporary examples of this are found easily on the internet. In this context it is interesting to note that, rather surprisingly, when John F. Kennedy, a Catholic, was elected president of the United States in 1960, SDA speculation about the end-time joining of Roman Catholicism and the American political machine seemed to go into reverse—see further Malcolm Bull and Keith Lockhart, *Seeking a Sanctuary: Seventh-day Adventism & the American Dream* (San Francisco, Calif.: Harper & Row), 50–5.

4. See Newport, *Apocalypse and Millennium*, 172–96, for details and bibliography.

5. The precise number of ATF agents is not clear. Reavis gives it as between seventy-five and ninety, which is in tune with all other estimates (Reavis, *Ashes of Waco*, 138).

6. See e.g. Hardy, *This is Not an Assault*, 173ff.; Reavis, *Ashes of Waco*, 177–84 *et passim*; *Final Report*, 124–43 *et passim*; and there are sections too in most of the other standard academic literature on Waco.

7. *Report*, 8; the warrant (ref. W93–14M) was for the arrest of Vernon Wayne Howell aka David Koresh.

8. The warrant (ref. W93–15M) was issued on the probable cause to believe that unregistered machine guns and destructive devices were being concealed in violation of both 18 and 26 USC.

9. Warrant ref. W93–19M.

10. USC 26, sec. 5845 (f) defines a 'destructive device' as: '(1) any explosive, incendiary, or poison gas (A) bomb, (B) grenade, (C) rocket having a propellent [*sic*] charge of more than four ounces, (D) missile having an explosive or incendiary charge of more than one-quarter ounce, (E) mine, or (F) similar device; (2) any type of weapon by whatever name known which will, or which may be readily converted to, expel a projectile by the action of an explosive or other propellant, the barrel or barrels of which have a bore of more than one-half inch in diameter, except a shotgun or shotgun shell which the Secretary finds is generally recognized as particularly suitable for sporting purposes; and (3) any combination of parts either designed or intended for use in converting any device into a destructive device as defined in subparagraphs (1) and (2) and from which a destructive device may be readily assembled.'

11. The affidavit runs to *c.*6,500 words and copies of it can be found on the internet. To avoid confusion from differing formats, no page numbers are used here.

12. David Block was recruited by Steve Schneider, who, it seems, had known him for some time. Block's first defection took place a few months after that of Breault. However, Block returned to the Branch Davidians for a while before defecting once more, this time for good. During the initial conversations the ATF had with Breault, they used some of Breault's records to track Block down and spoke also to him. (Information from Marc Breault, email to Kenneth Newport, 2 September 2003.)

13. From material which, at the time of writing, is at www.rickross.com/reference/waco/waco1.html

14. Moore, *Davidian Massacre*, 61, takes such a position, suggesting that the explosions were related to the excavation of an underground tornado shelter. No hard evidence has been produced to support this view.
15. See e.g. *Davidian Massacre*, 47–8.
16. Reavis, *Ashes of Waco*, 36.
17. See further, 'Pair who sold guns to Koresh say the ATF had made life difficult', *St Louis Post-Dispatch*, 29 Jan. 2000. The report is based upon an interview with McMahon, who at the time of the interview was living in Bonners Ferry, Idaho.
18. See Reavis, *Ashes of Waco*, 37; that McMahon was selling gun parts to Koresh is also confirmed in the report cited in the previous note.
19. Ibid. 38.
20. Affidavit.
21. According to Reavis (*Ashes of Waco*, 34), in 1993 some 234,000 Americans held fully automatic weapons (machine guns) quite legally. Koresh could not be one of them since he had not registered any nor paid the fees. If he had any, then, they were illegal.
22. See further *Final Report*, 175. Some of this was produced as evidence at the criminal trial (see *Civil Trial Transcripts*, 2078, for one of numerous examples). The 'civil trial' to which reference is here made (civil action number W–96–CA–139) took place in Waco, beginning on 19 June 2000, and was heard by Judge Walter Smith. The plaintiffs were attempting to prove that government agents had wrongfully killed the Branch Davidians who died at Mt. Carmel. An electronic copy of the trial transcripts is in my possession. (The action was unsuccessful.) Some photographic evidence is also in the *Report of The Department of the Treasury on the Bureau of Alcohol, Tobacco, and Firearms Investigation of Vernon Wayne Howell also known as David Koresh* (Washington, DC: Dept. of the Treasury, US Government Printing Office, September 1993); see especially figs. 4, 36–9.
23. The above account does appear properly to reflect the weight of evidence. The conclusion, that the search and arrest warrants were justified on the basis of Aguilera's affidavit, also seems properly supported by the information to hand. This is not to say that no legitimate questions can be raised regarding the process by which the warrants were obtained. For example in the affidavit the issue of suspected child abuse is fairly prominent, although this was entirely outside the jurisdiction of the ATF. It is apparent to anyone who reads the affidavit that Aguilera seems almost to go out of his way not to say anything at all about the outcome of the child abuse allegations. Rather the issue of 'child abuse' slides into a discussion of whether the children dreamed of carrying guns. This was not simply a matter of adding something in the affidavit that was superfluous and/or failing to report fully that the child abuse allegations were found to be groundless. Child abuse is an emotive issue and might well have affected the decision to issue the warrants (though there is no evidence that it did). Some have argued also that Aguilera did not fully understand the mechanics of some of the alleged weaponry he was investigating, and as a result made mistakes about the use which could be made of some of the hardware at Mt. Carmel. However, even allowing for these

questionable inclusions and some factual mistakes in the affidavit, it does seem that there was 'probable cause' for the ATF to suspect that Koresh was in control of serious weaponry, some of which may have been illegal, and, importantly, the Davidians were not planning simply to use such weaponry (legal or not) for purposes that would give no cause for concern.

24. *Final Report*, 127–8.
25. Ibid. 129–32.
26. Reavis, *Ashes of Waco*, 123.
27. Ibid. 125–6.
28. Ibid. 125.
29. Discussion of this point can be found extensively in the secondary literature on Waco, where it is generally argued (or at least stated) that the decision was not only heavy-handed, but also unnecessary (see, e.g. Hardy, *This is Not an Assault* 173–84). The other side of the argument can be found in Department of the Treasury, *Report of the Department of the Treasury on the Bureau of Alcohol, Tobacco, and Firearms Investigation of Vernon Wayne Howell also known as David Koresh* (Washington, DC: U.S. Government Printing Office, Sept. 1993), part 2. I have drawn here on material from that report.
30. The counter-argument, that Koresh had once invited the inspection of his weapons and that this illustrates an underlying good will on his part, cannot be sustained. On that occasion Koresh made the invitation by telephone knowing full well that if the agents had taken the offer up he would have had ample time to conceal any firearms he did not want drawn to the attention of the authorities (see further Reavis, *Ashes of Waco*, 38).
31. *Treasury Report* (I have used the web-based version of this document, which does not include page numbers).
32. Thibodeau, *A Place Called Waco*, 158.
33. The details on Jones are in the general literature on Waco. They were confirmed by Clive Doyle (Interview with Kenneth G. C. Newport, Waco, Nov. 2001).
34. See e.g. Moore, *Davidian Massacre*, 113–5; Hardy, *This is Not an Assault*, 175–81.
35. See further Reavis, *Ashes of Waco*, 43.
36. Ibid. 67.
37. According to *Final Report*, 125, Agent Rodriguez first made contact directly with the Davidians in late January.
38. Ibid. 133.
39. Hardy, *This is Not an Assault*, 24.
40. Ibid. 24 n. 32. The question of exactly what Jones had said to Koresh and what Koresh said in the presence of Rodriguez is important. How precise was Rodriguez's information and, consequently, how specific could he have been in warning his superiors that the Branch Davidians knew that the ATF were coming? *Final Report*, 133, is quite clear on this point: Rodriguez reported to his supervisors that 'Koresh knew about ATF's operation'. The decision to be made by the ATF was hence an informed one: should the raid proceed even though the Branch Davidians had now had some time to prepare?

41. *Civil Trial Transcripts*, 1436.
42. *Final Report*, Appendix C, 26, *Civil Trial Transcripts*, 1440; the Davidian view is found in, among other places, Thibodeau, *A Place Called Waco*, 177, *et passim*.
43. Thibodeau, *Place Called Waco*, 166.
44. Ibid.
45. Reavis, *Ashes of Waco*, 142.
46. See *Civil Trial Transcripts*, 2194, where Ballesteros states: 'I continued to run to the front door, and I reached to the porch. I jumped on the porch and I tried to open the front door. At that time I heard a burst of gunfire and I observed holes in the front door coming from the inside out.'
47. The testimony of agent Kris Mayfield given at the civil trial (*Transcripts*, 1536ff.) is also worth considering.
48. Although the claim is not made outright, this is the clear implication in Reavis, *Ashes of Waco*, 140–2. It is stated more explicitly by Moore, *Davidian Massacre*, 128–9.
49. Reavis, *Ashes of Waco*, 142.
50. *Civil Trial Transcripts*, 1548.
51. There is extensive discussion on this point in *Civil Trial Transcripts*; see also Reavis, *Ashes of Waco*, 132–6, *et passim*; Hardy, *This is Not an Assault*, 189–201.
52. On the same day Renos Avraam, Brad Branch, Jaime Castillo, Kevin White Cliff, Graeme Craddock, Livingston Fagan, and Ruth Riddle were all convicted of using or carrying a firearm during a conspiracy to murder federal officers. Craddock was also convicted of possessing an explosive grenade, and Paul Fatta of conspiring illegally to possess and manufacture machine guns and aiding and abetting the illegal possession of machine guns. Three others, Norman Allison, Clive Doyle, and Woodrow Kendrick, were acquitted of all charges (*Final Report*, 181–2).
53. *Final Report*, 182.
54. Koresh can be heard clearly to make this claim on the KRLD tape. According to Moore (*Davidian Massacre*, 142), Castillo later argued (rather implausibly) that some of Jaydean Wendell's blood had fallen onto a child and that it was this that led Koresh to make the 'mistaken' claim.
55. See Thibodeau, *A Place Called Waco*, 176–8, for his account of the deaths of five of the Branch Davidians. The death of Michael Schroeder is discussed on 186–7. A different version of events surrounding the death of Schroeder is in *Final Report*, 28 n. 32.
56. Carol Moore, *Davidian Massacre*, 129–31, discusses the death of Jones from a perspective highly critical of the official report. As often in Moore's work one has the impression that there is little hard evidence to support the bold statement of an extremely contentious theory. In this case Moore has to depend upon the reader being willing to assume, with her, that the autopsy report was wrong (either by intention or simple incompetence) or else that the FBI switched Jones's body for another one to get the 'right' report.

57. See Thibodeau, *A Place Called Waco*, 176; Autopsy report (MC 80). All references to Waco autopsies given here are from *Final Report*, Appendix J, which contains a summary and discussion of the original autopsy reports conducted in 1993. Those original reports are available on the internet and have been also consulted.
58. Autopsy report (MC 80).
59. Jones's body was recovered and stored in a cooler at the medical examiner's office. This cooler later failed, giving rise to a claim that the reason the 'other' injuries to Jones were not apparent at the autopsy was that the body had decomposed (e.g. Thibodeau, *A Place Called Waco*, 176). The summary of the autopsy in *Final Report* indicates that there was a cooler malfunction, but that this had occurred only after the autopsy was complete.
60. Moore, *Davidian Massacre*, 160; Thibodeau, *A Place Called Waco*, 178.
61. Thibodeau, *A Place Called Waco*, 178.
62. *Final Report*, Appendix C, 46.
63. *Civil Trial Transcripts*, 2086–7.
64. Thibodeau, *A Place Called Waco*, 177.
65. I am dependent upon secondary sources for information on the UK autopsy report since, despite a number of requests to the Manchester Coroner's Office, the relevant document never came into my hands.
66. Derek Lovelock, interview with Kenneth G. C. Newport, Manchester, UK, Nov. 2003.
67. *Final Report*, Appendix J, 137.
68. Michael Schroeder was twenty-nine when he died in Feb. 1993. He was born a Lutheran, but had become a Baptist and then joined the Church of God before developing an interest in Seventh-day Adventism. He and his wife Kathy came into contact with Steve Schneider, who brought them into contact with Koresh. Kathy Schroeder had three children by a previous marriage and one with Michael (information from Reavis, *Ashes of Waco*, 192, and *St. Petersburg Times*, 28 Feb. 2000).
69. Reavis, *Ashes of Waco*, 193, has some interesting detail on Allison, apparently gained from interview. In essence Reavis reports that Allison was from Manchester, UK, where he had been a taxi driver. He was persuaded to go to Waco by Derek Lovelock (also from Manchester and a fellow Seventh-day Adventist) in autumn 1992. Allison was very interested in music and had been a part-time singer in the UK, but his voice was not appreciated by Koresh. Allison hence left Mt. Carmel to seek his fortune in California. When he left he was apparently warned that he might miss out on the events that would lead to the end of the world and his response was (according to Reavis) oft repeated by Mt. Carmel residents: 'That's all right,' he said, 'I'll watch it on TV.' In Jan. 1993 Allison returned to Waco but was not admitted to Mt. Carmel itself. He had taken up residence on a discarded bus seat at the Mag Bag.
70. The *Report*, 25, states: 'At approximately 4:55 p.m., several agents were ambushed by three individuals as the agents crossed a field near the compound. The ATF

agents returned the gunfire, killing one individual and capturing another. The third individual escaped . . . All three individuals were Branch Davidians who had been at another location called the "Mag Bag" and were attempting to shoot their way into the compound.'

71. *Final Report*, 134.
72. Kendrick was eventually arrested on 9 March.
73. *Final Report*, 28 n. 32.
74. Moore, *Davidian Massacre*, 178.
75. *Final Report*, Appendix J, 148.
76. See e.g. Reavis, *Ashes of Waco*, 197; Hardy, *This is Not an Assault*, 32.
77. Hardy, *This is Not an Assault*, 32 n. 41.
78. A copy of the 911 tapes is in my possession. Some, but not all, are also in TXC, Mark Swett Collection. Martin's estimate of 'about seventy-five men' is remarkably accurate (it should be remembered that the estimate was arrived at within two minutes of the arrival of ATF and amid a hail of gunfire), though there is nothing to suggest it was anything other than a lucky guess.
79. See also the time line at Appendix C to the *Final Report*.
80. *Civil Trial Transcripts*, 329.
81. The initial request from the ATF for the assistance of the FBI appears to have come between 10 a.m. and 11 a.m. when Dan Harnett, Deputy Director of the ATF, phoned Douglas Gow, Associate Deputy Director of the FBI. Experts in crisis management (including Byron Sage) were dispatched immediately. The time of the request from Harnett to Gow and the subsequent dispatching of Sage to Waco is given as 11.30 a.m. in the timeline (Appendix C to *Report*), which then indicates that Sage arrived in Waco at 12.05. These times cannot both be accurate; Sage took the call from home and it is a good hour's drive from Round Rock, where he lived, to Waco. Later that day it was agreed that the Hostage Rescue Team (HRT) would become involved as would the Special Weapons and Tactics teams (SWAT). The official request from the Treasury Department that the FBI assume responsibility for what was by now a major crisis came at approximately 10.00 a.m. on the morning of 1 March.
82. KRLD tape.
83. In this context it is worth noting that on 14 April Koresh sent a letter to Dick DeGuerin warning of the coming of an earthquake in the Waco area. A copy is in Appendix E of *Report*.

13

'A Call for the Endurance of the Saints'
(cf. Revelation 14.12): Mt. Carmel,
28 February–19 April 1993

In the mind of the general public the events of Waco are largely condensed into two days: 28 February and 19 April 1993. Between these two dates, however, is a period of fifty-one days, during which various efforts were made on the part of the authorities to get the Branch Davidians to leave the Mt. Carmel property. Some of what happened during this period was reported by the world's media, especially in the first week or so of the stand-off. Eventually, however, interest in what was happening at Mt. Carmel dwindled, until that is, the dramatic climax to events propelled Waco back onto centre stage.

Opinion about what happened during those fifty-one days is polarized. On the one hand the government voice states unequivocally that the intention was to get the Branch Davidians to exit peacefully, and that everything that could be done was done to see that this came about. Those who accept this view argue that the fifty-one days were taken up, by and large, with real efforts on the part of the negotiation team to bring the situation to a peaceful end. No stone was left unturned in an effort to find a solution; concessions were made, reasonable demands met, and assurances given. Where strong-arm tactics were employed, it was in the Branch Davidians' own interests.[1]

On the other side of the debate there are those who argue that during the fifty-one days the FBI negotiators engaged in psychological warfare partly, perhaps, as a means of wearing down Branch Davidian resolve, but also to punish the Branch Davidians for killing the four ATF agents, and perhaps even in a concerted effort to get the movement to self-destruct. The playing of loud music, the constant glare of high-powered lighting, and the cutting off of electricity and all means of communication with the outside world were a part of this plan and designed to achieve these ends. Behind such tactics, it is sometimes said by those on this side of the debate, was a fundamental machismo coupled, perhaps, with a determination to 'get straight' with these religious fanatics who had dared take on the government.[2]

Religious studies experts have in general come somewhere between these two poles, though perhaps closer to the second position (the FBI were acting in a machismo fashion) than the first (the FBI did everything in their power to bring the crisis to a peaceful resolution). In the discipline, however, a further ingredient is quite often added: the suggestion that if scholars trained in the nature and dynamics of religious groups had been brought in, some better outcome could have been engineered. Indeed, in such sources it is generally assumed, sometimes specifically argued, that with proper handling the Branch Davidians could have been talked out and that the FBI were remiss in not achieving this. According to this view, the methods employed by the FBI were born more of ignorance than of malice.[3]

It is not the intention here to attempt a full analysis of the ways the FBI conducted the negotiations with the Branch Davidians, nor to address directly the issue of whether the tactics employed at Waco were, in general, the right ones, though some remarks will be made on these central concerns.[4] It is only fair to state unequivocally at this early point, however, that the reading of the material presented here rather favours the FBI account. There is little evidence that the FBI negotiators were determined to 'get straight' with the Branch Davidians or to get the group to self-destruct. The extensive tapes bear witness rather to a really quite remarkable concern on the part of the negotiators to meet Koresh half way and to work for the peaceful resolution of the conflict. Neither was the failure to consult with religious experts complete, although doubtless more could have been done in this area in an effort to increase the negotiators' level of understanding of the kind of persons they were dealing with. However, it seems to have been the FBI view that you do not debate delusions with those who hold to them, and they were probably right to take this line. There seems no possibility that any negotiator, however skilled or aware, could have argued Koresh out of the view that he was the Lamb of God. Tabor's case is much more finely nuanced than that, of course; he and Arnold saw the 'ambiguity' of the situation as an area that might be exploited to good ends.[5] This is possible, but, as is argued in this book at considerable length, Koresh's view was that the situation that had come about as a result of the events of 28 February was not ambiguous at all.

What can be treated in a little more detail, however, is how the Branch Davidians themselves saw and reacted to the events. This is a very important aspect of the process of negotiations (as will become painfully clear in the chapters on the fire) and one frequently misunderstood. To be brief, there are clear and early hints in what was said by the Branch Davidians, and some of the plans they evidently already had in place, of what was to come. In fact by the time the FBI arrived the situation was already at crisis point, and probably at the point of no return. That evening Koresh had spoken on air about 'going back to his father' and 'coming back' (after his death). He was already thinking 'this is it': this was the breaking of the fifth seal and the coming of the time when the souls must go under the altar (Rev. 6.9–11). As the siege wore on this conviction seems to have increased, to the point where the Branch Davidians began to speak about 'going back en masse'. Finally they (some of them at least) set fire to their home in an effort to live out what they considered to be their God-ordained destiny.

It is fortunate for the researcher that a number of sources relating to the conduct of siege have survived. While these come in several formats, by far the most important are the audio tapes that were recorded from the beginning of the initial raid by the ATF to the point at which contact was lost during the fire on 19 April. There are three distinct subdivisions to these. First, there are the '911' tapes, that is the recordings of the sometimes frantic discussions between a number of Branch Davidians (principally Wayne Martin, Steve Schneider, and David Koresh) and the McLennan County sheriff's office which began at 9.48 a.m. on 28 February, a few minutes after the raid began.[6] These tapes are useful; they are unguarded and give some insight into how the raid was seen during and immediately after the initial shootout. Chapter Twelve has already noted some of these. Second, and most substantially, there are the official recordings of the negotiations between the FBI and the Branch Davidians that were made during the siege itself. Third, and very important, are the 'bug' tapes. These are the often poor-quality recordings that resulted from the placing inside Mt. Carmel of a series of concealed transmitters.[7] This final set of recordings has been at the centre of some of the most aggressive debate, for it is these that have been thought to show that the fire on 19 April was the result of actions taken by the Branch Davidians themselves. Some of the material from these bug tapes will be discussed briefly in this chapter. A more sustained analysis of them appears in Chapters Fourteen and Fifteen. There are also one or two other recordings which do not fall into any of the categories above. Such materials are separately and clearly identified in what follows.

It was noted in the previous chapter that on the night of 28 February Koresh made contact with KRLD News Radio in Texas, and spoke extensively to the station on two separate occasions.[8] The quality of the resulting audio tape is good. As an indication of the general context in which the Davidian–FBI negotiations began, the content of those KRLD recordings is worth examining further.

There is very little that, on reflection, would have brought much comfort to those even then devising a negotiation strategy. The potential importance of much of what Koresh said during the interviews would not have been apparent to the average listener. However, to anyone with a sense of the biblically informed world to which Koresh belonged, the tape presents some unwelcome clues as to what was going on in his mind. For example, already he seemed to have decided that the end of this siege would be death; or, more accurately, death followed by resurrection/return. At a number of points Koresh can be heard to refer explicitly to this. He talked not only of 'going home' (where 'home' clearly means 'heaven'), but also of returning. He spoke of the events of the fifth seal being even now underway, which meant that the souls of the faithful must go under the altar, and the events of the sixth seal, Matthew 24, and Joel 2 as being the next to take place. Crucially, and very problematically to those facing the task of getting him to come out, he seems already by now to have taken a huge step: what was happening was the beginning of the end, and that 'end' was fast approaching. Had someone versed in Branch Davidian theology been on the negotiating team, he or she might with good reason have tried the argument that what was happening could not be 'the end' since the community were still in Waco and not in the Holy Land. If the contents of the tape are anything to go by, however, such an argument would probably have fallen on deaf ears. There is no hint of any expectation that the move to Jerusalem would now take place; nor of any expectation that a war in the Middle East must come first—in fact quite the contrary. God was about to put this nation (the USA) to shame. He was about to hold them up as an example of infidelity and its rewards. Koresh plainly saw the events now occurring as fulfilling Psalm 2. Indeed, at one point on the tape Koresh was asked specifically by the interviewer if what is found in that Psalm was now being fulfilled at Mt. Carmel. 'Definitely', said Koresh, 'I am the anointed one ... this is the fulfilment of prophecy, this is it, this is the end'.

It would be a mistake to think that Koresh had come to the view that he would have to die only once the siege began. In other parts of the taped material he left behind one can see that he was anticipating his own death, and at the hands of the King of the North, whom he identified as the United States, for several years before 1993. For example, on the tape 'The Bird', recorded in August 1987, Koresh went into some detail on the question of the fate of 'the bird' (the reference is probably to Isa. 46.11), namely himself. 'The bird' would be killed by the King of the North on account of the bird's polygamous activities and his claim to be the Son of God. 'But that's all right', said Koresh, 'he gets the last laugh, because he is strictly biblical.' If one combines this with the contents of the tape 'Letter to Steve Schneider', the same basic outline becomes apparent as that which emerges in the negotiation transcripts and other materials during the siege. Koresh would be killed, but he would return ahead of an army to destroy God's enemies. The Branch Davidians in general and Koresh (and Steve Schneider) in particular went into the siege with the expectation that what was happening would result in communal death.

Despite the (in retrospect) fairly ominous contents of the KRLD tape, FBI negotiators might justifiably have drawn some comfort from a clear promise that Koresh gave very early on the morning of 2 March. He had been thinking about this at least since the evening before; Thibodeau remembers the group being gathered together to hear of the plans.[9] In effect Koresh set up a deal. If the FBI would see to it that a tape recording of an extended message was played on national radio at prime time, the Branch Davidians would exit. The promise is heard on the tape itself. Right at the beginning Koresh said 'I, David Koresh, agree, upon the broadcasting of this tape, to come out peacefully with all the people immediately.'[10] Later that day the negotiators informed Koresh that the message would be played as he had requested, and the taped message was sent out with Catherine Matteson, Margaret Lawson, and two of the Martin children, Kimmie and Daniel.[11] The tape was played at 2.30 p.m. What should have happened then was that the Branch Davidians left. Thibodeau comments that many of them had even got as far as preparing some food supplies to last them through the day ahead.[12] They waited in anticipation expecting soon to be leaving. Koresh had discussed some of the practical arrangements:

Koresh: You know. And then, you know, I'll space them at a long enough distance to where . . . and you can see there's a steady line of them. And—

Garcia: OK.

Koresh: —I'll have them walk up to the, to the front of the property there at the gate. Then the guys will come out, and I'll have them hold their hands up.

Garcia: OK. And single file.

Koresh: And—OK. Like—yeah, single file. Not two at a time.

Garcia: Um-hum.

Koresh: Their hands up. And, and—well, do you have like—

Garcia: We can turn—

Koresh: —warm vehicles and stuff like that?

Garcia: What we'll do is we'll, we'll turn on the lights, and they can walk towards the lights. And then we'll have people, you know, ready to, to assist them[13]

However, at approximately 6.00 p.m. on the evening of 2 March a key turning point in the siege was reached when, rather than leaving Mt. Carmel, Koresh sent a message to the negotiators indicating that God had told him to wait.[14] It was Schneider who broke the news, talking to FBI negotiator Jim Cavanaugh:

Schneider: Be careful who you're dealing with. Read Psalms 2.

Cavanaugh: This has been—this has been four hours.

Schneider: He says his God says that he is to wait because that which was played on the air is given for everyone to hear—

Cavanaugh: Right.

Schneider: —that they might be proven or not. That's exactly what he said to me. Did you hear me? . . . But that same God is saying to him, 'wait'. It's not that he's not going to do what he said, not at all. In fact, he's not said—he's not recanted from that. His God said to him—he prayed a long time and there was a voice that did— said nothing else to him but, wait. . . . I mean he was told to wait. He said—so the same God that showed him the seals and gave him the seals is the same one that said wait. So, that's—right at this moment, that's all he can do, right at this moment.[15]

It was a catastrophic blow.

There has been much discussion about this decision by Koresh to 'wait'. Some have understandably argued that this was simply a matter of Koresh breaking his word. He had promised to come out, but he did not. Perhaps he had never even meant to keep his word; it could all have been a lie from the beginning. Others, however, have argued that Koresh was being entirely genuine here. He had meant it when he said he and the others would come out but, for whatever reason, he had now come to the view that he must wait on God's next signal.[16]

There is another view, however. At the criminal trial in 1994 two Branch Davidians, Kathy Schroeder and Vickie Hollingsworth, testified clearly that the plan for the 'exit' on 2 March was a plan for mass suicide. The testimony of Hollingsworth on this point is worth quoting at some length:

Greg Summers was to go out with Koresh with hand grenades strapped around his waist. Those inside the building knew that the ATF would try and enter it and that there would be another shootout, and that they [the Branch Davidians] would 'blow the place up.' And it was Annetta—Annetta Richards, Doris Fagan and Zilla Henry, the three ladies—because, you know, it's four black ladies—was four black ladies in our message. I am the fourth one, four of us. So, the rest of them were together and I was sitting—I was sitting a little away from them. And Annetta says to me, she said, 'Vickie you know, don't stay away from us, you know, come and join us, that we all will go home to mother, you know, together.' . . . And at that time, you know, we were there, I stand up with them and we're talking. Mrs. Evette Fagan came out and she brought a green thing, and she give it to her mother-in-law, Mrs. Doris Fagan. And Annetta Richards said to me, she said, 'Vickie,'—you know—she said—well, she said all to—you know—to all of—all of us, she says that, 'This would be a quick death and we will all go home to mother.' I said to her that I want to be—I want to be—I want to be put to sleep. Because before then, Paullina Henry, she came and she said to me— she know that I was afraid of the—you know—what went on—you know—what went on with the—the raid and the siege and all that. So, she came and she said to me, she says, 'Vickie, Marguerita [sic] has a[n] injection and that injection would put you to sleep,' that when David goes out and the ATF comes—comes in to us, we will—the ATF comes in to us, we would have a shootout, because we girls all upstairs would only—would only waste away, and then we would blow the—you know—we would blow the place up. My answer to her, I said to her that I wanted to be put to sleep. But when I said that I want to put to sleep, I didn't mean that, you know, for the injection, because in all—you know—all the—all the time in the raid and the—and the siege and all of that, I'd been praying, asking that my—my heavenly—because I believe that we have a heavenly mother and a heavenly father, so I was praying, asking them if they could put me to sleep. And that was the sleep that I meant, that I said, you know, to them, that I want to be put to sleep, because I know that if I commit suicide, I would not be—I would not, you know, be saved, you know, to have a place in God's kingdom. So, when I said that I wanted to be put to sleep, that was what I meant. She joined the other men and women in the serving area on the first floor where they all held hands and prayed loud. They were happy because they were all going to heaven—they were going to be translated to die.[17]

Even clearer is the testimony of Kathy Schroeder, which, given the importance of this point, is again worth quoting in full. Schroeder was being asked about the events of 2 March, and responded:

Schroeder: Neil Vaega told me that there had—there was a plan that David was making a tape, that when it was aired—after it was aired, we were all going to come out, David on a stretcher that the FBI had sent in, and fire and draw fire.

Q: OK. Fire at whom?

Schroeder: The agents.

Q: OK. What was Mr. Koresh's condition to be when he was carried out on the stretcher?

Schroeder: If he was not already dead, we would shoot him.

Q: OK. And what was the intention of firing and drawing fire?

Schroeder: That we would all be killed.

Q: OK. Did there come an alternative plan—or possibility?

Schroeder: A couple of alternatives.

Q: All right. What were those alternatives?

Schroeder: These were all just methods that we could go, we didn't have any idea exactly how it would happen. But Neil gave me a grenade for the purpose …

Q: For the purpose of what?

Schroeder: Blowing up the girls that were in the room with me.

Q: OK. Who were the girls in the room that you spoke to about it?

Schroeder: Sheila Martin, Jr., Vanessa Henry, Sandra Hardial, and I believe Marjorie Thomas, I'm not sure.

Q: OK. What was their reaction to the prospect of blowing themselves up with a hand grenade?

Schroeder: They didn't really have much of a reaction, they were like, 'Kathy, you can do this.'

Q: OK. Was there any discussion in the event that 'Kathy' Schroeder couldn't do it? Was there any discussion in the event that—that you could not take it upon yourself to—to blow people up with a hand grenade?

Schroeder: I—I discussed that with the girls and I was asking them, 'What are we going to do if I can't?' But they were just reassuring me that I could.

Q: OK. Was there any discussion about people who did not have a hand grenade or people who could not inflict death upon themselves, as to how they might be translated?

Schroeder: If the hand grenade was not used, if that was not the plan or if there was not one available, yes, there was another plan?

Q: And what was that?

Schroeder: The women could be shot by a male.

Q: Did you discuss that prospect with anyone?

Schroeder: Yes, I did.

Q: With whom?

Schroeder: Neil Vaega.

Q: And what was his response?

Schroeder: That he would take care of me.[18]

This seems clear. The plan, according to these witnesses, was for a number of persons to exit Mt. Carmel on 2 March, carrying the possibly already dead Koresh on a stretcher. If he was not dead, they were to shoot him and also at the agents outside. This would draw gunfire and they would all be killed. Those not involved in the shooting were to huddle together, some still inside Mt. Carmel, and blow themselves up with grenades. Vaega would see to it that Schroeder did not survive by shooting her himself if need be.

The expectation here (as with 19 April, it will be argued) was not that the Branch Davidians were simply committing suicide. Death was a gateway to life.

Schroeder: We started praying. I don't remember why or how, we just started praying.

Q: OK. Can you describe the prayers? Were they joyful, sorrowful?

Schroeder: Oh, joyful. Everybody was ready to be translated.[19]

Schroeder and Hollingsworth may have been lying of course. However, there seems no reason why they would do that.

It seems likely that the planned exit from Mt. Carmel on 2 March was an exit also from this world. If so, the decision to 'wait' might just indicate that Koresh had decided to back down on this occasion. Perhaps he now had doubts that death, or perhaps just death at their own hands as opposed to waiting for God's enemies to bring it, was not in keeping with what God wanted. Indeed there are later references on the tapes where Schneider states categorically that suicide is wrong; Koresh too hints at this sort of thinking.[20] These statements sit very awkwardly with the testimony of Schroeder and Hollingsworth and, indeed, with what appears to have happened on 19 April when, even if the Branch Davidians did not set fire to Mt. Carmel (and it will be argued here that they did), it is entirely evident that some took their own lives by gunshot. Alternatively, perhaps Koresh simply looked around and caught a glimpse of the horror of what was being planned and thought better of it. Was it really the case that God wanted all these people—men, women and children—to suffer the violence that, according to Schroeder and Hollingsworth, was now being prepared for them? If either of these things (shrinking from suicide for moral reasons and/or backing away simply on the grounds of the horror it inspired) is what happened, then the breaking of the promise to 'come out' is quite understandable. Leaving Mt. Carmel to go to the Father was one thing; leaving Mt. Carmel to go into the hands of the FBI was something quite else.

In any event the exit was cancelled and the fact that Koresh had, in the eyes of the negotiators, broken his promise made things all the more difficult from this point on. Over the next few days others left the complex. With the departure of David Jones's nine-year-old daughter, Heather, on 5 March, however, the departures of children stopped, and no more left Mt. Carmel after this date. There were twelve further adult departures: Kathy Schroeder and Oliver Gyarfas on 12 March, Kevin Whitecliff and Brad Branch on 19th, Rita Riddle, Gladys Ottman, Sheila Martin, James Lawton, Ofelia Santoya, Victorine Hollingsworth, and Annetta Richards on 21st, and Livingstone Fagan on 23rd.[21]

The pattern of departures is important to note. Twenty-one of the thirty-five who exited Mt. Carmel were aged twelve or younger (often much younger), while six were over the age of sixty, and Victorine Hollingsworth was fifty-nine. A number of the others who left were mothers who, one suspects, had maternal instincts that were proving difficult to override. Kathy Schroeder may have been an example of this, though she claimed that she had been ejected from Mt. Carmel for smoking. If so, that too is interesting. It is probably a sign that Koresh would not tolerate disobedience at this point. He needed the community to stick together. If Schroeder disobeyed on the question of smoking, it was a sign of disloyalty to Koresh and to the whole group, and she was ejected as a result. Fagan, on the other hand, appears to have been sent out by Koresh as a theological ambassador.

The other side of this coin is that the children who did remain inside Mt. Carmel were mostly Koresh's own and there were only two persons in Mt. Carmel at the time of the fire who were over sixty (Raymond Friesen and Floyd Houtman). The younger mothers who had not left during the siege almost all had their children, or some of their children, with them (Yvette Fagan was an exception, but far from wanting to leave to be with them she expressed the view that it had been a big mistake to send them out. They would have been better off, and safer, she said, had they remained with the community).[22]

The overall impression given by this profile is that there was a determined effort to firm up the group. Children and older people in particular were shed. The social group left at Mt. Carmel was now all the stronger, prepared, perhaps, for the tough time that lay ahead. Throughout all this the negotiations went on, with the FBI team talking not only to Koresh and Schneider but to a number of the others too. Those discussions are frequently very one-sided. This is certainly so when the Branch Davidian is either Koresh or Schneider for these two sought, as would be anticipated, to explain to the FBI the biblical significance of what was happening. One can drop in almost at random and get a sense of what is going on. The following, from 7 March, is a typical extract. Koresh had evidently got his negotiator, Dick Rogers, reading from the book of Revelation:

Rogers: He planted his right foot on the sea and his left foot on the land.

Koresh: That's the Book of Revelation. That's what we're dealing with right now. Go ahead.

Rogers: And he gave a loud shout, like the roar of a lion. When he shouted, the voices of the seven thunders spoke.

Koresh: Uh-huh.

Rogers: And when the seven thunders spoke, I was about to write, but I heard a voice from heaven say, seal up what the seven thunders have said and do not write it down.

Koresh: OK. Go ahead.

Rogers: Then the angel I had seen standing on the sea and on the land raised his right hand to heaven, and he swore by him who lives forever and ever—

Koresh: That's the Father.

Rogers: Who created the heavens and all that is in them, the earth and all that is in it and the sea, and all that is in it, and said, there will be no more delay. But in the days—

Koresh: Time no, time no longer, in other words.

Rogers: But in the days when the seventh angel is about to sound his trumpet—

Koresh: Uh-huh.

Rogers: The mystery of God will be accomplished, just as he announced to his servants, the Prophets.

Koresh: Exactly. OK? Now, whatever the prophets have stated, remember, these events of revelation are the previews of the events that are to soon take place against this great nation known as Babylon. Now, remember, in Daniel 2, Babylon is a cessation, a continuation of the empires that will rule over Israel to the end of time when God will break the yoke of all nations from off his people, that God may set himself up a kingdom... [there follows an extensive discourse by Koresh on the meaning of the passages][23]

Obviously there are many other sections where something much closer to a real conversation is going on. As one reads the transcripts of the tapes, and even more listens to the tapes themselves, it becomes evident just how hard the negotiators were trying to get the Branch Davidians to listen to reason. The problem was that 'reason' was not what drove this particular group.

On 9 March the FBI cut the power to Mt. Carmel. It was first cut for a period of about eight hours and then restored. The following day it was cut once more and this time not restored.[24] It is evident that the cutting of the power was a source of great frustration to the Branch Davidians; psychologically it must have been damaging, reinforcing as it did the sense of loss of control. Koresh immediately threatened to stop talking to the negotiators, sending a message via Steve Schneider that he would not come to the telephone until the power was back on.[25] But it was a practical issue too. Without refrigeration some of the food would have deteriorated quickly. This would not have been such a problem for the adults, as there were plenty of MREs in stock.[26] However, it was much more serious for the young children, as the milk they depended on soon began to sour.[27]

On 15 March a face-to-face meeting took place outside the Mt. Carmel buildings between Byron Sage (chief negotiator), Sheriff Jack Harwell, who had played a key role in dealing with the initial 911 calls, Wayne Martin, and Steven Schneider.[28] Sage was wearing a microphone and the conversation was hence captured.[29] The meeting progressed reasonably well. Martin was concerned with legal matters relating to the preservation of evidence and the question of who would be conducting the investigation. He was assured by Sage and Harwell on both points: the evidence would be preserved and the investigation would be handled primarily by the Texas rangers. Sage worked hard to persuade Martin and Schneider to bring the people out. Medical attention and legal representation was promised and a good deal of what Sage said, backed up every now and then by Harwell, seemed to be sinking in. However, the direction changed significantly when Martin suddenly said that there was another party in the negotiations, God, and God had told them to wait. As soon as this was introduced into the conversation Schneider, who had been relatively quiet to this point, became vocal in support of Koresh's view that God has communicated to him that the community should wait. Listening carefully to Schneider's voice and, where audible, that of Martin, from this point on there seems little cause for optimism. No firm commitments were made on the part of the Branch Davidians, though Schneider did agree to report back to Koresh what had been discussed.[30]

From this point on the negotiation tapes do not contain much that could be considered evidence of a willingness to leave Mt. Carmel on Koresh's part, or of any real progress being made towards bringing that end about on the part of the FBI. It is true that there were still some 'successes'; ten persons left the complex between 15 and 23 March. But, as has been said above, this was probably more to do with Koresh battening down the hatches and preparing for an assault by sending out the weaker members of the community than his being persuaded by any skilful negotiation.

All the time the pressure was increasing. On 15 March the FBI had requested the loan of two Zeon pedestal-mounted searchlights.[31] These were used to flood the Mt. Carmel complex with light and hence, together with loud-speakers over which a variety of unpleasant sounds were broadcast, frustrate sleep.[32] There must have been considerable frustration on the part of the FBI negotiators too, who, despite their best efforts, seemed able to achieve little beyond driving the community into an even greater determination to stay with what in their minds had now become an eschatological course. For their part the Branch Davidians continued with their daily routine of extended Bible study, efforts to keep Mt. Carmel clean (no mean feat given that there had never been internal plumbing and sewage systems were extremely basic even in better times). But frustration is clearly evident: at one point Koresh expresses the view (regarding those who turned off the electricity) that 'we need to send guys up there and blow their heads off,[33] and Schneider comes to the point of suggesting to the negotiators that they set fire to Mt. Carmel in an effort to force the residents out.[34] This latter remark is very significant. It is preceded by the statement that he was not planning suicide and that, in his view, no one else would now be leaving Mt. Carmel. In this context, given what else Schneider taught regarding the coming of a fire at the end of the age to cleanse the people of God, a doctrine examined in some detail in the next chapter, it seems he had reached the point of wanting to force the FBI's hand. It may be speculation, but it is not wild, to suggest that it was Schneider's view that while suicide is wrong, accepting a martyr's death wrought by the actions of another is not. Schneider may here have been looking for death; in effect inviting the FBI to take on the role of sacred executioner.

As the siege wore on there were some further developments, though nothing to suggest that a peaceful end was in sight. On 24 March the FBI lines were breached when Louis Alaniz, described by Thibodeau as 'a twenty-five-year-old Pentecostal telephone operator from Houston',[35] got into the Branch Davidian complex.[36] He remained in Mt. Carmel until 17 April and hence had good opportunity to become acquainted with the community.[37] The second visitor went by the name of Jesse Amen.[38] He arrived on 26 March, but stayed only a little over a week, leaving on 4 April. He was by all accounts an interesting figure who claimed a special relationship with God (whom he called 'Lord Lightning Amen' and who lived in heaven with his companion 'Cherry Lightning Amen'). According to Jesse Amen a biblical army some 50,000 strong was amassing on the banks of the Colorado River and would come to free the Branch Davidians from their current situation if Koresh would hang a red flag outside his door.[39]

The visits of Alaniz and Amen were not the only ones during the siege; several were made also by lawyers who had agreed to represent the interests of the Branch Davidians, chief among them being Dick DeGuerin. Between 29 March and 4 April DeGuerin entered Mt. Carmel on at least six or seven occasions to speak with those whom he had agreed to represent. Still, however, the impasse could not be broken. A month had now passed since the failure of Koresh to come out with his people on 2 March and the discussion had, in truth, hardly moved on.

There was another highpoint, however, when on 14 April Koresh informed his lawyers by telephone that he would not come out until he had written out his interpretation of the seven seals.[40] This verbal statement was followed by a letter, part of which reads:

I am presently being permitted to document, in a structured form, the decoded messages of the *7 Seals*. Upon the completion of this task I will be freed of my 'waiting period'. I hope to finish this as soon as possible and to stand before man to answer any and all questions regarding my actions.[41]

Koresh's written interpretation of the seals was never completed, although part of it was undertaken and survived the fire on a floppy disk found on the person of Ruth Riddle. Only the first of the seven seals is actually discussed by Koresh in this; what he says is in keeping with the sketch of his theology given in Chapter Eleven. Tabor and Gallagher published the document as an appendix to their own work; they estimate that the whole work would have taken Koresh about a further week to write and would have run to between fifty and seventy-five pages.[42]

It is possible that Koresh would have come out had he been allowed the time to complete his work on the seven seals. The FBI doubted it, however, at least partly on the grounds that Koresh had made such a promise once before. He had said quite categorically that he would exit Mt. Carmel if his message was played on the airways at prime time; it was and he did not leave. The FBI suspected that this too was a delaying tactic. However, this understandable suspicion aside, there is other harder evidence to suggest that exiting Mt. Carmel was still not Koresh's intention. This is detailed in the next two chapters.

In the event, however, things came much more rapidly to a head than perhaps the Branch Davidians had anticipated. On the morning of 19 April an assault was launched on Mt. Carmel that would end in the deaths of all but nine of those still inside. The plan that was put into effect on the morning of 19 April had been under discussion for some considerable time. As early as 10 March it had been formulated, in outline form for further discussion.[43] A revision of the plan was made on 14 March.[44] It was not particularly complicated, though it was tactically difficult. Over a period of time, and it might be several days, tear gas would be introduced into Mt. Carmel. This would do two things: first, it would put the members of the community under some considerable physical pressure as the very unpleasant effects of the tear gas were felt; second, it would cause psychological pressure, especially on the mothers, since, inevitably, the children too would be affected. No parents, so the FBI gambled, would be prepared to stand by and see their children suffer if it was within their power to do something about it. Instinct would take over as parents sought to remove their children from the source of danger.

The gas that was to be used would be unpleasant, but not lethal. It was a necessary act of force to bring about the desired end. On 17 April a number of those centrally involved in the plan, including the deputy assistant to the Attorney-General, the director of the FBI, the assistant director of the FBI, and the deputy assistant director, met together to prepare for a meeting with Attorney-General Janet Reno at which they would explain the plan and seek her approval. On the same day she was duly informed and the 'rules of engagement' were outlined, together with the gas option. The plan was approved, a decision communicated by the Attorney-General to President Clinton the following day.[45]

Preparations were now made. Cars and other obstructions in the perimeter area of the Mt. Carmel buildings that might potentially impede the progress of the operation were cleared away. Schneider observed some of this action and commented: 'Do you see that there? Right here—down. You see that? Do you want to know what that is there? Do you know what that's for? You don't huh? It's for—ah—the people that are here. You know—Joel 2 and Isaiah 13 whose faces are like flames.'[46] The stage was now set for the apocalyptic drama that was to unfold the next day. 'An end' to the events that had begun with the arrival of the ATF some fifty days before was in sight. The only question was what it would look like.

NOTES

1. This is the line followed in *Final Report*, 140–3.
2. Such a view is found, e.g. in Moore, *Davidian Massacre*; see especially 222–34.
3. An early statement of this view is found in Tabor and Gallagher, *Why Waco?*; and see also Tabor, 'The Waco Tragedy'.
4. The most substantial study of these negotiations is Docherty, *Learning Lessons from Waco*; see also Eugene Gallagher, 'Negotiating Salvation', *Nova Religio: The Journal of Alternative and Emergent Religions*, 3, no. 1 (Oct. 1999): 27–35. Also very useful is J. Phillip Arnold, 'The Davidian Dilemma'.
5. See Tabor and Gallagher, *Why Waco?*, 13.
6. Copies of these tapes are in my possession. Some, but not all, are also found in TXC, Mark Swett Collection.
7. Legal permission to place recording devices inside Mt. Carmel was requested and received on 4 April and the first device was introduced into Mt. Carmel on the same day; *Final Report*, Appendix C, 38–9.
8. Other important events were recorded during the same show, including a telephone call from Paul Fatta who wanted help to get back into Mt. Carmel.
9. Thibodeau, *A Place Called Waco*, 199.
10. A copy of this tape is found in TXC, Mark Swett Collection; see also *Final Report*, Appendix C, 36.
11. Thibodeau, *A Place Called Waco*, 201; also exiting on that day were Joann Vaega and Natalie Norbrega.
12. Thibodeau, *A Place Called Waco*, 201. According to the same source, on the evening before there had even been something of a party at Mt. Carmel, though neither Koresh nor Schneider seem to have taken any part. Koresh is reported as being quite upset with the revellers, asking why they were 'letting down the message'.
13. NT 13.
14. *Final Report*, Appendix C, 37; Thibodeau, *A Place Called Waco*, 202.
15. NT 19.
16. Thibodeau, *A Place Called Waco*, 203.
17. Testimony of Victorine Hollingsworth, Criminal Trial, Waco, 1994 (Swett, *Ultimate Act of Faith*, 62–3; this is a web-based paper; it can be accessed at www.hope. ac.uk/humanities/theology/branchdavidians.)

18. Testimony of Kathy Schroeder, Criminal Trial, Waco, 1994 (Swett, 'Ultimate Act of Faith', 63–4).
19. Testimony of Kathy Schroeder, Criminal Trial, Waco, 1994 (Swett, 'Ultimate Act of Faith', 64).
20. Bug tape, 16 March, SA 66–1 (Swett, 'Ultimate Act of Faith', 67); NT 10b.
21. Details from *Final Report*, Appendix C; the only two departures after 23 March were of Louis Alaniz and Jesse Amen, neither of whom were Branch Davidians, who had somehow managed to dodge through FBI lines and enter Mt. Carmel during the siege.
22. Thibodeau, *A Place Called Waco*, 222. Thibodeau's reference is to the evidence on a video tape recording of the Mt. Carmel residents that had been taken by Schneider during the stand-off and sent out to the FBI. (A copy is in my possession.)
23. NT 181.
24. *Final Report*, Appendix C, 41.
25. NT 97.
26. Thibodeau, *A Place Called Waco*, 225.
27. NT 103.
28. See photograph in Moore, *Davidian Massacre*, 242/3.
29. A copy is in my possession.
30. The bug devices picked up something further of the response of Schneider and Martin to the meeting with Sage and Harwell. Both were complimentary about the persons they had met, but doubted their ability to see through what had been discussed since; it was stated that both Sage and Harwell were not the ones really driving the negotiations forward but were fronts for much more senior persons in the USA administration. A second meeting was set for 17 March, but it did not take place. See further Swett, 'Ultimate Act of Faith', 83–6.
31. *Final Report*, Appendix C, 44.
32. Thibodeau, *A Place Called Waco*, 228, 236, lists the sounds as 'the noise of sirens, seagulls, bagpipes, crying babies, strangled rabbits and crowing roosters', followed by 'howling coyotes'.
33. Bug tape—as quoted in *Final Report*, Appendix C, 43.
34. *Final Report*, 142, and Appendix C, 49.
35. Thibodeau, *A Place Called Waco*, 232.
36. *Final Report*, Appendix C, 48.
37. Reavis, *The Ashes of Waco*, 247–51, has considerable information on Alaniz, apparently gained from an interview with him.
38. *Final Report*, Appendix C, 49.
39. Reavis, *Ashes of Waco*, 250; Thibodeau, *A Place Called Waco*, 232.
40. *Final Report*, Appendix C, 58.
41. Letter of David Koresh to Dick DeGuerin, 14 April. A copy of that letter is in Appendix E of the *Report*.

42. See Tabor and Gallagher, *Why Waco?*, 189–211, for an introduction, the document itself, and a commentary on it.
43. *Final Report*, Appendix C, 42.
44. Ibid. 43.
45. Ibid. 62–3.
46. Bug tape, SA72–28 (which is discussed more fully in the following two chapters).

14

'The Ultimate Act of Faith?' The Cause of the Waco Fire

The negotiations that took place at Waco from 28 February to 19 April were not a success. There were failings on both sides. For their part the FBI failed to understand the nature of the community they were dealing with, and failed also to grasp the extent to which the thought world this community inhabited far outweighed in importance the reality of the situation they were facing on the ground. Those inside Mt. Carmel, on the other hand, made no serious attempt to bring about a peaceful resolution to the conflict. The broken promises to 'come out' (or, as the Branch Davidians would have seen it, the overriding by God of a human commitment made in error) did not help the situation, but neither, on the other hand, did the treatment of those who had exited, even if that treatment was intended to be good (such as the giving of hamburgers to Branch Davidian children). In effect a line had been drawn in the sand on 28 February and despite some early apparent successes neither side was really able to cross it.

The question of whether the negotiations could have brought about a less catastrophic outcome is important, and there will doubtless always be division about it. Certainly there was a lack of real communication during the fifty-one days. The early observations of Tabor and Arnold, followed by the more detailed work of Docherty, are valuable in this context, and it is apparent with the benefit of hindsight that the FBI did not handle the situation as well as they might. However, while the shortcomings of the FBI team ought to be acknowledged, it must also be admitted that it is quite possible, perhaps even probable, that the Branch Davidians were never planning to come out. It may be that really from day one of the siege, or perhaps a little later, but not much, a decision had been taken by some in Mt. Carmel community to bring on the Apocalypse—or, from their perspective, play out their assigned apocalyptic role. As was seen in the previous chapter, there is evidence in the negotiation transcripts that points in this direction, and some of the actions of the Branch Davidians can also be taken with hindsight as suggesting 'the ultimate act of faith',[1] an intention to stick the siege out to its God-determined end, which would be the dawn of the kingdom.

In this context the question of who started the fire is pivotal. Understandably this is a question that raises huge passions, and rightly so. By the time the fire subsided, most of those in Mt. Carmel when it broke out were dead. The body count included a significant number of children, and two foetuses. The mode of some of those deaths was particularly horrifying. It was a very sad day for all concerned, and those on both sides of the divide have cause to remember it.

In this chapter and the next an account of the fire is given and a particular case is argued regarding its origin. It will quickly become apparent that the case advanced here is not the one that has in general been argued in scholarly circles, at least not at any length. Nevertheless, the case is both consistent with the unassailable evidence, and best able to account for that part of the evidence that is not so clear; it would not have been put forward otherwise. In essence the argument is that the Davidians set fire to Mt. Carmel themselves, and did so with a clear goal in mind, which was not simple suicide. Furthermore the fire, while it may have been started on the orders of David Koresh, was not just his idea. Rather, it is argued here, in the tradition to which Koresh and his followers belonged it had long been taught that the community would have one day to pass through a cleansing fire shortly before the dawn of the new kingdom. Indeed, it was the means by which that kingdom could be born. It is this doctrinal conviction, based on biblical texts, that perhaps best accounts for the actions of the Branch Davidians on 19 April.

The conclusion that the Branch Davidians set fire to their own home is not pleasant; neither is it simple. Indeed, unlike the easy option of arguing that they (or perhaps just Koresh) were deranged and set fire to themselves in an act of unfathomable madness, it takes effort to seek to understand why a perfectly sane group of individuals, which included the leaders of the community if not the community in its entirety, would come to the conclusion that it was in their longer-term interests to be incinerated.

There are four plausible explanations of how the fire started. These are that: (1) the Branch Davidians set fire to Mt. Carmel on purpose (the view supported here); or (2) government agents set fire to Mt. Carmel on purpose; or (3) the Branch Davidians set fire to Mt. Carmel by accident; or (4) government agents set fire to Mt. Carmel by accident.[2] Not all of these explanations have attracted significant support. In particular option three (the Branch Davidians set fire to Mt. Carmel by accident) has rarely been raised as an explanation and never argued for extensively, though it must be theoretically possible. Survivors of the fire have stated openly that they were making Molotov cocktails to throw at the tanks.[3] Perhaps, then, an accident occurred as one was being lit or thrown and it was this that started the chain of events.

Option two, on the other hand (the fire was started by government agents), has been given vociferous expression. Examples can be found on the internet, but one finds it too in non-web sources, for example the video *Waco the Big Lie*. Here one apparently sees footage of tanks, modified to carry flame-throwers, purposely setting fire to Mt. Carmel (a view that has been contested by government and non-government sources alike).[4] At another point in the video a figure dressed in black fire-protective clothing is shown moving away from the building just recently put on fire. The direction of the commentary on the video is unmistakeable: government agents in tanks and on foot set fire to Mt. Carmel; they intended to do it, drew up a plan to do it, and executed that plan with clinical efficiency.

Those who adopt such views generally argue that the reason for this act of murderous arson was either revenge or else to make sure that the evidence indicating the initial crimes of the ATF, in firing first (through the doors) and firing on Mt. Carmel from helicopters, was destroyed. Some supporters of this theory will also argue that there is evidence to suggest that the FBI both blocked escape routes and shot at individual Branch Davidians as they were seeking to escape the flames. David Hardy, for example, thinks that there was hard evidence to support the view that government agents actually fired either tear-gas rounds or live ammunition into 'the pit'. The FBI thought (incorrectly) that this was where the women and children were holed up, though perhaps in a bus that had been buried underground to connect 'the pit' to the main building rather than in 'the pit' itself.

This allegation ought not to be passed over lightly. What Hardy appears to be arguing is that government agents first set fire to Mt. Carmel (he stops short of saying that this was by intention), then ascertained where the women and children were likely to be, and finally shot directly into that area—knowing full well that they would thereby be at least preventing the escape of such innocents if not actually killing them.[5]

The question of whether, in fact, there was a blocking of exit points either by accident or design has been much discussed in the literature, and there is no space to deal with this issue in detail here. Suffice it to say, however, that the evidence clearly points to the fact that there were numerous avenues of escape open to the Branch Davidians had they wished to leave the burning building, and some members of the community (though not those in the 'bunker' area)[6] probably had a good fifteen to twenty minutes to make their way out. Similarly, the claim that shots are visible on the footage is much disputed. The *Final Report* provides the counter-evidence.[7]

In general the very limited academic debate on the question of how the fire started has been focused on options one and four: either the Branch Davidians themselves set fire to Mt. Carmel on purpose, or else the government caused the fire accidentally; though, to repeat, the academic literature rarely deals directly with the issue at all.[8] Most scholarly authors leave the question open, though reading between the lines, it seems that some lean towards the view that the Davidians were responsible, but stop short of actually saying it.[9] Those who take the view that the FBI caused the fire by accident, on the other hand, are more vociferous, and some go on to argue that this outcome may have been predictable in some sense (in which case was it really an accident, if it could have been foreseen and hence avoided?). For example, it should have been obvious to all, some have argued, that Mt. Carmel was a tinderbox, especially after the gas had been inserted. Firing pyrotechnic rounds into Mt. Carmel was hence either wantonly and criminally negligent or an act of gross stupidity.[10]

In theory it ought not to be difficult to narrow down the options set out above. After all, it is not as though the events of 19 April went unrecorded. Not only does video tape survive, but there are also bug tapes that give some indication of what was going on inside Mt. Carmel shortly before and during the outbreak of the fire. Many of these are of poor quality; however, a careful analysis of them, the video evidence, the investigative fire reports, and the testimony of survivors and officers who were at the scene ought to be able, one would think, to bring us somewhere near the truth of the matter, and in a way not really open to fundamental dispute, even if some of the detail might be open to question and reinterpretation.

The evidence relied upon by the United States government that the Branch Davidians set fire to Mt. Carmel themselves and did so intentionally is extensive, unequivocal, and detailed. Any contrary conclusion necessarily depends upon a successful challenge to the reliability of that evidence. The conclusion that the Branch Davidians started the fire intentionally is found as early as the October 1993 initial *Report*. While some of the detail in that work has been amended, and account has been taken of some very obvious short-comings on the part of Government officials, the basic position argued in the initial *Report* has undergone no fundamental change.[11] While the text of the *Final Report* itself (8 November, 2000) is only 200 pages long (relatively short given the complexity and magnitude of the events being discussed), the appendices, which contain the findings of numerous fire, weapons, video tape, audio tape, and other experts, run to several thousand pages and all this evidence pulls in the same direction: the Branch Davidians set fire to Mt. Carmel themselves. The FBI did not set fire to the complex and they did not shoot at persons seeking to exit.

The *Final Report* is the result of huge investigative efforts by experts based both in the USA and further afield, for example, Sweden.[12] One ought not to underestimate the sheer scale of the cover-up that would need to be involved if one is to argue that the *Report* is fictional. Scores, perhaps hundreds, of people were involved in producing the documentation, either as authors or co-researchers or interviewees. So uniform and unequivocal are the basic findings that it would require nothing short of a Herculean effort to overturn it. Indeed, some of the raw data is so fundamental that the only way to dispute it would be to say that it was fabricated. For example, the Arson Report (Appendix D) states clearly that both an accelerant detection dog and laboratory analysis indicate that flammable liquids had been spread in many parts of Mt. Carmel and that the extent and pattern of distribution is not consistent with simple spillages that might have occurred as kerosene lamps were being refuelled. This is either true or not true, and if it is true then it seems that (as other parts of the report also argue) the Branch Davidians themselves were responsible for the spread of the fuel. If it is not true, then someone has tampered with the evidence or someone is lying.

One could continue this line of argument. If the bug tapes record those inside Mt. Carmel shouting, 'keep that fire going', then it is difficult not to conclude that they were responsible for the fire. Similarly, the *Final Report* states, on the basis of evidence supplied by investigative officers and backed up by photographs, that among the debris at Mt. Carmel were some thirteen punctured fuel cans, in addition to many unpunctured ones. It is further stated that the holes in those cans were made with a sharp instrument, perhaps a screwdriver or a blade, and that the shapes of the holes are not consistent with the cans having been used for target practice (which is what has been argued by those on the other side of the debate).[13] What purpose would there have been in puncturing cans in this way other than to create a mechanism for the efficient spreading of the fuel those cans contained?[14] This is not so much a matter of the interpretation of evidence as it is of the very existence of it.

If the *Final Report* is wrong in its conclusions, then, the only explanation would be to argue (as some have) that it is a huge cover-up. But, to repeat, if this line is taken, one should not underestimate the scale of what would be required. To carry it off, the compliance of scores if not hundreds of different individuals would be required. Evidence would not simply have to be misinterpreted; it would need to be manufactured, on a huge scale. Somebody would have had to first puncture and then plant the fuel cans, someone would have had to spread fuel at key points in the Mt. Carmel debris, and—surely least plausible of all—someone would have had to manufacture or somehow tamper with the bug tapes. All this is possible; but is it likely?

None of this is to say that there are not some problems with the official account of what happened. Why was it maintained that the FBI used only ferret rounds to deliver the CS gas when in fact they fired at least two pyrotechnic devices? (Actually, it is clear now that the FBI were not at fault in this—this is discussed further below.) Why was it not disclosed that there was a FLIR tape from the earlier part of the morning of the 19 April?[15] Such tapes are produced using Forward Looking Infrared technology, which records heat as white images—the hotter the fire the brighter it appears on the tape. What of other video evidence that appears certainly once to have been in place, but is now absent?[16] These are serious questions and Hardy (and others) are entirely right to draw them to the attention of the general public. There may well have been some interests being protected and some mistakes covered up. This is not the same, however, as saying that in the years after the fire, the FBI and other government agencies have sought consistently to cover up the fact that it was they (the FBI) who either deliberately or accidentally set fire to Mt. Carmel and have manufactured the evidence needed to shift the blame over to the Branch Davidians themselves.

What seems reasonably certain, and potentially very important, is that the fire did not start in one place only. Such a case was argued already in the 1993 *Report* and the evidence to support this view has increased significantly since then. It now seems almost certain that there were three separate fires: one in a second-floor room at the south-east corner of Mt. Carmel, one in the dining room area, and one in the chapel. In the 1993 *Report* the suggestion is that the fire in the second-floor room was the first to start (12.07 p.m.), followed one minute later by a fire in the dining room area and a third in the chapel at 12.09.[17] The principal source of evidence to support these times and locations is a FLIR tape. An aeroplane with this technology was flying over Mt. Carmel when the fire(s) broke out and hence a record of what happened is in existence. (The reason for its being there has been debated. However, FLIR-equipped aeroplanes had over-flown Mt. Carmel on numerous occasions; this flight may therefore have been nothing out of the ordinary).[18]

Initial examination of the FLIR tapes and other evidence relating to the fire became the responsibility of a government-appointed team led by Paul Gray, who quickly produced a report.[19] The team's analysis of the evidence led to the conclusion given above: that three separate fires broke out within two minutes of each other and in three different locations. A much more substantial examination of the video, FLIR, and other evidence is included in *Final Report*. This repeats much found in earlier sources. For example, very near the beginning the case is summarized: 'Government agents did not start or materially contribute to the spread of the fire. During the morning of April 19, 1993, several Davidians spread accelerants throughout the main structure of the complex, and started fires in several locations.'[20] The difference between this and the earlier reports comes in the form of the substantial appendices that have been added. Four of these relate directly to the question of the fire, and there is much other material in that mass of information that has a bearing upon it.

In his contribution to the *Final Report*, Appendix D, Walter Wetherington subjected to scrutiny the previous findings of the fire investigations conducted at the government's instruction, and sought to answer the obvious key questions: 'did agents of the United States start or contribute to the spread of the fire?'; 'did the United States Government's independent fire investigation accurately and completely define the cause of the fire and its point(s) of origin?'; 'can additional information be developed concerning the cause and/ or point(s) of origin of the fire?'; and 'could firefighters have controlled or stopped the spread of the fire?'[21] In order to address these questions, Wetherington re-examined the materials from the fire scene along with video evidence, previous reports, maps and charts, and other relevant materials. The conclusion is plain: 'From my examination of all the evidence, I conclude with absolute certainty that there were three points of fire origin within the Branch Davidian complex. Evidence further supports that each of these fires was intentionally started by the Davidians.'[22] Wetherington's report continues along this basic line. Great stress is put upon the presence among the debris of the large number of fuel cans.[23] Wetherington concurred with earlier claims that these punctured cans had been used by Branch Davidians to spread fuel inside Mt. Carmel in preparation for the fire and noted that there was a direct correlation between the location of the cans and the location of the three fires.[24]

The next appendix, Appendix E, of the *Final Report* is also focused on the question of the fire. It contains the expert testimony of Ulf Wickström of the Swedish National Testing and Research Institute. Wickström similarly reviewed the evidence from a number of sources. His conclusion is as clear as that of Wetherington:

Based on my review of all the available evidence, analysis of the fire, and after consideration of the final reports and opinions of Drs. Quintiere and Mowrer, Mr. Kennedy, and others, I conclude that fires were started by means of accelerants at many locations throughout the building. The fires commenced within a very short time interval, evidencing that occupants of the Branch Davidian complex deliberately started the fires. Many of the fires went out by themselves when the combustible liquid was consumed. Fires did, however, continue to develop in three separate locations, which can be concluded with certainty with or without support of the FLIR tape imagery.[25]

Wickström went on to give an account of the three fires. His summary is worth quoting in full:

The first fire, denoted *Fire A*, started at the stage in the rear of the chapel. The first visible heat image on the FLIR occurs at 12:04:23 on the catwalk over the stage. This fire spread quickly in the debris of the crushed building. When the fire spread to the asphalt felt roof a lot of black smoke developed. This fire spread slowly against the wind direction towards the chapel and merged at a rather late stage with the fire that started in the southeast corner Red/White tower, i.e. *Fire C*.

The second fire, denoted *Fire B*, started in the cafeteria/kitchen area of the Branch Davidian complex. This fire was very dangerous, as most of the Davidians seem to have taken shelter and were found dead near this part of the complex. Fire B was first discovered on the FLIR as a heat image at 12:08:10. TV footage of Fire B shows smoke streaming out from the north side of the cafeteria at 12:08:11. Ground photos of the cafeteria taken between 12:08:10 and 12:08:58 also show flames penetrating through the north wall of the cafeteria at the same position as the heat images on the FLIR.

The third fire, denoted *Fire C*, started on the second floor of the southeast tower of the Branch Davidian complex. This fire was first observed on the FLIR as a heat image at 12:07:41, and the first flames were seen on TV footage at 12:09:42. This fire developed quickly as mainly accelerants and other easily ignitable items burnt. The wind, however, cooled this fire thereby delaying its burn through of the structure and its spread into the complex.[26]

Wickström further concluded that most of those inside Mt. Carmel could have escaped had they made an effort to do so. Those inside the 'bunker' (a concrete room at the base of the tower) would have had only a limited chance of escape since one of the fires had started outside the only possible exit. Further, the fire could have been fought had fire trucks been on hand and firefighting begun immediately. By the time the trucks did arrive (after 12.30 p.m.), however, the situation was too far gone and no effective control of the fire was possible.[27]

Both Wetherington and Wickström, then, agreed on the issue of there being (at least) three separate fires at Mt. Carmel all starting within a few minutes of each other. This agreement is not limited to the *Final Report*, but is found elsewhere too. Indeed, while the cause of those fires, and the relationship between them (did one spark the others?), is much disputed in the literature, one of the few things very widely accepted is that there were three and that they did start in three different places.[28]

The question of how the fires started still needs to be addressed in detail, though the government's position has been set out above. The relevant evidence comes in various forms. The principal and potentially the most important is from the bug tapes. Indeed, putting to one side the view that these tapes were manufactured after the event, it is this body of evidence that may well hold the key to what really took place inside Mt. Carmel on the morning of 19 April. There are, however, two problems with the evidence from these tapes: audibility and context.

Some of the material on the tapes is actually quite clear. For example, on the morning of 19 April Byron Sage's voice was often broadcast over the loud-speaker system giving information about what was happening and, now famously, telling the Davidians 'this is not an assault'. He can be heard very easily and clearly, which is hardly surprising given that it was being broadcast over good quality sound equipment. What is not always so obvious is what the Branch Davidians themselves are saying. The tapes heard in the extracts played on *Waco: The Rules of Engagement* are not difficult to understand at all. One suspects that they have been professionally enhanced to give far greater clarity than is evident on other tapes. But others are so unclear as to render them highly problematic, and it would be very unwise to base too much upon them.

A further problem arises when working with the tapes/transcriptions. Sometimes if the context of what is apparently being said by the Branch Davidians is not known, it is very difficult to be confident of the meaning of the words. Here it is particularly important to note that a number of surviving Branch Davidians claim that references on the tapes to fuel being poured and something being lit are to be understood not as referring to a planned fire, but the making and throwing of Molotov cocktails. (And it is perhaps significant that they are not disputing that such things were being discussed.) There is in fact no evidence of Molotov cocktails actually being thrown, and some of what is said, for example 'is there a way to spread fuel here?', cannot be reconciled with the view that this was all just about Molotovs.

Both of these precautionary concerns (audibility and context) must be kept clearly in mind in the narrative given below, which is at best a well-informed and critically-arrived-at best guess at what the bug tapes reveal of the events. The form of the tapes given is in every instance indicated in the notes and is drawn either from the work of Mills or that of Mark Swett.[29] Where possible (i.e. where they have been available) reference is made to the bug tapes themselves.

A key tape is SA73 5, the last to be recorded. There are several apparent statements on it that are potentially critical to this discussion. Very important are the last reasonably clear words, which would appear to be: 'keep that fire going'.[30] Both Mills and Swett agree that these are the words spoken, though Swett has 'let's keep that fire going'. On the tape itself the words do seem fairly plain. Shortly afterwards the bugs failed and approximately ten minutes later fire was visually detected by FBI agents. About ten minutes before the apparent shout to 'keep that fire going' there are some other potentially very important words, which again are reasonably clear, though not entirely so. Swett, who thinks the words are spoken by Cohen, renders the words as 'I want a fire around the back!', whereas Mills has 'I wanta [*sic*] fire on the front.'[31] The two transcriptions are hence somewhat different, and listening to the tape itself it is difficult to say which is the better.[32] The statement 'I want a fire' is reasonably clear, even if the desired location is not. A little earlier still (approximately twenty-seven minutes before the call 'keep that fire going'), the bug also picks up the words 'do you think I could light this soon?'[33] Of course the 'it' could have been a Molotov cocktail. Swett also thinks that at one point on the tape one can hear the words, 'Look out! Look out! It's already lit!'[34] But here Mills had 'get out...get out...no, they've already (moved)',[35] which illustrates again the difficulty of working this material.[36] Similarly, Swett thinks that at approximately 11.30 a.m. the words 'he said to light it' can be heard, though Mills had nothing even approaching this in his transcription.[37]

It is the US government's position that the kind of remarks cited above indicate that the Branch Davidians set fire to Mt. Carmel and that (following the timing of the tapes) this process began at approximately 11.30 a.m.[38] This conclusion is then set in the broader context of what was apparently taking place inside Mt. Carmel earlier in the day, namely preparations for the fire. This is also recorded, imperfectly, on the bug tapes.

The initial assault on Mt. Carmel began just before 6.00 a.m. when two Combat Engineer Vehicles (hereinafter 'CEV/CEVs) approached the complex. Sage telephoned into Mt. Carmel at 5.58 and, a few minutes later, spoke to Steve Schneider. Sage told Schneider that although the 'tactical operation' was about to begin, 'this is not an assault'. Sage then switched to the loudspeaker system and made several further announcements. The insertion of the gas began some minutes after this (hence the Branch Davidians had possibly as much as ten minutes' warning before the gassing began). Sage encouraged the Branch Davidians to exit peacefully.[39] According to the *Final Report* the Branch Davidians replied with gunfire.[40]

By the time Sage was making his appeals over the public address system, however, the situation inside Mt. Carmel had probably already reached the point of no return; the Branch Davidians had already begun to act. At 6.09 a.m. the following conversation was picked up. (Byron Sage's voice over the loudspeaker can also be heard. It is not actually relevant here and so has been omitted).

UM:[41] Have you poured it yet?

UM: Hm.

UM: Did you pour it yet?

UM: In the hallway, yes.

UM: David said pour it right

UM: D'you need . . .

UM: Come on, let's go.

UM: David said we have to get the fuel on.

UM: Does he want it poured already?

UM: We want the fuel.

UM: Yeah.

UM: We want some here.

UM: We need a gas mask.

UM: Gonna need fuel.

UM: More fuel.

UM: . . . fuel . . . I've got (no fuel) . . .

UM: Did you get any yet?

UM: . . . water . . .

UM: Help me (pour) it.

UM: Yeah.[42]

And shortly thereafter we hear:

UM: Go get another mask.

UM: Have you got the fuel, the fuel ready?

UM: I've already poured it.

UM: It's already poured.[43]

It is difficult to see how such conversations could mean anything other than that the Branch Davidians were already preparing for something to be set alight. This does not necessarily mean that there was a plan to burn Mt. Carmel to the ground. This could have been an attempt to block the progress of the government agency vehicles through the tactical use of fire; if this is the case it was extremely rash. Again, according to some surviving Branch Davidians the conversation here recorded relates to a plan to use Molotov cocktails in an attempt to stop the progress of the CEVs. But, to repeat, this is unlikely given the reference to something being poured 'in the hallway'. Over the next hour and quarter (i.e. from *c*.6.10 a.m. to 7.25 a.m.), bug tapes picked up several further potentially very important conversations and phrases. These include the following exchange at *c*.7.23 a.m.:

UM: Is there a way to spread fuel here?

UM: OK...what we do...you don't know...

UM: I know that won't spread...Get some more.

UM: So we only light it first when they come in with the tank right...right as they're coming in...

UM: Right.

UM: That's secure...we should get more hay in here.

UM: I know.[44]

A moment later:

UM: You have to spread it so get started OK.

UM: Yeah...got some cans there.

UM: Right here...two cans here...and that's...and the rest can take 'em...

UM: Sometimes we don't know that...

UM: Somebody took one can and spilled...on the ground.[45]

Again it is important to remember the claim that there was a plan to use Molotov cocktails; this might explain some of what is being said. However, it is difficult to see how it could explain, 'Is there a way to spread fuel in here?', or 'We should get more hay in here.' Similarly, the intention of the additional words 'real quickly you can order the (fire) yes?'[46] seems plain enough.

As the morning progressed, the situation got worse. The initial insertion of tear gas had begun shortly after 6.00 a.m. The gas used was 'a liquid aerosol of CS powder dissolved in methylene chloride.'[47] There has been a great deal of discussion on whether this gas was potentially lethal to either the adults or children inside Mt. Carmel, and opinion is greatly divided. An extensive report on this question is found as Appendix L to *Final Report*.[48] That concludes that the gas was potentially lethal, but only if the persons affected had not been able to leave the area where the gas was present. A short period of exposure to the gas, even in a high dosage, would not have resulted in death. The assumption on the part of the FBI was that the Branch Davidians would flee Mt. Carmel rather than face the gas; this is not what happened.[49] There has also been discussion about whether this gas might have contributed to the outbreak of the fire. Again, while there are voices to the contrary, the most reliable evidence suggests that the gas itself was not a contributing factor, especially since there was a very strong wind that day (up to thirty-five knots according to one report),[50] which had the effect of dissipating the gas to the point where the FBI began to wonder whether it was really going to have the effect that they desired.

By 6.04 a.m. the code word 'compromise' had been broadcast by one of the FBI agents. This indicated that the agent had reported that he had seen

Branch Davidians firing at the CEVs.[51] A request was made by Hostage Rescue Team commander, Rogers, that this be confirmed, and the confirmation came at *c*.6.07 a.m. The effect of this was significant. The original plan had been to introduce the tear gas into Mt. Carmel only slowly, and it was anticipated that it might take several days to bring about the exit of the Branch Davidians. However, according to the operations plan that had been drawn up and approved by Attorney-General Janet Reno, if the FBI came under fire, the operation to insert tear gas and force the Branch Davidians out of Mt. Carmel was to be escalated. The crucial passage reads:

If during *any* tear gas delivery operations, subjects open fire with a weapon, then the FBI rules of engagement will apply and appropriate deadly force will be used. Additionally tear gas will immediately be inserted into all windows of the compound utilizing the four BV's as well as the CEVs.[52]

Consequently the operation was stepped up. In addition to the continued insertion of gas by the CEVs already at the building, agents in the four BVs began shooting 40 mm rounds of CS tear gas through the windows. The operation ceased at 6.31 a.m. when the report was made that the whole of Mt. Carmel had now been gassed. Rogers ordered his agents to stand by.[53] At 6.45 a.m. Sage broadcast again over the loudspeaker saying the Branch Davidians were to exit Mt. Carmel or else face further insertions of tear gas. That began a few minutes later with further ferret rounds being fired in through the windows. According to the *Final Report* this was met with further gunfire from the community and the cycle continued. Between 7.30 a.m. and 8.00 a.m. more gas was inserted by the now reloaded CEVs while the ferret rounds also continued. Still the Branch Davidians refused to come out.

As was noted briefly above there has been significant discussion on whether the FBI used 'pyrotechnic' devices to deliver tear gas into Mt. Carmel. That question cannot be dealt with in full here, but some remarks are certainly called for since it is sometimes claimed that pyrotechnic devices were responsible for the start of the fire.[54]

The outline of the situation seems plain enough. It is not disputed that in addition to using the booms on the CEVs the FBI did employ hand-held grenade-launchers to deliver tear gas into Mt. Carmel. The question is what was fired out of those launchers, the crucial issue being whether they were used to deliver pyrotechnic or non-pyrotechnic tear-gas rounds. Non-pyrotechnic rounds depend upon the force of impact to ensure dispersal of the gas (the ferret round hits a wall, smashes upon impact, and releases its load into the atmosphere). Pyrotechnic rounds, on the other hand, use heat as the means by which the gas is released, and that heat is generated as chemicals are mixed together in the ferret during its flight from the launcher to the target. Pyrotechnic rounds get very hot and are known to be a fire hazard. Non-pyrotechnic rounds do not heat up and can no more cause a fire than could a splattered tin of beans.

Many non-pyrotechnic rounds were used at Waco. What is now clear, however, is that pyrotechnic rounds were also employed. It is often claimed that the FBI 'denied' this until 1998, when the denial became untenable because Mike McNulty (the person behind the video *Waco: Rules of Engagement*) discovered a pyrotechnic military tear gas projectile in the 'Waco evidence storage facility'.[55] In fact, however, as early as November 1993 hostage rescue team operators had provided full details of their use of such rounds at Waco. The problem was that the person to whom this information was given did not pass it on (and was later charged with lying to the Federal Grand Jury). The name of this person is deleted from the redacted version of the *Final Report* that has been available for this research, though it is fairly clear who is meant. The report addresses this question very directly and at great length and the conclusion is clear. Pyrotechnic rounds were fired at Waco, this was made known by the FBI at an early stage, but concealed by the person to whom the information passed. As a consequence the FBI came under suspicion of 'covering up' the use of pyrotechnic devices, and the worst was assumed—that it had been covered up because it explained how the fire started.

The question still remains, of course, as to whether those rounds did cause the fire. The answer is surely 'no', and it is very difficult to see how anyone who has looked at the evidence could come to any other conclusion. At most only three were used. This was at approximately 08.08, a good four hours before any fire started. The time lag alone is enough to rule out the suggestion that it was these pyrotechnic rounds that caused the fire. However, there is another point. The rounds were used in one very specific situation: to try to deliver gas into the area known as 'the pit', a little way north of the main Mt. Carmel structure. They were used here because the ferret rounds were not able to penetrate this area; permission was hence sought and given for the use of pyrotechnic rounds. But these did not work either; all three bounced off the roof. Two dispersed their contents, but with little effect.[56] In short, then, the FBI fired three pyrotechnic rounds four hours before the fire, all at a distance from the wooden structure that was Mt. Carmel. They could not have started the fire.

By this point the FBI had used all the available non-pyrotechnic ferret rounds and a call was put out for more. At *c*.9.20 a.m. some forty-eight further rounds were delivered from the Houston FBI. One of the CEVs was now suffering mechanical problems and went out of service. The crew was redeployed to another CEV, which had not been converted to enable it to deliver gas. Over the course of the next two hours the operation continued: more ferret rounds were fired and holes were made in the Mt. Carmel structure, both to facilitate the insertion of gas and also, according to the FBI, to enable the Branch Davidians to exit their home. (And in fact seven of the nine who did escape the fire at Mt. Carmel came through one of those routes.)

The operation was not going well. There was no sign whatsoever that those inside Mt. Carmel were planning to come out, and most worrying of all there was no sign of the children. This presented a huge problem for the FBI since it was largely on the basis of a concern for the welfare of the children that Janet Reno had agreed the plan, and she had done so only after very specific assurances had been given with regard to the children's well-being.

It was on this point that the FBI negotiators made a fundamental and ultimately catastrophic error of judgement. They may have had an arsenal at their disposal, but the weapon they were banking on most was maternal instinct. Their reasoning was that once the tear gas had been inserted into Mt. Carmel the mothers would sense the danger to their children and instinctively seek to remove them from that environment. Maternal instinct would override allegiance to Koresh (throughout the FBI seem to have been working on the assumption that the group functioned through allegiance to Koresh rather than through a shared identity as members of a remnant community). Surely then they would at least send the children out even if the mothers did not exit themselves.[57] But the FBI were wrong. No children and no mothers exited.

Later investigations revealed that most of the mothers and children died close to one another inside or very close to the bunker. Juliet Martinez died there alongside her five children Crystal, Joseph, Isaiah, Audrey, and Abigail; Rachel Jones with her twins Chica and Little One, and Serenity; Lorraine Sylvia with Hollywood and Rachel, and Rachel Howell with Star, Cyrus, and Bobbie. Some of these were killed by the effects of the smoke, some from wounds apparently inflicted by other members of the community (and it is particularly horrible to note that one child died from a stab wound to the chest), and others of undetermined causes. In fact once the fire had taken hold, the people inside the bunker may have had little chance of escape (a few minutes at the most), though they could presumably have left at any point during the six hours that elapsed from the start of the raid and the first evidence of fire. The tear gas plan simply did not work. There must surely have been maternal instincts at work inside Mt. Carmel that morning, but if so it appears to have directed the mothers to keep their children safe as part of God's treasured remnant community rather than expose them to the uncertainties and dangers of the outside world. (Or they may, of course, simply have feared breaking ranks.)

The gassing plan, then, was a total failure. It achieved nothing other than, perhaps, further heightening the sense the Branch Davidians had that the end was indeed nigh. The FBI were serious—this was the showdown and the community faced a clear choice: leave Mt. Carmel and, in their minds, effectively turn their back on God who had told them to wait and hold out despite the apparently overwhelming odds. The leaders of the community at least must also have been aware that to go out would be to abandon communal and individual goals. Despite any reassurances to the contrary (some had been given at the meeting on 15 March) they probably feared that the community would be imprisoned, dispersed, and made homeless. The group would be broken up and how then would the kingdom come?

In retrospect and with the benefit of access to the enhanced bug tapes, it seems very unlikely that the FBI had even an outside chance of bringing things to a satisfactory conclusion through the actions they adopted on 19 April. It was a plan more or less doomed from the start. Their failure to grasp the level of each individual Branch Davidian's commitment to the communal goals or to the community leadership, especially Koresh, has been noted already; mothers may well have placed their fear of putting their children's eternal salvation in jeopardy above any concern they might have had for their physical survival. (The remarks of Yvette Fagan quoted in the previous chapter are worth remembering here.) The group was as strong now as it ever had been; indeed, if anything it was stronger because they had suffered together the tactics employed during the siege. Here was real hard evidence that the prophecies in which they had for so long believed were indeed coming to pass. It was hence very unlikely that the Branch Davidians could be forced out in this way. All the FBI did on that morning may only have strengthened the group's resolve further. It is guesswork, but not wild, to suggest that the thought if not the precise texts of some of what Jesus said came to their minds: 'ye shall be hated of all men for my name's sake [but] he that endureth to the end shall be saved' (Matt. 10.22).

The only possible way that force might have worked would have been for the FBI gradually to strip away Mt. Carmel until the community within it was left exposed to the elements. This would have been completely impractical, however: Mt. Carmel was no garden shed. Even if what was above ground could have been safely dismantled (highly unlikely given the complexity of the building and the fact that it was on more than one floor), there was the underground tornado shelter and buried bus to contend with. If Koresh and the community were going to come out, they would have to be talked out, and so far all attempts to pursue that course of action had yielded little result.

Further, what the FBI did not know was that the Branch Davidians probably already had a plan to bring the siege to a close and that the details of that plan had been discussed by some of the members of the community in the days before the fire. The actions undertaken on 19 April did nothing to head this plan off; indeed, if anything they brought its execution forward.

Again it is important to note that some of the evidence upon which the previous comment is based is not entirely clear. However, it cannot simply be overlooked altogether even if it needs to be approached with caution. Some of it has already been presented; it was noted that the bug tapes contain reasonably clear indications that within minutes of the initial actions of the FBI some of the Branch Davidians were already preparing to set Mt. Carmel alight. Indeed, so quickly was this course of action adopted that it seems obvious that it must have been planned well in advance.

Some of that planning may well be seen in the action taken on 15 March, when Koresh ordered that substantial quantities of diesel fuel should be transferred from tanks outside Mt. Carmel to five-gallon containers. The operation was tricky, involving the use of a long hose, and undertaken at some considerable risk. Now it may be that the diesel was intended for use in powering a generator, or for lamps; that cannot be ruled out. Nevertheless, if other evidence can be found of incendiary intentions it may put the concern to draw down the diesel in another perspective.[58]

The bug tapes again may be useful. It appears from information on the tapes that on 18 April some sort of plan was in place and being discussed among some of the more central figures in Mt. Carmel. On that day the FBI began moving vehicles from around Mt. Carmel to facilitate the actions planned for the following morning. Those inside Mt. Carmel had been told that this was purely a precautionary measure to enable the Branch Davidians to exit safely when the time came. However, Koresh and others correctly perceived that something was afoot. As Swett notes, 'there was an air of excitement. There was an increase in talk of "graduation" and "going home"'.[59] The same day the bug tapes recorded the following conversation:

UM:	I hope so God … I hope so.
UF:[60]	Want filling up.
UF:	Anything good?
Schneider:	I think that … It may be scary.
UM:	Oh yeah Ok … it may be scary.
UM:	Oh yeah Ok … the way in.

Schneider:	Yeah well you've been hearing he's been saying about that for 2 or 3 days . . . now we're making efforts I think . . . he did say that . . . we'll make an effort if he goes back on that.[61]
UM:	I said that is my position now.
Schneider:	You always wanted to be a charcoal briquette. [laughs]
UM:	He told 'em . . . he goes . . . you, your prophecy will be . . . [chuckles]
Schneider:	That's your price if you take that.
UM:	I hear your prophecy not going to say nothing happened, er, they're never going to say this to my . . .
UM:	I know that there's nothing like a good fire to bring us to birth.
Schneider:	I know it.
UM/F:	Oh I was getting a little . . .
UM:	Ow—ow—ow—ow—ow—ow.
Schneider:	My impression of the first man landing on the sun; ow—ow—ow—ow—ow—ow—ow—ow.
UM:	Yeah, got it right.
UM:	Darn our controls are jammed . . . here comes Mr. Sun.[62]

The conversation then continues for some time, but is so broken up as to make it almost impossible to follow. Then towards the end of the conversation Schneider is heard again.

Schneider:	Boy . . . wait 'til I get my scrawny hands on your scrawny little neck . . . I'm coming back and when I do you are gonna . . . cos there's nowhere you're gonna be able to hide.[63]

A conversation like this needs some interpretation and any such interpretation may be wrong. However, the reference to the 'charcoal briquette' is reasonably plain:[64] there is an expectation that the speaker in this conversation will find his desire fulfilled. Further a 'good fire' will bring 'us' to birth and Schneider will 'come back' from something/some state and, apparently, wring the scrawny neck of the FBI.[65]

On the same day (18 April) the bug tapes record Schneider talking apparently to a small group of people in the course of which he states 'definitely a fire around the back'.[66] At this point Scott Sonobe joins in saying, 'If we're gonna have a fire we'd better get some fuel in here'.[67] Schneider then finishes up the conversation by saying 'At least we're going up. I'd rather go up in a puff of smoke than out the door and in a Bradley. At least we will get away from all this crap . . .'[68] That same day the FBI sent in a package of material that consisted of seventeen pints of milk, dog biscuits, Milky Way chocolate bars, Casio typewriter ribbons, and another recording device. Scott Sonobe wanted to save the boxes, commenting, 'These boxes will make for good burning material.'[69]

As the FBI manoeuvred outside there was some discussion about whether it was safe to look out of the windows. The instructions were to stay away, but Schneider told his fellow Branch Davidians to look out if they wanted to. Schneider then apparently joined someone at the window, and said,

Schneider:	Do you see that there? Right here—down. You see that? Do you want to know what that is there? Do you know what that's for? You don't huh? It's for—ah—the people that are here. You know—Joel 2 and Isaiah 13 whose faces are like flames.
UM:	I was always wondering how that was brought about.
Schneider:	It is—Isaiah 33.
UF:	Is that from scripture?
Schneider:	Huh?
UF:	Is that from the scriptures?
Schneider:	Yes it is.
UM:	We will run through the fire.
UF:	God said to do this?
Schneider:	That's what David said to do and it's fine with me. Wherever you want to be . . . all his ways are directed as far as I am concerned. If he goes down . . .
UF:	I'm just wondering if that's what he said.
Schneider:	Yeah that's his direction.[70]

The reference to Joel 2 is particularly important here. In that chapter we read:

Blow ye the trumpet in Zion, and sound an alarm in my holy mountain: let all the inhabitants of the land tremble: for the day of the Lord cometh, for it is nigh at hand; A day of darkness and of gloominess, a day of clouds and of thick darkness, as the morning spread upon the mountains: a great people and a strong; there hath not been ever the like, neither shall be any more after it, even to the years of many generations. A fire devoureth before them; and behind them a flame burneth: the land is as the garden of Eden before them, and behind them a desolate wilderness; yea, and nothing shall escape them. The appearance of them is as the appearance of horses; and as horsemen, so shall they run. Like the noise of chariots on the tops of mountains shall they leap, like the noise of a flame of fire that devoureth the stubble, as a strong people set in battle array (Joel 2.1–5)

A little more of the implication of the Branch Davidian reading of this passage is set out in Chapter Fifteen; here we note only that as Schneider looked out of the window on 18 April, it was this passage which came to his mind and to which he drew others' attention. The forces were assembling for battle and the alarm was to be sounded in God's holy mountain; the day of the Lord was coming, a day when a fire would be both before and behind 'a great people and a strong'. This is not a matter of reading back into Schneider's mind what we think might have been going on; we know he looked out of the window and saw the movement of the FBI and said: 'Do you know what that's for? You don't huh? It's for—ah—the people that are here. You know—Joel 2 and Isaiah 13 whose faces are like flames.'

It is unsurprising, then, given this apparent context, that when the FBI did make a move the next day the Branch Davidians reacted almost instantaneously. They were prophetically primed and practically ready. There was an expectation that the events of Joel 2 were about to be fulfilled and that there would be a 'good fire' to bring birth. At least one person was anticipating becoming a charcoal briquette and Schneider was looking forward to 'coming back' (which means he would have to be going somewhere first). Fuel was available as a result of the actions taken more than a month earlier, and some of the detail of where that fuel was to be spread had been worked out ('definitely a fire round the back'). The Branch Davidians sprang into action and spread the fuel; some of the fuel remained on the clothes of survivors.[71] By 7.30 a.m. Mt. Carmel was a potential inferno.

While the chaos of the moment might well have given the Branch Davidians reason to begin the spreading of the fuel, only a clear direction from Koresh himself would be enough to authorize the actual lighting of the fire. In this context the fact that some sort of semi-secret meeting took place beginning at approximately 7.30 a.m. on 19 April is important. The bug tapes again:

UM (1):	Pablo (?) do you know where David is?
Pablo Cohen (?):	Upstairs.
UM (1):	One guy at a time, go upstairs—down the hallway to where David said (is?) OK?
UM (2):[72]	A meeting about what.
UM (2):	I wonder what the meeting is about.
Pablo Cohen (?):	Did you hear about going up to David?
UM:	Hmmm?
Pablo Cohen (?):	Did you hear about going up to see David?
UM:	No.
Pablo Cohen (?):	OK. When the next guy comes down you go up to see him, OK?
UM:	Umm-hmm.
Pablo Cohen (?):	We have to talk to David.[73]

This kind of conversation continues for several more minutes and the overall impression is reasonably clear: David Koresh was conducting some sort of personal interviews with several of the male members of the community. What was said during those interviews is not known, but given the crisis of the moment they must surely have discussed how the current situation (and one must remember that ferret rounds of tear gas were coming through the windows as they spoke) should be dealt with.[74]

The spreading of the fuel continued. By 9.20 a.m. supplies were running low.

UM:[75]   They got two cans of Coleman fuel right there? . . . Huh?

UM:[76]   Empty.

UM: All of it?

UM: Think so.

UM: Can you check?

UM: There isn't anything showing . . . nothing left.

UM: Out of both cans?

UM: I got this . . . (going) on air.

UM: You want some mineral oil . . .

UM: Don't know . . . I'll have to think . . .

UM: Hm.

UM: I got some mineral oil.

UM: Don't think I got any.[77]

Just who was involved in the meetings with Koresh cannot be ascertained. Probably it was a select few who knew the time had come to act out the Branch Davidians' predetermined part in the coming Apocalypse and actually set fire to Mt. Carmel. However, although only a few seem to have been directly involved in executing the plan, a much wider group seem to have known that it was a part of God's plan that the Branch Davidians would one day have to die and, in some cases, that an inferno was a part of that process.

It appears, then, that the bug tapes indicate that the fire may well have been the direct result of actions taken by the Branch Davidians themselves. It certainly looks as though they were planning to set fire to the centre. Many will want to argue with this reconstruction, but to do so effectively such persons will need to access the material and argue at least one of three things: (1) that the transcriptions given here are inaccurate; (2) that the interpretation of the transcriptions implied here is implausible; or (3) that the tapes themselves are the result of some sort of conspiracy. What cannot be done is simply to ignore the tapes. They must be dealt with, even if only to argue that they are manufactured. (And if such an argument is advanced, evidence to support it must be presented. It will not be enough simply to say that the US government is a wicked institution that as a matter of course fabricates evidence.)

To the evidence of the bug tapes must be added two other sets of data: the testimony of the survivors of the fire, and of others who were at Mt. Carmel when the fire broke out. It is surely the first body of evidence that is likely to be the most persuasive, but the latter cannot be ignored.

As potentially important as it is disturbing is some evidence from the children of Mt. Carmel. The testimony of Kiri Jewell has been in the public domain for some time: it was she who stated on live television that she had been shown how to commit suicide and in a way that had no chance of failure. She was to place a gun into her mouth and fire.[78] Jewell's testimony does not lend any weight to the view that the Branch Davidians set fire to Mt. Carmel, but it does suggest a broader context in the light of which other evidence of an inclination to communal self-destruction might be viewed.

More recently, however, further evidence has come to light. On 17 April 2003 *Primetime Live*, a regular news programme produced by ABC News, aired 'Witness: The Children of Waco'. On that show seven of the Branch Davidian children who exited Mt. Carmel during the siege were interviewed; among them was the now twenty-two-year-old Kiri Jewell, who repeated the earlier testimony. Importantly, the show aired for the first time video evidence of the children at play shortly after their departure from Mt. Carmel but before 19 April. There was talk of death and a rhyme was sung: 'we've got to fight, someday we have to die, we gotta, gotta hold up the blood stained banner'. There was talk also of a battle between 'good guys and bad guys' with the bad guys winning at first; 'but then the good guys win' said Landon Wendell (then three or four years of age), 'because they get up the angels and burn the bad guys'. Later in the show we hear of Jaunessa Wendell (then aged eight). She was asked to draw a picture of Mt. Carmel, which she did, then added some flames and some steps (the video, it is worth repeating, was filmed before the fire.) Psychiatrist Bruce Perry stated:

And I said, 'what's that?' She said 'that's what's going to happen.' And I said, 'well what is that?' She said, 'that's a fire. There's an explosion.' 'And what are these steps?' 'Those are steps up to Heaven.' And I said, 'well, what does that mean?' And she said, 'Well, you'll find out.'

Adult testimony is also important. In 1999 Graeme Craddock was interviewed by the Office of Special Counsel in the context of the impending wrongful death lawsuit. According to Craddock a number of other Branch Davidians poured fuel in the chapel area of the complex on the morning of 19 April. He stated that he saw another Davidian, Mark Wendell, arrive from the second floor, yelling: 'Light the fire.' According to Craddock, Cohen said 'wait, wait, find out', and there was then a further conversation Craddock could not hear.[79] Similarly, Clive Doyle told the Texas rangers that the Branch Davidians had spread Coleman fuel in designated locations throughout the complex, though Doyle offered no explanation as to the precise start of the fire.[80]

There is one other possible source of information on the start of the fire from a survivor, though one that must be treated with great caution. This is an account by 'Branch Bill', an unidentified individual who claimed that his information came from Renos Avraam. ('Branch Bill' claims to have been a cell mate of Avraam at one point). In the hand-written account, it is stated that Avraam was the last one to see Koresh alive—when 'he and Steve [Schneider] had just come down the hall and passed me'. 'I followed them into a room', the account continues; 'Koresh had a yellow can of gasoline in his hand which he threw against the wall of the room and said "the fifth seal is set—prophecy will be fulfilled—we must all die—we must wound the beast in the head"'. The account then describes how Avraam panicked at the words 'we must all die', and fled the building.

This, then, is an interesting document indeed. To be sure there are major problems with it: its authenticity cannot be verified and in any case the document stops short of actually stating that the fire was lit by the Branch Davidians themselves (though intention to do so seems clearly to be implied). The document is worth mentioning here, however, if only to draw it to the attention of other researchers. If it is a fake, it tells us nothing. If it has a direct link with Avraam, however, it is potentially of exceptional importance.[81] Probably we will never know.

The *Report* also refers to evidence provided by witnesses on the scene at Mt. Carmel, which it summarizes:

> Observations by government witnesses support the conclusion that the Davidians started the fire. FBI agents who had the opportunity to observe activity within the Branch Davidian complex on April 19, using field glasses or spotting scopes, saw Davidians engaged in activity which they later concluded to be pouring fuel to start a fire. Some of these sightings were noted contemporaneously by the agents in FBI logs. Also, an FBI agent observed an unidentified Davidian ignite a fire in the front door area of the complex shortly after noon. This observation was also reported contemporaneously.[82]

This evidence could be followed up; however, that is not done here. This is so since the arguments above build up a case based upon hopefully much harder evidence; if that evidence, which comes from expert analysis of the fire scene, the FLIR tapes, the bug tapes, and the Davidian depositions, is not persuasive,[83] comments made by FBI agents looking at Mt. Carmel through field glasses are unlikely to convince.

The basic conclusion reached in this chapter is not new. There have been previous expressions of it—the *Final Report*, of course, and also the work of Mark Swett. However, to say that the Branch Davidians set fire to Mt. Carmel themselves is only to raise a second and far less well researched question: why did they do it? Was it perhaps, as some have suggested, Koresh's last act of manipulative dominance? Alternatively, perhaps the Branch Davidians did not really know what the purpose of the fire was, but simply believed it would in some way force God's hand. (While such an argument has not been advanced in this specific context, it is worth considering as a religious motive. On occasions it has even been put forward as an explanation for the actions of Judas in betraying Jesus.) Others might want to explore the possibility that the group became self-destructive once it perceived that its communal goal, the establishment of the kingdom, had come under serious threat. Perhaps it had not always been the plan of the Branch Davidians to go out with a bang rather than a whimper, but once the ATF had surrounded their home, such a course of action began to form in their minds. Here, however, another view is advanced: the fire was very much part of the overall eschatological scheme that the Branch Davidians believed themselves to be acting out during these last days. It had a well-defined function and was expected to accomplish several things. Precisely what those things might have been are outlined in the following chapter.

NOTES

1. I owe this apt description of the events of 19 April to the title of Mark Swett's web-published and privately circulated paper, 'The Ultimate Act of Faith?: David Koresh and the Untold story of the Branch Davidians', which has been of great value in the preparation of this chapter. The paper is widely available on the internet (at the time of writing for example at www.rickross.com/reference/waco/waco299.html) and has been placed also on the website that supports this book: www.hope.ac.uk/humanities/theology/branch davidians.
2. There is one further option: that the fire started independently of actions (intentional or otherwise) by either the Branch Davidians or the government agencies. It might, for example, have begun with an electrical fault, or some accident of weather. There is no evidence to support such a view.
3. Such a view was communicated to me by Derek Lovelock in a personal interview.
4. It is worth pointing out that this allegation has no hard evidence to support it. Following the release of *Waco: The Big Lie*, extensive checks were conducted on the

vehicles used at Mt. Carmel, and their maintenance records, to see if there was any evidence to suggest that any had been adapted to carry flame throwers: there was not. The 'flame' to which the video points has been identified as a piece of Mt. Carmel's insulation material which had an aluminum backing and stuck to the tank as it backed away. This can apparently be seen fairly clearly if the video footage is allowed to run on rather than freezing it at the point at which the 'flame' appears. As early as 1994 Thompson's views were being questioned even by non-government sources. In the Feb 1994 issue of *Machine Gun News*, for example, hardly the kind of publication that might be thought to support the government line, a columnist wrote of the longer video footage: 'In the COPS version, rather than stopping the video at the point where the illusion of flame is most apparent, as in the AJF [American Justice Federation] tape, the camera continues to follow the vehicle as it backs clear of the building...As [the] tank turns away from [the] camera, [the] reflection spreads to reveal what appears to be a large section of tan wallboard leaning against [the] turret.'

5. See Hardy, *This is not an Assault*, 291–2.
6. See *Final Report*, Appendix D, 20–1; Appendix D has its own appendices, and Appendix N (to Appendix D) provides some photographic evidence of escape routes available.
7. Ibid. 17–29
8. In Wright, ed., *Armageddon in Waco*, for example, the origin of the fire is scarcely mentioned, while the neutral comments in Tabor and Gallagher *Why Waco?* seem fairly typical: 'Around noon, smoke was seen coming from the second-story windows' (2–3, and see also 21–2).
9. See e.g. Catherine Wessinger, 'Varieties of Millennialism and the Issue of Authority', in Lewis, ed., *From the Ashes*, 60, where she raises the possibility that the Branch Davidians set fire to Mt. Carmel themselves. In a later study, however (*How the Millennium Comes Violently* (New York and London: Seven Bridges Press, 2000), 102–3), she seems less sure.
10. See e.g. Hardy, *This is Not an Assault*, 286. Hardy is actually very cautious on the question of how the fire started and never really states his view clearly in his book. However, what he does argue is that the use of pyrotechnic rounds to deliver tear gas into Mt. Carmel indicates that at the very least the FBI were 'recklessly indifferent that its methods would cause a lethal fire'.
11. See *Report*, 295–307.
12. Ulf Wickström, who produced an analysis of the fire (Appendix E of the *Report*), was from the Swedish National Testing and Research Institute in Borås, Sweden. Lena Klasén and Sten Madsen, the authors of Appendix H ('Image Analysis and Video Authentication'), were from Orlunda Agro & IT and Aservice i Linköping respectively.
13. See *Final Report*, Appendix D, 14, where the author (Wetherington) states that the holes in the cans were most probably made by 'a knife blade or a bayonet'.
14. An alternative view that has been put forward is that the cans were designed as portable showers; this seems possible but implausible, since some were in the

chapel area (not the place to take a shower one presumes) and, even more telling, some had fuel residue (rather than water) still in them.

15. See Hardy, *This is Not an Assault*, 80–1.

16. Ibid. 272.

17. *Report*, 330–1.

18. One other view is that the FBI sent the plane up as a precaution. The bug tapes had picked up a conversation the previous day in which the possibility of a fire was mentioned. Accordingly the FBI decided to record the events using FLIR imaging in order to safeguard their own position should a fire actually break out. If one accepts this argument, the remark of Reavis is surely worth considering: would it not have been better to ensure that fire trucks were on standby rather than sending up a FLIR equipped aircraft? Reavis, *Ashes of Waco*, 272–3.

19. 'Fire Investigative Report, Branch Davidian Compound, Waco, Texas, April 19, 1993', prepared by Paul Gray, John T. Ricketts, William S. Cass, and Thomas W. Hitchings, 13 July 1993 (*Report*, Appendix D).

20. *Final Report*, 6.

21. Ibid., Appendix D; the questions are raised on page 4.

22. Ibid. 8.

23. Ibid. 15.

24. The basic data relating to the cans is gathered together in Danforth, *Final Report*, Appendix D, 14–15.

25. Ibid., Appendix E, 2.

26. Ibid.

27. The reason given by government sources for the delay in the arrival of the fire trucks was that it was not safe for the fire-fighters to approach (*Final Report*, 170).

28. Reavis, *Ashes of Waco*, 273, refers to an independent analysis of the FLIR tapes that suggests that the fire started a few seconds before twelve o'clock. Quite what that report is, is not clear and (as normal) Reavis gives no reference; hence it cannot be checked. It may well have been the same analysis as the one referred to on *Waco: The Rules of Engagement* (a video in which Reavis appears several times). This suggestion appears not to have won much support, though it is mentioned also in Thibodeau, *A Place Called Waco*, 264. So close is the wording in Thibodeau to that in Reavis, however, that it is highly likely that Thibodeau is directly dependent upon Reavis at this point (and indeed on others).

29. Swett, 'The Ultimate Act of Faith'. Mills's work is in *Final Report*, Appendix G. This contains details on the bug tapes and transcriptions of them. The references given here are those at the bottom left of the pages of that appendix.

30. *Final Report*, Appendix G, 73, Day 2—Tape 5/37. See also Swett, 'Ultimate Act of Faith', 145. On the copy of the tape used here, the words are 36 mins and 30 secs into side 2.

31. Swett, 'Ultimate Act of Faith', 144; *Final Report*, Appendix G, 73, Day 2—Tape 5/35.

32. Tape SA73 (5); the words are approximately 26 mins into side 2.

33. *Final Report*, Appendix G, 73, Day 2—Tape 5/28.

34. Swett, 'Ultimate Act of Faith', 144; SA73/5; the words are 11 mins and 45 secs into side 2.
35. *Final Report*, Appendix G, 73, Day 2—Tape 5/30; Mills uses parentheses to indicate 'sounds like'.
36. Listening to the tape does not clarify matters, though Swett's transcription does seem at the very least possible.
37. Swett, 'Ultimate Act of Faith', 144; the words are not at all clear on the tape used here, though there is something audible that could be what Swett suggests.
38. SA73/5 side 2, the very last tape, is nearly 40 minutes long, though the recording actually finishes about two minutes before the end. It appears that the recording device failed at approximately 12.00 noon. Since the words 'look out...it's already lit' come 11 mins and 45 secs into the tape (around 26 mins before the end), the 'it' that had been lit was lit by *c.*11.34. If 'it' is a fire (rather than a Molotov cocktail) this may have been one of the fires that did not spread (see *Final Report*, Appendix E, 2).
39. *Final Report*, 155.
40. Ibid. 156.
41. Unidentified Male.
42. *Final Report*, Appendix G, 73, Day 2—Tape 2/11.
43. Ibid., Tape 2/15.
44. Ibid., Tape 3/4.
45. Ibid., Tape 3/5.
46. Ibid., Tape 2/42.
47. *Final Report*, 9–10.
48. Uwe Heinrich, 'Possible Lethal Effects of CS Tear Gas on Branch Davidians during the FBI raid on the Mount Carmel Compound near Waco, Texas, April 19, 1993' (*Final Report*).
49. The exact concentration of gas is impossible to ascertain. The winds, coupled with the holes in the building created by the CEVs, would have dissipated the gas significantly. It has been pointed out by some that whereas gas masks appear to have been used early in the attack (and hence the conversations heard on the tapes are somewhat garbled) later the conversations are much clearer. This may suggest that the masks had been removed and hence, presumably, the effects of the gas were not now feared. It is also surely worth noting that of the nine persons that did come out of Mt. Carmel on 19 April, not one needed medical treatment for the effects of tear gas. On these issues see further *Final Report*, appendices F and L.
50. *Report*, 292.
51. It is worth noting here that in private correspondence with me, Byron Sage was very clear that shots were being fired. He wrote, 'I am one that observed the rounds ricochet off the tracked vehicle...I saw those rounds bouncing/sparking as they struck the armoured vehicles' (a copy of Sage's remarks is in my possession).
52. *Report*, 288.
53. *Report*, 289.

54. See e.g. Moore, *Davidian Massacre*, 373–4.
55. *Final Report*, 193.
56. Ibid. 158–60.
57. Byron Sage states that this was the case very clearly on the TV show *Primetime Live* (17 April 2003). At the time of writing a transcript of the show is available at www.transcripts.net. The source used here is the video itself.
58. Swett, 'Ultimate Act of Faith', 82–3, drawing on material from the bug tapes.
59. Ibid. 112.
60. Unidentified Female.
61. Swett thinks that 'going back on that' is in fact 'going back en masse'. This is a major difference and worth highlighting. Listening to the tape itself makes things no clearer, but Swett's reconstruction does at the very least seem quite possible.
62. This transcription is based upon *Final Report*, Appendix G, SA72, Tape 28, 2–3, but has been changed a little on the basis of information supplied by Mark Swett and from listening to the tape itself.
63. This transcription is from *Final Report*, Appendix G, SA72, Tape 28, 3, 6. The tape is very clear and most of the words are certain.
64. Given the importance of this statement it is worth noting that the tape is very clear; the words 'you always wanted to be a charcoal briquette' are unmistakable.
65. On the probability that this reference to wringing the neck of the FBI is related to Schneider's conviction that he and his fellow co-religionists would one day make up part of the avenging army described (in Schneider's understanding) in Rev. 9.16ff., see further below.
66. Swett, 'Ultimate Act of Faith', 114.
67. Ibid. 115.
68. Ibid. (citing tape SA73–1).
69. Ibid. (citing tape SA72–28).
70. Tape SA72–28. The transcription is based upon the work of Mark Swett with some minor modifications that seem more accurately to reflect the recording.
71. See *Final Report*, Appendix D, 17 for details.
72. Swett thinks that this is possibly Graeme Craddock.
73. Swett, 'Ultimate Act of Faith', 138–9.
74. That this 'semi-secret' meeting took place was confirmed to Mark Swett by Clive Doyle, though Doyle insisted that he was not part of it and did not know what was being discussed. See Swett, 'Ultimate Act of Faith', 140.
75. In *Final Report*, Appendix G, this is identified as Koresh, but listening to the tape suggests that this is not correct.
76. In *Final Report*, Appendix G, this is identified as Schneider, but listening to the tape suggests that this is not correct.
77. Swett, 'Ultimate Act of Faith', 142.
78. Donahue transcript # 3682 (10 March 1993). Jewell's precise words, according to the transcript, were, 'You were supposed to stick a gun in your mouth because if you stuck it to your head, you'd—there would be a chance you could survive'.

79. *Final Report*, 9; the reference is to the oral and video-taped deposition of Graeme Craddock taken in the FCI Oakdale, Louisiana. The crucial section reads: 'I went back inside, sat back where I was at. It seemed like about two minutes later I heard the same call coming from Mark Wendell, who said the building was on fire. This time I looked out. I looked up in the sky. I could see smoke around. It was—I couldn't see it coming from any, any particular area. I could see black bits of debris falling, like snow, black snow, but I, I couldn't see any general direct area where the smoke was coming from, but I could tell the building was on fire somewhere. Again I pulled my head back inside; and it was, like, a few seconds later I heard Mark Wendell again. He said this time, "Light the fire." At that point—Pablo said in response, he said, "Wait. Wait. Find out." And there was some conversation that then took place between Pablo and—I'm sorry. I've forgotten his name—Mark Wendell.' Craddock Deposition, 202–3.

80. *Final Report*, 9; Doyle's interview was conducted in Parkland Hospital in Dallas, Texas, on 20 Apr. 1993 by Texas ranger Bobby Grubbs. A summary of the interview was filed as RF093021Z.24 with the Texas Department of Public Safety, Criminal Law Enforcement Division, and a copy of that report is in my possession.

81. The document itself, dated 27 Apr. 1996, can be found in TXC, Mark Swett Collection, box 4, folder 'Renos Avraam'. It is identified in the writer's hand as two pages in length, but only one is found in TXC. There are two other items in the folder that appear to be from a similar origin. On one, clearly a fax, a hand-written note indicates that the document has been sent to Dr Phillip Arnold from 'Kevin McCrary'. The handwriting in this note is similar to that of the account of the start of the fire. E-mail and telephone conversations with Mark Swett, and all other attempts to investigate the origin of this material, have proven fruitless.

82. *Final Report*, 9.

83. There is also the evidence given by the children, though in this case all that could really be established is that the Branch Davidians expected a fire, not that they actually set one.

15

'For Behold the Lord Will Come with Fire' (cf. Isaiah 66.15): Theology and the Waco Inferno

The previous chapter surveyed some of the evidence relating to the start of the Mt. Carmel fire. The conclusion reached is not pleasant. Precisely who was involved in setting the fire(s) cannot be established with complete certainty, but it seems reasonably clear that the fire was started by the Branch Davidians themselves and not by persons external to Mt. Carmel. To be sure this conclusion is based in part on the interpretation of debatable evidence. However, in some cases the evidence is very plain. So strong is the evidence that the conclusion that the Branch Davidians were responsible for the fire could really be overturned only if the very existence of that evidence could be proven suspect (i.e. if it was fabricated). Apparently hard facts, then, seem to point in one direction: that the Branch Davidians were responsible for the fire.

The circumstantial evidence also seems important. For example, it does seem reasonably clear that well before the events of 19 April there was an expectation on the part of the Branch Davidians that Mt. Carmel would be consumed by flames. Of course, expecting something to happen, or even planning to bring that 'something' about, does not necessarily mean that those concerned were actually responsible for what did eventually come to pass. Taken together with the harder 'facts', however, it does seem as though there was a move from expectation to plan to action. Hence in this chapter an attempt is made to establish a coherent framework within which those actions might have taken place.

As has been argued throughout this book, the Davidians/Branch Davidians were driven by theology. This was a Bible-obsessed religious tradition that sought always to base whatever its adherents did on the words of the Bible. If Branch Davidians did set the fires that burnt Mt. Carmel to the ground, and did so only after careful planning, they must have had some sort of biblical-interpretative understanding of what they were doing and why they needed to do it. It will not do simply to say that they set fire to Mt. Carmel but we are not sure why. It will not do either to say that the reason they acted in this way was because the crazed David Koresh told them to do so. Given the profile of the group and its leader, the presumption must surely be that if they set fire to Mt. Carmel it was for some theological reason.

The basic point made in this chapter is a simple one: that from the beginning of the movement with Houteff, the Davidians/Branch Davidians expected that an important part of the events leading up to the coming of the literal kingdom of God and the cleansing of the earth would be the outbreak of a cleansing fire through which they would have to pass. The detail of that expectation changed somewhat through the course of the movement, but the core remained constant: there would be a fire; this was part of God's plans; and those plans, including the fire, could be seen clearly prophesied in scripture. At the very least such a belief probably explains why some Branch Davidians reacted to the fire as they did. Many made no obvious attempt to escape; indeed, according to the *Final Report*, one of those who did manage to flee the flames, survivor Ruth Riddle, at one point came out of the building only to turn around and run back in again, where she would surely have died had she not been pulled from the flames against her will by FBI agent James McGee.[1] Further, Wayne Martin, a man of considerable intellectual ability who must have known that his life was in imminent danger, simply sat down amid the smoke to 'wait on God'. However, the belief in the coming of a cleansing fire as the gateway to the new kingdom probably explains more than just the reaction of the Branch Davidians to the fire once it had started; it may well account for how it was that the fire started in the first place.

Victor Houteff's views on the coming of a fire through which the faithful would have to pass are reasonably clear.[2] In essence he argued that this fire would be a means of cleansing; it would cleanse the people of God, who would survive it, and destroy the wicked, who would not. According to Houteff, there would be three points in the progress of the plan of salvation when fire would be the (or at least 'a')[3] means by which the wicked would be destroyed. The last of these would be the final destruction of the wicked, when all the wicked who had ever lived would be finally and permanently destroyed by God. When this fire came, said Houteff, the Lord would protect the righteous from the effects of the fire so that they would be completely unharmed by it.

This final destruction of the wicked, however, was some way off, for Houteff adopted the traditional SDA view that the wicked would be sent only temporarily to the grave at the start of the millennium.[4] According to Houteff, as to mainstream SDA doctrine, during the millennium itself the wicked would remain in their graves while their cases were examined by the righteous (now inhabiting the heavenly kingdom), but at the conclusion of the millennium the wicked would be resurrected and together with Satan make one last

PLATE 12 The Waco fire: Branch Davidian Ruth Riddle is pulled away from the fire by FBI agent Jim McGee

attempt to overthrow God. Unlike traditional Seventh-day Adventism, however, Houteff put a definite time period on this final act of rebellion: it would last, he said, 100 years (the period is taken from Isa. 65.17–20). At the conclusion of this period God would finally, completely, and eternally destroy the wicked with fire.[5]

However, Houteff argued that this post-millennial destroying fire was to be prefigured by events prior to the millennium. He was very clear on this; speaking of the destruction of the wicked after the 100-year period of rebellion he wrote:

Since not only Satan, but also 'whosoever was not found written in the Book of Life, was cast into the lake of fire,' the fire in the lake simply continues the same destruction wrought by the fire which comes 'down from God out of heaven.' Rev. 20:9. After the thousand years, in other words, the fire which comes 'down from God out of heaven,' results in 'the lake of fire' (Rev. 20:10) and in eternal extermination of all sinners. Of this final destruction, a pre-millennial demonstration is to be given when the beast and the false prophet are cast into the 'lake of fire'—their grave for the thousand years. And as the fire does not, of course, keep burning during the thousand years, the statement, 'the devil . . . was cast into the lake of fire and brimstone, where the beast and the false prophet are' (Rev. 20:10), shows therefore that there are both a typical and an antitypical destruction; the lake of fire before the millennium, being a type of the one after the millennium.[6]

One can follow Houteff's thinking here. At the start of the millennium fire comes down from heaven and results in 'the lake of fire' (cf. Rev. 19.20) and it is into that lake that the devil and the false prophet are thrown. Houteff apparently took the view that the false prophet was an individual who would prophesy the second coming of Christ, an event in fact 'fulfilled' by the manifestation of Satan as an angel of light (cf. 2 Cor. 11.14).

It is important to recall, however, that in the scheme of the Davidians and Branch Davidians the onset of the millennium comes only after the establishment of the kingdom and that will itself come about through an extremely violent rite of passage. This has been discussed already above, but in summary the Davidians and Branch Davidians expected that the Church of God (the Seventh-day Adventists) would be cleansed, and that after this cleansing the remnant would take the gospel to the world; to this point the gospel had been for the SDA community only. This cleansing of the Church, during which the unfaithful would be literally slain, would happen at the conclusion of a further act of very visible violence, namely war in the Middle East and the slaughter of the Jews and the Arabs (which would leave Jerusalem empty in preparation for the arrival of the 144,000, and then the great multitude).

Potentially importantly for the later Branch-Davidian understanding of the role of fire in the eschatological plans of God, Houteff argued also that fire would be a factor at this point. What is in view here is the point at which the kingdom is established—a premillennial and very much 'this worldly' event. It would precede the move of the Branch Davidians from Waco to the Holy Land.

In talking about this rite of passage (but not when talking about the other two destroying fires), a key text for Houteff is Isaiah 66.15–20. The text is quoted in whole or in part many times in his voluminous writings; it reads:

For, behold, the Lord will come with fire, and with his chariots like a whirlwind, to render his anger with fury, and his rebuke with flames of fire. For by fire and by his sword will the Lord plead with all flesh: and the slain of the Lord shall be many... For I know their works and their thoughts: it shall come, that I will gather all nations and tongues; and they shall come, and see my glory. And I will set a sign among them, and I will send those that escape of them unto the nations, to Tarshish, Pul, and Lud, that draw the bow, to Tubal, and Javan, to the isles afar off, that have not heard my fame, neither have seen my glory; and they shall declare my glory among the Gentiles. And they shall bring all your brethren for an offering unto the Lord out of all nations upon horses, and in chariots, and in litters, and upon mules, and upon swift beasts, to my holy mountain Jerusalem, saith the Lord, as the children of Israel bring an offering in a clean vessel into the house of the Lord.

Houteff thought that this passage relates to the time when the 'eleventh hour' people were called, that is, when the 144,000 would be gathered in readiness for the taking of the gospel to the world. This would also be the time of the slaughter of Ezekiel 9. It is at this time too that the Lord will come 'with fire' to rebuke 'with flames', and 'by fire' to plead with all flesh.

The events of Isaiah 66.15–20, then, will happen as the 144,000 are gathered. Fire will come to destroy the unfaithful (which in this context means Seventh-day Adventists who have not accepted the *Shepherd's Rod* message). However, the fire will also do something else. It will purify the people who do escape it, and so be the means by which the 144,000 are made ready for the work ahead.

Such a scheme comes across in Houteff's detailed arguments concerning the statement made by John the Baptist in Matthew 3.11–12:

I indeed [says John] baptize you with water unto repentance: but he that cometh after me is mightier than I, whose shoes I am not worthy to bear: he shall baptize you with the Holy Ghost, and with fire Whose fan is in his hand, and he will thoroughly purge his floor, and gather his wheat into the garner; but he will burn up the chaff with unquenchable fire.

According to Houteff this prophecy does not relate to the ministry of Jesus, for Jesus, like John, baptized only with water and not with the Holy Ghost and fire. Hence unless the prophecy is wrong (which would be inconceivable to Houteff) the statement 'he will baptize you with the Holy Ghost and with fire' must relate to some event still future.[7] In fact the Christian rite of baptism, said Houteff, is but a sign of what is to come. Christians are baptized in water but this is only the type. The antitype to which the type points forward is the end-time baptism which purifies God's people, a baptism in the Holy Ghost and with fire. Houteff was very clear on this point. The Davidians were now preaching the antitypical message of John the Baptist and thereby preparing people for the second coming of the Lord. And there would be an antitypical baptism too; a baptism in the Holy Ghost and with fire. And 'since', said Houteff, 'the proper form of baptism is by immersion, then those who are baptized with the Holy Ghost must be covered with the Holy Ghost. Likewise, for a person to be baptized with fire he must go through the fire.'[8]

On 24 April 1943 Houteff preached a sermon on this very subject, subsequently published in the Davidian publication *The Symbolic Code*.[9] Here he made clear his view that a time was coming when the people of God would be totally immersed in fire. He wrote:

John said that He who would come after him would baptize with the Holy Ghost and with fire. That baptism is still future. And if it is still future from John's time, it must be performed sometime before we get into the Kingdom, sometime when the Lord's fan is in His hand. We see, then, that after John's baptism comes the baptism of the Holy Ghost and fire; therefore John's baptism must be a symbol of another baptism, that of the Holy Ghost and fire. To find out more about what this means, let us turn to Mal. 3:1–3—'Behold, I will send My messenger, and he shall prepare the way before Me: and the Lord, Whom ye seek, shall suddenly come to His temple, even the messenger of the covenant, whom ye delight in: behold, he shall come, saith the Lord of hosts. But who may abide the day of His coming? and who shall stand when He appeareth? for He is like a refiner's fire, and like fullers' soap: and He shall sit as a refiner and purifier of silver: and He shall purify the sons of Levi, and purge them as gold and silver that they may offer unto the Lord an offering in righteousness.' Jesus used this scripture to identify John as being the messenger who was to prepare the way for His coming. In studying these verses we find that there is no difference in the event mentioned here in Malachi and the event mentioned by John himself other than that another symbolism was used in Malachi. We went through the baptism of water to show that we were sinners and have received forgiveness, but this baptism is a baptism of fire which is to purify us and cause us to emerge as silver and gold. Yes, we have been baptized with water, but when the Lord comes to His temple to baptize us with the purifying fire, who will be able to stand? This experience must come to take away the chaff and to save the wheat and to cleanse those who are God's people.[10]

Another important passage for Houteff was Zechariah 14 which, according to his understanding, also spoke of an eschatological battle to be fought over 'Jerusalem' (which, he argued, meant God's people). According to Houteff, when the battle breaks out, 'Jerusalem' will be surrounded by a 'wall of fire' (Zech. 2.5). But this is not the final battle, that is, not the battle that takes place one hundred years after the end of the millennium. Neither is it a battle to be fought at the coming of Christ. Rather, this battle will be fought at a point (just) prior to that at which the 144,000 gain entry to the Kingdom. Houteff wrote: 'In view of the fact that Jerusalem is to be protected by a wall of fire (Zech. 2:5) while the house of Judah reigns there, it is definite that the battle here described must be fought before the house of Judah is established.'[11]

Again Houteff's exegesis takes some effort to follow, but it is not impossible to do. What he seems to be saying is that as with David of old, so the antitypical king David would rule first over the 'house of Judah' and then over the 'house of Israel'. His eschatological expectations and typological interpretation of scripture get even more tortuous at this point. What he argued is that for the birthing of antitypical Judah, over which the antitypical King David will rule in Jerusalem, there will be a rite of passage through which the faithful must pass. In fact we are back with Ezekiel 9 and Matthew 3.11–12. There will be some sort of battle during which 'Jerusalem', God's people, will be protected by God as 'a wall of fire'.

At some point in this battle/cleansing/slaughter of the wicked, antitypical Judah will come into existence. It is antitypical Judah (i.e. the 144,000) over which antitypical David will first reign. When the message then goes to the rest of the world, antitypical Israel will come into existence and again the antitypical King David will rule over them until he hands the kingdom over to Christ. Elsewhere Houteff referred to the leaders of this antitypical Judah being 'like a hearth of fire among the wood and like a torch of fire in a sheaf' (Zech. 12.6). As we shall see, in later Branch Davidian theology this expectation is worked up considerably. According to Steve Schneider there would come a time when the people of God would burn like coals and yet not be consumed. Rather they would be able to destroy their enemies by touching them, for upon such a touch the enemy would burst into flames.

There is a good deal more in the work of Houteff that could usefully be explored here. However, though the detail is interesting, what he says elsewhere adds little to the general picture already gained. The conclusion, then, is plain: Victor Houteff, founder of the Davidian Seventh-day Adventists, expected that the kingdom would come with fire. This fire would accomplish at least two things: it would destroy God's enemies and at the same time refine God's faithful, who would emerge from the flames as silver refined in the furnace. While some of the detail of this changed between Houteff and Koresh, the basic scheme remains substantially intact: 'For, behold, the Lord will come with fire, and with his chariots like a whirlwind, to render his anger with fury, and his rebuke with flames of fire. For by fire and by his sword will the Lord plead with all flesh: and the slain of the Lord shall be many.' (Isa. 66.15–16.)

The extent to which the Davidians under Florence Houteff and the Branch Davidians under Ben Roden kept alive this expectation that the birth of the kingdom would be with fire is difficult to judge. There is nothing to suggest that it was important in Florence's eschatology. What is clear, however, is that Ben found a place for the burning up of Mt. Carmel. He had confidently announced this to the residents there in 1955 and on 11 October of that year had the TV on waiting for the news that it had happened.[12] Fire was important to him then, though not, as far as one can tell, in the same way that it was for Houteff.

However, when we get to Lois Roden the theme emerges again, and very strongly. This perhaps suggests that there was continuity on this point through the period of Florence and Ben Roden, even if that continuity is now undocumented. Lois's remarks on the fire issue are important. In fact in the immediate context of what happened on 19 April Lois may well have been a more important influence than Houteff; though to be sure she was aware of what had gone before her and referred frequently to Houteff on points relating to the cleansing/destroying fire. However, it was she and not Houteff who was Koresh's tutor. Neither ought it to be forgotten that she tutored others at Mt. Carmel, including Clive Doyle. Her influence was considerable on many points and her views on the fire ought therefore not to be passed over.

Some of what Lois had to say on the coming of the fire has been outlined briefly in Chapter Eight above. There it was noted that Lois put forward her views on the subject on one particular tape, and did so very forcefully.[13] There is no need to repeat that outline here except to note very briefly that, drawing on the work of Houteff, Lois Roden argued that Matthew 3.11–12 refers to a baptism to come which will be of fire and not water; it will be by immersion not sprinkling. This baptism, says Lois, will come upon Jerusalem, which for her meant Mt. Carmel. The fire that is to come, she states on the tape, is the gateway into the new kingdom and those who go through it are prepared for the transition thereby. The fire will also be a 'signal fire'. That is, it will attract the attention of the nations who will as a result flock towards it.

We turn now to the view of Steve Schneider. Schneider was an important figure in Koresh's Branch Davidianism and an individual whose views cannot be ignored. From the point of his conversion, Schneider became an able spokesperson for the Davidian cause and was kept busy in seeking to spread the word in Hawaii, Wisconsin, and England. In early 1990 Schneider visited Manchester where he succeeded in winning a number of converts, including five from one family. Some twenty British people died in the Waco fire, the majority from Manchester, and most, if not all, were recruited by Schneider. His influence within the movement, then, was great. He is frequently referred to as 'second in command' of the Koreshian Branch Davidian movement, and while this may not have been formally the case, it is almost certainly a fair reflection of what was happening on the ground. It was probably Schneider who shot Koresh at the end, a dramatic if gruesome pointer to the esteem in which he was held.

Fortunately for this research, several meetings Schneider conducted during the Manchester visit were recorded. This material amounts to about nine hours of very clear audio tapes and provides an excellent view of just what it was that the Branch Davidians thought was potentially appealing to would-be converts.[14] Schneider also played an absolutely key role during the negotiations with the FBI as the Waco siege progressed, and in fact it was he rather than Koresh who was the principal negotiator on the Branch Davidian side. He also appears frequently on the FBI bug tapes. We hence have quite a bit of first-hand information regarding his expectations of the end; from reviewing that material it is probably fair to say that his views on the coming of an eschatological fire were more pronounced than those of any other in the tradition, including Koresh himself.

Schneider's views come across very clearly indeed on the Manchester tapes. Summarizing the key points, it seems that he was of the opinion that this world was set for a cleansing by God (hardly a radical thought in the context of the movement). This cleansing would be total; it would cover the whole earth and eradicate all sin (and sinners). However, in keeping with the wider tradition Schneider took the view that God would not do everything at once. Rather, God would start in one particular place—'God's bit of real-estate' as Schneider often put it in the Manchester tapes—and from there spread out across the globe. This special place was known to some people, Schneider told his hearers, and known to him. And it is in this one place that the work of cleansing the earth will begin. Already a people are being gathered together there. Already a 'young man' is teaching there (Schneider clearly means David Koresh). This is no ordinary young man; in fact he is the 'young man' predicted in Zechariah 2.4, which reads 'And [an angel] said unto him, Run, speak to this young man, saying, Jerusalem shall be inhabited as towns without walls for the multitude of men and cattle therein'. The following verse is perhaps more important here: 'For I, saith the Lord, will be unto her a wall of fire round about, and will be the glory in the midst of her'.[15]

The thinking of Schneider regarding the coming of an eschatological fire is frequently set out on the tapes and what he has to say on the issue seems plain enough. Both the integrity of what he says (that is, the extent to which it agrees with itself) and the skill with which he put it across is impressive. He comes across as a preacher of real conviction. For Schneider there are no grey areas: if God said something will happen, then it will happen. So if God said he would be a wall of fire about Jerusalem, then that is what God will one day be; no ifs, no buts and no maybes.

Schneider's scheme is complex but understandable; in essence what he was expecting was what was already well known in the tradition as outlined above. His basic argument was that God would indeed cleanse his people by fire and that this cleansing would be the means by which the people of God would be made ready for entry into the kingdom (whether he thought that this was the baptism by fire spoken of by Houteff and Lois Roden is not clear in the sources that have survived).

Listening to the tapes, however, it is plain that Schneider took the tradition on somewhat and had a more developed view of the role these cleansed people of God would play in the bringing into existence of the kingdom of God. According to Schneider not only would this community be cleansed; they would be warriors in an avenging army that would wreak God's vengeance upon the earth. During their own cleansing, however, the people of God would die. Schneider did not pull back from this in any way. His statements are as clear as they are brutal. He did not argue that this was a spiritual death; for him the death that must be encountered is a literal earthly death that must come before the rebirth. At one point on the tapes his view is put very succinctly, stating that while the thought that he might have to die 'for a while' was scary, it was 'OK' with him since in the longer term he anticipated coming back riding on a white horse. The reference to the 'white horse' provides a way into Schneider's thinking here, for this and other statements on the tapes give some indication of the extent to which the book of Revelation informs what he has to say on these eschatological issues. Here he almost certainly has in mind the words of Revelation 6.2 and/or 19.11, which refer to a white horse and the rider thereof. In Branch Davidian sources these texts are themselves linked to Revelation 9.15–18:

And the number of the army of the horsemen were two hundred thousand thousand: and I heard the number of them. And thus I saw the horses in the vision, and them that sat on them, having breastplates of fire, and of jacinth, and brimstone: and the heads of the horses were as the heads of lions; and out of their mouths issued fire and smoke and brimstone. By these three was the third part of men killed, by the fire, and by the smoke, and by the brimstone, which issued out of their mouths (Revelation 9.15–18).

The rider on the white horse of Revelation 6.2/19.11 was seen as simply the leader of this army. This is Schneider's vision of the future for him and his fellow believers, and on the tapes he refers to the scheme a number of times. This is a major change in the tradition. God will still do the killing, but Koresh, Schneider, and the other faithful Branch Davidians will be instruments in God's hands and themselves take part in the slaughter. This is echoed again in the bug tapes where, as we saw, Schneider at one point (speaking of the FBI) said, 'Wait till I get my scrawny hands on your scrawny neck. I'm coming back and when I do you aren't gonna know where you're gonna be able to hide.' It is worth noting again that this portion of the tape is very clear.[16]

The reference to not knowing where to hide is probably also important. It may well be an echo of Revelation 6.16–17, which speaks of a time when the authorities of the earth will face the judgment of God and would say 'to the mountains and rocks, Fall on us, and hide us from the face of him that sitteth on the throne, and from the wrath of the Lamb: For the great day of his wrath is come; and who shall be able to stand?' This is during the period of the sixth seal (events for which Branch Davidians today are eagerly awaiting). The fifth seal, however, must come first and the events described be faced:

And when he had opened the fifth seal, I saw under the altar the souls of them that were slain for the word of God, and for the testimony which they held: And they cried with a loud voice, saying, How long, O Lord, holy and true, dost thou not judge and avenge our blood on them that dwell on the earth? And white robes were given unto every one of them; and it was said unto them, that they should rest yet for a little season, until their fellow servants also and their brethren, that should be killed as they were, should be fulfilled (Revelation 6.9–11).

Death will come. The souls must go under the altar. Those that 'should be killed' must be killed and thereby fulfill the condition only after which God will avenge the blood of the martyrs on the inhabitants of the earth. That number of 'fellow servants' is known. It is 200,000,000, the number of the army in Revelation 9.16.[17]

The question is how that death would come. Fire was certainly one possible means. We know for certain that one of those to whom Schneider was speaking on 18 April anticipated that he or she would be a 'charcoal briquette'. It may have been the same person, or perhaps another Mt. Carmel resident, who thought that 'there's nothing like a good fire to bring us to birth'.[18] Koresh too, as we shall see, also spoke of a time when the community must face death; that death might come, he said, in any one of a variety of ways. One of these was by being 'burnt'.[19] Hence fire was definitely on the agenda as one possible form that death would take.

Given the theological framework evident in Schneider's recorded statements (especially the Manchester tapes), it is not at all surprising that he seems not to have made any attempt to escape the fire. According to one unverifiable source his last words were, 'Come on, God where are you?' Shortly thereafter he took his own life using the method Kiri Jewell had spoken of on live TV: he put a gun in his mouth and fired upwards.[20] He was hence spared the pain of the flames, but probably went to his death in the full knowledge that the fire had been lit and that his body would soon be cleansed by it. He had said, very clearly, to his Manchester audience that he was anticipating death 'for a while', but looked forward to the resurrection that was soon to follow. When the time came he did not back down.

It is probable, though not certain, that it was Schneider who killed Koresh too. Koresh's body was found very near to Schneider's, and the shot that killed him was a low velocity gunshot wound, at close proximity, and direct to the head. This could have been self-administered, though given the weapon most probably involved (a rifle) this is unlikely: it is difficult, if not impossible, to shoot oneself in the forehead with a rifle. By the time he died Koresh had apparently been exposed already to smoke. He too knew that the fire had started and may well have instructed Schneider to spare him its ravages.[21]

There is little to admire in Schneider; if the tapes are anything to go by, he was looking forward with some relish to his part in the latter-day slaughter of the wicked. (At one point on the tapes he can be heard talking about how the enemy were going to 'crap their pants' when they saw the army of God coming, in a way that suggests he took some pleasure in the thought.) One cannot know precisely what he was thinking as he dispatched himself to the grave. Perhaps it was that he would soon be back to 'wring the scrawny necks' of the FBI.

To this point very little has been said about the views of David Koresh himself regarding the fire that would cleanse the people of God. This has been deliberate, for it is important to challenge the view that it was Koresh, and Koresh alone, who was uniquely responsible for the events of 19 April. To be sure he did have a part to play in preparing the people theologically for those events, but the view that it was he who was solely responsible for what happened is at the very least disputable. As we have seen, it had long been argued in the tradition to which Koresh belonged that the kingdom would be brought about only violently. The details did not remain constant as the tradition developed, but there can be no disputing that from Houteff to Koresh the view was that at the point at which the kingdom was set up there would be a slaughter of those who had rejected the message and at the same time a 'baptism by fire' for the righteous. The baptism would be literal, total, and by immersion. Earlier in the tradition this baptism by fire seems not to be seen as resulting in the deaths of those who underwent it. Schneider, however, and, as we shall see, Koresh too, went further. Death was the means of rebirth. The faithful would have to 'die for a while'.

Like all the others in the tradition Koresh argued that those who were faithful would receive a great reward. However, before that day there would be a time of great distress. Koresh himself would be killed. The community would suffer, the fifth seal would be opened and the souls would go under the altar. They would soon return as an avenging army when the sixth seal opened:

And I beheld when he had opened the sixth seal, and, lo, there was a great earthquake; and the sun became black as sackcloth of hair, and the moon became as blood; And the stars of heaven fell unto the earth, even as a fig tree casteth her untimely figs, when she is shaken of a mighty wind. And the heaven departed as a scroll when it is rolled together; and every mountain and island were moved out of their places. And the kings of the earth, and the great men, and the rich men, and the chief captains, and the mighty men, and every bondman, and every free man, hid themselves in the dens and in the rocks of the mountains; And said to the mountains and rocks, Fall on us, and hide us from the face of him that sitteth on the throne, and from the wrath of the Lamb: For the great day of his wrath is come; and who shall be able to stand? (Rev. 6.12–17.)

Koresh's views on the necessity of death as a means by which the faithful could gain a new status before God, go under the altar, and then return as the events of the sixth seal unfolded are reflected in a number of sources. Reference has already been made to a number of these earlier in this book and a careful analysis of such sources as the negotiation tapes will reveal more. However, on one occasion Koresh seems to have been particularly clear on this issue. This was when he delivered a particularly direct sermon at Mt. Carmel a week before the final day of the siege. Unfortunately the sermon itself was not recorded; however, it is possible to reconstruct at least some of what was said since it was the subject of conversation inside Mt. Carmel, some of which was picked up on the bug tapes. For example, at one point on the tapes Scott Sonobe is heard summarizing what David Koresh had said:

And that's because everybody here when...whether by tanks, fire, bullets, or being taken out of here as living wave sheaf. You know he says those four things, and I'm going 'Well. You know there always hope—hope upon hope. And he brought that up too. But you know the whole thing really revolved around travailing—to give birth. That's for everybody here. Having given birth to an experience that is on and about the truth. He said whether we like it or not. You're impregnated. You're going to bring forth a baby because it's too late to turn back. That's basically what he said. 'Ask any of these girls what it feels like to have a kid.' He goes, 'OK girls. Tell 'em. Do you feel like you're gonna make it when you have a kid?' And they go, 'No. It feels like you're gonna die.' He goes, 'Exactly. Your flesh is gonna go through that. You're gonna get to the point where you see no way out—you know you're gonna die, and then your gonna trust God. Even if it's the last second before the tank hits you. Even if it's a foot away and you go 'God!' Even if it's for a second—the last second before it runs you over, or you burn, or you get shot or whatever. You're gonna bring forth, buddy'.[22]

Fairly clearly Koresh was expecting some sort of major confrontation in which the Branch Davidians may well be called upon to die for their faith, though interestingly he seemed to think that some at least would be taken out of Mt. Carmel as a 'living wave sheaf' and presumably escape death itself. For the majority, however, death awaits, and might well come as a result of fire. He refers explicitly to the possibility that some might be burnt. However, and this is important in the light of what actually happened on 19 April, this was but one way that death might come to the faithful: other methods by which death might come include being run over by a tank or getting shot. The important thing it seems was the acceptance of death, in whatever form it came, as the way to glorify God. In that second or two before death there would be a moment that would give the opportunity for life-giving faith. In the few seconds between knowing for sure that death was about to embrace the believer and that death actually coming there would be the opportunity for absolute pure faith. As the believer looks down the barrel of the gun, sees the approaching tank tracks, or feels the heat of the flames upon the skin, he or she can now rely totally on God and on God alone. The believer accepts God's way not knowing for sure, but believing wholeheartedly, that God will not forget the faithful who go into death, but will reward them for what they have done.

Elsewhere in Koresh's teaching it is possible to gain a more rounded view of just what he expected to happen. There are further indications that he thought that the exit of the faithful from Mt. Carmel would not be a simple matter of walking out of the door. For example, on the KRLD tape (the one recorded on the night of 28 February) he made several statements indicating what was going on in his mind. As has been noted above, at one point on the tape Koresh stated unequivocally 'I am going home... I'm going back to my Father'. Earlier he had talked about how he, as Christ, would be struck again, as predicted in the actions of Moses in Numbers 20.11. 'Christ should not have to die again,' he said, but the implication is that he would. Further, Koresh said, 'As I said to my disciples in Matt. 24 where the carcase would be [there will the eagles be gathered together]'. Already on the night of the ATF raid death is in the air at Mt. Carmel. The events of the fifth seal are now being opened up. 'People are going to lose their lives over this.'[23] Koresh was clear on this: 'we're in the fifth seal right now'. But the sixth seal was about to open and he would be back. There is a basic consistency here with the views of Schneider. The faithful will depart to God and then return in some other form. (And to repeat, with Koresh it seems to be the departure and not the mode by which one is dispatched that is important.)

Also on the KRLD tape we hear Koresh talking about being 'taken up' by God, quoting Psalm 27.10 to prove his point: 'When my father and my mother forsake me, then the Lord will take me up.' Koresh was not going out, he was going up. A little later in the siege (on 7 March) Koresh was speaking to a member of the negotiating team. The subject under discussion was the situation that the FBI and the Branch Davidians were facing, and Koresh was linking what is happening to numerous biblical prophecies. He then said, 'Look at this world we're coming out of. We're getting out of here, friend. You can stay back here and die if you want to, but we're not going to.'[24] Koresh was saying (and this time he included his co-religionists too) that he was set to depart the world.[25]

So how would this departure, this 'going up', take place? Might it be that, as with the ascension of Jesus, a cloud would come and transport the Branch Davidians to their (temporary) celestial home? The answer must be 'no', for as we have seen both Schneider and Koresh reckoned seriously with the reality of their own deaths and those of the other members of the community (though at one point Koresh was at least open to the possibility that some might be taken as a 'living wave sheaf'). The departure would be violent.

There is much in the negotiation tapes that points in this direction, but one very clear example comes on NT 75, a tape recorded on 7 March from

12.31–1.18 a.m. (the lateness of the hour perhaps explains why the negotiator did not pick up the danger signals). Koresh is talking on the tape about the status of himself and his co-believers as 'the apple of God's eye' and then accuses the negotiator of trying to poke God in the eye by harming his remnant. But God would not stand for it, says Koresh, and would:

shake [his] hand upon them and they shall be a spoil to their servants. Like in the Book of Nahum. The belligerent power comes in to scatter, you know, and God's people were there at the mercy of God because they in—like in Psalms 18, they're too strong for us. What happens is God intervenes and makes an example of the belligerent power, brings that nation to an end and all other nations realize that there is a living and true God.

Koresh then goes on to say that this relates to Psalm 18:

Now, so we know the Father's going to rise up off his throne, don't we? Like in Psalms 18. Now, we know this man on the red horse was Christ before he became flesh. We know that the subject is God's still going to rule in Jerusalem, but one of the signs is going to be, he's going to be a wall of fire around about Jerusalem. We need to know about it ahead of time.

This is fairly dense material, but with a bit of effort one can see the big picture that emerges from the detail. The basic parts of Koresh's narrative are that he and the other Branch Davidians were preparing to 'get out of here' by going to the Father. That departure would be marked by violence and entail the deaths of many, if not all, of the faithful (some might be taken up alive). At that time God would be a 'wall of fire' around Jerusalem and destroy those who are seeking to scatter the faithful.[26] The purpose of their destruction is that they will be a sign to the rest of the nations who will 'realize that there is a living and true God'. At what point exactly the events of Matthew 24 take place is unclear, but it will be soon ('like I say the next thing that you will see according to Matt. 24 is the Son of Man').

Some of what Koresh taught on the coming of death to the community, which might be by fire but could be by other means is, then, fairly easy to reconstruct from Koresh himself. Other material is found in reports of what Koresh had said by other Branch Davidians, such as Sonobe's summary of Koresh's sermon picked up by the bug tapes. Further, Branch Davidian survivor Marjorie Thomas also remembered that David Koresh had once stated in a Bible study that fire would be the means by which the faithful would ascend to heaven. What she said was that during the Bible study (at which she was present) Koresh had said that fire would transcend[27] the Branch Davidians to heaven during the 'battle' with Babylon, and that, further, Koresh considered the US government to be Babylon.[28] Similarly, survivor Kathy Schroeder recalled that, shortly after the confrontation with the ATF on 28 February, Koresh told the Branch Davidians he had a dream that they would burn in a great fire, their skin would burn off, and they would 'transcend' to heaven.[29] There is also the widely reported incident that on 16 April, a Branch Davidian (it is not clear who) held a sign outside a window of the complex that read 'the flames await: Isaiah 13'. That was the text that came to Schneider's mind when he looked out of the window on 18 April and saw the FBI clearing away obstacles from the front of Mt. Carmel.

More could certainly be said regarding the biblical-interpretative context of the probable actions of some of the Branch Davidians on 19 April. As was argued in the previous chapter, the fire was most likely started by the Branch Davidians themselves and not by the FBI either by intent or by accident. Why did they do it? Because they had been theologically primed (which is not the same as brainwashed) to expect such a conflagration and looked upon it as a means by which they would enter into the kingdom. These were desperate times: the enemy was at the gate. Tear gas was coming through the windows while tanks demolished parts of 'God's bit of real estate'. One cannot know precisely what went through the mind of Koresh, Schneider, Cohen, Sonobe, and the others as the decision was taken to 'light the fire'. In all probability they would have preferred to wait for God to strike the match, but time was rapidly running out. What was called for was not cowardice and surrender to the beast, but loyalty to God and a determination to stick with him no matter what. Perhaps this was the final test. Perhaps matters had to be taken into the Branch Davidians' own hands. Perhaps, as Swett has put it, it was time for 'the ultimate act of faith'.

This act of faith was a communal one. We do not know precisely how many Branch Davidians were involved in the actions that appear to have led to the fire. We do know, however, that it was not just a small group, but the membership as a whole, who knew that they would one day be called upon to die for their faith. The commitment of the group was not just to Koresh, although of course he was an extremely influential figure and it might well have been within his power to steer the community along another course. Thus had he suddenly said, 'the period of waiting of over—it is time for the Babylonish captivity to begin' (cf. Jer. 20.6), and walked out of the door, he might well have taken all the other community members with him. However, there is much about Branch Davidianism, even the Branch Davidianism during the period of Koresh's leadership, that can only be understood if one sees it not as a personality cult, but as a fully functioning interpretative community. A failure to do this was a big mistake on the part of the FBI negotiators. It was an error for the 'HRT' (Hostage Rescue Team) to be rapidly deployed and become the driving force in deciding upon and putting into practice the tactics. There was no point trying to drive wedges between Koresh and the other members of the group. To be sure the Koreshian Branch Davidians were committed to him as leader and prophet. However, an even stronger allegiance in Mt. Carmel was that of all those inside, including Koresh, to the vision of the coming of the new kingdom. As we have seen, the expectation that the kingdom would be brought into existence violently had long been held in Davidianism and Branch Davidianism, even if views regarding the level, extent, scope and agency of that violence were subject to development. Specifically, the coming of a fire that would effect the cleansing of the faithful can be found firmly embedded within Branch Davidianism well before Koresh came on the scene. Lois Roden had said the kingdom would be entered through a portal of fire and Houteff too had spoken of this 'baptism' that was to come. Schneider did not draw back from the implications in what he told would-be converts and we know for a fact, since we have the tapes and they are clear, that the Manchester converts were told by him that death would come their way if they decided to join the movement. The act of faith was then a communal one and not just Koresh's. To argue otherwise is seriously to misunderstand how this group functioned. To misunderstand this group is to risk not learning 'the lessons of Waco' (as the learning process argued for here is so often referred to in other literature), and to do that is to invite further catastrophe in the future.

NOTES

1. *Final Report*, Appendix C 98. See also plate 11 and note the testimony of McGee given at the Civil Trial: 'Q: I'm showing you Government's Exhibit 1451. Can you tell us what's happening there?' 'A: Right here I have Ruth Riddle and I'm carrying her out of the compound.'

2. James Trimm, 'Fire in Branch Davidian Theology', an unpublished, undated paper, a copy of which is in my possession.

3. During the first of these three purifications by fire, the sword would also be used as an instrument of destruction. See further below.

4. SDA views on the millennium are discussed in Kenneth G. C. Newport, 'The Heavenly Millennium of Seventh-day Adventism', in Stephen Hunt, ed., *Christian Millennialism* (Indiana: Indiana University Press, 2001), 131–48.

5. Houteff refers to this period a number of times, e.g. in *All Things New*, 36. It is clear that at least some of this was still taught in Koresh's Davidianism, since this 100-year post-millennial, pre-second-death period was specifically mentioned to me in an interview with Derek Lovelock.

6. Houteff, *All Things New*, 38.

7. 12 SC 6–7, 4–5.
8. 12 *SC* 6–7, 9.
9. Houteff, 'Baptism with Water, Baptism with Fire and the Lord's Supper', 12 *SC* 6–7, 3–19.
10. 12 *SC* 6–7, 9–10.
11. 1 *TG* 19, 3.
12. See Chapter Six.
13. The tape was recorded on 21 Mar. 1978 at the Mt. Carmel centre. A copy is in my personal possession.
14. Copies of these tapes are in my personal possession. They may be accessed too in TXC.
15. Koresh himself also claimed to be the 'young man' of Zech. 2.4, e.g. on the tape 'The Bird', where he stated unequivocally that he, the young man, went to Israel in 1985 and measured the temple (cf. Zech. 2.1–2).
16. See Chapter Fourteen.
17. David Koresh also mentioned the army of 200 million horsemen several times during the negotiations (examples are found on NT 10a, 47, 80, 81).
18. See Chapter Fourteen.
19. See below.
20. *Final Report*, Appendix J 50.
21. Ibid. 52.
22. FBI bug tape, 13 April, SA 72–14.
23. KRLD tape.
24. NT 85 (7 March).
25. It would be a mistake to think that Koresh came to this view only during the siege. Elsewhere in his taped messages he refers to the necessity of his own death. He had come to this view several years before.
26. Cf. Zech. 2.
27. The word might have been 'translate', which is commonly used in SDA circles when speaking of the departure of the faithful from this world to be with Christ during the millennial period in heaven.
28. *Final Report* 16.
29. Ibid.

16

'Prophecies shall Fail' (cf. 1 Corinthians 13.8): Post-1993 Branch Davidianism

In the spring of 1993 the Branch Davidian movement suffered a truly catastrophic sequence of events. By the time those events concluded, more than eighty members of the group were dead. Among the dead were most of the key players, including David Koresh himself.

Public interest is notoriously fickle and it was not long after the fire that the attention of the general public was lost. 'Waco' had come and gone and it was time for the press and other media to move on. From time to time, of course, what had happened at Waco did come back into the news. The several attempts by Branch Davidian families and survivors to progress an unlawful killing suit through the US courts were occasionally reported by the international media,[1] while the annual memorial services at Mt. Carmel also gained some press attention, albeit primarily local.

By far the most dramatic re-entrance of Waco and the Branch Davidians into public consciousness was on 19 April 1995, when, precisely two years after the Waco fire, Timothy McVeigh bombed the Alfred P. Murrah Building in Oklahoma City. The link between this outrage and the events in Waco two years earlier is direct. McVeigh is known to have been very concerned about the actions of the government at Waco, and to have taken part in some of the anti-government meetings that quickly became focused on what happened at Mt. Carmel. At one such meeting he was inadvertently caught on camera by an amateur photographer, sitting on the bonnet of a car handing out the now famous 'is your Church ATF approved' bumper stickers.[2] It is reported that after his arrest McVeigh told two persons at the prison in which he was being held that he had been motivated to set the Oklahoma bomb by the events of Waco and Ruby Ridge (where the wife and child of Randy Weaver, a right-wing extremist, had been shot dead by government agents). He also gave this motive in a letter to Fox News. In that letter McVeigh also said that he considered assassinating Janet Reno and Judge Walter Smith—the Waco connection is obvious.[3] Later, as McVeigh's scheduled execution date of 16 May 2001 drew near, Waco and the Branch Davidians again hit the headlines as documentaries detailing McVeigh's crime sought to explain his motives. Such events, however, came and went and soon Waco slipped again into the background of public consciousness.

For the surviving Branch Davidians themselves, and the families and friends of the dead, however, the events of February to April 1993 could not be so quickly forgotten. The ways in which the families and friends sought to cope with the loss of those they held dear would be well worth detailed examination, not just from a purely academic but also from a pastoral perspective. This is not the concern of the present chapter, however. Rather, a brief account is given of how the Branch Davidian movement itself has sought to come to terms with the events of 1993. As we shall see, the picture is by no means uniform; different sections of Branch Davidianism have reacted in quite different ways. Neither has the movement remained static; there have been new converts, albeit on a very small scale. But while numerically the movement may now be judged to be insignificant, as a case study, the developments that have taken place within it since 1993 are illuminating. Just how has this disappointed, not to say devastated, religious group sought to come to terms with its crisis? How successful have such attempts been? And what, if anything, can those interested in tracking such troubled religious trajectories learn about the mutability of religious communities?

The attempt by surviving Branch Davidians to come to terms with the severe cognitive dissonance (not to mention in many cases considerable physical hardship) that 19 April 1993 brought with it began almost immediately. Members of the group sought to explain to themselves and to others why it was that God's remnant people, the Branch Davidian community, had been all but wiped from the face of the earth. The problem was severe; David Koresh, the Lamb of Revelation 5 and the mighty angel of Revelation 14, lay dead. The chances of the new kingdom now coming, one would think, had become remote. This was not, however, how the survivors saw things.

Without doubt the process of coming to terms with what happened was facilitated by some aspects of Koresh's theology, which left considerable room for manoeuvre. For example, when Koresh died no final, fixed date for the Apocalypse was in place. To be sure specific events were anticipated, but no definite timescale for their occurrence had actually been given. There was hence no make or break point for the community; no point beyond which they could not feasibly go. The crisis that hit the movement post-1993 was hence theologically unlike what their spiritual father, the Davidian Seventh-day Adventist movement, had suffered in 1959, although it was on a larger scale in terms of the percentage loss of membership. As we have seen, Florence Houteff had confidently predicted that the battle of Armageddon, and probably the resurrection of her husband, would occur on 22 April that year. She had set a definite date. Koresh, on the other hand, had not been so rash. He had left some credible prophetic space for the post-1993 Branch Davidians to inhabit without their having to go through exegetical gymnastics of too great an order.

It was potentially helpful also that some of the things Koresh and other leading figures in the movement had said before 1993 were capable of being interpreted as finding fulfilment rather than contradiction in the events of that year. For example, on numerous occasions Koresh had said that it was his role to die.[4] For a long time he thought that this death, and that of his followers, would be in Jerusalem. On one study tape he can be heard to say:

After the [fourth] seal is the fifth seal. The thing that seals every last one of us is death. So do you wanna be sealed? It's because—you go to Israel and you get killed. That's your seal of approval. They loved not their lives unto death. Right? We're gonna have to first kick some butt, buy and sell, and death and hell will—follow to the world. And the world ain't gonna do a thing about it. The guys that are with me—we're gonna bust the city down aren't we? Right, guys? We're gonna die, right?[5]

However, it is clear on the negotiation tapes that Koresh adjusted this expectation in the light of the events that had come upon the community, and began to speak about the death he would now suffer in Waco. In any case, on the most basic point, that Koresh had died, the post-1993 Branch Davidian community could and did refer back to Koresh's own statements about himself and from them build up a biblically saturated account of how prophecy clearly shows that Koresh was to die and would subsequently rise again. One can see examples of this in numerous sources.[6] This is not simply a case of the community claiming things about Koresh that have no basis in what he actually said in an effort to release the pressure of the cognitive dissonance. Koresh said that he would die, and he did—his prophecy was fulfilled. Further, the fact that he died at the age of thirty-three and around Passover time could be seen as prophetically encouraging. Jesus had also died at this age and at this time of year. Koresh was hence in chronological step with Jesus. There is no evidence to suggest that Koresh actually manipulated events so that he would die at thirty-three; it was probably just a coincidence. For the theological well-being of those Branch Davidians who did not die in the Mt. Carmel fire, however, it was a fortunate one.

There were of course some more difficult obstacles to negotiate, and adjustments needed to be made in the light of what had happened. How could it be, for example, that not all of the community had been killed? If the fire that razed Mt. Carmel to the ground was the cleansing fire that had been expected, why had not all be cleansed? And, as time wore on, the obviously linked question needed to be addressed: how could the present delay in the coming of the kingdom be explained? But difficult as these questions were, they were not so problematic as to mean that the surviving group had no option but to abandon its core beliefs, and quite quickly some moderately successful theological salvage operations were begun. Some further details on the forms these took are given later in this chapter.

Despite outward appearances, then, it was relatively easy for the faithful Branch Davidians to detect God's hand at work in the tragic events that had taken place. God had not planned it, but he had predicted it thousands of years ago and hence could be seen to be in control. This apparent fulfilment of prophecy has been the source of some considerable strength to post-1993 Branch Davidians, and given rise to optimism. Not only does it explain the past, it gives hope for the future and enables the believers to pin-point their place on the eschatological timescale and hence sustain a level of expectation as a result.

Such expectation, sometimes intense, fervent, and sharply focused, is seen throughout the post-1993 Branch Davidian tradition. For example, in conversation with two Branch Davidians in Manchester, UK, the topic of where precisely the Branch Davidians consider the world to be on the prophetic timetable came up.[7] It was clear that this was an issue of great importance to them, and the conversation was excited. It was clear also that they had a very precise view, based upon the belief that the events at Waco could be seen in scripture and that what was now soon to take place could also be seen there. Particular attention was drawn to the fifth and sixth seals, which were read out from a heavily marked Bible. (This conversation took place in a restaurant, but the Bible was produced from the pocket of one of the believers the moment it was needed.) The fifth seal, they said, described what had happened on 19 April:

When he opened the fifth seal, I saw under the altar the souls of those who had been slaughtered for the word of God and for the testimony they had given; they cried out with a loud voice, 'Sovereign Lord, holy and true, how long will it be before you judge and avenge our blood on the inhabitants of the earth?' They were each given a white robe and told to rest a little longer, until the number would be complete both of their fellow servants and of their brothers and sisters, who were soon to be killed as they themselves had been killed. (Rev. 6.9–11.)

But the conversation moved on quickly. The next event was the sixth seal. That text was read out too:

When he opened the sixth seal, I looked, and there came a great earthquake; the sun became black as sackcloth, the full moon became like blood, and the stars of the sky fell to the earth as the fig tree drops its winter fruit when shaken by a gale. The sky vanished like a scroll rolling itself up, and every mountain and island was removed from its place. Then the kings of the earth and the magnates and the generals and the rich and the powerful, and everyone, slave and free, hid in the caves and among the rocks of the mountains, calling to the mountains and rocks, 'Fall on us and hide us from the face of the one seated on the throne and from the wrath of the Lamb; for the great day of their wrath has come, and who is able to stand?' (Rev. 6.12–17.)

This is the event for which some in the tradition are waiting. It is also of course anticipated by literally millions of other prophecy believers in the world today, especially, perhaps, in the United States. But there is a big difference. Outside the Branch Davidian tradition the Lamb here spoken of is Christ, who will one day return to destroy evil and take the faithful to himself. According to the two Branch Davidians in Manchester, however, the Lamb is David Koresh and the event here spoken of is the same as that in Revelation 9.16ff. This is a picture, so they argue, of the return of those they lost at Waco, and indeed all who have been slain for the Word of God (200,000,000 in total). They are led by Koresh on a white horse—the 'King of Kings and the Lord of Lords.'[8]

The expectation that Koresh would return is not without focus. There have even been some precise dates set.[9] The first of these fell in December 1996, a date worked out on the basis of Daniel 12.12, which speaks of a period of 1,335 days.[10] Some surviving Branch Davidians took this to mean that 1,335 days after the death of David Koresh, he would return. But nothing happened: the December date simply came and went. The response to the failure of the prophecy was not uniform. Some simply saw this as a test that God had set to try the faith of those who claimed to believe in him. There was another reaction that was equally predictable: a recalculation. Among those who adopted this position attention settled on Daniel 8.14 and the 2,300 days mentioned there. This text had long been important in the tradition; it was primarily (though not exclusively) on the basis of this text that Miller came to the view that Jesus was to return to this earth in October 1844. However, some of the post-1993 Branch Davidians took an entirely different view. According to them the text spoke not of the chronological distance between the decree of Artaxerxes that Jerusalem should be rebuilt and the return of Jesus (measured in so many literal days as prophetic years), but of a literal period of 2,300 days between the death of David Koresh and his return. This pushed the date to late August 1999.[11]

There is here the formula for disaster. It should be remembered that the Branch Davidians placed great emphasis upon the working out of the seven seals, and according to them the world is currently placed somewhere between seals five and six. Further, the fifth seal states that before God will 'avenge our blood on the inhabitants of the earth' something further must happen: the 'number' must be complete. This number is that of 'their fellow servants' and 'their brothers and sisters who were soon to be killed as they themselves had been killed' (Rev. 6.10–11). The logic is plain: before Koresh returns all of his followers must die and go under the altar as he did. Only then could they receive the white robes necessary for salvation.

The extent to which the biblical text has exerted an influence here is worth considering. The KJV clearly says that the 'fellow servants' will be 'killed'. There is a huge potential difference between being killed and dying. Had the text read differently, events in August 1999 might have run a different course; one cannot say for sure. In the event, however, August 1999 like December 1996 passed without event. For several years the only discernible response from those who had focused attention on the date was silence.

It is perhaps surprising to outsiders that anyone has the sheer spiritual energy to go on with this sort of thinking. However, as we have learnt from Festinger and the work done in response to that now classic (if disputed) study, believers who have as much at stake as the Branch Davidians will seldom simply admit defeat.[12] Those who did not die in the fire themselves nevertheless lost a great deal: family, friends, leader, home, and, in some cases, many years of their lives now to be spent in prison. Anyone who has invested so much in a belief system is very unlikely to give it up easily. To do so would be to undervalue what has already been committed and to say, in effect, that the deaths of family and friends were futile.

It is perhaps this kind of pressure that puts into context the views of Livingstone Fagan regarding the non-appearance of Koresh on the 1996 date.[13] It would be easy to mock his remarks, but one has to remember where he is coming from. His wife is dead, his mother is dead, his children are several thousand miles away and at the time he wrote he was serving a forty-year prison sentence (now reduced to fifteen). When questioned specifically on the 'failure' of the prophecy that Koresh would return in 1996, the answer he gave was ingenious. The failure of Koresh to return as prophesied, he stated, was completely in accord with the Bible. After all, 1 Corinthians 13.8 states quite unequivocally that 'prophecies shall fail'. An example of this was Koresh's non-appearance on the prophesied date—which according to Fagan's logic was a case of the prophecy being wrong, not of a human misunderstanding of what the prophecy actually said. The failure of the 1,335 days prophecy fulfilled the one that says that 'prophecies shall fail'. Fagan went on to say that this was a time of great testing of the faithful. He likened it to Noah getting into the Ark and waiting seven days for it to rain.[14] There was nothing to sustain Noah and his family during this period but faith that God would do what he said he would do. In the same way during this waiting period the Branch Davidians must rely solely upon God; and show that they can do this even without the focus that prophecy can give.

Theologically, then, the fact that Koresh fell into the category of a 'dead Messiah who did not come back' appears not to have been a theological impasse for the movement. There were ways of coming to terms with this without abandoning core beliefs or group identity. In fact seen from a purely theological point of view one might reasonably have expected that the Branch Davidians would have undergone a period of significant growth during the 1990s when events were fresh in the minds of potential converts. The leader was dead, but that could be shown to be just how it was supposed to be according to God's prophecies, and the next event was any time now. An even more finely tuned sense of eschatological urgency would, one would think, drive the group on. Perhaps God had given further time for repentance, perhaps he had exercised more mercy than justice, or perhaps he had allowed human frailty to misunderstand the clear revelation of scripture in order to test, and thereby strengthen, the faith of those he had chosen. And in addition, of course, as the 1990s progressed and the new millennium dawned there were some hard facts that supported Branch Davidian claims. Key among these were the developing crisis in the Middle East in general and, more specifically, the events of 9/11 and the war in Iraq. While it is true that many eschatologically focused groups look in a general way to the Middle East as the place where the events leading to the coming of Christ will begin, the Davidians and Branch Davidians have always had a very finely tuned expectation in this regard. From the beginning the Davidians/Branch Davidians have confidently predicted that there will be a war in the Middle East and that this will involve America (identified as the 'King of the North' spoken of in the book of Daniel). Koresh himself spoke very clearly about this; about the 'good old American boys' with their 'Budweiser and mom's apple-pie' being in the Middle East making war, an event to occur shortly before the coming of the kingdom.[15]

Theologically then the Branch Davidian movement is easily sustainable. It is very easy to see ways in which the Branch Davidians could, and in fact do, extricate themselves from the difficulties of their position. If, as will be here suggested, this movement is coming to an end, it will not be for theological reasons. Movements such as this do not collapse as a result of theological incongruity. Other factors must be sought.

In this context the sheer scale of what happened ought not to be forgotten. The Davidian/Branch Davidian movement has never been numerically great. Even if we trace the trajectory back to what may well have been its high point (before the 'Branch' movement as a separate entity as born), the numbers are comparatively small. About 1,000 Davidian Seventh-day Adventists turned up at Mt. Carmel in the run-up to 22 April 1959, and from then on the direction was probably downwards. The literal loss of blood at Mt. Carmel was simply too great for the corporate body to sustain and it became terminally anaemic. Add to this the fact that those inside Mt. Carmel were the key players, Koresh among them obviously, and one can appreciate that the situation was serious indeed.

Perhaps the single most important factor in what was to become the break up and eventual (one suspects) collapse of Branch Davidianism was the lack of a strong leadership once Koresh was dead. Here it was particularly problematic for the movement that Steve Schneider, the one person who might have emerged as heir apparent had he survived, also died. In fact, in post-1993 Branch Davidianism no real prophet has arisen, or at least none widely accepted.[16] As a consequence the leadership of the movement has become weak and fragmented.

One person who can justifiably be called a leader, but not a prophet, is Clive Doyle (see plate thirteen). Doyle had long been associated with the Branch Davidian movement and had played a key role under Lois Roden. He survived the fire, albeit with some serious burns; he also survived the trial and was released from jail. As much by default as by specific intent he became the spokesperson of the survivors who have remained in the Waco area. Doyle claims no prophetic status. In a sense he is a caretaker, both quite literally of the Mt. Carmel property (the legal ownership of which has been the subject of much dispute) and in seeking to sustain the spiritual life of the small group of believers in Waco who have remained faithful to the message. His presence at Mt. Carmel has been constant since his release from jail; it was he (together with one or two others) who was responsible for the Waco visitors' centre now housed in a small wooden building to the right of the main entrance. Doyle has also seen the rebuilding of a Branch Davidian church at the Mt. Carmel site, an impressive achievement for such a shattered community. Services are held there on some Saturdays; it is the site too of the memorial services that take place each 19 April, and, beginning in 2003, each 28 February. Numbers are small; probably less that a dozen regulars, with perhaps as many as two dozen normally turning up for the memorial services on 19 April.[17]

Interviews with Doyle in fact suggest something of a waning of eschatological interest. It is also apparent that as time has passed he has come to see the message of Koresh as very much related to the context in which it was delivered. There is a definite sense that Doyle is more interested in telling the story of how things were rather than how they will be. At the tenth anniversary memorial service he publicly lamented the fact that there seemed (to him) to be fewer and fewer Branch Davidians in attendance each year. Some of course have died. Doyle lost his own mother the previous year. In late 2003

Tillie Friesen died. She was the widow of Raymond Friesen, who died in the fire, and at ninety-six was the oldest Branch Davidian alive. Doyle's group, then, gives the definite sense of being in decline. It has reached a point where memorials are more important than missions.

If there is a waning of eschatological expectation in what Doyle has to say, there is not a hint of it, nor any question over the continuing validity of the message of David Koresh, discernible in the work of Livingstone Fagan. (Although at Mt. Carmel on 28 February, Fagan left before the end of the siege.) A careful analysis of his theological work does, however, reveal a definite shift, a shift that might be important for the future of the movement, if it has one, and also as a contemporary example of how some leader-focused religious traditions can develop. Since April 1993 Fagan could reasonably be said to be the most important theological spokesperson for what Gallagher rightly described as 'Koreshian orthodoxy'.[18] His literary output has been significant.[19]

Fagan's writings employ the same style as that so familiar in the work of Koresh. Long quotations from the Bible, sometimes whole chapters, are interspersed with comments on what to Fagan's mind is the text's self-evident meaning. Much of what he has to say is by way of seeking better understanding of the content of the faith already received. However, his work also exhibits some significant development of the tradition, for in it one can discern an increased emphasis upon Koresh the person as opposed to Koresh's message. In other words in Fagan's writings the proclaimer is becoming the proclaimed.

To be sure there is continuity here. Koresh did see himself as important; he even thought that his importance was not just in the message he had to give, but in his person. Indeed, he thought that he was in some way ontologically related to Jesus, though from the evidence that has survived he did not have a very well developed view on this. Nevertheless, for the most part he put great stress on the fact that he was a messenger with a message, even if he seldom got down to saying what that message was (at least in the surviving material). It is the importance of the message that gives importance to the messenger, and hence his importance is more functional than ontological. However, Fagan seems increasingly to be giving Koresh—as person rather than as messenger—a key place in God's plans. In one place, for example, Fagan, picking up on things Koresh said about himself, goes into some significant detail about how according to Numbers 20.11 Moses struck the rock not once but twice and how in 1 Corinthians 10.4 Paul says explicitly that the rock that Moses struck was 'Christ'. The rock was struck twice, reasons Fagan, and hence Christ must also be struck twice: once on the cross and once at Waco. Koresh said something very like this on the KRLD tape. However, Fagan is

PLATE 13 Clive Doyle, survivor of the fire and effective leader of the Waco-based post-1993 Branch Davidians

much clearer than Koresh was regarding the reason for the latter's death: like Jesus, Koresh was a bearer of our sins. Later Fagan also says that the two goats from the Day of Atonement ceremony foreshadow God's plans. The first is a type of Christ, the second, the one led away into the wilderness, is Koresh.[20] There is a good deal more of this sort of thing in what Fagan has to say, but it is unnecessary to explore it further here as the trend has already been indicated: Fagan puts greater and greater stress on who Koresh was/is and what he did (die for our sins) than on what he said.[21]

Fagan is also important in another way. He does not have a group of his own in any identifiable sense, but it is clear that many Branch Davidians do look to him for theological guidance. It is common when talking to Branch Davidians both in the UK and elsewhere for his name to crop up and for the believers to be in contact with him. Many of his letters (he is a prolific writer) are heavily theological in nature, but some are in fact very pastoral, as he seeks to encourage the surviving Branch Davidians to keep in contact with one another and with him and to maintain the faith.[22] When he is released it will be very interesting to see what effect he will have on the group to which he has remained committed during the past very difficult decade, a good deal of which he seems to have spent in solitary confinement.

Neither Doyle nor Fagan have claimed the prophet's mantle. Renos Avraam, on the other hand, has. Avraam, who is from the UK, though of Greek origin, began claiming the prophetic status soon after the events of April 1993. He was convicted of various offences and sentenced to a long prison term, now reduced to fifteen years. It was, in all probability, he who was responsible for a very large two-volume Branch Davidian work that was for a while available on the internet.[23] According to Avraam he is now the 'chosen vessel', Koresh's rightful successor, and it is through him that the final message will come. The claim is made frequently in Avraam's writings. As far as can be ascertained, the group led by Avraam is very small indeed; attempts to contact him have gone unanswered.

Like a number of other Branch Davidians, Avraam was clearly looking forward to Koresh's return in 1999; the date is easily arrived at by following the exegetical logic found in the books that Avraam (almost certainly) wrote. It is also stated in those sources that the 'rest of the bride' (which means the surviving Branch Davidians) would have to be killed before Koresh's return. When this did not happen the group said nothing. Avraam's group is out of tune with some other Branch Davidian factions, as a letter written to Avraam by Waco survivor Catherine Matteson clearly shows.[24] The Manchester Branch Davidians also appear sceptical of Avraam's claims.

After a period of relative inactivity, the 'Avraamite' Branch Davidians have more recently relaunched one of the older websites, which gives a rather different account of things from previously. At the time of writing (early 2004) the website is far from complete, but an outline at least of some new directions in their eschatology can be seen in what has already been established. The claim that there is a 'living prophet' who is 'the chosen vessel' and who can now reveal what the future holds is unchanged. However, a new date has come to the fore: March 2012, at which point, so the web site confidently predicts, a large comet will strike the earth. The impact of the comet will cause a huge earthquake and the opening up of a caldera (though quite how the caldera appears as a result of a comet striking elsewhere is difficult to imagine). This caldera is in Yellowstone National Park, and out of it will billow smoke and ash which will darken the land. For the next five months (the influence of Revelation 9 is easily discernible at this point) the plagues of God will rain down upon the earth until, at the conclusion of the period, molten lava will spew out and eventually consume the whole world. Before the comet strikes, however, 'the Chosen Vessel's church and the 144,000 are imbued with the power of the spirit'. They will escape the plagues and the lava and go out of the earth (precisely where is not clear in the materials so far posted). A new earth will be created and those who have been prepared for it will now inhabit the new creation, it seems through the natural process of (re)birth. Who the parents are is not clear, but the earlier work of this group spoke of a new Adam and a new Eve being created and these new creations being the parents of all who are to be (re)born.[25] All births in this new earth are of twins.[26]

The three persons named above (Doyle, Fagan, and Avraam) are the most significant players in post-April 1993 Branch Davidianism, but not the only ones. Charles Pace, for example, a Canadian Branch Davidian who split with Lois Roden in the early 1980s, moved back onto the Mt. Carmel site in 1998 in an attempt to gain the allegiance of the Branch Davidians still associated with the property. His efforts have so far been fruitless, it seems, though he is still active. He remains on speaking terms with Doyle and others, as his presence as a 'guest' at Tillie Freisen's funeral shows.[27]

A definite claim to leadership and indeed to prophetic status was made by Ron Cole, a post-1993 convert. Cole claims that it is he who will now bring to a close the seventh angel's message, a message that Koresh did not complete before his death. There is no evidence to suggest that he has been taken very seriously by the Branch Davidians, and his status as a post-1993 convert must hold him back somewhat.[28]

And there are others too. They include Teresa Moore,[29] Amo Roden,[30] Doug Mitchell,[31] and the man who goes by the name of Andrew X98.[32] None has a sizeable following, and in fact at least two of them are probably loners. Some of these would-be leaders (Amo Roden for example) are very much opposed to Koresh. Others, like X98, see themselves as loyal to Koresh but wanting to take his work on, or at least preserve it from corruption. Actually in X98's case it is probable that the end of the line has been reached. His views are so extreme and, to be frank, so bizarre, that even people prone to religious beliefs of the kind we are here discussing will probably judge him to have gone too far.

This chapter has outlined some of what appear to be the more important developments in the Branch Davidian tradition since 1993. Reflecting upon those developments might bring one to the conclusion that this is a movement that has now had its day. The group has not regained its stability, and, despite some apparent successes, such as the rebuilding of the Branch Davidian church in Waco—which was probably as much an act of political protest as one of religious commitment—the movement has been in steady decline. The theological, social, and psychological pressure caused by the dissonance has been resolved in a number of ways, but none has been very successful. In some cases alleys have been explored that have turned out to be blind; such may well turn out to be the case with the small group that now give allegiance to Avraam. The more sober approach of Doyle will probably sustain at least the core group at Waco for a while, but, one suspects, his energies are not now going to be channelled towards recruitment. When Fagan and the other imprisoned Branch Davidians are released there may be a change in the movement's fortunes; one can never tell. But this seems unlikely, for the group has now become so fragmented and so small that it is difficult to see how it could survive.

In short the future does not look bright; in fact survivor David Thibodeau seems to have been on the right track when he wrote some time ago of his experiences in the immediate aftermath of 1993:

The sheep were scattering; our cohesion seemed to be weakening. Most of us felt that David's teachings couldn't continue without him, and without David there was no strong, motivating force. He was the heart and the soul of our community, and we were the truncated body, helpless to move on.[33]

We are indeed witnessing the demise of a religion here. The death blow came in 1993, probably self-administered. In the decade since, the body has twitched somewhat, and even shown some signs of life now and then. But we are now in the closing stages. And soon, one suspects, the Branch Davidians, a movement that was started by Ben Roden some fifty years ago, will be no more.

NOTES

1. The details of this lengthy process will not be discussed. Over the course of several years a number of survivors and the relatives of some who died sought to bring an unlawful killing lawsuit against the US government. On 22 Mar. 2004 that process came to an end when the Supreme Court declined, without further comment, to listen to appeals regarding the alleged conduct of federal judges during the hearings of two previous cases of unlawful killing, one in Waco and the other in California.
2. Hamm, *Apocalypse in Oklahoma*, 105.

3. See Hamm, *Apocalypse in Oklahoma*, 121–2, and 'McVeigh Considered Killing Reno' by Karen Gullo (Associated Press, 27 Apr. 2001).

4. For some of the references in the surviving material see generally Chapter Thirteen.

5. David Koresh, 'Bible Study Tape #8', 1989; a copy of this tape is in my possession.

6. For example, for Fagan Isa. 26.19–20 is particularly significant. The text reads: 'Thy dead men shall live, together with my dead body shall they arise. Awake and sing, ye that dwell in dust: for thy dew is as the dew of herbs, and the earth shall cast out the dead. Come, my people, enter thou into thy chambers, and shut thy doors about thee: hide thyself as it were for a little moment, until the indignation be overpast.'

   These verses, according to Fagan, speak of the experience at Mt. Carmel. As they had been previously taught, those who were slain at Mt. Carmel now rest in the grave assured of resurrection. This is also, said Fagan, the event predicted in Rev. 11.3–13—the resurrection of the two witnesses. (Letter of Livingstone Fagan to Kenneth G. C. Newport, 19 Feb. 2001.)

7. This record is based upon a personal conversation between Kenneth Newport, Derek Lovelock, and another unnamed Branch Davidian, in Oct. 2002.

8. Such thinking sustains other Branch Davidians too, including a post-1993 convert Branch Davidian in Nottingham, UK. He too verbally tripped over himself with excitement in an effort to explain what was about to happen (interview with Kenneth G. C. Newport, July 2002). In this part of the Branch Davidian community, then (though not in all) there is still a real sense of eschatological expectation. The biblical text is interpreted in ways that give an explanation of what has gone before, an account of where we are now and, of course, real hope for the future.

9. On this see generally Eugene Gallagher, 'The Persistence of the Millennium: Branch Davidian Expectations of the End After Waco', *Nova Religio*, 3 (2000): 303–19; Marc Breault, 'The Return of David Koresh' unpublished paper, n.d. A copy of this paper is in my possession.

10. According to the logic, the date set for Koresh's return should have been 13 December, though I have not been able to confirm this.

11. The precise date is not given in any of the literature I have been able to access. The expectation that Koresh would return at the end of the period was, however, very clear on materials that were on the web site www.branchdavidian.com and its sister web site www.sevenseals.com. These web sites reflected the views of Waco fire survivor Renos Avraam and his small group of followers, but both sites became defunct some time after Aug. 1999. At the time of writing (2004) the second site has come back online and its content, while still very obviously generated from the same source as the original www.sevenseals.com, is now rather different in its focus.

12. See Leon Festinger *et al.*, *When Prophecy Fails*, and Stone, ed., *Expecting Armageddon*.

13. Open letter of Livingstone Fagan (n.d.). A copy of this document is my possession.

14. Fagan evidently understands Genesis 7.1–10 to indicate that there was a period of seven days after Noah's getting into the ark before the rains began to fall.

15. In this context, Koresh stated: 'You see? I mean these American troops, you know their good old American boys. I mean, they're over there cussin', and stuff you know. It's all a religious war. Girls, boys, you know. Mom's apple pie, and Budweiser, and a little religion, you know, and praise to the Lord and all that kind of stuff ... Just like Joel 1 says. You see? So in other words, the American troops come in and totally devastate Jerusalem, take all their food. Joel 1 tells us ('Shower Head Tape' [1987]).'

16. Two persons, Renos Avraam and Ron Cole, have made an explicit claim to the prophet's mantle, but neither has had much success. A few further remarks on them are found below.

17. In 2003, the tenth anniversary, at least 150 persons attended the memorial service. Most of these were not Branch Davidians but people who for one reason or another felt it appropriate to attend. Anecdotal evidence suggests that in previous years there had been a high concentration of people who might best be described as sympathetic to a general anti-government agenda. This was not so evident in 2003. There were four main speakers for the principal service in 2003: Ramsey Clark, Philip Arnold, Cathy Wessinger, and Kenneth Newport.

18. See Gallagher, 'Persistence of the Millennium'.

19. A good deal of what Fagan has written can be accessed via the internet. At the time of writing, the site www.start.at/mtcarmel has a gateway into Fagan's materials.

20. Livingstone Fagan, 'Christ', unpublished MS, n.d., a copy of which is in my possession.

21. It is not just in the work of Fagan that such a move is discernible, though Fagan is without doubt the most able exponent of it. In an interview with Branch Davidians in Manchester I once asked whether work was done on the Sabbath at Mt. Carmel. It was confirmed that this was sometimes the case. When asked to explain how this fitted with the traditional SDA/Davidian SDA/Branch Davidian insistence that the Sabbath was sacred to the Lord, the respondent answered, 'yes, but David is the Lord of the Sabbath' (cf. Mark 2.28).

22. One such letter was shared with me by a Branch Davidian in Nottingham. It included a reference to the necessity of offering hospitality to other Branch Davidians should they visit and reminded the reader that in so much as he did this for others, he was doing it also for David (cf. Matt. 25.40).

23. This was on www.branchdavidian.com but the original site is now not available; a hard copy of those two very large volumes is in my possession.

24. Catherine Matteson left Mt. Carmel on 2 Mar. 1993. The letter itself can be found at www.hope.ac.uk/humanities/theology/branchdavidians.

25. This is found in the original 'Book Two' that was posted on www.branchdavidian.com.

26. This reflects the poorly documented but very definite Branch Davidian view that 'a human being' is made up of one man and one woman—the two together making one 'unit' of humanity (cf. Gen. 1.27: 'So God created man in his own

image, in the image of God created he him; male and female created he them'). All births, some Branch Davidians have said, were originally twins and these twins were, quite literally, each other's 'other half'. They were also a unit of procreation so from those twins would come others. This all became corrupted through sin with the result that the vast majority of births now are of one child only or of same-sex twins. Almost all human beings are hence destined to wander the earth feeling 'incomplete' as a result of being estranged from their other halves. The outline of this doctrine can be found on the Schneider tapes. It was also communicated to me directly by Derek Lovelock during an interview in Manchester in Oct. 2002.

27. On Pace see further Dick Reavis, 'Davidian claims Koresh fulfilled prophecy of doom', *San Antonio Express-News*, 27 Feb. 2000. A small amount of material by Pace is located in TXC, Mark Swett Collection, box 3. It includes an affidavit by Pace dated 28 July 1994, stating that he had been a member of the General Association of Branch Davidian Seventh-day Adventists since Dec. 1973. The affidavit itself was part of Pace's attempt to win control of the Mt. Carmel property from the followers of Koresh and place it in the hands of 'the last, living, original trustee, George B. Roden'. The folder also contains two booklets by Pace: *The Revelation of Jesus Christ as the Second Adam* (1994) and *Christ the Branch: The Brazen Serpent* (n.d.).

28. There is a small amount of material by Cole in TXC, Mark Swett Collection, box 3. It includes *The Future of the Wave Sheaf* (New York: Cyrus Productions, 1996) and *Sinister Twilight: A Tragedy Near Waco, and a Sinister Twilight in America* (n.p., 1994). An additional publication by Cole, an information booklet on 'The Colorado First Light Infantry ... and its Affiliate The General Association of the Seventh Angel's Message' is in TXC, Bill Smith Collection, box IP144.

29. Teresa Moore considers herself as the rightful successor to Lois Roden and has been in the background of Branch Davidian history for a number of years. It is probably she who is still active in the two 'Living Waters' churches in East Texas today. A photograph of one of those churches is located in TXC 2D217.

30. Amo Roden was the wife of George Roden. Ever since 1993 she has been making a claim to the ownership of the Branch Davidian property. She continues to write tracts. See e.g. her *Miracles, Mysteries and Messiahs*, n.d. [2003]; TXC 2D214.

31. See Doug Mitchell, *The Warfare of Vernon Howell (a.k.a. David Koresh), et al. against The Branch Davidian Seventh-day Adventists* (1993, revised edn. 1995), copy in TXC 2D216, Vernon Howell folder. Here Mitchell argues that Koresh started a new group in 1983–4 and that his views are not in keeping with the true Branch Davidian message.

32. 'Andrew X98' is a post-1993 convert in dispute with Clive Doyle; he spends a good deal of his time outside the Mt. Carmel gate passing literature to visitors. He is of the view that all Koresh taught was in complete accord not only with the Bible, but also with the Koran. He is viciously anti-Semitic and intemperate in the language he uses to express his views.

33. Thibodeau, *A Place Called Waco*, 329.

17

Concluding Observations

In this book the religious trajectory that gave rise to the Davidians and Branch Davidians has been examined in some considerable detail. Indeed, some might say that too much time has been taken, too much energy expended and too many pages spent on dealing with a religious tradition that never amounted to much numerically. After all, despite the exaggerated claims of some in the movement, there has probably never been a time when the combined membership of all of the various factions rose above 1,000 in total. What is more, for most of the time, and in most of its forms, this tradition existed without anyone else really noticing that it was there, except in Waco itself, where in decades now long gone its size relative to that of the population gave it more significance.

All that was to change, however, on 28 February 1993. What happened then propelled the Branch Davidians into the public domain in a way that few religious communities have ever experienced. Reaction was quick and individuals and organizations lined up to give advice to the authorities on how to handle the crisis that had now come about. As was noted in Chapter One, several books came from the presses in a matter of months, all of which sought to explain what the Branch Davidians in general, and David Koresh in particular, were about.

This book has been longer in gestation. It also has a rather different focus from much of what has gone before. In particular the story presented is not of a group that began with Koresh, or indeed ended with him. The Davidian/ Branch Davidian tradition is much more complex than that and any serious attempt to understand this movement will need to take account of that fairly long history. To see Koresh in isolation is to misunderstand him and, more worryingly, to misunderstand how this community as a whole functioned. And if that is misunderstood, the oft talked about 'lessons of Waco' will not have been learned. A book of this size was hence necessary.

Research in the area of religious studies quite often brings to the surface fundamental differences in the way people see things. However, even if one is used to working in this area, the level of disagreement over what happened at Waco still comes as something of a shock. There is good reason for this situation of course: the events of 28 February to 19 April 1993 were very troubling. The thought of so many people dying, some very young and some dying in quite horrid ways, ought to be taken very seriously indeed and with that seriousness come passionate points of view, not all of which can be right. Trying to figure out 'what really happened at Waco' is not an intellectual game. It matters what happened, and it matters fundamentally. If it was, as so many have said, the result of either bungling or deliberate wrongdoing on the part of the ATF/FBI ('wrong' here meaning either mistaken or simply immoral), then this needs highlighting. At the very least society needs to learn from the experience and be aware that even government agencies can at times get things badly wrong. Others would go further. Some might argue that we need to be aware of the propensity of government agencies not simply to get things wrong, but to run amok; such would no doubt argue further that where this does happen the offending parties need to be brought to book.

It should be clear by now, however, that this is not the view presented here. To be sure, there were some mistakes made by both the ATF and FBI and there are some lessons to be learned. But when looked at as dispassionately as possible the hard evidence simply cannot be said to support the view that the fire at Waco, or even the catastrophic outcome of the siege in general, was the result of either malice or ignorance on the part of the authorities. At worst ignorance (and there was plenty of that) may have played a small supporting role, by pushing forward at a somewhat faster rate a course of action that seems to have been set in motion within days, if not hours, of the start of the siege, and set in motion by the Branch Davidians themselves. It might well have been better if the negotiators had understood better the nature of the Mt. Carmel community, but would it have made any difference? It is very doubtful: from day one Koresh was set on 'going home' and the fulfilment of the dreams of the community was confidently expected. Reason, and certainly any attempts at clever argument (even if based upon the same texts that the Branch Davidians held sacred), would have been swept away in a tide of religious excitement. One can see that process in train in the negotiation tapes: negotiators want to talk about medical care for the injured, Koresh wants to talk about the seven seals and why it is that these people have come to 'break his bands asunder'.

There is of course one argument that would indeed prove all this wrong. If the Danforth *Final Report* were in fact the result of a huge cover-up then much of what has been argued in this book would be groundless. There are no doubt some who will seize upon this immediately and argue that this is in fact precisely the case. Indeed, such a counter-argument can confidently be anticipated on the part of some subsections of those who still spend time and energy thinking about Waco, and will come as no surprise. However, if it is going to be argued in a credible way by members of the academic community it will take some doing. As has been made abundantly clear in this study, if Danforth is a cover-up it is on a truly breathtaking scale, so breathtaking in fact that it is scarcely possible to conceive of it.

This is important. If the academic community wants to understand Waco there is one thing that, in all probability, must be taken into account: the Branch Davidians themselves set fire to Mt. Carmel. This cannot be ignored. Whatever one makes of the community it must be able to account for this very unpleasant fact. The work presented in this book is able to account for this act of apocalyptic self-destruction (in anticipation of new birth) and if the general flow of the argument is to be overturned (there will of course always be room for discussion on details) then some other credible explanation must be given. It will simply not do to ignore it. It will simply not do to say, as some have in essence, 'and then the fire started'. The fire is the end point and it must be explained. If it cannot be explained by arguing that it was the work of the FBI or accident, then it must be explained with reference to the workings of this group.

In the end Waco was indeed a tragedy and the result of some fundamental mistakes. The ATF made a mistake in going ahead with the raid once the element of surprise had been lost. The FBI made a mistake in thinking that maternal instinct would override physical well-being and force the mothers and children out of Mt. Carmel if enough tear gas could be inserted. But this is not the end of the list of big mistakes. In a post-modern intellectual climate it has become rather unfashionable in academic circles to say that people's religious beliefs or their interpretation of the Bible are wrong. But at Waco this was surely the case. The Branch Davidians were wrong in thinking, however sincerely, that God was about to set up a kingdom to be ruled over by the antitypical King David. They were wrong also in thinking that this kingdom would come through a fiery rebirth of the chosen, prophetically led, remnant people. They were wrong in thinking that Koresh was who he said he was: the seventh angel of Revelation who could reveal the secrets of the end time and the person to whom the book of Psalms pointed. They were wrong also to believe Schneider, who in the Manchester tapes promised them unequivocally that they would come back riding on white horses as an avenging army if they were willing to face a short-term death. Now one could argue that most religious people are wrong in what they think. That might well be so. Unfortunately, however, in the case of Waco being right or wrong turned out to be a matter of life or death.

Appendix A

A PERSONAL VIEW: DEREK LOVELOCK[1]

In the first part of this manuscript Derek Lovelock gives an account of his early life in Manchester, where he was born 13 August 1955. He talks a little about his family and indicates that he was brought up in a religious home. Sadness came with the death of his brother from a brain tumour, and of his uncle, who died of stab wounds in an alley. After leaving school at the age of fifteen he went from one job to another, and it was at this time, he says, that he began his search for truth. The manuscript then continues as follows.

As life went on my hunger for understanding led me through the doors of the Seventh-day Adventist Church. I believed this church had the truth and the answers to my questions. I came into contact with the church by mere chance through a friend of my younger brother Paul. This was the first church of which I actually became a member, although I had been christened in the Church of England. I was invited to attend the church's Revelation Seminars. These took place every Sunday evening and as an encouragement to attend I was given some Adventist literature, which explained certain Bible passages. At the time I was of the view that of all the books of the Bible, it is the book of Revelation that seems the most mysterious. (I was later to learn that in fact all the books of the Bible begin and end in Revelation.) I was quite impressed by the literature and the seminars and things seemed a little clearer. Finally I began to make frequent visits to the church.

Then in 1984 I was baptised into the Seventh-day Adventist faith. I was proud to be a member of the true church of God. Every Sabbath I made my way to church; no secular work was performed during Sabbath hours from sunset to sunset. I became involved in church activities. I enrolled as a literature evangelist, going from door to door with literature that contained the truth. I also became a children's Sabbath School teacher.

Following my marriage in 1985, I transferred my membership from the Fallowfield to the Old Trafford Seventh-day Adventist Church, where my wife was a member. Things did not work out and I moved out of our married home and into a flat. Shortly afterwards I was knocked down by a car and woke only after eight days of being in a coma. I thought that God had spared me and became even more determined to find the truth. As my Christian experience continued, I became somewhat dissatisfied with the Seventh-day Adventist church. It became a place where one would meet every Sabbath as if it were a social club. Despite the many activities that the church organized, including coach trips and large district camp meetings, I became increasingly frustrated. It seemed to me that I was getting the milk but never the meat; as if I was forever leaning towards, but never coming to a full knowledge of, the truth (2 Tim. 3). I would sit in church listening to the Bible being read and asking myself what does it all mean? ... [2]

I remember one Sabbath afternoon as I returned to church for the evening service there were about five people in the kitchen area. I could not help overhearing a conversation concerning the Holy Spirit being female. I thought 'this is new. I haven't heard this before'. I found it fascinating to listen to and it made sense to me. I asked where this information came from and I was told by one of the persons there who had previously made a visit to Waco, Texas, that the teaching had come from David Koresh, who is believed to be a messenger of God. Well, I wanted to know more, so I was invited to attend one of the study groups. A date was made for the following week.

When we met for the study, I was asked if I thought that God has rebuked and chastised me. I thought for a moment and then said 'yes', (but to be honest I was not sure). I was pointed to the book of Revelation chapters 4–5, which clearly show the judgement scene. One is sat on the throne. The twenty-four elders are the grand jury. As I began to look up these references the very words of my Bible danced before my eyes. I began to read the Bible more and more. I found it fantastic to read; it was a revelation.

At our next meeting there was talk of a trip to Waco, Texas. I just had to meet this man and see for myself. So in September 1990 I made arrangements for a trip to Waco. I left with ten other people from Gatwick airport to travel to Waco via Dallas. On arriving at Dallas airport we were met by a group of Davidians, some of whom had been followers for quite some time. We introduced ourselves and boarded a minibus and made the 180-mile journey through the dusty Texas summer heat. It must have been around 90 degrees. We arrived in Waco in the late afternoon. I recall seeing people walking around by the lakes, children were laughing and playing. I was greeted by other Davidians who helped unload my luggage. We talked for a while, but my thoughts were on that man David Koresh. I was then taken to the male quarters, into a house with a veranda and shown a room with white walls and a comfortable single bed. It was a beautiful place to be, away from the city. It was peaceful. There were 75 acres of land to roam on and I could hear the chirp of crickets through the open window of my room.

In the communal refectory I was given half a watermelon, which was quite large, and a bowl of popcorn. A bit weary after the long journey I ate, sat and watched what was going on around me. Then someone nudged me and whispered excitedly 'David's here; he's over there'. I took a long look at the man who would show me things from the Bible that were mind blowing, the mysteries of God. He was wearing a white T shirt, blue jeans and trainers. He looked right into my eyes, as if to say 'I know everything about you'. It really felt strange. I felt as though I was in the presence of a messenger of God. We were about 25 yards apart, but he looked straight through me.

That night David gave a study to the somewhat exhausted British pilgrims. It lasted six hours. It was awesome. He explained the Bible like I had never heard it explained before and it made me sit up in my chair for the whole of the six hours.

I introduced myself to David. We shook hands. He had a strong but firm hand-shake, yet somewhat gentle. I told David about my car accident. 'I can't do miracles' he said 'I'm not Christ'. Then I mentioned my little boy Hayden and asked David 'if I am saved, will he be saved'? 'You bet' said David 'he's my son'. That made me feel as though I belonged.

As I became more acquainted with everyone, it was as if I had known these people all my life. I stayed for two weeks and during that time learned more than I had in my previous seven years in the Adventist church. I wanted more truths of God. The studies were so deep it was mind-blowing, yet it made sense; it was logical.

No-one at Mt Carmel was lazy. We all had things to do. It was like one big family; a community. I miss those times now. I remember hearing the bell ring. If it rang for a long time then you knew it was time for study. The studies made one fear God; God is real.

I recall the time when those of us who had come from England were asked if they would like to stay. Some decided that they would stay and learn more, but I wanted to return to England. (I guess I had to come back to think these things over). As my stay in Waco continued I began to believe that this man was special, that he was no ordinary man. He showed me things that no other person ever has. It was as if the presence of God's Spirit rested upon him. We were told not to look at the man himself, but to see what was behind him. I found him to be the most compassionate person I have ever met. His love was strong and deep and it was a privilege to be in the company of such a person. Everything he put his hand to he did perfectly. Just to be around him was an honour.

The best studies were when he did not use the Bible at all. Those were the best studies. He would go so deep in detail, explaining how the sun is formed from matter and anti-matter. I would often sit outside David's office listening with others through the door that had been left ajar as he gave studies to newcomers, revealing some of the deepest mysteries of God. Things which made you listen with attention. It was a fearful message, yet a message of grace. He was like any other man in the sense that he ate, slept, worked, exercised, and pointed you to good moral standards which the world no longer considers of any value. He supervised us during working hours, making sure that we did the task correctly. David Koresh was a humanitarian; he had a burden for souls. He had the wisdom of God. There were so many questions that I wanted to ask, but never seemed to get round to asking them.

Many people paid visits to Mt Carmel. Some would leave the next day, others would stay just a few hours. David would speak with them concerning scripture. Later they were shown hospitality. They were served refreshments and made welcome.

Our main diet was a variety of foods: popcorn, bananas, millet, granola (a mixture of fresh fruit and cereal) and plenty of watermelon, which one needed in such a hot climate. We also had chicken, vegetables, pinta beans and plenty of water from our own well. I was happy to be amongst such people who cared for each other's welfare. It was the best two weeks of my life.

The time came for me to leave. Plans were made that day and the plane tickets booked. I would leave on the next available flight, which was around 2.30 pm the following day. I felt that I should stay, but I just had to return to England to think things over. The next morning as I said goodbye to everyone it was as if I knew that I would see them again soon. Standing at the main entrance of the building with the hot Texas sun beating down, one could see the heat rising off the dusty path that leads to the Mt. Carmel Centre. I asked David what would he have me do; 'fear God' came the simple reply.

For the next eighteen months I did just that by immersing myself in the Bible. Slowly and painfully I began to make what I felt was even greater sense of those things that I had learned in Waco and I knew I had to return. While in England, my thoughts were always on the things that I had now been privileged to receive. It was as if I was being oppressed by the very words of the Bible; it made me restless. I spent a few sleepless nights and kept thinking 'if this really is true, do you know what it means'! I met together with others to have studies to go over notes and seek to understand even further the things that we had learned. I was seeing more and more of the Bible come alive before me.

The next trip I made to Waco was March 23rd 1992 and I made sure that I had a return ticket. There were four of us who went, so we booked as a group and travelled together. We had booked flights from London Heathrow to New York JFK. I made arrangements for my uncle to meet us in New York. We stayed with him in New York overnight and then caught the Greyhound bus from New York. This was a very long journey across the states and down into the deep south. The journey was a very tiresome one. It took four days.

We finally reached Waco in the late evening of the fourth day. On arriving at Mt. Carmel, I noticed that the place had changed somewhat. Gone were the small houses with the verandas and there stood now a huge complex which had been built by the residents of Mt. Carmel itself. It reminded me of the ark of safety. This was my first time back for almost two years. It had changed so much. There were so many exits. The building was built so that wherever you were situated you could see for miles.

After eating I and some newcomers were told that David would like to speak with us. After a short study, we retired for the night. I was shown to my room, which was on the ground floor; the women's quarters were upstairs. There was a kitchen area with a large dining hall with storage for food goods. The office was situated at the main entrance of the building. There was a computer room and work shop. At the back of the complex we had our own well. We raised chickens and so had fresh eggs. There were three lakes full of 5lb–8lb bass and we had our own bee hives for honey. We also grew tomatoes, figs, [and] pecan butter nut trees.

As the days and weeks and months passed by, I really got to know David and my new-found friends. Our next task was to build a swimming pool and gym, which I took part in myself. The next thing was to build a storm shelter. Texas is known for its hurricanes and when it rains, it really rains. Some other times it would be so hot that it was unbearable. It can reach 110 degrees and even in the shade it was still quite hot. Plenty of cold drinks and water melon kept one from dehydrating.

We had a work rota; we would wake around 6.30 am for breakfast and lunch would be at 1.30. Dinner was at 7.30. No men were allowed to work in the kitchen area. There were also times for entertainment. David would play his guitar (he owned about ten altogether).

There were so many talented people at Mt. Carmel. There were chefs, doctors, nurses, lawyers, builders, painters and farmers. Most people were ex-Adventists, but there were some others from different denominations. They came from as far apart as Australia, China, New Zealand, Hawaii and Great Britain, but the vast majority were from the United States.

After finishing work it was down to some hard studies. A study could be called any time and no matter what you were doing, you would drop it and attend the study, unless, that is, you were feeling unwell. David liked everyone to attend the studies because he saw them as uncovering the mysteries of God, which are the most important things to know. Such knowledge is vital to one's eternal truth—one must know what the truth is. Material things would come last. Sometimes we would not eat for some hours and even stay up for long hours so that we could receive more of the truths of God. The word of God comes first; it is more important than food, sleep or drink. However, no-one was ever under-fed or suffered from lack of sleep or exhaustion. We had a balanced life style. As the months went by we were shown clearly from Nahum 2 that what happened at Mt. Carmel was prophesied thousands of years ago; all of the minor prophets spoke of it.

David spoke of an evil beast with two horns which looked like a lamb, but speaks like a dragon and forces all the world to wonder after the beast (read the whole of Revelation 13). David Koresh taught that the beast in Rev 13 is the United Nations and the power of the shadow of the USA. David felt very strongly that our freedoms guaranteed by the United States Constitution were being destroyed. He knew that those opposing the new world order would be oppressed. He knew that war would be made against him by the lamb-like beast of Rev 13 and he made no secret of it. Everything David taught was designed to prepare himself and his followers for the judgement that was soon to come and to be ready to recognise and face the deception and tenacity of the beast.

February 28th 1993—A Day of Infamy

This part of the manuscript begins with a lengthy quotation from the first of the 911 tapes (Wayne Martin and Lt Lynch). Lovelock then continues as follows.

I had risen for breakfast. It was millet and bananas. It was around 9.00 am, perhaps a little later. Women and children were also having breakfast. I could hear something in the distance. It sounded like the rhythmic humming of engines, but it could have been anything and so it did not concern me. As we spoke this humming got louder and louder. I realised that it was being made by helicopters and later learned that these were under the control of the BATF. The BATF were raiding Mt. Carmel with the intention of arresting David Koresh for stockpiling illegal arms. (Actually the arms that David had were all entirely legal and he had not violated any law). On one occasion he had invited the authorities to come out to Mt. Carmel and inspect the weapons there, but the authorities refused.

There was an assault under way at the front of the building; agents were leaping from two cattle trailers that had driven up the Mt. Carmel driveway. Suddenly a hail of gun fire began to shower Mt. Carmel and there were bullets coming through the ceiling and walls. Bullets were flying everywhere. Women and children were screaming, mothers clutched their young children and everyone dived for cover. I made a run for the men's dormitory, but was stopped by the bullets that were ripping through the thin plasterboard and the wooden walls. I threw myself to the floor and cowered in terror. I believed I was going to die there and then. I was down the corridor and I heard David shout 'there's women and ..'; that is as far as he got. Later I heard that they had opened fire on him, despite the fact that he was unarmed. What I heard was that he had run into the cafeteria and had said to David Thibodeau, who was working on the lyrics for a new song, 'they are on their way. Don't anybody do anything stupid. I'll go and talk to them'. He then went down the hall and headed for the front door. David opened the door and at about the same time the agents began to rush forward. David shouted 'Wait, we have women and ..', at which point gunfire ripped through the door, knocking it back and throwing David off balance. David tried to leap clear of the burst, but was struck in the groin and the right wrist. Perry Jones was standing behind David at this time. Perry had accompanied David to the door to give him moral support. Perry was not as quick as David and was shot three times through the stomach and once in the right elbow. He fell to the floor screaming as David ran down the hall to his right. (I myself saw Perry as he lay bleeding to death on the floor). Brad Branch watched Perry fall only a few feet in front of him. He turned around and headed back into the chapel area as bullets ripped past him through several walls. Another blast of gunfire ripped through the wall to the right of the door in the direction of David. The BATF seemed to be firing at random, just hoping for a lucky kill.

Two helicopters passed overhead. They were so low that Annetta Richards thought that one had landed on the roof. These two helicopters peppered the roof with gunfire and this accounted for several casualties. Peter Gent had been working inside the old water tower since early in the morning. The tank was riddled with gunfire from one of the helicopters and he was shot twice in the head and once through the heart. He was not armed. Whinston Blake was sitting on his bed in his room when he heard the first shots fired. Bullets tore through the roof above him and struck him in the head. He was armed only with a piece of French toast. His body was found by me and he was definitely dead when I found him.

As the magnitude of the situation became apparent to us inside Mt. Carmel people slowly began to react. Wayne Martin called 911 in an attempt to get a cease fire. Others ran round trying to find guns to defend themselves. There were a few guns that were already loaded. These belonged to the die-hard patriots among those that lived at Mt. Carmel. In fact the vast majority of the rifles that had been at Mt. Carmel in the previous weeks had been taken by Paul Fatta to Austin that very morning as he was attending a gun show. There were some others, however. Many of these were still in boxes and had never been fired and there were no magazines to hand.

Most people in Mt. Carmel just ducked under beds or took some other form of cover. Some shots were fired by the Branch Davidians at the BATF, but by the time everyone who wanted to be armed was armed, the BATF already had all the windows covered by gunmen and every time a BATF agent saw movement at a window the agent would shout 'window, window' and several other agents would pepper the area with shots. It appears to me (though I had no way of telling this at the time) that most of the injuries and casualties suffered by the BATF were the result of friendly fire; perhaps some were even self-inflicted. For example Robert Williams was one of the agents on the roof. He entered what the BATF thought was the gun room on the second floor. He received some wounds while he was inside the supposed gun room and left by the window he had entered. Another BATF agent shouted, 'who's on the roof?' and a shot rang out and Williams was shot in the face. I think that he was shot (in error) by one of his own fellow agents.

However, there is little doubt that the Branch Davidians did inflict some damage. It is more likely than not (but I do not know for sure) that those agents who entered the gun room were killed or wounded by Davidian fire. (But Texas State law allows citizens to defend themselves even against law enforcement officers if the officers are using unnecessary force).

There follows in the manuscript a lengthy section dealing with the question of who fired first and the tactics employed by the ATF and the FBI. It is reasonably clear that some of this has been derived from video and other sources that Lovelock has studied since his release from prison. The manuscript then returns to the narrative and continues as follows.

After 45 minutes the firing stopped as suddenly as it had started. David had been hit twice, once in the groin and once in the right wrist and he was by now propped up on a mattress. There was blood all over his lower body and the nurses that were in the building were attending his wounds. There were already two telephones by his side and he had a mobile phone. He was talking to the authorities and trying to negotiate. He said 'anyone can go now if they want to. Who wants to leave? Who wants to go?' In the end some 25 men, women and children went out from Mt. Carmel during the first part of the standoff, but I feared God more than I feared the authorities and I was prepared even to die if necessary. It was a personal thing, David made it clear that whoever wanted to could leave and whoever wanted to could stay. It was up to them.

David immediately took charge and commanded us to store water and clear the place up. 'Get organised' he said. We went round checking rooms for survivors. There were women and children in the dormitories shivering with shock. (It was at this time that, as I mentioned earlier, I found Whinston Blake. He was in my own room. He was dead). At the end of that first day David told us that God had told him that he had to wait. I for one knew exactly what that meant. David based his teachings on the book of Revelation and especially to the mention made in Revelation of a book in the right hand of God. This book is sealed with seven seals and contains the mysteries to be revealed to the people on the earth. Only he who is worthy may open the seals and reveal these mysteries in the final days of life on earth. I believe David Koresh was chosen by God to open the seals and discover the events that would come to pass. Accordingly later on in the standoff he informed the authorities that he would lead his people out only after he had written the interpretation of the seals down and not before.

No one slept that first night. Many of us prayed, convinced that this was the long-prophesied end of the world. It was a deeply personal thing. Anyone could have left, but we were all determined to stay. David began negotiations with the FBI. He told them to read their Bibles and that Lake Waco was going to burst its banks in a tidal wave caused by an earthquake. I and others believed him. His word was truth. When he was not negotiating with the FBI, David gave Bible studies from his mattress. We felt we were in the presence of the Messiah.

We organized ourselves and buried our dead fellow Branch Davidians in makeshift graves which we dug with shovels and our bare hands in the hard winter earth. David handed out ex-Israeli gas masks that he had purchased for this eventuality and organized drills so that we would know what to do should tear-gas come raining down. On the tenth day the power was cut off. This meant the water was cut off too, since the water supply was dependent upon an electric pump at the well. Kerosene lamps were hung and we had a small cooker that was used to heat food and water for more than one hundred people. David rallied us and kept us going by telling us we were strong and that we would be delivered. We studied the Bible and talked about what was going to happen. There was no going back now. They put floodlights on us. This was quite handy actually as it meant we were not entirely dependent upon the kerosene lamps. Food was rationed, but David had bought in enough food so that he could complete his work on the seven seals. As the days passed, tempers often frayed to snapping point. It was a bizarre situation, but there was order. No wild sex orgies, no abuse of children, and we still all slept apart segregated except for husbands and wives. They tried to drown us with loud music, the sound of rabbits being slaughtered and Tibetan chants. It went on night and day, but it did not bother us as we used ear plugs. We stuck together determined to get through it. We prayed for deliverance. We held out for fifty-one days.

April 19th 1993: A Day of Death

At 5.45 am on the morning of April 19th I awoke to the sound of a loud noise coming from somewhere outside the building. This time it was a low reverberating sound, not the kind of sound that the helicopters had made on the 28th February. I barely had time to wake up those around me before the shell-like tear-gas canisters began smashing through the walls and ceiling. My eyes started to burn as the gas hit me. It was still dark. I struggled to get my gas mask on. They just kept bombarding us with the canisters for what seemed like five or ten minutes. When that was over, an FBI voice announced on a loudspeaker that the siege was over and that we should come out with our hands up. The voice said 'This is not an assault. Do not retaliate. You are all under arrest. Come out with your hands up'. No-one moved inside the building, despite the repeated demands that we surrender.

People regrouped in the canteen area. The gas masks that we had were not small enough for some of the children so we drenched towels in water and wrapped them around the children's heads and then put the masks over them. There were some little children as young as three and they were crying and coughing with tears streaming down their faces as they struggled to breathe. David came down and asked if everyone was OK. We told him no one had been hurt. Then after fifteen to twenty minutes they started gassing the place again. A tank with a specially designed nozzle came up to the front wall and punched a hole through it and poured tear-gas in. People were screaming and crying and huddling together. The gas masks that we had would last about half and hour before they started to fail. When they do, you can feel the gas getting to you and your eyes begin to burn.

Someone said the petrol tank outside had been bulldozed and that it was leaking fuel everywhere. The tanks started smashing the upper floor and the roof came in. People were in the chapel praying for God to help us. Then a tank smashed a hole in the side of the wall. Another tank came through the gymnasium wall and another right through the front door, pushing the walls before it. No-one could escape. The whole building was buckling and shaking and crumbling. I thought I was going to die. Then someone shouted 'fire'! 'Oh no' I thought 'there's no chance'. Ever since the power had been turned off we had used kerosene lamps in almost every room and most of them were still lit. The makeshift barricades were made of thick bales of straw. A thick, black, acrid smoke began to creep through the building. The wind funnelled down the corridor, bringing clouds of smoke with it. The flames licked along the wood and plasterboard walls. There was fuel in the kitchen area. Within seconds Mt Carmel was an inferno. You could not see your hand before your face in the chapel, which is where I still was. I stood transfixed. There was a hole in the wall and the black smoke was billowing through it. I could see the light of day outside. However, I stood rooted to the spot wondering if I would be shot if I walked out of the building through the hole I could now see. However, I thought that it was better to take a chance since if I stayed in the chapel it would be certain death. Suddenly the heat hit us and I felt the pain of burning flesh on my right arm. I headed for the hole in wall and went out into the open with my hands up. I could see two tanks and FBI agents, who had raised rifles; 'keep your hands up' they shouted 'and walk—walk'. I did not look back, though I could hear the screams of others still inside.

There were three of us that had come out of that hole. We voluntarily lay face down on the ground. The agents told us to get up and run. It was about 50 yards to the tanks. The agents checked us for guns and then lashed our hands together with cable straps. One agent asked me where the children were. Another said 'God damn you, you will go to prison for ever'. Medics bandaged my badly burnt arm and I was then taken to the ATF headquarters at the Waco airport base, where I was fingerprinted and had my photograph taken. A Texas ranger asked me if I still thought that David Koresh was the lamb of God. I simply replied 'read Revelation chapters four and five'.

There follows in the manuscript a section dealing with the perception of David Koresh among those who did not know him. Lovelock argues that contrary to popular perception, Koresh was a kind and thoughtful individual who was very concerned for the welfare of his followers and for the underprivileged of society. Lovelock then continues by giving an account of what he thinks happened to some of his colleagues as they sought to flee the burning building. There follows a section on Koresh's theology and a description of the accusations made by Marc Breault. Some further details of the period leading up to the siege are given. The manuscript ends with an account of how he was released from custody in order to attend the funeral of his father.

Notes

1. The material in this chapter is taken from a much longer MS composed by Branch Davidian survivor Derek Lovelock. It is used with permission. Grammatical slips have been corrected and there has been some rewriting in the interests of clarity, and deletion of material that would perhaps have been outside the immediate concerns of this book. The final form of the transcription, printed here, has been discussed with Lovelock who has agreed all amendments, clarificatory additions, deletions and other changes. The full version of this MS can be found at www.hope.ac.uk/humanities/theology/branchdavidians.
2. There follows a substantial section outlining the way in which Lovelock felt increasingly unhappy with the church. His view of Ellen White, however, was entirely positive.

Appendix B

DAVIDIAN SEVENTH-DAY ADVENTISTS, 1961–2003

It was argued in the concluding chapter of this book that the Branch Davidian movement may well be on the verge of extinction. The original Davidian Seventh-day Adventists, however, seem rather better placed to face the challenges of the twenty-first century. Since the fiasco of 1959 they have fragmented into several groups, none of which has a really charismatic leader. However, the very fact that despite these obstacles Davidian Seventh-day Adventism has already survived for more than forty years is evidence of staying power. This Appendix briefly examines the history and current state of the movement; partly to put this information on the record, for no such study currently exists elsewhere,[1] and partly to show the contrast to the Branch Davidian situation.

Serious as the failed prophecy of 1959 was, it was not in itself the issue upon which the Davidian tradition began to splinter. In fact the first major issue came not so much with the failed prophecy, but with Florence's attempt to explain it. As was noted above, according to her, one explanation for the non-arrival of the kingdom was that the Davidians had not spread the message widely enough. The truth was for all Protestants, she said, and not just Seventh-day Adventists. This dangerous theological move on her part in effect cancelled out much the tradition had stood for. The Davidians had always seen it as their God-given role to call the 144,000 out of the wider membership of the SDA Church. Florence went against this tradition, and to take her views on board the Davidians would have had to effect a paradigm shift.

Many of those at Mt. Carmel were unable to accommodate so radical a transformation—to say in effect that Brother Houteff had been wrong. Consequently, some time in 1961 a meeting was called, to take place in Los Angeles. The movers appear to have been Warden and Bingham.[2] Perhaps sixty to a hundred people were present, including such long-standing Davidians as Don Adair himself. After discussion a decision was taken to establish a separate Davidian Association in Riverside, California. (Those meeting would not have seen it this way of course; their view was that Florence was the one who had in effect separated from the original movement by so radically altering its central mission.) Warden was elected vice-president of the Association, and Bingham was appointed as editor of the publications once again being planned, publications designed strictly for the work among Seventh-day Adventists and not Christians in general.

But further problems soon came. Bingham decided that the move from Mt. Carmel had brought to fulfilment the prophetic statement found in Amos 1.2: 'the top of

Carmel shall wither'. He said the Davidians had now gone into a new spiritual pasture, spoken of in the Old Testament as a move from the pastures of Carmel to those of Bashan (Mic. 7.14). The physical move was but a sign of the spiritual—the Davidians had now entered a new phase of their ministry and were feeding upon the fresh spiritual pastures of Bashan.[3]

The problem some Davidians perceived here is that it suggests progression. If they were to move from the (spiritual) pastures of Carmel into those of Gilead before the setting up of the kingdom (via Bashan), then Houteff could not have been the last prophet, the one who brought the final light. And that is exactly what Bingham said: Houteff was a prophet, but he (Bingham) was a 'porter-prophet' who, upon hearing the command of the great shepherd so to do, would open the door of the sheepfold and allow the sheep access to new pastures (cf. John 10.3).

Bingham's views hence struck at the heart of the movement as much as the suggestion by Florence had done. Both in effect questioned Houteff's place as the last prophet and/or the validity of his message. Bingham's views became a major issue. He wrote an article setting them out, which he then wished to see published in the organization's media. The standing committee simply refused to publish it, despite the previous assurances that Bingham as editor would have the final say. As a result some of the Davidians became suspicious of the standing committee's motives and sided with Bingham, who by now was claiming prophetic status. Indeed, on one occasion (says Adair) Bingham, unable to show from scripture the truth of what he was arguing, simply gave up trying to make the exegetical argument and said 'All right, I'll tell you how I know … I know because I'm inspired of God, and he told me.'[4] Some left Bingham in the light of this claim, but others remained loyal despite (or perhaps because of) his newly claimed prophetic status.

This was in fact the third attempt by Bingham to gain control of the Davidians. The first had been in 1938, when he tried to seize the leadership during Houteff's visit to his native Bulgaria. The second was immediately following Houteff's death in February 1955. On that occasion Bingham may have lost out as a result of being in the West Indies at the crucial time. However, his work in that part of the world was now about to bring fruit. He had married a Davidian Bible worker from Trinidad. The two embarked on an evangelistic tour of the West Indies, with great success. Most of the Davidians from those islands now accepted the Bashan message. This success in the West Indies would eventually change the shape of Davidianism.

In 1969 Bingham moved with about thirty-five of his followers to a site in Exeter, Missouri, which he named 'Bashan Hill'.[5] Soon thereafter he died, but not before he had nominated his wife, Jemmy Rohoman, as the next leader. At the time of writing the Bashan Hill headquarters still exists and is still under Rohoman's leadership.

But the Bashan group too was to split. In 1979 one of Bingham's close supporters, M. T. Jordan, a Bible worker from Trinidad, rebelled against the Bashan movement, arguing that just as the Carmel pasture had withered, so now also had the Bashan and that the period of Gilead had come (cf. Micah 7.14). Jordan and his followers moved to Canada and established another Davidian splinter group. Don Adair has stated quite clearly that his understanding is that the Gilead Davidians are the most numerous of the several Davidian factions. He has also stated that they accepted Jordan as the antitypical King David.[6]

The Bashan split was a serious blow to the Riverside group, who lost a good number of members to the faction, including the central figure of Bingham himself. During the next several years, however, the Riverside Davidians stabilized. The location was good in terms of opportunities for evangelism for there were, and still are, a number of significant SDA institutions within a 10 mile radius, and the potential for conversions seemed great.

Things appear to have been going well when, rather oddly, in 1969 a decision was taken to move the headquarters from Riverside to Salem, South Carolina. According to Adair this decision was taken purely on the basis of Bible study, the key passage being Ezekiel 47.1. According to the Riverside Davidians this passage spoke of how they must progress towards the east. Houteff, they said, had known this and moved his headquarters from Los Angeles to Waco (which was east as well as south); in coming back to the west coast they were seriously out of tune with biblical teaching. What was needed was a property even further east than Waco and there was an option. In 1949 Victor Houteff had overseen the establishment of a Davidian rest home in Salem, South Carolina, which was certainly in the east. In 1970, at a meeting held in Salem, the decision to move there was confirmed. The group who moved were about fifty in number, and perhaps another twenty-five or so (though they did not move physically to Salem) placed their allegiance there.[7]

Not all were agreed, however. Some executive council officers were opposed to the move, including the vice-president, H. G. Warden. An election to the vice-president's post took place in 1970 and Warden was this time defeated. The new vice-president was Sump Smith, who was re-elected in 1972. But Smith came to the same view as Florence Houteff, that the *Shepherd's Rod* message was for everyone and not just Seventh-day Adventists. Consequently, in 1973 Smith was replaced by Warden again. Warden was in Salem for the election and went back to Riverside to collect his belongings. However, he did not return. Some of the Salem members went to investigate what had happened to Smith and discovered that Warden and others were actually in favour of moving back again to Riverside. The ensuing squabble resulted in another split and the formation, in 1974, of yet another Davidian Association, at first headed by Warden himself, though the leadership passed into the hands of Adair's ex-wife, Wanda Blum (later Wanda O'Berry).[8] There were now three Davidian Associations in existence: the Salem Association, the California Association, and Bingham's 'Bashan' Association in Exeter, Missouri. This would increase to four in 1979 with the formation of the Gilead Association by M. T. Jordan.

But more developments were yet to come. In 1974 Adair went to the West Indies to study with the Bashan believers there in an effort to bring them back on board. This resulted, he said, in some considerable success and many of those who had been converted to the Bashan message were won over to the Salem Association. One such was Tony Hibbert, a Jamaican Davidian who moved to join the Salem group and was sent to take charge of the work in New York. In 1981, while Adair was conducting studies in New York, Hibbert disputed a doctrinal point; this dispute continued (a cover, one suspects, for a power struggle) and in 1982 Hibbert and some others sympathetic to his views (all West Indian) decided to separate from the Salem Association and set up their own Davidian group in New York. The New York faction is today an important part of Davidian Seventh-day Adventism and its very professional website is informative.[9]

One final change came in 1989 when a number of the New York Davidians decided that the time was right to return to Waco, and a majority voted for the move. The decision caused some considerable dispute. In the end the Waco group secured some property on the old Mt. Carmel site, principally a former Presbyterian church, and the move took place. According to Adair the Presbyterian church was itself a conversion from the original Davidian print shop. From the old Presbyterian church the group now run a very professional printing operation and literature campaign, targeted, as one would expect, only on Seventh-day Adventists and not the wider Christian Church. In 2004 the leadership of the Waco group was in the hands of Pastor Norman Archer.[10]

Despite some serious setbacks, then, the Davidian Seventh-day Adventist movement currently appears to be in a fairly healthy state. The six known major factions (there may be others who have not come to the surface in this review) are independent of each other in terms of formal structures, but all seem nevertheless to be viable. Unlike the Branch Davidians they have managed to maintain critical mass and indeed have probably grown somewhat. In contrast to the probable fate of the Branch Davidians, then, the Davidian Seventh-day Adventists are an example of how a group can survive even against the odds. Some storms have been weathered; there may be others ahead. And there are certainly some obstacles to further success; not least the notoriety that the 'Branch Davidians' now have, for the 'Davidians' have been tarred with the same brush without recognition of the firm historical and theological boundaries between the factions. This may cause the general public to react negatively to those who call themselves 'Davidians'. However, this is not the real issue, which is rather the even greater hostility of the only group of potential converts that matters. The publicity shy mainstream SDA Church has understandably reacted with horror to the events of 1993 and the mere mention of the name 'Davidian' is enough to put the average Seventh-day Adventist onto the defensive. Through no fault of their own, then, the Davidian Seventh-day Adventists now have a mountain to climb if they are to have any success in calling out the 144,000 from the SDA Church. It is on this very point, the need to present the *Rod* message exclusively to the Seventh-day Adventists and not to the world in general, that the Riverside group split away in the first instance. Limiting evangelistic activity to a group who are fundamentally antagonistic to messengers of the proposed 'new light' is not a recipe for success.

On the other hand, the Davidians do have some cards to play. As the situation in the Middle East continues to deteriorate and the events of 9/11 remain unblurred, the argument can be made that the Davidian understanding of biblical prophecy stands up in the light of current events (Seventh-day Adventists have always been keen to see a correspondence between prophecy and history; such reasoning might appeal to them in a way the outsider might find difficult to understand). The group in Waco in particular has now found stability and is clearly a financially viable organization with a keen sense of mission and, importantly, the physical facilities (including printing equipment) to engage in it. In the person of Archer they have a solid, dependable, even if far from prophetic, leader, and for this group at least the future looks reasonably positive. The Salem community is small, as is the one in New York, but the Bashan Davidians in Exeter and (according to Adair) the Gilead Davidians in Canada continue to do reasonably well. Hence despite the fragmentation, and the failed prophecy, Houteff's vision lives on.

Notes

1. This appendix is a summary by Kenneth G. C. Newport, ' "Thy Kingdom Come": The Davidian Seventh-day Adventists and Millennial Expectation, 1959–2004', in Crawford Gribben and Kenneth G. C. Newport, eds., *Expecting the End: Millennialisim in Social and Historical Perspective* (Waco, Tex.: Baylor University Press, forthcoming).
2. Adair, *Davidian Testimony*, 227; 'Interviews', 57–8.
3. Adair, 'Interviews', 58–9.
4. Ibid. 62.
5. Pitts, 'Davidians and Branch Davidians', 38.
6. See further Adair, 'Interviews', 181.
7. Ibid. 171.
8. According to Adair, this group grew fairly well and lasted at least until the early 1980s; Adair, 'Interviews', 192–3.
9. www.shepherds-rod-message.org.
10. Adair, 'Interviews', 77, 80, indicated that Norman Archer was a Davidian in Jamaica before leaving for the United States.

Appendix C

DEATHS AT WACO

A. ATF Agents who died on 28 February 1993 (Total 4)

Name	Age	Nationality	Cause of Death
Conway LaBleu	30	American	Gunshot
Todd McKeehan	28	American	Gunshot
Robert Williams	26	American	Gunshot
Steve Willis	32	American	Gunshot

B. Branch Davidians who died on or shortly after 28 February 1993 (Total 6)

Name	Age	Nationality	Cause of Death
Whinston Blake	28	British	Gunshot
Peter Gent	24	Australian	Gunshot
Peter Hipsman	28	American	Gunshot
Perry Jones	64	American	Gunshot
Michael Schroeder	29	American	Gunshot
Jaydean Wendell	34	Hawaiian-American	Gunshot

C. Branch Davidians who died on 19 April 1993 (Total 74, plus unborn babies Gyarfas and Gent)

Name	Age	Nationality	Cause of Death
Katherine Andrade	24	American	Smoke Inhalation
Chanel Andrade	1	American	Suffocation
Jennifer Andrade	19	American	Smoke Inhalation
George Bennett	35	British	Smoke Inhalation
Susan Benta	31	British	Smoke Inhalation
Mary Jean Borst	49	American	Gunshot Wound
Pablo Cohen	38	Israeli	Smoke Inhalation
Abedowalo Davies	30	British	Unclear
Shari Doyle	18	American	Gunshot Wound
Beverly Elliot	30	British	Unclear

Continues

Table *Continued*

Name	Age	Nationality	Cause of Death
Yvette Fagan	32	British	Smoke Inhalation
Doris Fagan	51	British	Unclear
Lisa Marie Farris	24	American	Gunshot Wound
Raymond Friesen	76	Canadian	Smoke Inhalation
Sandra Hardial	27	British	Unclear
Zilla Henry	55	British	Unclear
Vanessa Henry	19	British	Unclear
Phillip Henry	22	British	Gunshot Wounds
Paulina Henry	24	British	Unclear
Stephen Henry	26	British	Gunshot Wound
Diana Henry	28	British	Unclear
Novellette Hipsman	36	Canadian	Gunshot Wound
Floyd Houtman	61	American	Compound
Sherri Jewell	43	Asian-American	Smoke Inhalation
David M. Jones	38	American	Unclear
David Koresh	33	American	Gunshot Wound
Rachel Koresh	24	American	Suffocation
Cyrus Koresh	8	American	Smoke Inhalation
Star Koresh	6	American	Smoke Inhalation
Bobbie Lane Koresh	2	American	Inhalation of Carbon Monoxide
Jeffery Little	32	American	Unclear
Nicole Gent Little and unborn child	24	Australian	Gunshot Wound
Dayland Gent	3	American	Stab Wound
Page Gent	1	American	Unclear
Livingston Malcolm	26	British	Smoke Inhalation
Diane Martin	41	British	Unclear
Wayne Martin, sen.	42	American	Smoke Inhalation
Lisa Martin	13	American	Unclear
Sheila Martin, jun.	15	American	Unclear
Anita Martin	18	American	Unclear
Wayne Martin, jun.	20	American	Unclear
Julliete Martinez	30	Mexican-American	Smoke Inhalation
Crystal Martinez	3	Mexican-American	Unclear
Isaiah Martinez	4	Mexican-American	Unclear
Joseph Martinez	8	Mexican-American	Smoke Inhalation
Abigail Martinez	11	Mexican-American	Gunshot Wound
Audrey Martinez	13	Mexican-American	Suffocation
John-Mark McBean	27	British	Inhalation of Carbon Monoxide
Bernadette Monbelly	31	British	Unclear
Rosemary Morrison	29	British	Smoke Inhalation
Melissa Morrison	6	British	Smoke Inhalation
Sonia Murray	29	American	Smoke Inhalation
Theresa Norbrega	48	British	Unclear
James Riddle	32	American	Gunshot Wound
Rebecca Saipaia	24	Asian-British	Thermal Burns
Steve Schneider	43	American	Gunshot Wound

Table *Continued*

Name	Age	Nationality	Cause of Death
Judy Schneider	41	American	Unclear
Mayanah Schneider	2	American	Suffocation
Clifford Sellors	33	British	Smoke Inhalation
Scott Kojiro Sonobe	35	Asian-American	Smoke Inhalation
Floracita Sonobe	34	Filipino	Unclear
Gregory Summers	28	American	Smoke Inhalation and Burns
Aisha Gyarfas Summers and unborn child	17	Australian	Gunshot Wound
Startle Summers	1	American	Unclear
Lorraine Sylvia	40	American	Gunshot Wounds
Rachel Sylvia	12	American	Suffocation
Hollywood Sylvia	1	American	Inhalation of Carbon Monoxide
Michele Jones Thibodeau	18	American	Smoke Inhalation
Serenity Jones	4	American	Smoke Inhalation
Chica Jones	2	American	Unclear
Little One Jones	2	American	Unclear
Neal Vaega	38	Asian-New Zealander	Gunshot Wound
Margarida Vaega	47	Asian-New Zealander	Unclear
Mark H. Wendell	40	Asian-American	Thermal Burns

D. Unidentified Bodies

The following bodies remain unidentified. They are referred to by the numbers assigned them upon their discovery at the compound.

ID	Gender	Age Range	Cause of Death
Doe 13	Female	30–50	Blunt Force Trauma
Doe 14	Female	30–39	Smoke Inhalation
Doe 15	Male	35–50	Thermal Burns
Doe 16	Female	22–28	Smoke Inhalation
Doe 17	Female	22–40	Smoke Inhalation
Doe 18	Female	17–35	Smoke Inhalation
Doe 19	Female	35–50	Smoke Inhalation
Doe 24	Female	20–50	Smoke Inhalation
Doe 26	Female	15–19	Thermal Burns
Doe 28	Female	*c.*50	Smoke Inhalation
Doe 29	Female	35–50	Burns
Doe 31DE	Not determined	11–14	Gunshot

Continues

Table *Continued*

ID	Gender	Age Range	Cause of Death
Doe 44	Male	27–40	Gunshot
Doe 47a	Male	22–28	Gunshot
Doe 51a	Female	2	Smoke Inhalation
Doe 53	Female	5–6	Gunshot Wound
Doe 57	Female	6	Suffocation
Doe 59	Female	14–19	Blunt Force Trauma
Doe 63	Female	1	Blunt Force Trauma
Doe 64	Female	1	Smoke Inhalation
Doe 65	Female	Baby	Smoke Inhalation
Doe 67–7	Not determined	2	Unknown
Doe 67–8	Not determined	Infant	Gunshot Wound

Appendix D

WACO SURVIVORS[1]

A. Left during the Siege (Total = 35)

Name	Age	Nationality	Date of Departure
Brad Branch	35	American	19 March, 7.15 p.m.
Livingstone Fagan	34	British	23 March, 10.05
Nehara Fagan	4	British	28 February, 9.42 p.m.
Renae Fagan	6	British	28 February, 9.42 p.m.
Oliver Gyarfas	19	Australian	12 March, 6.00 p.m.
Victorine Hollingsworth	59	American	21 March, 12.15 a.m.
Heather Jones	9	American	5 March, 8.39 a.m.
Kevin Jones	11	American	4 March, 7.25 a.m.
Mark Jones	12	American	3 March, 4.26 p.m.
Margaret Lawson	75	American	2 March, 8.10 a.m.
James Lawton	70	American	21 March, 2.15 p.m.
Christyn Mabb	7	American	1 March
Jacob Mabb	9	American	1 March
Scott Mabb	11	American	1 March
Daniel Martin	6	American	2 March, 8.10 a.m.
Jamie Martin	10	American	1 March, 11.05 p.m.
Kimberley Martin	4	American	2 March, 8.10 a.m.
Sheila Judith Martin	46	American	21 March, 2.15 p.m.
Catherine Matteson	77	American	2 March, 8.10 a.m.
Natalie Norbrega	11	American	2 March, 1.20 a.m.
Gladys Ottman	67	American	21 March, 11.00 a.m.
Annetta Richards	60+	British	21 March, 12.15 a.m.
Rita Fay Riddle	35	American	21 March, 11.00 a.m.
Ofelia Santoya	62	American	21 March, 2.15 p.m.
Bryan Schroeder	3	American	1 March, 8.27 p.m.
Kathryn Schroeder	34	American	12 March, 11.50, a.m.
Angelica Sonobe	6	American	28 February, 8.55 p.m.
Crystal Sonobe	3	American	28 February, 8.55 p.m.
Joshua Sylvia	7	American	1 March, 11.05 p.m.
Joann Vaega	7	Asian-New Zealander	2 March, 1.20 a.m.
Jaunessa Wendel	8	American	1 March
Landon Wendell	4	American	1 March
Patteon Wendell	5 months	American	1 March
Tamara Wendell	5	American	1 March
Kevin Whitecliff	31	American	19 March, 7.15 p.m.

Continues

B. Survived the Fire

Name	Age	Nationality
Renos Avraam	29	British
Jaime Castillo	24	American
Graeme Leonard Craddock	31	Australian
Clive Joseph Doyle	52	American
Misti Ferguson	17	American
Derek Lloyd Lovelock	37	British
Ruth Riddle	29	American
David Thibodeau	24	American
Marjorie Thomas	30	American

Note

1. This list does not include the names of those Branch Davidians such as Paul Fatta who, while normally resident at the Mt. Carmel property, were not on site on when the siege began.

Select Bibliography

A Note on Primary Sources

This book has made extensive use of primary materials relating to the Davidians and Branch Davidians. Most of this material is located at the Texas Collection at Baylor University in Waco, Texas. Every attempt has been made in the notes to the chapters to make clear where this material is and how it may accessed, but readers are alerted to the fact that much of the material was not in a fully catalogued state when this research was carried out, and consequently precise location references may change. A number of other items are in my own possession. Audio tapes, for example the more than thirty cassettes by David Koresh and the similar number by Lois Roden, are not listed in this bibliography since they have no formal title by which to list them, but again a full location reference will be found in footnotes. A brief listing of these tapes is also found on www.hope.ac.uk/humanities/theology/branchdavidians. Some other primary materials have also been excluded from this bibliography due to the rather complex way in which they must be referenced, often including questions about authorship, date, and where relevant place of publication (though many such sources are in fact unpublished). Again the reader is referred to the footnotes where details of location can be found.

ADAIR, DON, *A Davidian Testimony* (privately published, 1997).
—— , series of three interviews, 1993–4 (Baylor University, Institute of Oral History, Oral History Project); see further Chapter One, n. 46.
ARASOLA, KAI, *The End of Historicism: Millerite Hermeneutic of Time Prophecies in the Old Testament* (Uppsala: University of Uppsala, 1990).
ARNOLD, J. PHILLIP, 'The Davidian Dilemma—To Obey God or Man?', in Lewis, ed., *From the Ashes*, 23–2.
BAILEY, BRAD, and DARDEN, BOB, *Madman in Waco: The Complete Story of the Davidian Cult, David Koresh and the Waco Massacre* (Waco: WRS, 1993).
BRADY, DAVID, *The Contribution of British Writers between 1560 and 1830 to the Interpretation of Revelation 13.16–18 (The Number of the Beast): A Study in the History of Exegesis* (Tübingen: J. C. B. Mohr (Paul Siebeck), 1983).
BALDWIN, DALTON, 'Experiences at Loma Linda', *Adventism Today,* 1 (May–June 1993).
BREAULT, MARK, *Preacher of Death: The Shocking Story of David Koresh and the Waco Siege* (Victoria, Australia: Signet Books, 1993).
BROMLEY, DAVID G., and SILVER, EDWARD D., 'The Davidian Tradition: From Patronal Clan to Prophetic Movement', in Wright, ed., *Armageddon in Waco*, 43–72.
CLAIRBORNE, WILLIAM, and MCGEE, JIM, 'The Making of David Koresh', in *Spectrum* 23/1 (May 1993), 18–25.

The Committee on Defense Literature of the General Conference of Seventh-day Adventists, *The History and Teachings of 'The Shepherd's Rod'* (1955).

COURT, JOHN M., *Revelation* (Sheffield: Sheffield Academic Press, 1994).

Department of the Treasury, *Report of the Department of the Treasury on the Bureau of Alcohol, Tobacco, and Firearms Investigation of Vernon Wayne Howell also known as David Koresh* (Washington, DC: US Government Printing Office, September 1993).

DOCHERTY, JAYNE SEMINARE, *Learning Lessons from Waco: When the Parties Bring their Gods to the Negotiation Table* (Syracuse: Syracuse University Press, 2001).

ELLISON, CHRISTOPHER G., and BARTOWSKI, JOHN P., 'Babies were being Beaten: Exploring Child Abuse Allegations at Ranch Apocalypse', in Wright, ed., *Armageddon in Waco*, 111–52.

FAUBION, JAMES, *The Shadows and Lights of Waco: Millennialism Today* (Princeton and Oxford: Princeton University Press, 2001).

FESTINGER, LEON, RIECKEN, H. W., and SCHACHTER, S., *When Prophecy Fails* (Minneapolis: University of Minnesota Press, 1956).

Final Report to the Deputy Attorney General Concerning the 1993 Confrontation at the Mt. Carmel Complex, Waco, Texas (Washington, DC: Office of Special Counsel, 8 Nov. 2000).

FROOM, LE ROY EDWIN, *The Conditionalist Faith of our Fathers* (Washington, DC: Review and Herald Publishing Association, 1963).

—— *The Prophetic Faith of Our Fathers*, 4 vols. (Washington, DC: Review and Herald Publishing Association, 1946–54).

Interim Report to the Deputy Attorney General Concerning the 1993 Confrontation at the Mt. Carmel Complex, Waco, Texas (Washington, DC: Office of Special Counsel, 21 July 2000).

GALLAGHER, EUGENE, 'Negotiating Salvation', *Nova Religio: The Journal of Alternative and Emergent Religions*, 3, no. 1 (October 1999), 27–35.

GRIBBEN, CRAWFORD and NEWPORT, KENNETH G. C., eds., *Expecting the End: Millennialism in Social and Historical Perspective* (Waco, Tex., Baylor University Press, forthcoming).

HAMM, MARK S., *Apocalypse in Oklahoma: Waco and Ruby Ridge Revenged* (Boston: Northeastern University Press, 1997).

HARDY, DAVID T. and KIMBALL, REX, *This is Not an Assault: Penetrating the Web of Official Lies Regarding the Waco Incident* (Philadelphia: Xlibris, 2001).

HARPER, BRIAN, 'God, Guns and Rock and Roll: David Koresh as seen from the Church Pews and Bar Stools of Downtown Waco', *Spectrum*, 23/1 [May 1993], 26–9.

HAUS, CARI HOYT, and HAMBLIN, MADLYN LEWIS, *In the Wake of Waco: Why Were Adventists among the Victims?* (Hagerstown, Md.: Review and Herald Publishing Association, 1993).

HOKAMA, DENNIS, 'Koresh and Ellen White', *Adventism Today*, May–June 1993.

HOUTEFF, VICTOR, *The Shepherd's Rod* (vol. 1, 1930; vol. 2, 1932. Privately published).

—— *Christ's Greetings* (1933).

—— *The Pre-Eleventh Hour Extra* (1933).

—— *The Great Paradox of the Ages* (1933).
—— *The Judgment and the Harvest* (1934).
—— *The Latest News for Mother* (1934).
—— *Final Warning* (1935).
—— *Why Perish?* (1936).
—— *The Great Controversy over the Shepherd's Rod* (1936).
—— *Mount Sion at the Eleventh Hour* (1937).
—— *Behold I Make All Things New* (1940).
—— *The Sign of Jonah* (1940).
—— *God's Titles Not Restricted to One Language* (1940).
—— *The World Yesterday, Today and Tomorrow* (1941).
—— *War News Forecast* (1943).
—— *Fundamental Beliefs and Directory of Davidian Seventh-day Adventists* (1943).
—— *The Answerer* (1944).
—— *The Entering Wedge* (1946).
—— *To the Seven Churches* (1947).
—— *Cookright Cookbook* (1947).
—— *General Conference Special* (1950).
—— *The White-House Recruiter* (1951).
—— *Jezreel Letters* (n.d., *c.*1953).
—— *Reporting Un-Adventist Activities* (n.d.).
HUNT, STEPHEN, ed., *Christian Millenarianism* (Bloomington, In.: Indiana University Press, 2001).
JOHNSSON, WILLIAM G., 'Pain and Perspective', *Adventist Review* (3 June 1993), 4–5.
KING, MARTIN, and BREAULT, MARC, *Preacher of Death: The Shocking Inside Story of David Koresh and the Waco Siege* (Victoria, Australia: Signet Books, 1993).
KOPEL, DAVID B., and BLACKMAN, PAUL H., *No More Wacos: What's Wrong with Federal Law Enforcement and How to Fix it* (New York: Prometheus Books, 1997).
LAWSON, RONALD, 'Seventh-day Adventist Responses to Branch Davidian Notoriety: Patterns of Diversity within a Sect Reducing Tension with Society', *Journal for the Scientific Study of Religion*, 34 (1995), 323–41.
LEPPARD, DAVID, *Fire and Blood: The True Story of David Koresh and the Waco Siege* (London: Fourth Estate, 1993).
LEWIS, JAMES R., ed., *From the Ashes: Making Sense of Waco* (Lanham, Md., Rowman and Littlefield, 1994).
—— 'Self-fulfilling Stereotypes, the Anticult Movement, and the Waco Confrontation', in Wright, ed., *Armageddon in Waco*, 95–110.
LINEDECKER, CLIFFORD L., *Massacre at Waco, Texas: The Shocking True Story of Cult Leader David Koresh and the Branch Davidians* (New York: St Martin's Paperbacks, 1993).
MADIGAN, TIM, *See No Evil: Blind Devotion and Bloodshed in David Koresh's Holy War* (Fort Worth, Texas: The Summit Group, 1993).

MOORE, CAROL, *The Davidian Massacre: Disturbing Questions about Waco which Must be Answered* (Franklin, Tenn.: Legacy Communications, and Springfield, Va.: Gun Owners Foundation, 1995).

NEWPORT, KENNETH G. C., *Apocalypse and Millennium: Studies in Biblical Eisegesis* (Cambridge: Cambridge University Press, 2000).

—— 'The Heavenly Millennium of Seventh-day Adventism', in Stephen Hunt, ed., *Christian Millennialism* (Bloomington, Ind.: Indiana University Press, 2001), 131–48.

—— ' "Thy Kingdom come": The Seventh-day Adventists and Millennial Expectation, 1959–2004', in Crawford Gribben and Kenneth G. C. Newport, eds., *Expecting the End: Millennialism in Social and Historical Perspective* (Waco, Tex.; Baylor University Press, forthcoming).

NICHOL, FRANCIS D., *The Midnight Cry: A Defense of William Miller and the Millerites* (Washington, DC: Review and Herald Publishing Association, 1944).

NUMBERS, RONALD L. and BUTLER, JONATHAN M., eds., *The Disappointed: Millerism and Millenarianism in the Nineteenth Century* (Bloomington and Indianapolis: Indiana University Press, 1987).

ODDY, J.A., 'Eschatological Prophecy in the English Theological Tradition, *c.*1700–*c.*1840' (University of London, Ph.D. Thesis, 1982);

PAULIEN, JON, *What the Bible Says about the End-Time* (Hagerstown, Md.: Review and Herald Publishing Association, 1998).

Pay Attention to Daniel's Prophecies (New York: Watch Tower and Bible Tract Society of New York, Inc., 1999).

PENTON, M. JAMES, *Apocalypse Delayed: The Story of the Jehovah's Witnesses* (Toronto: University of Toronto Press, 1985).

PITTS, WILLIAM, 'Davidians and Branch Davidians: 1929–1987', in Wright, ed., *Armageddon in Waco*, 20–42.

—— 'The Lord's Return to Mt. Carmel: Davidian Seventh-day Adventists, 1935–1961', a paper presented to the Southwest Meeting of the American Academy of Religion, Dallas, Tex., 1987.

—— 'The Mount Carmel Davidians; Adventist Reformers, 1935–1959', a paper presented at the American Academy of Religion, Kansas, 1991.

POWER, MARY ELIZABETH, 'A Study of the Seventh-day Adventist Community, Mount Carmel Center, Waco, Texas' (MA thesis, Baylor University, 1940).

RASMUSSEN, STEEN RAABJERG, 'Roots of the Prophetic Hermeneutic of William Miller', (MA thesis, Newbold College, Bracknell, Berkshire, 1983).

REAVIS, DICK J., *The Ashes of Waco: An Investigation* (Syracuse: Syracuse University Press, 1995).

REEVES, MARJORIE, *The Influence of Prophecy in the Later Middle Ages: a Study in Joachimism* (Oxford: Clarendon Press, 1969).

Report to the Deputy Attorney General on the Events at Waco, Texas, February 28 to April 19, 1993 (Washington, DC: Department of Justice, 8 October 1993).

RICE, RICHARD, *The Reign of God* (Berrien Springs, Mich.: Andrews University Press, 1985).

RICHARDSON, JAMES T., 'Manufacturing Consent about Koresh: A Structural Analysis of the Role of Media in the Waco tragedy', in Wright, ed., *Armageddon in Waco*, 153–76.

ROBBINS, T., and ANTHONY, D., 'Sects and Violence', in Wright, ed., *Armageddon at Waco*, 236–59.

ROBERTSON, J. J., *Beyond the Flames* (San Diego, California: ProMotion Publishing, 1996).

RODEN, BENJAMIN, *Branch Sabbath School Lessons* (n.d.).

—— *Revelation 14* (n.d).

—— *The Delivery of the Church from the Wilderness* (n.d).

—— *The Mighty Angel of Revelation 18.1* (n.d.).

—— *Vatican Built Watergate Frame-Up* (n.d.).

—— *We're Fed up with Catholics Crucifying Nixon* (n.d.).

—— *The Final Atonement* (1962).

—— *The Loud Cry: Rev. 18:1* (1964).

—— *God's Holy Feasts* (1965).

—— *The Man on the White Horse* (1965).

—— *Can You Count to Five?* (1967).

—— *The Flying Scroll: Zechariah 5* (1969).

—— *The Leviticus of The Davidian Seventh-day Adventists: Branch Supplement* (1972).

—— *Festival of the Purim* (1973).

—— *The Pentecost* (1973).[1]

—— *The Daily: Part 1* (1976).

—— *The Daily: Part 2* (1978).

—— *Tyre and Zidon* (reprint 1979).

—— *The Pentecost: What is It?* (1973).

—— *Seven Letters to Elder R. R. Figuhr* (Waco: The Universal Publishing Association, 1976).

—— *Deliverance In Mount Zion and in Jerusalem and in the Remnant: Whom the Lord Shall Call* (1977).

—— *Seven Letters and the Executive Council of the Davidian Seventh-day Adventist Association by The Branch* (1978).

RODEN, LOIS, *A Story of Shavuot* (n.d.).

—— *By His Spirit* (n.d.).

—— *In Her Image* (n.d.).

—— *Christ and the Holy Spirit* (1978).

—— *A Master Plan for America* (1979).

—— *Behold Thy Mother*, 3 parts (1980).

—— *As an Eagle* (1981).

—— *In Her Image* (1981).

—— *Merkabah*, 3 parts (1983–4).

—— *The Bride of Christ*, 3 parts (1986).

Rowe, David L., *Thunder and Trumpets: Millerites and Religious Dissent in Upstate New York, 1800–1850* (Chico, California: Scholars Press, 1985).

—— 'Millerites: A Shadow Portrait', in Numbers and Butler, eds., *The Disappointed*, 1–16.

Saether, George, *Oral Memoirs* (Waco, Tex.: Baylor University, 1977).

Sandefur, Joel, and Liu, Charles, 'Apocalpyse in Diamond Head', *Spectrum*, 23/1 (May 1993), 30–3.

Seventh-day Adventist Bible Commentary, 8 vols. (Washington, DC: Review and Herald Publishing Association, 1953–60).

Seventh-day Adventist Encyclopedia, 2nd revised edn., 12 vols. (Hagerstown, Md.: Review and Herald Publishing Association, 1976–2000).

Seventh-day Adventists Believe: A Biblical Exposition of 27 Fundamental Doctrines (Washington, DC: The Ministerial Association of the Seventh-day Adventist Church, 1988).

Shupe, Anson, and Hadden, Jeffrey K., 'Cops, News Copy and Public Opinion: Legitimacy and the Social Construction of Evil in Waco', in Wright, ed., *Armageddon in Waco*, 177–202.

Standish, Colin, 'Lessons from Waco', *Our Firm Foundation*, June 1993, 5–6.

Stark, Rodney and Bainbridge, William Sims, *The Future of Religion: Secularization, Revival, Cult Formation* (Berkeley, Calif.: University of California Press, 1985).

Stone, Jon R., ed., *Expecting Armageddon: Essential Readings in Failed Prophecy* (London: Routledge, 2000).

Swett, Mark, 'The Ultimate Act of Faith?: David Koresh and the Untold Story of the Branch Davidians', www.hope.ac.uk/humanities/theology/branchdavidians.

Tabor, James D., 'The Waco Tragedy: An Autobiographical Account of One Attempt to Avert Disaster', in Lewis, ed., *From the Ashes*, 13–21.

—— and Gallagher, Eugene V., *Why Waco? Cults and the Battle for Religious Freedom in America* (Berkeley and Los Angeles: University of California Press, 1995).

Thibodeau, David, and Whiteson, Leon, *A Place Called Waco* (New York: Public Affairs, 1999).

Wainwright, Arthur W., *Mysterious Apocalypse* (Nashville: Abingdon Press, 1993).

Waite, Albert C., 'From Seventh-day Adventism to David Koresh: The British Connection', *Andrews University Seminary Studies*, 38 (2000), 107–26.

—— and Osei, Laura, 'The British Connection', *Spectrum*, 23/1 (May 1993), 34–8.

Wessinger, Catherine, *How the Millennium Comes Violently* (New York and London: Seven Bridges Press, 2000).

—— 'Varieties of Millennialism and the Issue of Authority', in Lewis, ed., *From the Ashes*, 55–65.

Wright, Stuart A., ed., *Armageddon in Waco: Critical Perspectives on the Branch Davidian Conflict* (Chicago and London: The University of Chicago Press, 1995).

—— 'Construction and Escalation of a Cult Threat: Dissecting Moral Panic and Official Reaction to the Branch Davidians', in *idem.*, ed., *Armageddon in Waco*, 75–94.

Film and Television Sources

Ambush in Waco: In the Line of Duty (Culver City, Calif.: Patchett Kaufman Entertainment, 1993).

The FLIR Project (Produced and Directed by Mike McNulty, COPS productions, PO Box 8068, Fort Collins, Col. 80526; copyright 2001 to COPS productions LLC, Los Angeles, Calif.).

Madman of Waco, A Current Affair Special (Nine Network Australia, 1994).

Waco: A New Revelation (Fort Collins, Col.: MGA films Inc., 1999).

Waco: The Big Lie (Indianapolis, Ind.: American Justice Federation, *c.*1993).

Waco II: The Big Lie Continues (Indianapolis, Ind.: American Justice Federation, *c.*1994).

Waco—The Rules of Engagement (Los Angeles, Calif.: COPS/Somford Productions, 1997).

Electronic sites accessed over the Internet

All of these sites were active at 14 June 2005
http://members.aol.com/karenwmp/waco/neil.htm
www.adventist.org
www.branchdavidian.com
www.davidian.org
www.hope.ac.uk/humanities/theology/branchdavidians
www.rickross.com/reference/waco/waco1.html
www.rickross.com/reference/waco/waco299.html
www.sevenseals.com
www.shepherds-rod-message.org
www.start.at/mtcarmel
www.transcripts.net

Index